Studies in Regional and Local History

General Editor Jane Whittle

Previous titles in this series

Founding Editor Nigel Goose

Volume 1: *A Hertfordshire demesne of Westminster Abbey: Profits, productivity and weather* by Derek Vincent Stern (edited and with an introduction by Christopher Thornton)

Volume 2: *From Hellgill to Bridge End: Aspects of economic and social change in the Upper Eden Valley, 1840–95* by Margaret Shepherd

Volume 3: *Cambridge and its Economic Region, 1450–1560* by John S. Lee

Volume 4: *Cultural Transition in the Chilterns and Essex Region, 350 AD to 650 AD* by John T. Baker

Volume 5: *A Pleasing Prospect: Society and culture in eighteenth-century Colchester* by Shani D'Cruze

Volume 6: *Agriculture and Rural Society after the Black Death: Common themes and regional variations* by Ben Dodds and Richard Britnell

Volume 7: *A Lost Frontier Revealed: Regional separation in the East Midlands* by Alan Fox

Volume 8: *Land and Family: Trends and local variations in the peasant land market on the Winchester bishopric estates, 1263–1415* by John Mullan and Richard Britnell

Volume 9: *Out of the Hay and into the Hops: Hop cultivation in Wealden Kent and hop marketing in Southwark, 1744–2000* by Celia Cordle

Volume 10: *A Prospering Society: Wiltshire in the later Middle Ages* by John Hare

Volume 11: *Bread and Ale for the Brethren: The provisioning of Norwich Cathedral Priory, 1260–1536* by Philip Slavin

Volume 12: *Poor Relief and Community in Hadleigh, Suffolk, 1547–1600* by Marjorie Keniston McIntosh

Volume 13: *Rethinking Ancient Woodland: The archaeology and history of woods in Norfolk* by Gerry Barnes and Tom Williamson

Custom and Commercialisation in English Rural Society

Revisiting Tawney and Postan

Edited by
J.P. Bowen and A.T. Brown

University of Hertfordshire Press
Studies in Regional and Local History

Volume 14

First published in Great Britain in 2016 by
University of Hertfordshire Press
College Lane
Hatfield
Hertfordshire
AL10 9AB
UK

British Library Cataloguing in Publication Data
A catalogue record for this book is available from the British Library

ISBN 978-1-909291-44-7 hardback
ISBN 978-1-909291-45-4 paperback

Design by Arthouse Publishing Solutions Ltd
Printed in Great Britain by Henry Ling Ltd, Dorchester

Contents

Part IV: ACCOMMODATING CHANGE

Figures

Tables

Contributors

Dr James P. Bowen is a Postdoctoral Research Associate based at the Department of Geography and Planning, the School of Environmental Sciences, University of Liverpool. He is working on 'Spaces of experience and horizons of expectation: the implications of extreme weather events, past, present and future', a three-year project funded as part of the 'Care for the Future' programme of the Arts and Humanities Research Council (AHRC). He completed a PhD at Lancaster University supervised by Professor Angus J.L. Winchester and held the Economic History Society's Tawney Fellowship in 2012–13.

Dr John Broad is an Affiliated Researcher of the Cambridge Group for the History of Population and Social Structure (CAMPOP) at the University of Cambridge. Since publishing *Transforming English Rural Society: The Verneys and the Claydons 1600–1820* (Cambridge University Press, 2004) he has edited *A Common Agricultural Heritage?* (2009), *Bishop Wake's Summary Visitation Returns* (2012) and (with Anton Shuurman) *Wealth and Poverty in European Rural Societies* (2014).

Dr A.T. Brown is an Addison Wheeler Fellow at Durham University, having previously held the Economic History Society's Postan Fellowship in 2012–13. His book *Rural Society and Economic Change in County Durham: Recession and Recovery, c.1400–1640* was published in 2015 with Boydell Press. He co-edited (with Andy Burn and Rob Doherty) *Crises in Economic and Social History: A Comparative Perspective* (Boydell Press, 2015) and has published articles on the ecclesiastical estates of Durham in the *Economic History Review* and *Northern History*.

Professor Christopher Dyer, Emeritus Professor of History at the University of Leicester, has written on various aspects of agrarian, landscape and rural history, mainly in the later Middle Ages. His most recent book, published by Oxford University Press in 2012, is *A Country Merchant, 1495–1520: Trading and Farming at the End of the Middle Ages*.

Dr John Gaisford wrote his PhD on 'Capital in the Countryside: Social Change in West Wiltshire, 1530–1680', supervised by Professor Vanessa Harding at Birkbeck, University of London. His study investigated the social impact of the Western broadcloth trade, with particular reference to contact with the London merchant community and the Exchequer, and the effects of competition and co-operation amongst entrepreneurs in the West Country.

Dr Tom Johnson is Lecturer in Late Medieval History at the University of York, having previously held a research fellowship at Emmanuel College, Cambridge. He has published articles on medieval law and society in *Law & History Review* and *American Historical Review*, and is currently working on a monograph about popular legal culture in fifteenth-century England.

Dr David Rollison is a Research Associate at the University of Sydney. He is the author of *The Local Origins of Modern Society: Gloucestershire 1500–1800* (Routledge, 1992), *A Commonwealth of the People: Popular Politics and England's Long Social Revolution, 1066–1649* (Cambridge University Press, 2010), *Commune, Country and Commonwealth: the People of Cirencester 1117–1643* (Boydell Press, 2011) and a wide-ranging series of articles on popular politics and vectors of change in early modern England.

Dr Simon Sandall is Lecturer in Early Modern British History at the University of Winchester, having previously held positions at the University of East Anglia and the Centre for English Local History at the University of Leicester. He completed a PhD in 2009 at the University of East Anglia as part of an Arts and Humanities Research Council-funded project on popular memory, upon which his book *Custom and popular memory in the Forest of Dean, c.1550–1832* (Cambridge Scholars Press, 2013) is based.

Dr Alexandra Sapoznik is Lecturer in Late Medieval History at King's College London. Her publications include 'Resource allocation and peasant decision making: Oakington, Cambridgeshire, 1360–99', Agricultural History Review, 61 (2013), pp. 187–205 and 'The productivity of peasant agriculture: Oakington, Cambridgeshire, 1360–1399', Economic History Review, 66 (2013), pp. 518–44. She held the Economic History Society's Postan Fellowship in 2009–10.

Dr William D. Shannon is an independent researcher. His PhD on 'Approvement and Improvement in Early-Modern England: Enclosure in the Lowland Wastes of Lancashire c.1500–1700', supervised by Professor Angus J.L. Winchester, was awarded by Lancaster University in 2009. His publications include 'Approvement and Improvement in the Lowland Wastes of Early-Modern Lancashire', in R.W. Hoyle (ed.), *Custom, Improvement and Landscape in Early Modern Britain* (Ashgate, 2011); 'The Survival of True Intercommoning in the Early-Modern Period', *Agricultural History*, 84/4 (2012), and 'Risks and rewards in wasteland enclosure: lowland Lancashire *c.*1500–1650', in Jane Whittle (ed.), *Landlords and Tenants in Britain, 1440–1660: Tawney's Agrarian Problem Revisited* (Boydell Press, 2013).

Dr Sheila Sweetinburgh is Senior Research Fellow in the School of Humanities at Canterbury Christ Church University and an Associate Lecturer in Medieval Studies at the University of Kent. Much of her published work on medieval society adopts a microhistory approach. She is the editor of *Negotiating the Political in Northern European Urban Society c.1400–c.1600* (Brepols, 2013); and, with Boydell Press, *Later Medieval Kent, 1220–1540* (2010) and *Early Medieval Kent, 800–1220* (forthcoming). She is also the author of *The Role of the Hospital in Medieval England: Gift-giving and the Spiritual Economy* (Four Courts Press, 2004).

Professor Andy Wood is Professor of Social History at Durham University. He is the author of *The 1549 Rebellions and the Making of Early Modern England* (Cambridge University Press, 2007), T*he Politics of Social Conflict: The Peak Country, 1520–1770* (Cambridge University Press, 1999) and *The Memory of the People: Custom and Popular Senses of the Past in Early Modern England* (Cambridge University Press, 2013).

Publication grant

Publication has been made possible by generous grants from the Marc Fitch Fund and the Scouloudi Foundation in association with the Institute of Historical Research

Studies in Regional and Local History

General Editor's preface

Volume 14 of Studies in Regional and Local History is an innovative collection of essays put together by two early career researchers, James Bowen and Alex Brown. The authors revisit the classic works of M.M. Postan and R.H. Tawney on the economy and society of late medieval and early modern England through the lens of two important characteristics of the pre-modern economy, custom and commercialisation. Custom and commercialisation have typically been seen as opposites. 'Custom' has been used to describe pre-capitalist economies, where traditional practices and oral culture formed the basis of legal structures. 'Commercialisation' on the other hand describes the spread of market forces, which have been characterised as undermining customary practices, typically through the actions of landlords and other wealthy individuals. This book challenges these ideas. It provides examples of custom being used to further the commercial exploitation of resources, such as Simon Sandall's illuminating study of coal-mining in the Forest of Dean, and of custom being upheld by lords against tenants in arguments over rights to property. It also reveals the many ways is which customary practices have been understood by historians, for instance sometimes as oral rather than written rules, or as payment in kind rather than in cash, but the research presented here adds to this, showing that custom could involve written rules about cash payments, when those payments are long enough established or agreed by representatives of the community. We might wonder when, if ever, a commercial economy is truly free from customary practices.

The collection provides a number of new perspectives on the pre-modern economy. Christopher Dyer surveys and compares the work of Postan and Tawney: they were very different types of historian but perhaps had more in common than is often allowed. In doing so he also opens a discussion on the contrasts and similarities between England's medieval and early modern economies. John Broad revisits the classic topic of developments in land tenure, but he does so over the long *dureé*. His chapter is particularly important in relating the changes that Tawney focused on in the fifteenth and sixteenth centuries to what happened between the seventeenth and nineteenth centuries, when the transformations were no less significant, but shaped by the earlier changes. The remaining chapters are local studies. Rather than concentrating on arable agriculture as the rural history of England has classically done, they focus on relatively neglected economic resources and activities: iron production, the exploitation of marshlands, the maritime economy, common land, timber, coal, the cloth industry and the market town. And rather than looking at the Midlands and East Anglia, the studies are drawn from the west of England (Wiltshire, Gloucestershire and Shropshire), the north (Yorkshire, Furness in Lancashire and county Durham), and the periphery of eastern England (the Suffolk coast and the marshlands of Kent). What is revealed is an economy where agriculture was supplemented with varied occupations in which people drew a living from the sea, from mining and metallurgy, and from cloth production; and where the pressures were not only to feed the population, but to provide fuel, housing, tools and clothing. It is a richer and more varied picture of the pre-industrial economy.

There are many insights into the social relationships created by these economies: tensions and conflicts over rights and power were ever-present. There were conflicts between lords and tenants, as we would expect, but often alliances and discontents reveal other fault-lines. John Gaisford's examination of the Wiltshire cloth industry explores relationships within the elite, demonstrating just how powerful and wealthy leading clothiers had become by the second half of the sixteenth century with strong links into the gentry and the royal government. David Rollison's study of Cirencester illuminates a long running conflict between a lord and the community of townspeople that was characteristic of so many medium-sized towns between 1300 and 1700, while James Bowen demonstrates that conflicts over common land were often between communities rather than between lords and tenants. William Shannon, with regard to timber, and Alex Brown, for coal, demonstrate that lords were not always effective at exploiting the resources they notionally had control over: tenants and the resident lords of neighbouring properties often had a more detailed local knowledge that offered them an advantage. Conflict over resources was present alongside cooperation within occupational groups, such as the seafaring captains and crew innovatively explored by Tom Johnson, and the medieval iron miners illuminated by Alexandra Sapoznik. The variety of land tenures combined with an active landmarket, which Sheila Sweetinburgh illustrates for Kent's marshlands, offer another explanation for the complexity of socio-economic relationships in rural England. It is fitting that the volume ends with the thoughts of Andy Wood on the future direction of economic and social history, encouraging the reintegration of the social and the economic, closer connection of the medieval to the early modern, and reasserting the importance of 'small' history or local history alongside 'big' history. The volume as a whole builds on the ideas of Postan and Tawney to show that the economic transformation of rural and small town England between the late medieval period and the eighteenth century cannot be reduced down to simply the dispossession of the peasantry, or the rise of capitalism. Changes in the economy and society involved many strands and are best understood through the richness of regional and local history.

Jane Whittle
October 2015

Preface

This book arises from a colloquium held at the Institute of Historical Research, University of London, in July 2013. It brings together leading academics and early-career researchers exploring the role of agriculture, industry, custom and commercialisation in the rural development of England from the thirteenth to the eighteenth centuries, showcasing the latest research on the issues originally discussed by Tawney and Postan in their 'classic' works: *The Agrarian Problem in the Sixteenth Century* and *The Medieval Economy and Society: An Economic History of Britain, 1100–1500*, first published in 1912 and 1972 respectively.[1] It was decided to focus on the work of Tawney and Postan given our similar research interests in rural agrarian history and because, at the time, we held the Economic History Society's Tawney and Postan Junior Research Fellowships (2012–13) while based in the Departments of History at Lancaster and Durham Universities. Hence we sought to collaborate, organising the colloquium after an initial suggestion from Professor Miles Taylor, then Director of the Institute of Historical Research, and also subsequently publishing this volume.

Many people contributed to both the colloquium and this volume. We would like to thank those who kindly agreed to speak at the colloquium and everyone that attended and contributed to the discussion. Speakers included Sheila Sweetinburgh, Andy Wood, William Shannon, Tom Johnson, Richard Hoyle, John Broad, Christopher Dyer and Brodie Waddell. James Lees, formerly Fellowships Officer at the Institute of Historical Research, helped with its practical organisation and offered advice regarding funding. The Economic History Society awarded a grant from their initiatives and conference fund. The British Agricultural History Society and the Royal Historical Society advertised the colloquium. The publication of the volume was made possible by grants from the Scouloudi Foundation in association with the Institute of Historical Research and from the Marc Fitch Fund.

With regard to the volume, thanks go to all those who attended the colloquium and agreed to contribute to the book. We would like to thank those who we approached since we started putting the proposal together asking for papers that would complement those which we already had. The addition of these papers has added to the overall coherence of the volume and broadened the subject and themes explored, as well as the geographical and chronological range. Jane Whittle, in her role as series editor of the University of Hertfordshire Press's Studies in Regional and Local History, provided useful guidance and a critical but constructive assessment of the original book proposal which greatly improved the book's structure. Suzanne Yee of the School of Environmental Sciences, University of Liverpool produced the maps. Jane Housham and Sarah Elvins at the University of Hertfordshire Press provided assistance from the proposal stage, advising regarding funding and throughout the publishing process.

James P. Bowen and Alex Brown

---

1 R.H. Tawney, *The agrarian problem in the sixteenth century* (London, 1912); M.M. Postan, *The medieval economy and society: economic history of Britain, 1100–1500* (London, 1972).

Introduction

Custom and commercialisation in English rural society

James P. Bowen and A.T. Brown

> In that happy balance between the forces of custom and the forces of economic enterprise, custom is powerful, yet not so powerful that men cannot evade it when evasion is desired; enterprise is growing, yet it has not grown to such lengths as to determine the security which the small man finds in the established relationships and immemorial routine of communal agriculture.[1] R.H. Tawney

> A society like that of medieval England would nowadays be classified and described as pre-industrial. Its income came mostly from agriculture, and by far the largest proportion of its people was engaged in growing food. The numbers occupied in trade and industry formed a relatively small proportion of the total; and even those so occupied often combined their industrial and commercial occupations with some agricultural pursuits. This does not, however, mean that industrial and commercial activities were wholly insignificant and played little part in shaping the economic geography of the country or in directing the course of its economic development.[2] M.M. Postan

Revisiting Tawney and Postan

The enduring impact of the work of Tawney and Postan and their contributions to the discipline of economic history mean that they continue to provide inspiration for twenty-first-century historians. Although they worked with fewer sources than are readily available to historians today and their interpretations have been subject to substantial revisions, their views of late medieval and early modern society have endured. For instance, Christopher Dyer has recently noted that he often assumed Tawney had omitted some analysis of the period 'which I imagined to be relatively new, only to find the thought had already occurred to him'.[3] Similarly, areas of their work have been significantly developed. For example, an appreciation of the degree of

1 R.H. Tawney, *The agrarian problem in the sixteenth century* (London, 1912), p. 136.

2 M.M. Postan, *The medieval economy and society: economic history of Britain, 1100–1500* (London, 1972), p. 205.

3 C. Dyer, 'The agrarian problem, 1440–1520', in J.C. Whittle (ed.), *Landlords and tenants in Britain, 1440–1660: Tawney's agrarian problem revisited* (Woodbridge, 2013), p. 19.

custom and community within local society has gone hand in hand with an increasing acknowledgement of the degree of commercialisation in English rural society.[4] This collection focuses on the twin themes of custom and commercialisation, areas that Tawney and Postan lay the foundations for, but which have been significantly built upon since.

More typically, historians have approached Tawney and Postan's legacy in rural history through the lens of lord–tenant relationships, but what does custom and commercialisation as an approach offer that a central focus on lords and tenants does not?[5] Custom had multiple definitions depending on its context, primarily because it was 'a discursive field: a body of ideas that sanctioned claims to rights, office, space, land and resources'.[6] Custom was, therefore, fundamentally important as a contested area governing the behaviour of various aspects of economic and social life in English rural society in this period. By comparison, commercialisation is the process whereby a growing proportion of goods and services are being traded in the market so that people become increasingly dependent upon buying and selling for their livelihood.[7] This growing dependence upon the market could involve land, labour and goods and have a transformative effect upon medieval and early modern society not only through the growth of markets and towns and the quantity of money in circulation but also through important changes in people's mentality. Some of the chapters provide new perspectives on long-debated issues, while others focus upon neglected activities that took place in the countryside, particularly the growth of early industry and the use of commons resources and woodlands, ranging from the salvage of shipwrecks washed up on the Suffolk coast to the use of wood for charcoal in Lancashire. The volume is divided into four parts that explore the changes that rural society underwent from the medieval to the early modern period: new perspectives on the field; land and mobility in rural England; custom and commerce in non-arable areas of the countryside; and the ability of rural society to accommodate these significant changes. After first considering some general issues, this introduction offers an overview of the themes raised in each of the four sections.

Research into custom and commercialisation in this period of English history faces a number of challenges in terms of the nature of the sources available, the geographical biases of existing research, the tensions between demographic change and other aspects of economic development, and the chronological framework which divides medieval and early modern England. The types of documents available for studying custom and commercialisation, and their availability, vary over time. In 1955 Rodney Hilton bemoaned that between the Peasants' Revolt of 1381 and the

---

4 For one of the most important works on the increasing commercialisation of medieval England see R.H. Britnell, *The commercialisation of English society, 1000–1500* (Cambridge, 1993). For a recent volume on custom see R.W. Hoyle (ed.), *Custom, improvement and the landscape in early modern Britain* (Farnham, 2011).

5 J.C. Whittle (ed.), *Landlords and tenants in Britain, 1440–1660: Tawney's agrarian problem revisited* (Woodbridge, 2013).

6 A. Wood, *The memory of the people: custom and popular senses of the past in early modern England* (Cambridge, 2013), p. 2.

7 Britnell, *Commercialisation of English society*, p. xiii.

Dissolution of the Monasteries of 1536–40 lies 'one of the most formidable gaps in our knowledge of English rural life' because of the almost universal leasing of manors.[8] In the 1990s Bruce Campbell and Mark Overton still remarked that the fifteenth and early sixteenth centuries were 'a murky, ill-documented and under-researched period'.[9] Despite work crossing this period in the intervening years there is much that remains unknown, especially with regard to the commercialisation of English rural society and the tensions this caused. The expansion of rural industry took place in precisely this murky and poorly documented period, as, for example, in Kent, Essex and Devon between the late fourteenth and early sixteenth centuries.

Tawney and Postan carried out much of their work with limited access to the local archives that historians now take for granted; nevertheless, their works were perceptive and lucid accounts of economic and social change written in a style that is still readable today, ensuring their enduring importance. But their views of medieval and early modern England have often been debated based upon the traditional geographic areas of historical attention: the 'classic' arable-orientated commercialising agricultural regions of the Midlands, southern England and East Anglia. To what extent are their views applicable to parts of the country that they did not explore in detail? Many of the chapters in this volume examine regions outside the highly commercialised open-field areas of the English countryside, with contrasting landscapes, farming and rural economies. The diversity of the English landscape was acknowledged by Tawney and Postan, but it was not until the works of W.G. Hoskins, Joan Thirsk and subsequent historians that this regional diversity came to prominence.[10] This volume contributes to the picture of regional diversity of the English countryside by drawing upon research from the mixed economies of south-western, western and northern England, and by looking at the role of coastal and urban communities within the rural economy.

Postan was acutely aware of the importance of demography in creating or compounding many of the challenges facing people in the English countryside. He argued that medieval England suffered a Malthusian crisis in the late thirteenth and early fourteenth centuries because marginal land was brought into cultivation and peasant holdings became so fragmented that the fertility of the land was compromised.[11] For Postan, a significant proportion of the population was vulnerable to the effects of harvest failures when the Great Famine struck in 1315–17 because population pressure had caused diminishing yields. Although many of these conclusions have been questioned over the years, including the representativeness

---

8 R.H. Hilton, 'The content and sources of English agrarian history before 1500', *Agricultural History Review*, 3 (1955), p. 6.

9 B.M.S. Campbell and M. Overton, 'A new perspective on medieval and early modern agriculture: six centuries of Norfolk farming, c.1250–c.1850', *Past & Present*, 141 (1993), pp. 47–8.

10 W.G. Hoskins, 'Regional farming in England', *Agricultural History Review*, 2 (1954), pp. 3–11; J. Thirsk, 'The farming regions of England', in J. Thirsk (ed.), *The agrarian history of England and Wales. Volume IV: 1500–1640* (Cambridge, 1967), pp. 1–112.

11 M.M. Postan, 'Medieval agrarian society in its prime: England', in M.M. Postan (ed.), *The Cambridge economic history of Europe, vol. I: the agrarian life of the Middle Ages* (Cambridge, 1966), pp. 555–66.

of Titow's yield data that Postan used, population change undoubtedly had a strong effect on rural society during the pre-industrial period.[12] The population of England reached a medieval high of between 4.7 and 6 million in the early fourteenth century, but this was sharply reduced by the Black Death in 1348–50 and subsequent outbreaks of pestilence to just 2.5 million people by 1377.[13] Postan analysed many of these shifts in the population of medieval England and wrote several articles on the problems stagnant population levels caused society in the fifteenth century.[14] While, if anything, Postan over-emphasised the importance of demography, Tawney was more interested in what is now referred to as human agency – most notably the relations between landlords and tenants – than he was in population change, about which there was no clear consensus at the time he was writing. There is a much greater appreciation of the role played by demographic growth in the early modern period; population increased from around 2 million at the end of the fifteenth century to over 5 million by the time of the English Civil War.[15] In his introduction to the 1967 edition of the *Agrarian Problem* Lawrence Stone, for example, described how for many early modernists 'population pressure has replaced the wicked enclosing or rack-renting landlord as the *diabolus ex machina*'.[16]

While custom and commercialisation are studied by medieval and early modern historians in the context of their respective periods rarely are links made between them, despite clear parallels. There is, therefore, a need for a study of these topics, which bridges the medieval and early modern divide. Much work in recent decades, such as Christopher Dyer's *An Age of Transition?* and Richard Britnell's *The Commercialisation of English Society*, has emphasised the commercialised nature of the medieval economy.[17] Dyer notes how 'the supposed turning point around 1500 has been given excessive importance' despite the fact that 'many of the features of the early modern period can be observed well before 1500 and even before 1300', including some of the features of a 'consumer society', which can be traced back

12 J.Z. Titow, *Winchester yields: a study in medieval agricultural productivity* (Cambridge, 1972); Campbell and Overton, 'New perspective', pp. 38–105.

13 For an estimated figure of pre-plague population of 6 million see Postan, 'Medieval agrarian society', pp. 549–632; for a lower estimate of around 4.7 million see S. Broadberry, B.M.S. Campbell, A. Klein, M. Overton and B. van Leeuwen, *British economic growth 1270–1870* (Cambridge, 2015), p. 26.

14 M.M. Postan, 'The fifteenth century', *Economic History Review*, 9 (1939), pp. 160–7, and M.M. Postan, 'Some economic evidence of declining population in the later Middle Ages', *Economic History Review*, 2nd ser., 2 (1950), pp. 221–46.

15 W.G. Hoskins, 'Harvest fluctuations and English economic history, 1480–1619', *Agricultural History Review*, 12 (1964), p. 31; C.J. Harrison, 'Grain price analysis and harvest qualities, 1465–1634', *Agricultural History Review*, 19 (1971), pp. 147–51.

16 Lawrence Stone's introduction to the Harper Torchbooks version of R.H. Tawney, *The agrarian problem in the sixteenth century* (London and New York, 1967), p. xi.

17 C. Dyer, *An age of transition? Economy and society in England in the later Middle Ages* (Oxford, 2005); Britnell, *Commercialisation of English society*, pp. 79–228.

to the 'fourteenth century, if not earlier'.[18] Nonetheless, it can be argued that early modern England was more commercially oriented than the medieval economy, as evidenced by increasing regional specialisation in agricultural production and the rapid growth of rural industry after 1500. Although the process of these changes may have been slow and gradual, evolutionary rather than revolutionary, there can be little doubt that eighteenth-century England was a different world to that of the thirteenth century: industrialisation, urbanisation and commercialisation had produced significant changes in cultural, as well as economic and social, life.

Land and tenure

One of the most important themes to have emerged from Tawney, and to a lesser extent Postan, is that of landlord–tenant relations, specifically the issue of tenure. Tenurial change, with the decline of serfdom and the emergence of copyhold and leasehold tenures, was one of the most significant and earliest of these developments, hence the focus hitherto on landlords and tenants. This has been seen as one of the most important factors in the emergence of agrarian capitalism in the late medieval countryside, with the slow redistribution of incomes lower down the social scale enabled by the Black Death and depopulation.[19] Mark Bailey has recently estimated that perhaps 2 million of the 5 million people living in England in 1300 – approximately half of the rural population – were serfs, but by 1500 serfdom had 'simply withered away'.[20] He went on to argue that:

> there is no doubt the dissolution of villein tenure was a significant and beneficial contributor to economic development, because conditions in late sixteenth-century England were much better suited to the accumulation of wealth among the peasantry than they had been in the late thirteenth century.[21]

The evolution of these tenures into the copyholds and leaseholds which so vexed Tawney is a murky but indisputably important part of English agrarian history. As Whittle has noted, 'forms of land tenure were the most significant legacy of the manorial system to the sixteenth century and beyond'.[22] Indeed, it is necessary to recognise both the continuation of medieval forms of tenure well into the early modern period and the clear regional dimension to their survival, including the broad geographical divisions between copyholds for life, copyholds of inheritance and tenant right.[23]

---

18 Dyer, *Age of transition?* p. 3.

19 See, for example, C. Dyer, 'A redistribution of incomes in fifteenth-century England', *Past & Present*, 39 (1968), pp. 11–33.

20 M. Bailey, *The decline of serfdom in late medieval England: from bondage to freedom* (Woodbridge, 2014), p. 5.

21 Ibid., p. 8.

22 J.C. Whittle, *The development of agrarian capitalism: land and labour in Norfolk, 1440–1580* (Oxford, 2000), p. 64.

23 See, for example, R.W. Hoyle, 'Tenure and the land market in early modern England: or a late contribution to the Brenner debate', *Economic History Review*, 43 (1990), pp. 1–20.

Many of the factors in the development of agrarian capitalism across this period originated from the interaction between custom and commercialisation in English rural society: a freer and more widely accessible land market, relatively secure tenure and increasing urbanisation. Tawney and, more recently, Robert Brenner argued that the sixteenth century was particularly significant for the transformation of rural society as commercialising landlords sought to increase their incomes by evicting copyhold tenants, converting their lands to leasehold and, subsequently, rack-renting their lands.[24] However, copyhold tenure, especially copyholds of inheritance, provided tenants with more security than earlier historians acknowledged, with evidence from Earls Colne (Essex) leading Richard Hoyle and Henry French to argue that freeholding yeomen 'farmed much larger areas' and 'were significantly wealthier' than their forebears, holding freehold and copyhold land which gave them 'the security of tenure they required to invest and innovate' and allowing for 'capital formation in the form of the acquisition of further land'.[25] Compared with their medieval predecessors, who Postan and Hilton thought had 'next to nil' opportunities for wealth accumulation, even to the extent of exhausting the fertility of the soil, there were significant potential gains for these copyholding tenants in the early modern period.[26]

More recently, however, there has been a tendency to ascribe many of the same protections that custom afforded to sixteenth-century tenants to their thirteenth-century villein counterparts. This poses an interesting parallel between the two periods. For example, John Hatcher has suggested that English serfs were 'a protected, even privileged, tenurial group' because the 'restraint exercised by custom afforded a considerable measure of protection from the full force of the market'.[27] Similarly, Junichi Kanzaka concluded that 'seigniorial power and market forces were commonly restrained by community custom' in thirteenth-century England because villein rents did not increase in line with the competitive market rents for freehold land.[28] Bailey also observed that the 'gap between the theory of villeinage and its actual practice was maintained by custom' and that regional customs were highly important in 'the consistency with which certain exactions and standard fines were applied on manors

---

24 Tawney, *The agrarian problem* (1912), pp. 177–260. For recent views on Tawney, see the essays in Whittle, *Landlords and tenants*. R. Brenner,'Agrarian class structure and economic development in pre-industrial Europe', *Past & Present*, 70 (1976), pp. 34–70; see also the essays in T.H. Aston and C.H.E. Philpin (eds), *The Brenner debate: agrarian class structure and economic development in pre-industrial Europe* (Cambridge, 1985).

25 H.R. French and R.W. Hoyle, *The character of English rural society: Earls Colne, 1550–1750* (Manchester, 2007), p. 12.

26 M.M. Postan, 'Investment in medieval agriculture', *Journal of Economic History*, 27 (1967), p. 585; R.H. Hilton,'Rent and capital formation in feudal society', in R.H. Hilton (ed.), *The English peasantry in the later Middle Ages: the Ford Lectures for 1973* (Oxford, 1975), pp. 199–200.

27 J. Hatcher,'English serfdom and villeinage: towards a reassessment', *Past & Present*, 90 (1981), p. 24 and p. 5.

28 J. Kanzaka,'Villein rents in thirteenth-century England: an analysis of the hundred rolls of 1279–1280', *Economic History Review*, 55 (2002), pp. 593–618.

of different lordships'.[29] This customary restraint upon the actions of landlords and tenants is a hallmark of the sixteenth century, posing the question as to why the formation of capital took a decidedly different form in early modern England. The thirteenth and sixteenth centuries provide much scope for comparative work because these two centuries both witnessed rapid population growth, inflationary trends, the expansion of markets and increasing commercialisation, but with notably different outcomes: in the first case rural England was pushed to the edge of subsistence in the thirteenth and early fourteenth centuries, whereas in the latter, if the Malthusian cycle was not broken, then at least the foundations were laid for commercial expansion and the agricultural revolutions. Why did population growth in the thirteenth century produce a fragmentation of holdings, whereas in the sixteenth century it produced the dichotomy of engrossed holdings, increasing rural poverty and widespread vagrancy?

There are also problems relating to a lack of consistency both in the use of the terms 'custom' and 'commercialisation' and in discussions surrounding the relationship between the two concepts by medieval and early modern historians. For example, the language used by some medieval historians to describe custom and market forces has focused upon the notion of 'restraint' or 'constraint' provided by custom, portraying what is, at its centre, a conflictual relationship between custom and commercialisation. Kanzaka thought that 'the custom under which unfree tenants held their lands might have protected them against the chill wind of market forces', while Hatcher believed the 'demise of custom gave a freer rein to market forces'.[30] Of course, these historians refer to the protection that custom often provided tenants from rent increases created by competitive market forces for land. In contrast, early modernists such as Richard Hoyle have focused more specifically on custom's tendency to 'limit a lord's income from his tenants', 'lords therefore ha[ving] every reason to want to escape from these customary relationships into market relationships'.[31] But, significantly, custom does not seem to have protected tenants from market forces *in general*; rather, it opened tenants up to commercialisation on a much larger scale than had previously been possible. For example, custom often led to tenants retaining a larger portion of their agricultural profits from the land, leading to wealth accumulation and capital formation among the tenantry of the English countryside. Tenants could buy and sell their tenements, bequeath and inherit them and even sublet them at a market or 'rack' rent, often because of the security enshrined in local customs, thus allowing them to benefit directly from increasing commercialisation. So, in reality, custom and commercialisation were not necessarily conflicting forces, with custom often leading to market penetration much further down the economic and social ladder than ever before specifically because it protected many customary tenants from rent increases and so gave them a larger disposal income.

---

29 M. Bailey, 'Villeinage in England: a regional case study, c.1250–c.1349', *Economic History Review*, 62 (2009), p. 452.

30 Kanzaka, 'Villein rents', p. 593; Hatcher, 'English serfdom', p. 39.

31 R.W. Hoyle, 'Introduction: custom, improvement and anti-improvement', in R.W. Hoyle (ed.), *Custom, improvement and the landscape in early modern Britain* (Farnham, 2011), pp. 4–5.

Custom, community and the law

Aside from issues of tenure, debates surrounding custom have emerged most strongly under the influence of the cultural turn on social history, and there is a considerable focus upon the character of the popular politics of custom and the community, particularly with regard to the enclosure of common land and the loss of common rights, legal or customary. At the centre of these arguments are issues surrounding the changing perceptions of community, custom and law, reflecting the divergent interests of lords and tenants.[32] The economy of pre-industrial England was essentially 'organic' up to the eighteenth century; hence the value of fuel rights and other resources was pre-eminent in local customary economies.[33] Migration and population growth, changes in living standards, increased competition for resources and attempts at commercial exploitation, have been identified as resulting in the more intensive utilisation of resources over time.[34] But how was custom articulated in this period and how did it evolve in the face of these challenges? Custom was a set of rules which, despite drawing upon historical precedent and past practice for legitimacy, often evolved over time and was rooted in the locality. Rural communities relied on custom that was often transmitted orally, although it could be codified through the production of custumals or surveys – a written statement of the economic, social and political customs of a manor – perhaps when it was contested. Much emphasis has thus been placed on the language of custom in the early modern period, with contemporaries referring to custom as having existed 'in the memory of man', since 'time out of mind' and 'time immemorial'.[35] Tawney emphasised the significance of the manorial court as the upholder of manorial custom and in overseeing the regulation of common interests. He defined the custom of the manor as:

> a body of rules which regulates the rights and obligations of the peasants in their daily life. It is a kind of law. It is a kind of freedom. And since it is the custom [of the manor] which most concerns the mass of the peasantry, it is not the state, or the law, but the custom of the manor which forms their political environment and from which they draw their political ideas.[36]

---

32 For example: A. Wood, 'The place of custom in plebeian political culture: England, 1550–1800', *Social History*, 22 (1997), pp. 46–60; N. Whyte, 'Landscape, memory and custom: parish identities c.1550–1700', *Social History*, 32 (2007), pp. 166–86; B. McDonagh 'Negotiating enclosure in sixteenth-century Yorkshire: the South Cave dispute, 1530–1536', in J.C. Whittle (ed.), *Landlords and tenants in Britain, 1440–1660* (Woodbridge, 2013), pp. 52–66.

33 E.A. Wrigley, *Continuity, chance and change: the character of the industrial revolution in England* (Cambridge, 1988).

34 D. Woodward, 'Straw, bracken and the Wicklow whale: the exploitation of natural resources in England since 1500', *Past & Present*, 159 (1998), p. 44.

35 See, for example, Wood, *Memory of the people*, pp. 247–86; E.P. Thompson, *Customs in common: studies in traditional popular culture* (London, 1991), pp. 97–184.

36 Tawney, *Agrarian problem*, pp. 159–62, 244–6.

Manor court records have, therefore, received the attention of both medievalists and early modernists, being interpreted not just as a tool which lords could use against tenants but often as a guarantee of tenants' rights and customs.[37]

It is in the context of enclosure and common rights that the significance of custom is best demonstrated. The enclosure process to which Tawney referred, later outlined by Thirsk and others, brought about transformative agricultural change, shifting conceptions of law and property from the community to the individual, which, in effect, created the development of a modern form of individual private property rights.[38] For commoners, the loss of commons access had a substantial impact on their outlook, producing a significant focus upon the complex and overlapping notions of custom, folklore and memory of past use-rights.[39] The exploitation of commons resources, whether of grazing or pasture land, forms of fuel for domestic or industrial use, or other natural resources, was a means of subsistence and informal relief, access to which was highly contested. Although custom was based upon precedent it was often malleable, as it was grounded in the collective community memory and could be disputed, not only among landlord–tenant interests, but also within village communities, often reflecting attempts to exclude the economically marginal. Indeed, the codification of custom was not a simple process of writing down these customs but was often an arena for the construction of customary practices, providing 'claims to "ancient" customs with a spurious authenticity', often despite their relatively recent

37 For manor courts in the medieval period see P.D.A. Harvey, *Manorial records* (London, 1999); M. Bailey, *The English manor c.1200–c.1500* (Manchester, 2002); For early modern manor courts see C.J. Harrison, 'Manor courts and the governance of Tudor England', in C.W. Brooks and M. Lobban (eds), *Communities and courts in Britain, 1150–1900* (London, 1997), pp. 43–59; A.J.L. Winchester, *The harvest of the hills: rural life in northern England and the Scottish Borders, 1400–1700* (Edinburgh, 2000); B. Waddell, 'Governing England through the manor courts, 1550–1850', *Historical Journal*, 55 (2012), pp. 279–315; J.C. Whittle, 'Peasant politics and class consciousness: the Norfolk rebellions of 1381 and 1549 compared', in C. Dyer, P. Coss and C. Wickham (eds), *Rodney Hilton's Middle Ages: an exploration of historical themes* (Oxford, 2008), pp. 233–47.

38 J. Thirsk, 'Enclosing and engrossing', in J. Thirsk (ed.), *The agrarian history of England and Wales. Volume IV: 1500–1640* (Cambridge, 1967), pp. 200–55; A.J.L. Winchester, 'Property rights, "good neighbourhood" and sustainability: the management of common land in England and Wales, 1235–1965', in B. van Bavel and E. Thoen (eds), *Rural societies and environments at risk: ecology, property rights and social organisation in fragile areas* (Turnhout, 2013), pp. 301–29.

39 W.G. Hoskins, *The Midland peasant: the economic and social history of a Leicestershire village* (Chichester, 2008), pp. 190–1, 254–5, 267; G. Nair, *Highley: the development of a community 1550–1880* (Oxford, 1988), pp. 40–1, 88–9; D.G. Hey, *An English rural community: Myddle under the Tudors and Stuarts* (Leicester, 1974), pp. 31–9; A. Fox, 'Custom, memory and the authority of writing', in P. Griffiths, A. Fox and S. Hindle (eds), *The experience of authority in early modern England* (London, 1996), pp. 97–8; A. Wood, 'The place of custom in plebeian political culture: England, 1550–1800', *Social History*, 22 (1997), pp. 46–60; N. Whyte, *Inhabiting the landscape: place, custom and memory, 1500–1800* (Oxford, 2009).

creation.[40] The efforts of commoners and the rural poor more generally to defend or restore what they believed to be morally and sometimes legally valid common rights illustrate the effects that the loss of commons access had on local societies.

One way in which custom was defined and maintained was through the established administrative and legal structures. It was the dynamic interplay between the legal framework provided by the institutional network of manorial courts, as well as the higher central courts of Chancery and Exchequer, and local custom and manorial by-laws that resulted in the evolution of property rights. Manorial leet courts, as communal courts, were cultural and legal institutions which sought to uphold the private interests of lords while maintaining the customary expectations of tenants. It was the responsibility of the village community and, in particular, the officers of the manor court jury to maintain order through the administration of law and, more importantly, the enforcement of locally established by-laws and customs. Manorial by-laws, which have long been studied for the medieval period, notably by Warren Ault and, more recently, by early modern historians, were one way by which custom could be enforced.[41] For instance, regulations sought to ensure that the exercise of commons use-rights upheld the idea of 'good neighbourhood' in rural communities.[42]

The decline of manorial administration has traditionally been attributed to the rise of the parish following Elizabethan poor law legislation and their increasing domination by a nucleus of landholding tenant farmers. As a result, comparatively less work has problematised the importance of manor courts in the early modern and modern periods given this perceived decline following the end of serfdom and tenurial change in which new administrative units became prominent.[43] Village studies have shown that, by the late sixteenth century, developments which brought about enclosure marked the decline of communal relations, the breakdown of kinship lines and the polarisation of rural society on the basis of wealth.[44] Yet more work is required to ascertain the precise chronology of their decline, which is often viewed as congruent with commercialisation and enclosure.[45] It is widely agreed that the

---

40 See, for example, A. Wood, *Politics of social conflict: the Peak country 1520–1770* (Cambridge, 1999), p. 159.

41 W. Ault, *Open-field farming in medieval England: a study of village by-laws* (London, 1972); Winchester, *Harvest*, pp. 39–40, 45–7.

42 Ibid., pp. 39–40.

43 Bailey, *English manor*, pp. 11–8; J.M. Neeson, *Commoners: common right, enclosure and social change in England, 1700–1820* (Cambridge, 1996), pp. 134–57; Winchester, *Harvest*, pp. 146–51; M.K. McIntosh, *Controlling misbehaviour in England, 1370–1600* (Cambridge, 1998), pp. 34–45; M.K. McIntosh, *Autonomy and community: the royal manor of Havering, 1200–1500* (Cambridge, 1986), pp. 181–215.

44 French and Hoyle, *Earls Colne*; Nair, *Highley*; J.V. Beckett, *A history of Laxton: England's last open-field village* (Oxford, 1989); Hey, *An English rural community*; K. Wrightson and D. Levine, *Poverty and piety in an English village: Terling, 1525–1700* (London, 1979).

45 Harrison, 'Manor courts', p. 45; C.W. Brooks, *Law, politics and society in early modern England* (Cambridge, 2010), pp. 261–6; C.E. Searle, 'Customary tenants and the enclosure of Cumbrian commons', *Northern History*, 29 (1993), pp. 126–53.

sixteenth century saw an increasing polarisation of English rural society on the basis of landholding and wealth which, it is assumed, led to larger wealthier tenants siding with their landowners against the poorer members of the community.[46] This, it has been argued, further resulted in the apparent decline of custom and a diminishing sense of community, leading to a 'culture of local xenophobia'.[47] Arguably, however, where enclosure did not take place in the medieval or early modern periods, this traditional rural economy continued into the eighteenth and nineteenth centuries, until eventual parliamentary enclosure.

Agriculture and rural industry

While in the modern economy there is a clear distinction between the agricultural and industrial sectors it was, prior to the Industrial Revolution (c.1760–1840), often difficult to distinguish so clearly between them. In addition to arable cultivation and livestock production, pre-modern agriculture included the production of raw materials which were necessary for everyday life. For example, wool, flax, linen and hides were used for clothes; animal fat (tallow) was used for candles; feathers were used as quills for writing, which was undertaken on animal skins (*vellum*); and forms of transport were made from wood and relied on the power of oxen and horses. Some specialised industrial crops were grown commercially, such as hemp, hops, woad, weld, madder, saffron and teasels.[48] In the medieval and early modern periods most households were not employed in a single occupation but, rather, had dual occupations or by-employments in addition to being engaged in agriculture. These included brewing, brick-making, milling, tanning, soap boiling, rope-making, weaving, nail-making and a range of other crafts. By-employments were an aspect of rural society revealed after the work of Postan and Tawney, but have long since attracted historians' attention and been the subject of much historiographical debate. However, it should be noted that recent research that has sought to test the reliability of probate inventory evidence by comparing it with occupational data drawn from parish registers for the counties of Cheshire and Lancashire has argued that by-employments were not as widespread as has been previously assumed by historians.[49]

Postan recognised that in the medieval period there existed areas possessing a 'specialised economy' that were smaller in scale than pastoral regions, citing the examples of mining areas in Cornwall, the West Riding of Yorkshire, the Forest of Dean (Gloucestershire) and on the Northumbrian coast; seafaring and coastal fishing villages; areas of charcoal-burning in forests; and regions of localised metal-working around Coventry and the Midlands, and in parts of Yorkshire and Sussex.[50]

---

46 A. Wood, *The 1549 rebellions and the making of early modern England* (Cambridge, 2007).

47 K.D.M. Snell, 'The culture of local xenophobia', *Social History*, 28 (2003), pp. 1–30.

48 For the growth of saffron, for example, see John S. Lee, *Cambridge and its economic region, 1450–1560* (Hatfield, 2005), pp. 108–13.

49 S.A.J. Keibek and L. Shaw-Taylor, 'Early modern rural by-employments: a re-examination of the probate inventory evidence', *Agricultural History Review*, 61 (2013), pp. 244–81.

50 Postan, *Medieval economy and society*, p. 222.

This regional diversity often produced distinctive features of local society, with, for example, coastal and maritime communities experiencing low sex ratios and an exaggerated seasonality of marriages and baptisms because of their reliance on the sea.[51] Analysis of occupational data for the late medieval and early modern periods has revealed the falling proportion of the population directly engaged in agriculture and a rise in those employed in non-agricultural occupations, although the exact chronology of this has been the subject of recent debate.[52]

Custom has played a considerable role in the extractive industries in England since at least the thirteenth century, while the increasing commercialisation of these industries was one of the key features of early modern England which set it apart from other European countries. Andy Wood, for example, has traced the development of the customary rights of lead miners in the Peak District, from the 1288 *Quo Warranto* (by what warrant) proceedings which codified the existing rights of miners to dig for ore wherever it was to be found within the lead field to Lord Hardwick's declaration in Chancery in 1743 that the 'mineral laws and customs [of Derbyshire] were as old as and part of the common law of England'.[53] Similar rights of free mining in the Forest of Dean, again since 'time out of mind', still exist today thanks to the Dean Forest Mines Act of 1838, allowing those aged 21 or over who were born within the Forest and have worked a year and a day in a coal or lead mine to be deemed free miners.[54] Custom also played its role in the precocious development of large-scale commercial coal mining in the North East of England, as in 1619/20, when a dispute between the copyholders of Whickham and the Grand Lessees of the bishop of Durham's coal mines came to a head. Although the copyholders ultimately lost their court action, they cited the custom of the manor and the unreasonableness of the Grand Lessees' actions (which included digging mines on copyhold land without the consent of the sitting tenant) in their defence. As Keith Wrightson pointed out, however, this was not a 'straightforward case of law against custom', since the lessees made their own counter-claim based upon their customary rights as lords of the soil.[55]

Even in the medieval world, Hatcher has highlighted that 'mining was one of the few areas of economic activity where capitalistic organisation flourished'.[56] The mining of stream deposits of tin in mid-thirteenth-century Cornwall, for example, could employ

51 M. Kowaleski, 'The demography of maritime communities in late medieval England', in M. Bailey and S.H. Rigby (eds), *Town and countryside in the age of the Black Death: essays in honour of John Hatcher* (Turnhout, 2012), pp. 87–118.

52 E.A. Wrigley and R.S. Schofield, *The population history of England and Wales: a reconstruction* (Cambridge, 2002); E.A. Wrigley, R.S. Davies, J.E. Oeppen and R.S. Schofield (eds), *English population history from family reconstitution* (Cambridge, 1997); S. Broadberry, B.M.S. Campbell, A. Klein, M. Overton and B. van Leeuwen, *British economic growth, 1270–1870* (Cambridge, 2015).

53 Wood, *Politics of social conflict*, pp. 127–62, quotation p. 148.

54 A ruling in 2010 changed the 1838 proscription of males to male or female, allowing women to become free miners.

55 D. Levine and K. Wrightson, *The making of an industrial society, Whickham 1560–1765* (Oxford, 1991), pp. 120–31.

56 J. Hatcher, *English tin production and trade before 1550* (Oxford, 1973), p. 43.

upwards of 50 labourers, while the royal silver-lead mines of Devon and Cornwall employed more than 300 men in a single operation. There were few comparable examples of large-scale mining in the medieval period, but even landlocked coal mines which employed ten men could serve local markets.[57] From the evidence of the bishop of Durham's coal accounts, Britnell has shown how some of the coal won at such landlocked mines was sold to '*diversis hominibus patrie*' (different men in the country), who purchased coal by the wagonload at the pithead even during the depths of the mid-fifteenth-century recession.[58] By comparison, the expansion of the coal industry was a major driver of commercialisation and urbanisation in certain regions, especially the North East of England and the Midlands, from the late sixteenth century onwards. The annual production of coal from the former coalfields increased from some 65,000 tons in the 1550s to 1,225,000 tons by the 1680s, the output of the latter coalfields growing from a similar starting point to 850,000 tons across the same period.[59] This led to major changes in the coalfields themselves, as land was increasingly given over to the search for this subterranean wealth, but also in the surrounding areas because of the demand for food created by the large workforces needed to extract and transport coal.

Rural industry often coincided with pastoral farming, as livestock husbandry was less labour intensive and so provided the opportunity for by-employments in craft production or mining, with even full-time medieval tin miners usually keeping 'a few animals close to their tin work'.[60] Seasonality also played its part, especially given the propensity of mines to flood during bad weather. These links between the farming economy and industrial activity occurred within a regional framework, as Thirsk emphasised. Regional interpretations have been further enhanced by the use of the French geographical concept of '*pays*' to distinguish past historic landscapes based on economic, social, cultural and environmental factors in order to answer fundamental questions about the character of rural society.[61] The subsequent refining of the regional framework saw greater sub-division take place which considered not just farming practice but also the growth of rural industry and the commercialisation of agriculture, the latter being viewed as more specialised in the period 1640–1750 than in 1500–1640.[62] Work since has shown that early industrial regions whose

---

57 See, for example, the differences between the tin and coal industries: Hatcher, *English tin production*, and J. Hatcher, *The history of the British coal industry. Vol. 1, before 1700: towards the age of coal* (Oxford, 1993).

58 R.H. Britnell, 'The coal industry in the later Middle Ages: the bishop of Durham's estates', in M. Bailey and S.H. Rigby (eds), *Town and countryside in the age of the Black Death: essays in honour of John Hatcher* (Turnhout, 2012), pp. 447–50.

59 J.U. Nef, *The rise of the British coal industry, vol. 1* (London, 1932), p. 19. By the 1780s this had reached 3 million tons from the north-east coalfields and 4 million tons from the Midlands.

60 Hatcher, *English tin production*, p. 47.

61 A.M. Everitt, 'Reflections on the historical origin of regions and pays', *Journal of Historical Geography*, 3 (1977), pp. 1–19.

62 Thirsk, 'The farming regions of England', pp. 1–112; J. Thirsk, *England's agricultural regions and agrarian history, 1500–1750* (London, 1987).

economies were also agricultural experienced deindustrialisation later, such as parts of Cheshire and Lancashire, Essex, Berkshire, Kent, Sussex, Norfolk and East Anglia more widely. Today, the English landscape is still diverse but, historically, it was much more varied in terms of, for instance, farming systems, landscape, topography, field systems, landholding and property ownership, social structures and cultural experience.

Custom and commercialisation

The chapters that form this volume offer insights into the significance of custom and commercialisation in medieval and early modern England. An important aspect which distinguishes this collection from previous work is the focus upon commercialisation and the potential tensions this created in terms of custom and the moral economy, rather than upon the subsistence economy.[63] Instead of concentrating on a particular period or century, this volume intentionally has a broad chronological span, ranging from the thirteenth century through to the eighteenth, showing the interactions between custom and commercialisation at a key stage in what has conventionally been referred to as the 'transition from feudalism to capitalism'.[64] As Christopher Dyer points out in his chapter, historians do not often 'embark on elucidating the far-reaching, long-term, comparative vistas of the past which inspired Tawney and Postan'. In many respects the works of these two historians overlap thematically, and the former recognised the importance of the fifteenth century in providing the context for the agrarian problems of the sixteenth century, making this volume a natural extension and combination of their research interests.

Part 1 opens with several chapters exploring new perspectives and approaches to rural history across the medieval and early modern divide. Dyer (Chapter 1) provides an overview of Tawney and Postan's understandings of the pre-industrial economy and the way they applied theory to historical data, reflecting on their respective contributions and the continuing significance of their work for historians today. While Tawney was, for instance, concerned primarily with social structure and the way this changed with commercial pressures, by contrast Postan was more interested in prices, wages and rents, trends typically examined by classical economists such as David Ricardo as being indicative of economic change.[65] Both

63 E.P. Thompson, 'The moral economy of the English crowd in the eighteenth century', *Past & Present*, 50 (1971), pp. 76–136; Thompson, *Customs in common*, pp. 185–258.

64 S.R. Epstein, 'Rodney Hilton, Marxism and the transition from feudalism to capitalism', in C. Dyer, P. Coss and C. Wickham (eds), *Rodney Hilton's Middle Ages: an exploration of historical themes* (Oxford, 2007), pp. 248–69; See, for example, Maurice Dobb, *Studies in the development of capitalism* (London, 1946); R.H. Hilton et al., *The transition from feudalism to capitalism* (London, 1976).

65 R.H. Tawney, 'The rise of the gentry, 1558–1640', *Economic History Review*, 11 (1941), pp. 1–38; M.M. Postan, 'Money, population and economic change in late medieval Europe', *Economic History Review*, 12 (1959), pp. 77–82; M.M. Postan, 'Some economic evidence of declining population in the later Middle Ages', *Economic History Review*, 2 (1950), pp. 221–46.

were influenced by Marxism but significantly rejected it, the former writing from the perspective of a Christian socialist and the latter opposed to the Bolsheviks.[66] Nevertheless, Eric Hobsbawm acknowledged the strong theoretical underpinning of Postan's work, recounting that, although passionately anti-communist, he was 'the only man in Cambridge who knew Marx, Weber, Sombart and the rest of the great Russians and central Europeans, and took their work seriously'.[67] Moreover, their interpretations of economic change were linked to broader developments, with Tawney making a connection between economic changes and political and religious history, while Postan viewed change as a continuum of economic development from the Roman period up to the present day.

Alexandra Sapoznik (Chapter 2) readdresses the issue of rural industry in the peasant agrarian economy, considering the extent to which recent work on the iron industry might present a challenge to Postan's ideas of rural settlement and patterns of land use.[68] Although agriculture was the largest and most important sector of the late medieval economy, industry occupied a part of the rural labour force and was also a source of both investment and profit for agrarian capital. Drawing upon archaeological sources, she explores iron mining and related charcoal-burning in relation to increasing population and the intensification of agriculture as indicated both by the need for more tools and by settlement patterns in upland and wooded areas. In a wide-ranging essay, John Broad (Chapter 3) explores the relationship between small-scale producers and the land from the later Middle Ages through to the early twentieth century, when customary or feudal rights were finally extinguished with the passing of the Law of Property Act in 1925.[69] In doing so, he offers a framework for the development of an 'English system' of agriculture from the peasant point of view and shows how patterns of landownership were frequently very different from farm structures in English villages.

The book's remaining chapters are case studies addressing specific issues and themes, each highlighting the complexities of the transformations of rural England and demonstrating the value of local and regional approaches. Two chapters examine landownership, migration and identity in rural society across the late medieval and early modern periods, exploring the increasing commercialisation of the land. In Part 2, Sheila Sweetinburgh (Chapter 4) utilises the records of Christ Church Priory to investigate the changing nature of landownership after the Black Death in Kent, examining tenant landholdings, farming practices and the peasant land market. She studies the wills and possessions of tenants in the Kent marshlands to shed further light upon what Tawney called 'the plight of the husbandman'. James P. Bowen

66 For the background to R.H. Tawney and his writing of *The agrarian problem in the sixteenth century* see J.C. Whittle, 'Introduction: Tawney's agrarian problem revisited', in J.C. Whittle (ed.), *Landlords and tenants in Britain, 1440–1660: Tawney's agrarian problem revisited* (Woodbridge, 2013), pp. 1–18; L. Goldman, *The life of R.H. Tawney: socialism and history* (London, 2013), pp. 217–48.

67 E.J. Hobsbawm, 'A life in history', *Past & Present*, 177 (2002), p. 5.

68 Postan, *Medieval economy and society*, p. 205.

69 The Law of Property Act 1925 (c 20).

(Chapter 5) explores what Tawney referred to as the 'struggle for the commons' in the under-researched area of Shropshire. In particular, he focuses on the efforts that lords and tenants made to increase income from commons in the sixteenth and seventeenth centuries by leasing manorial rights and bringing areas of waste into more intensive usage, and also discusses the use of commons by cottagers on both a legal and a customary basis. Tawney recognised the impact of agrarian change on the peasantry and the links it had with the development of the poor relief system in England, as well as the problems that population movement presented, while not being aware of the effect of population change. This is one aspect which he got essentially right, although rather than migrating to the towns or becoming vagrants, those displaced by enclosure became craftsmen, labourers, industrial workers and sub-tenants, playing an equally important role as those employed in agriculture in a diversifying rural economy.

In Part 3, Tom Johnson (Chapter 6) begins by exploring the traditional dichotomy between commercial and customary forces in the valuations of shipwrecks in fourteenth-century Suffolk by a specialist court called the Hethewardmote that registered items found as shipwreck at sea and on beaches. Tawney and Postan did not consider maritime communities in detail in their works, although the medieval historian Maryanne Kowaleski has more recently emphasised the importance of these communities, showing how they adapted to their marine environment.[70] Johnson's chapter uses court records to show the relationship between customary and commercial valuations of shipwrecks and their importance for the second-hand market in coastal areas. The next two chapters explore the use of wood resources in early modern England. William D. Shannon's essay (Chapter 7) investigates the role of custom in disputes surrounding woodland resources in early modern High and Low Furness, Lancashire, drawing on the records of the courts of the Duchy of Lancaster. Wood resources were widely utilised not just for housebote (an allowance of wood made to a rural tenant for repairing the house and for fuel) and ploughbote (a similar allowance for instruments of husbandry), but also for fuel and the rights of browse for tenants' animals. The tenants of Low Furness could take all the timber they needed to repair the sea-defences of Walney Island, while tenants also had the right to all the coppice wood needed to make charcoal for the bloomeries and copper smelters of the region. Simon Sandall (Chapter 8) explores the power of custom in competition over resources in the Forest of Dean, Gloucestershire, stressing the political nature of traditional practices at the village level and in everyday life in the wider context of the large-scale socio-economic changes which took place in rural England in the sixteenth and seventeenth centuries. Building on work which has emphasised the power of custom in motivating and legitimating resistance to the loss of common rights, he shows how the idealised and often fabricated nature of timeless practices claimed the authority of antiquity.

70 M. Kowaleski, 'The demography of maritime communities in medieval England', in M. Bailey and S. Rigby (eds), *Town and countryside in the age of the Black Death: essays in honour of John Hatcher* (Turnhout, 2012), pp. 74–97.

The final three chapters explore the ability of rural society to adapt to changes, both exogenous and endogenous, in this transitional period of English rural history.[71] Although Postan considered the importance of trade, industry and towns, much of his work was focused on agriculture; likewise, Tawney focused primarily on agrarian themes.[72] In Part 4, Alex Brown (Chapter 9) explores the changing consumption patterns of Durham Cathedral across the dissolution and the effect this had on the local economy; after this period, all coal mines were leased out rather than kept in hand for the household consumption of the priory. This chapter also shows the shift from rents paid in kind, which dominated rental payments in the late fifteenth century, to rents paid in cash after the dissolution, exploring how far changes in the priory's demands precipitated the more commercial use of the cathedral's assets. Building on research that has explored the importance of 'industries in the countryside', a theme widely studied by historians since the 1960s, John Gaisford (Chapter 10) explores the role of Elizabethan clothiers in rural society.[73] He examines the businesses established in Somerset's Frome Valley by three outstanding entrepreneurs who marketed and sold the white broadcloth they produced to London merchants for export to the Low Countries and Germany, highlighting the link between commercial agriculture and merchant capital. In the last case study, David Rollison (Chapter 11) examines the changes undergone at Cirencester, Gloucestershire – a rural market town and important regional centre known for its role in the wool trade – from the twelfth to the eighteenth centuries and, using local sources, provides insight into the strategic connectedness and enterprise that drove England's developing urban network. Finally, in an afterword, Andy Wood discusses the recent literature on medieval and early modern English rural society, highlighting ways in which economic and social history can be reunited in the study of this period.

What, then, can we say about the relationship between custom and commercialisation in medieval and early modern England? One of the crucial themes of Tawney's *Agrarian Problem* was the 'struggle between custom and competition, which colours so much of the economic life of the period', and yet many of the following chapters show that, as Rollison argues, commerce was very far from being an enemy to custom.[74] When exploring the shipwreck economy of late medieval Suffolk, for example, Johnson concludes that custom and commercialisation were acting in tandem, with customary expectations shaping the way that shipwrecked goods were valued and distributed. Shannon shows how these two forces were deeply entwined

---

71 See, for example, Epstein, 'Rodney Hilton, Marxism', pp. 248–69; Hilton, *Feudalism to Capitalism*; D. Ormrod, 'Agrarian capitalism and merchant capitalism: Tawney, Dobb, Brenner and beyond', in J.C. Whittle (ed.), *Landlords and tenants in Britain, 1440–1660: Tawney's agrarian problem revisited* (Woodbridge, 2013), pp. 200–15.

72 The former highlighted the importance of towns as specialised localities offering products and services which they became known for: Postan, *Medieval economy and society*, p. 222.

73 J. Thirsk, 'Industries in the countryside', in F.J. Fisher (ed.), *Essays in the economic and social history of Tudor and Stuart England* (Cambridge, 1961), pp. 70–88. M. Zell, *Industry in the countryside: Wealden society in the sixteenth century* (Cambridge, 1994).

74 Tawney, *Agrarian problem*, p. 3.

in the Duchy of Lancaster in the early modern period: custom ensured that the Duchy could not commercially exploit its woods in Low Furness, but a new custumal in High Furness actually secured a charcoal supply for the copper-smelters of Keswick, thus promoting local industry and Duchy profits. The tenants were also able to benefit from this situation and, for them, 'custom and commercialisation were not in conflict, and there seems little doubt that they could and did manipulate custom for commercial advantage'. Sandall takes this further by arguing that the 'obscure world of custom, common right and tradition could also be deployed to aid rather than impede the commercialisation of local industry'. He questions the historical tendency to align the orality of custom with the 'weapons of the weak', showing how local gentry deliberately avoided the specificity of written record, using the nebulous nature of custom to assist their commercial industrial interests. Brown also questions the historical orthodoxy that custom was always beneficial to the tenantry of the English countryside, demonstrating how inflation could be detrimental to tenants paying fixed rents in kind, and highlighting the potential role a large landowner could play in the development of regional markets.

Although the views of Tawney and Postan have experienced extensive revisions over the years, Dyer argues that, without the questions they originally asked, historians would not have embarked 'with such energy and sense of purpose' on research into customary tenures and common rights in the early modern period and commercialisation in the later Middle Ages. According to Sweetinburgh, rather than witnessing a change from an agrarian regime governed by custom to one driven by commercialism between c.1300 and c.1500, the tenure of husbandmen in the Kentish marshlands gave them an advantage over Tawney's tenants in the Midlands. As Sandall notes, it is important that we do not idealise custom as an 'inert force' that protected a bucolic medieval England from the rapacious commercial interests of the early modern period: it is entirely possible that commercialism actually developed so precociously in the English countryside because of custom rather than in conflict with it. Indeed, the contested and often localised nature of custom may have not only enabled the accumulation of wealth further down the social scale than elsewhere in Europe but also provided sufficient scope for manipulation so that it did not impede private enterprise.[75] Broad, for example, highlights how use-rights embedded in English custom were distinctly different from property rights that developed in France, where manorial lords were granted much more autonomy, potentially providing opportunities in the English countryside that were not available on the Continent.

Moreover, the following chapters highlight the dangers of focusing predominantly upon arable and pastoral agriculture in the English countryside, with Sapoznik highlighting how arable growth into marginal lands had significant implications not only for woodlands but also for rural industry such as iron mining, which, in turn, was a pre-requisite for further arable growth. Rural industry and agriculture were thus co-dependent, and the commercialisation of one had a significant impact upon the other. Similarly, Gaisford develops upon work on the cloth industry by showing

---

75 For further discussion of some of these issues, see, for example: Thompson, *Customs in common*, p. 6; Wood, *Memory of the people*, pp. 183–7; Hoyle, 'Introduction: custom', pp. 4–5.

the importance of clothiers in providing the business enterprise required for the commercial expansion of the industry in Tudor England. Based upon a series of local and regional case studies of English rural society, this volume offers new perspectives for discussion and further research. Was there a conflict between custom and commerce across these centuries which saw a largely traditional society replaced by a more capitalist one? Or did the commercialisation of the English rural economy evolve alongside – or perhaps even because of – custom, rather than in conflict with it? How did English rural society respond to the increasing commercialisation of land, labour and resources, and, importantly, what drove these changes? Rural England was undoubtedly different in the eighteenth century from how it was in the thirteenth – much of this change being analysed through the Marxist discourse of the transition from 'feudalism to capitalism' – but, by focusing upon the role of custom and commercialisation, this volume sheds new light upon these fundamental changes in the English countryside.

Part I: Perspectives

Chapter 1

Tawney and Postan: two pathways to understanding the pre-industrial economy

Christopher Dyer

R.H. Tawney and M.M. Postan had a huge influence on twentieth-century interpretations of the pre-industrial economic and social history of England. The Economic History Society now acknowledges the contribution of these commanding figures by naming two post-doctoral fellowships after them. Tawney and Postan were very different in outlook and they represent two traditions that were brought together in the Society and which are still active in the practice of the subject today. They came to economic history along distinctive but parallel paths: their methods were not the same, but they were by no means complete opposites. Tawney was focused on social structures and attitudes, while Postan was more concerned with economic trends. Both were conscious of the dynamic changes indicated by long-term movements in prices, rents and trade. They depicted a rural society dominated by manors, from which the peasant population held land by a variety of tenures. They also appreciated that the state had at least a role, if only limited, in regulating the economy.[1]

Two lives compared

Tawney was the older, having been born in 1880, while Postan's year of birth was 1899. They both lived until the age of 82, so they died 20 years apart, Tawney in 1962 and Postan in 1981. In the early 1920s the middle-aged Tawney taught the youthful Postan and appreciated his qualities. Their lives were changed in different ways by the First World War, Tawney having been severely wounded on the western

---

1 Sources of biographical information used throughout this essay are: T.S. Ashton, 'Richard Henry Tawney 1880–1962', *Proceedings of the British Academy*, 48 (1962), pp. 461–82; J.M. Winter, 'Introduction: Tawney the historian', in J.M. Winter (ed.), *History and society. Essays by R.H. Tawney* (London, 1978), pp. 1–40; L. Goldman, *The life of R.H. Tawney: socialism and history* (London, 2013); E. Miller,'Michael Moissey Postan 1899–1981', *Proceedings of the British Academy*, 69 (1983), pp. 543–57; M.W. Flinn and P. Mathias,'Professor Sir Michael Moissey Postan, 1899–1981', *Economic History Review*, 35 (1982), pp. iv–vi; entries in *Oxford Dictionary of National Biography* (Oxford, 2004), under Postan, M.M. and Tawney, R.H. Both of the historians discussed here were consistently named on their publications by their initials and surnames, not by forenames, as is now the fashion.

Figure 1.1 Photograph of R.H. Tawney. The London School of Economics Library's collections, IMAGELIBRARY/1105.

Figure 1.2 Photograph of M.M. Postan. By kind permission of the Master and Fellows of Peterhouse College, University of Cambridge.

front, while Postan, then in his late teens, was caught up in the post-war turmoil of his native Russia, which forced him into exile in 1919. More important than these personal experiences, perhaps, was the change in the intellectual and cultural climate beginning before 1914, but accelerated in the war, which swept away established ways of thinking, such as the idea that historical change consisted of continuous progress and improvement.

The quintessentially English Tawney numbered among his ancestors the founder of a small provincial bank, and his father was an academic with a post in India. He was educated at Rugby School and Balliol College Oxford at a time when these institutions, though at the heart of the British establishment, were inspired by ideas of moral responsibility and social reform. Postan, the son of a landowner, was born in Bessarabia, of Jewish heritage, and always spoke with a slight Russian accent. Although Tawney could practise history in empirical style, he was interested in general ideas and criticised his fellow countrymen for their lack of conceptual thinking. He taught himself economic history, having taken Greats (classical studies) at Oxford. Postan gave theory a high priority, having studied various social science subjects at three Russian universities and at the London School of Economics (LSE). After an early phase of research on fifteenth-century trade, in which he used a great quantity of data deriving from the customs accounts, Postan was supported in gathering data from archives by others, especially his diligent student J.Z. Titow.[2] He once promised

2 M.M. Postan, 'Credit in medieval trade', *Economic History Review*, 1 (1928), pp. 234–61; E. Power and M.M. Postan (eds), *Studies in English trade in the fifteenth century* (London, 1933); J.Z. Titow, *Winchester yields: a study in medieval agricultural productivity* (Cambridge, 1972) is a substantial example of archival research that helped Postan to sustain his thesis.

to publish a book on manorial profits, which would have been based on manuscript sources, but it did not appear. Tawney spent time in the archives, though in the case of his first book he was helped considerably by assistants transcribing documents in the Public Record Office.[3] He edited collections of documents to make primary sources accessible to students, commented on a sixteenth-century treatise on usury, based a study of occupations on a Gloucestershire muster roll and used a large archive for his life of Lionel Cranfield, an early seventeenth-century merchant and financier.[4]

Tawney published books on sixteenth- and seventeenth-century history, beginning with his famous work on the *Agrarian Problem* in 1912, which was followed by the even better known *Religion and the Rise of Capitalism* in 1926, and then in 1958 the biography of Cranfield.[5] Interspersed with these were books on general political and social themes, notably *The Acquisitive Society* in 1921, *Equality* in 1931 and a study of China's economic problems in 1932.[6] All of these had an historical dimension, but their main purpose was to analyse the contemporary world and propose remedies for current ills. He wrote hundreds of short articles and essays, mostly on contemporary social and political concerns. His best-known article on early modern history, 'The rise of the gentry', appeared in 1941. Some of these shorter pieces of writing were collected and published in edited collections, two of them after his death.[7] His works were much read in the English-speaking world, and not just by academics. *Religion and the Rise of Capitalism* sold more than 100,000 copies, and *Equality* went through five editions.

Postan contributed to the official economic history of the Second World War (which was being written while the conflict was underway), and wrote a book about the post-war European economy. A rather unsatisfactory general survey of the medieval English economy was published in 1972. He made his mark most forcefully through a series of innovative and carefully reasoned articles from 1937 ('The chronology of labour services') to 1962 ('Village livestock in the thirteenth century'), which, taken together, proposed a new interpretation of economic and social change not just

---

3 J.C. Whittle, 'Introduction: Tawney's agrarian problem revisited', in J.C. Whittle (ed.), *Landlords and tenants in Britain, 1440–1660. Tawney's agrarian problem revisited* (Woodbridge, 2013), pp. 1–18, especially pp. 4–5.

4 A.E. Bland, P.A. Brown and R.H. Tawney (eds), *English economic history. Select documents* (London, 1914); R.H. Tawney and E. Power (eds), *Tudor economic documents* (London, 1924), 3 vols; R.H. Tawney (ed.), *Thomas Wilson, a discourse upon usury* (London, 1925); A.J. Tawney and R.H. Tawney, 'An occupational census of the seventeenth century', *Economic History Review*, 5 (1934), pp. 25–64; R.H. Tawney, *Business and politics under James I. Lionel Cranfield as merchant and minister* (Cambridge, 1958).

5 R.H. Tawney, *The agrarian problem in the sixteenth century* (2nd edn, New York, 1967; 1st edn, London, 1912); R.H. Tawney, *Religion and the rise of capitalism* (London, 1926); Tawney, *Business and politics*.

6 R.H. Tawney, *The acquisitive society* (London, 1921); R.H. Tawney, *Equality* (London, 1931); R.H. Tawney, *Land and labour in China* (London, 1932).

7 R.H. Tawney, *The attack and other papers* (London, 1953); Winter, *History and society* (which includes a reprint of 'The rise of the gentry'); R.H. Tawney, *The radical tradition* (London, 1964).

between the eleventh and sixteenth centuries but with a potential to explain the whole pre-industrial past. The more important essays and articles on the Middle Ages were collected in two volumes during Postan's lifetime, and he summed up his main conclusions firstly on trade and then the rural economy in his long contributions to the *Cambridge Economic History* (in 1952 and 1966).[8] Postan was not very well known in Britain outside academic circles, but he was read on the continent by academics, where his theoretical approach to the problems posed by cycles and crises was appreciated. His explanation of the growth of the twelfth and thirteenth centuries, and retreat after 1300, influenced a number of historians across the Channel.

Tawney and Postan had much in common. They taught at the LSE, where Tawney gained a lectureship in 1919 and served as professor until his retirement in 1949. Postan also held a post at the LSE from 1931 to 1935, afterwards moving to a lectureship at Cambridge. He was appointed to the chair in economic history in 1938, from which he retired in 1965. They were notable teachers. Eric Hobsbawm was among those who remembered the electrifying lectures given by Postan at Cambridge in the late 1930s decades after they were delivered, above all because they were expounding exciting ideas in an ebullient style.[9] Tawney attracted an enthusiastic following among adult students, among them potters, miners and industrial workers, for his economic history classes for the Workers' Educational Association (WEA) given in Longton (Stoke on Trent), Rochdale and other manufacturing towns between 1908 and 1914, and intermittently in subsequent years. His inspirational classes had the capacity to change the lives of his students, and often the debates he stimulated continued long into the night.[10]

In their lifetimes the Economic History Society became one of the most important historical organisations in Britain and beyond. Tawney was one of the two joint editors of the *Economic History Review* from 1926 until 1934, when Postan took over as sole editor until 1950, acting as joint editor for a further ten years. Through this long period as successive editors they helped to make the *Review* one of the major historical journals in the world. Tawney was also a pioneer of adult education and, through his own classes and as a leader of the WEA, promoted a knowledge of economic history to the wider public outside the universities. Although these strong, forceful characters moved in different circles, they had many friends and colleagues in common. They admired another charismatic economic historian, Eileen Power, but when he met her Tawney was already married to Jeannette, the sister of William (later Lord) Beveridge,

8 M.M. Postan, *British war production* (London, 1952); M.M. Postan, *An economic history of western Europe, 1945–64* (London, 1967); M.M. Postan, *The medieval economy and society: economic history of Britain, 1100–1500* (London, 1972); M.M. Postan, *Medieval agriculture and general problems of the medieval economy* (Cambridge, 1973); M.M. Postan, *Medieval trade and finance* (Cambridge, 1973); M.M. Postan,'The trade of medieval Europe: the north', in M.M. Postan and E. Miller (eds) *The Cambridge economic history of Europe, vol. II* (Cambridge, 1952), pp. 168–305; M.M. Postan, 'Medieval agrarian society in its prime: England', in M.M. Postan (ed.), *The Cambridge economic history of Europe, vol. I* (2nd edn, Cambridge, 1966), pp. 549–632.

9 E. Hobsbawm, *Interesting times. A twentieth century life* (London, 2002), pp. 110–11, 282–5.

10 Goldman, *Life of R.H. Tawney*, pp. 53–80.

and it was Postan who became her husband. She died prematurely in 1940, and both men were shaken by the loss.[11] Power lived at an elegant London address, Mecklenburgh Square, and when married to Postan they continued to live there. Only a few doors away the Tawneys also had a flat, notorious for its untidiness. The Square was in easy walking distance of the LSE, other parts of the University of London such as University College, the British Museum (which then housed the British Library), the Public Record Office (then in Chancery Lane), and the theatres, clubs and other facilities of Soho, Covent Garden and Shaftesbury Avenue.

Both had connections with the Labour Party. In the 1930s Postan had formed a friendship with Hugh Gaitskell, who was to lead the party in the 1950s, while Tawney helped to form party policy, especially on education.[12] Through such books as the *Acquisitive Society* and *Equality* he gave British socialism an intellectual underpinning which had an influence from the 1920s to the 1960s. As a Christian socialist he also contributed to the social thinking of the Church of England, and had a continued involvement with the church through, for example, his friendship, formed in their boyhood, with William Temple, archbishop of Canterbury between 1942 and 1944.

The achievements of both historians were recognised with the offer of honours. Both were elected Fellows of the British Academy. Postan received a knighthood in 1980, prompting a well-wisher to ask ironically if this made him 'a feudal island in a non-feudal sea' (parodying an aphorism used in *Medieval Economy and Society*).[13] Tawney rejected an offer of a peerage in 1933 with the famous retort 'What harm did I ever do to the Labour Party?'[14] The invitation had come from the prime minister widely believed to have betrayed the party, Ramsay Macdonald, but a more fundamental reason for the refusal lay in Tawney's opposition to privilege and his championing of the cause of equality. As their ideas challenged conventional interpretations, both Tawney and Postan stirred up opposition which could reach a pitch of virulence. The Cambridge professor G.R. Elton used his own inaugural lecture to denounce Tawney for allowing left-wing political prejudices to distort his historical judgement, and many others have registered their disagreement with both his use of evidence and its interpretation. After his death a former student wrote a whole book to expose his supposed errors on the security of customary tenure in the early modern period.[15] Of course, Tawney's socialist ideas led to the criticisms. His historical writing was inspired by a sympathy with the underprivileged classes and hostility towards those enjoying

---

11 M. Berg, *A woman in history. Eileen Power 1889–1940* (Cambridge, 1996), pp. 150–3.

12 M.M. Postan, 'Hugh Gaitskell: political and intellectual progress', in M.M. Postan, *Fact and relevance: essays in historical method* (Cambridge, 1971), pp. 169–82; R.H. Tawney, *Secondary education for all* (London, 1922); R.H. Tawney, *Education: the socialist policy* (London, 1924); Goldman, *Life of R.H. Tawney*, pp. 199–216.

13 The author of the message was R.H. Hilton. Postan had described medieval towns as 'non-feudal islands in the feudal seas' in *Medieval economy and society*, p. 212.

14 Goldman, *Life of R.H. Tawney*, pp. 158–9.

15 Ibid., pp. 217–18; E. Kerridge, *Agrarian problems in the sixteenth century and after* (London, 1969). The criticisms were linked, as Elton was the general editor of the series in which Kerridge's book appeared.

wealth and privilege. That did not mean that he abandoned objectivity or broke the rules about the use of evidence. Postan was less overtly political and, though he was very critical of the Soviet system in his native country, he claimed to find some useful ideas in Marxist historical analysis. His outlook was more conservative than Tawney's and, as we have seen, like the government which awarded him his knighthood, he admired the teachings of the classical economists. In the 1980s and 1990s Postan's views faced strong revisionist criticism, mostly respectful and good-natured, although an economic historian at LSE, again after the death of his opponent, objected to a move to set up a fund in his memory on the grounds that Postan had perpetrated historical errors.

Interpretations and achievements

Although the ideas of Tawney and Postan have to some extent been superseded, they are still remembered. One suspects that their original books and articles are not read very often now, but rather are known at second hand, because historians writing in the last 20 years will refer to the rise of the gentry or 'the Postan thesis' as part of the historiographical context for their own work. They caused a stir in their day, and we still feel the effects of their impact on historical thinking because (to use clichés) they proposed grand narratives and painted big pictures. Their ideas were developed from studies of particular places and times: both focused on England, and Tawney's work was so concentrated on 1540–1640 that those years have become known as 'Tawney's Century'. No-one has ever described a specific period as belonging to Postan, but they could well have used the phrase 'Postan's century' to describe the years 1250–1350. From these specific examples they felt able to learn lessons which were applicable in other times and places. They saw the parallels between pre-industrial England and the less-developed peasant societies of the twentieth century. For example, Tawney visited China in 1931, when the country was attracting the attention of the League of Nations. In *Land and Labour in China* he identified problems of small landholdings, the intensive application of family labour, a shortage of credit and a lack of capital. Part of his prescription of remedies, as well as the obvious need for better systems of land tenure and improved roads, was a radical reform of Chinese education, with less formal lectures and more emphasis on student learning. In similar vein, at an international economic history conference in 1962, Postan set out to advise the Indian government on the basis of Western Europe's experience of economic development, and advocated a focus on the improvement of the agricultural sector.[16] Closer to their home ground, each wrote about periods of British and European history outside the centuries on which they focused their most intense research. Tawney could apply his analysis of the social consequences of profit-seeking capitalism to the period after 1640, while Postan, having identified history as moving not in linear

16 The original conference proceedings has the title 'Agricultural problems of under-developed countries in the light of European agrarian history', but it was reprinted as 'Agriculture and economic development: a lesson of history', in M.M. Postan, *Fact and relevance. Essays in historical method* (Cambridge, 1971), pp. 103–18.

progression but in cycles of expansion and decline, could recommend that approach more generally. His grasp of economics gave Postan the authority and confidence to write about capital formation and technical development in the twentieth century.[17]

To characterise their main contribution to historical understanding, Tawney's great theme was the socially disruptive effects of the rise of early capitalism. Before the mid-sixteenth century peasant society was moving away from the equal division of land found before 1350, and there were signs of mobility, enterprise and 'petty commercialism'. Communities ran the open fields and commons in a flexible way, and relationships between neighbours, and between tenants and lords, were regulated by custom. There was a widespread respect for the 'common good' and writers on social and political matters believed that they were advocating the ideal of a 'commonwealth'.[18] Production was carried out in small units, mainly peasant holdings and artisan workshops, headed by masters who worked alongside family members and some employees. Those who did the work owned their own equipment and livestock. The church helped to unify society and to reinforce ideas of a collective purpose.

Tawney believed that society was undermined by depopulating enclosure and the increasing occupation by large capitalist farms of land that had previously been organised in open fields tilled by villagers living on holdings of modest size. Land was engrossed – that is, holdings were taken into the hands of an acquisitive owner.[19] An important stimulus for the changes came from the rise in prices in the sixteenth century. On the basis of commercialised agriculture, financial capitalism developed and industry expanded, which had the effect of separating people from the land as greater numbers were employed in manufacture. After the Reformation a shift in social attitudes put a new emphasis on the individual and led to harsh criticisms of the idleness and fecklessness of the workers. Greed and selfishness became the guiding lights of a wealthy profit-seeking minority. A social group who did well out of these changes were the landed gentry, who, unlike the continental nobility, invested in their estates, enclosed or encouraged enclosure, changed tenures, overthrew custom and generated increased income from their estates by embracing the new acquisitive spirit. This interpretation bears a close resemblance to Marx's account of the origins of capitalism, but Tawney found inspiration in the English progressives of the nineteenth century, such as Ruskin and Morris, and rarely referred to Marx. His Christian socialism gave his thinking a strong foundation in morality, and he did not subscribe to the Marxist emphasis on class and class struggle. He found evidence for peasant resistance to enclosure and oppression, but he believed in the powers of persuasion and argument to resolve differences.

Postan came from a different starting point, as he based his analysis on the principles which had been devised among the late eighteenth- and nineteenth-century classical economists, and especially David Ricardo. Ricardo argued that the rent of land would fall with repeated cultivation and the colonisation of poor-quality

17 M.M. Postan,'Recent trends in the accumulation of capital', *Economic History Review*, 6 (1935), pp. 1–12; M.M. Postan, *British war production* (London, 1952).

18 Tawney, *Acquisitive society*, pp. 51–6.

19 Tawney, *Agrarian problem*, pp. 260–5.

new land. Postan believed that the agricultural expansion of the twelfth and thirteenth centuries, with greater density of population, rising prices and increased rents, went too far. Repeated cultivation of the same land caused a deterioration in what he called the 'metabolism' of the fields, and when arable fields extended on to marginal land, such as hills and moors, or the sandy soils of parts of East Anglia, the yields soon declined.[20] Peasants kept animals, which played a vital role in maintaining the fertility of the fields through their manure, but the number of sheep and cattle fell far short of the quantity needed to keep the land in good heart. Technological improvement did not come to the rescue by raising productivity and feeding the surplus of population. The intellectual leaders of the period took little interest in science or farming practices, and levels of investment remained at a low level.[21] Growth contained the seeds of its own destruction, which came with the crisis of the early fourteenth century, leading to the abandonment of land, a falling population and an agrarian slump characterised by reduced prices for both produce and land. The tipping point had not been the Black Death of 1348–9, but earlier in the fourteenth century, when the Great Famine of 1315–17 played a major part.

Similar ideas had first been proposed by Abel in the 1930s on the basis of mainly continental evidence, and Postan, in turn, helped to form the thinking of a generation of historians throughout Europe. Le Roy Ladurie took up Postan's depiction of cycles and applied it to the whole of history, comparing the alternate expansions and contractions of population and the economy to the breathing of an immense beast.[22] Postan's great idea is now depicted as a population and resources model of economic change, and it owed little to analyses of social relations: serfdom and feudal obligations were interpreted as an integral part of society, but they had no fundamental bearing on the primary problem of numbers of people and finite landed assets.

The division between Tawney's social approach and Postan's economics are plain to see, yet again the contrasts are not as great as first appears. Postan's quantitative methods required long statistical series, but these were not as abundant as he would have wished. Figures for prices (especially of grain) and wages had been available since the 1860s, but good series of rents were scarce, while grain yields and year-by-year fluctuations in mortality were not researched until after Postan had formulated his ideas.[23] Tithe data that would confirm his argument of rising and falling levels of agricultural production were published as recently as 2007.[24] Tawney knew about the classical economists, and was aware of the need to demonstrate

20 Postan,'Agrarian society in its prime', pp. 552–9.

21 M.M. Postan,'Investment in medieval agriculture', *Journal of Economic History*, 27 (1967), pp. 576–87.

22 W. Abel, *Agricultural fluctuations in Europe. From the thirteenth to the twentieth centuries* (London, 1980) (original German version *Agrarkrisen und Agrarconjunktur in Mitteleuropa vom 13. bis zum 19. Jahrhundert*); E. Le Roy Ladurie,'L'histoire immobile', *Annales ESC*, 29 (1974), pp. 673–92.

23 Titow, *Winchester yields;* M.M. Postan (with J.Z Titow),'Heriots and prices on Winchester manors', *Economic History Review*, 11 (1959), pp. 392–417.

24 B. Dodds, *Peasants and production in the medieval north-east: the evidence of tithes, 1270–1538* (Woodbridge, 2007).

economic trends through statistical series. The background to the 'agrarian problem' was provided by evidence of rising prices in the sixteenth century, which was known well before 1912. Tawney, together with his wife, discovered a source for occupations in Gloucestershire in 1608 which supported his belief in a high level of industrial employment. Systematic nationwide evidence for rents was not published until five years after his death.[25] These pioneers of agrarian and economic history were willing to advance ideas on the basis of rather skeletal evidence, but they stimulated others to explore the sources more systematically and create sets of data on which further advances could be founded. Titow, a student of Postan's, worked on the voluminous records of the bishopric of Winchester, while Joan Thirsk, whose PhD had been supervised by Tawney, gathered evidence from sixteenth- and seventeenth-century probate inventories to define England's varied farming regions.[26]

'Postan's Century' – that is, the period 1250–1350 – which saw the end of growth in population and cultivation and the beginnings of retreat even before the Black Death, ushered in many decades of shrinking and low population, untilled land and low grain prices, which Postan depicted as a generally depressed and gloomy age in his article on the fifteenth century.[27] He emphasised the low values of land and poor market conditions for producers. His thinking connected in chronology with Tawney's work, which, although focused on the sixteenth century, went back before 1500 to set the scene for the great changes of enclosure and engrossing. Tawney's fifteenth century was very different from Postan's. He recognised that the majority of tenants were vulnerable to changes in their terms of tenure, but his emphasis was on the comparative prosperity of the peasantry and their participation in a land market. They invested in land and modified field systems, with some schemes for enclosure. Of course, Postan was reacting in the 1930s against the predominant view among many other earlier writers, such as Kingsley, that the fifteenth century was an age of well-being and progressive improvement. Although they disagreed on the character of agrarian society in the fifteenth century both scholars were making the centrepiece of their narratives two ages of growth, the thirteenth and the sixteenth centuries. In both periods prices and rent rose, trade and industry grew and cultivation was expanding in some parts of the country. It is worth noticing that they were writing in periods of economic and social troubles – in the period before 1914 and in the interwar years – and in such circumstances historians are drawn to make comparisons with happier and more prosperous times. Neither made an explicit comparison between the thirteenth and the sixteenth centuries, but rural society was affected in contrasting ways. In the thirteenth century landholdings would be subdivided or new cottage holdings formed, leading to a greater number of poor smallholders, but in the sixteenth century larger units of tenure remained intact and some of the most prosperous producers were

25 Tawney and Tawney, 'Occupational census'; P. Bowden, 'Agricultural prices, farm profits and rent', in J. Thirsk (ed.), *The agrarian history of England and Wales. Volume IV: 1500–1640* (Cambridge, 1967), pp. 593–695.

26 For Titow see n. 23 above; J. Thirsk (ed.), *The agrarian history of England and Wales. Volume IV: 1500–1640* (Cambridge, 1967).

27 M.M. Postan, 'The fifteenth century', *Economic History Review*, 9 (1939), pp. 160–7.

the farmers of lords' demesnes. The surplus population, many of them poor, were housed in cottages sited on the edge of common pastures. Clearly, institutions such as manors and the tenurial and legal framework had shifted between c.1300 and 1500 to such a degree that similar economic trends could have different consequences.

A distinctive feature of Tawney's writing was his willingness to adopt a moralistic attitude towards the past, leading him to show his disapproval of the greedy landowners and financiers who, in his view, damaged society in the early modern period. Although Postan adopted the detached objectivity typical of the social sciences, a hint of morality crept into his writing when he discussed the ecological implications of high population. According to him, nature punished mankind for its profligate use of resources. One also thinks of Tawney as having the greater concern with social attitudes and culture, but when Postan discussed the failure (as he saw it) of technological innovation to raise productivity, he mentioned the other-worldly preoccupations of medieval intellectuals.[28]

Tawney's breadth of historical vision led him to connect economic and social history with other dimensions of the past. The government legislated on economic matters, seeking to control the enclosure movement in the sixteenth century, and intervened to some effect in fixing the levels of wages.[29] New attitudes to those in poverty arose from the individualism associated with the new religion, and these, together with agrarian changes, paved the way for the Elizabethan poor law. The new emphasis on acquiring wealth was made possible by changes in religion, and in turn had implications for politics. In the long term the upheaval in the transfer of property when the monasteries were dissolved in 1536–40 helped to precipitate the revolution of the 1640s. All of this was relevant to the problems of the twentieth century, and Tawney recognised in the working men he encountered in his adult education classes and in the trenches of the Great War the successors of those he found in the historical records. Tawney was advising on current rates of pay in such industries as chain-making and coal mining in the 1910s and 1920s when he encountered employers or their supporters who believed, like their counterparts in earlier centuries, that low pay and high prices were beneficial because they forced workers to be more productive.

Postan contributed views about current concerns, such as expressing the opinion that the British economy would be healthier in the 1960s if there were fewer interfering economists.[30] He was more cautious than Tawney in connecting the economic history with which he was most familiar with other branches of history. For instance, he was sceptical about claiming that the Hundred Years War had important economic consequences, believing that the passage of the hundred years had a stronger

28 M.M. Postan, 'Why was science backward in the Middle Ages?' in M.M. Postan, *Medieval agriculture and general problems of the medieval economy* (Cambridge, 1973), pp. 81–6.

29 R.H. Tawney, 'The assessment of wages in England by the justices of the peace', in W.E. Minchinton (ed.), *Wage regulation in pre-industrial England* (Newton Abbot, 1972), pp. 37–91 (originally published in *Vierteljahrschrift fur Sozial- und Wirtschaftsgeschichte*, 11 (1913–14), pp. 307–37 and 533–64).

30 M.M. Postan, 'A plague of economists', in M.M. Postan, *Fact and relevance. Essays in historical method* (Cambridge, 1971), pp. 80–91.

influence than did the war.[31] He briefly suggested that falling landed incomes in the fifteenth century might have influenced the political behaviour of the aristocracy in the Wars of the Roses, and argued that in the same century the perpendicular style of architecture was appropriate to an age of economic recession, as the slender columns and large windows required less stone than had the monumental churches of the twelfth century.[32]

Critics of the 'big pictures'

The bold hypotheses of the two historians achieved such prominence that they attracted criticism. Mention has already been made of the more extreme responses, but other researchers who were not motivated by political or personal antagonism tested the ideas and found that they should be modified or even that they could not be sustained. It was a tribute to the quality of the arguments advanced by the two scholars that they provoked serious debate and questioning. The critics said that Tawney's *Agrarian Problem* was based on too narrow a range of sources, in that he made limited use of manorial court records, and his arguments had been overtaken by new advances in, for example, historical demography.[33] Nonetheless, the centenary of the book's publication was marked by a conference of agrarian historians and, while the participants found much to criticise and correct, they were able to engage with the book as a serious enquiry into the period that still commanded some respect.[34] The social and economic repercussions of religious changes in the century after the Reformation, and in particular the social significance of puritanism, have attracted much research and comment, leaving Tawney's work far behind.[35] The 'Rise of the gentry' provoked fierce reactions from which little of Tawney's idea emerged intact. The whole subject of the involvement of the gentry in the origins and conduct of the Civil War was given a stimulus by the debate about the 'county community', but that approach was also found wanting, leaving us with a new emphasis on political and religious ideas as the mainspring of the conflict.[36]

Postan's thesis was found to depend on uncertain statistical foundations, such as his calculations of village livestock. His negative view of demographic expansion was modified by the observation that a high population density could

31 M.M. Postan, 'Some social consequences of the Hundred Years War' and 'The costs of the Hundred Years War', in M.M. Postan, *Medieval agriculture and general problems of the medieval economy* (Cambridge, 1973), pp. 49–62, 63–80.

32 Postan,'Fifteenth century'.

33 L. Stone, 'Introduction to the Torchbook edition', in R.H. Tawney, *The agrarian problem in the sixteenth century* (2nd edn, New York, 1967; 1st edn, London, 1912), vii–xviii.

34 J.C. Whittle (ed.), *Landlords and tenants in Britain, 1440–1660. Tawney's agrarian problem revisited* (Woodbridge, 2013).

35 For example, G. Marshall, *In search of the spirit of capitalism. Max Weber and the Protestant ethic thesis* (London, 1982).

36 J. Eales and A. Hopper (eds), *The county community in seventeenth-century England and Wales* (Hatfield, 2012).

lead to an increase in productivity, as people were assets to the labour force rather than burdensome extra mouths to feed. His ideas about population change were challenged by those who saw the key factors as the age of marriage and fluctuation in the birth rate, which made the fourteenth-century crisis seem less catastrophically dependent on mortality.[37] Alternatively, disasters did occur but they were caused by an adverse climate and a virulent plague, which were visitations from the natural world, not the consequence of social and economic weaknesses.[38] The continuation of a low population and a sluggish economy into the fifteenth century could not be explained by a demographic crisis between 1315 and 1370 because economic circumstances favoured a recovery, as was the case in parts of continental Europe. A surge of interest in the history of technology, especially farming methods, showed that Postan underestimated the capacity of people to apply more intense cultivation by using the abundant supplies of labour. For example, it has been shown that in densely populated parts of Norfolk around 1300 the land was ploughed often, manure was applied, the crops were weeded and high yields were gained year after year, without much fallow.[39] Commercialisation gave historians an alternative model to Postan's picture of poor peasants struggling to provide their families with basic subsistence needs.[40] Crops and animal products were grown for the market and the cultivators were stimulated to change their cropping patterns to get the best prices. The apparently poverty-stricken smallholders might well have been employed in rural industries. Postan may have been mistaken, but much of the research which probed his weaknesses was stimulated by his generalisations about the driving forces behind the economy. His legacy includes a general acceptance that the period saw a cycle of expansion and contraction, and we still do not know the underlying causes. In some regions there may have been a problem of routine cultivation of soils with applications of inadequate quantities of manure, leading to low yields and peasant poverty, in line with his analysis.

Tawney and Postan enriched and enlivened debates on economic history. They inspired a new generation of scholars whose theses they supervised.[41] Undergraduates were drawn into an interest in economic history by these ideas, and their historical imaginations were stimulated by, for example, Tawney's suggestion that the decline of villeinage led to the introduction of the poor law, or by Postan's phrase about towns appearing as non-feudal islands in the feudal seas. Without the questions that they asked we would not have embarked with such energy and sense of purpose on studies of early modern enclosures, customary tenures and common

37 R.M. Smith, 'Plagues and people. The long demographic cycle, 1250–1670', in P. Slack and R. Ward (eds), *The peopling of Britain: the shaping of a human landscape* (Oxford, 2002), pp. 117–210.

38 B.M.S. Campbell, 'Nature as historical protagonist: environment and society in pre-industrial England', *Economic History Review*, 63 (2010), pp. 281–314.

39 B.M.S. Campbell, 'Agricultural progress in medieval England: some evidence from eastern Norfolk', *Economic History Review*, 36 (1983), pp. 26–46.

40 R.H. Britnell, *The commercialisation of English society, 1000–1500* (Cambridge, 1993).

41 Postan's research students included E. King and J. Titow; Tawney supervised F.J. Fisher and Joan Thirsk.

rights – in the case of Tawney – and without Postan's thesis we would not have given so much attention to historical demography, agricultural productivity, technology or commercialisation in the later Middle Ages.

Historians now seem too timid to embark on elucidating the far-reaching, long-term, comparative vistas of the past which inspired Tawney and Postan. We specialise, stick to short periods of time and focus on specific research questions and themes. They could offer contributions to current political controversies, but few historians venture into public engagement, even on such issues as constitutional change, for which past events have particular relevance. We are too insular, and are reluctant to make the comparisons between different parts of Europe, or outside Europe, that can be a fruitful source of insights, as Postan, in particular, showed. We sometimes forget that even a small local study can be given a universal significance if it applies a theory, preferably from a discipline outside history, such as the social sciences, in which both Tawney and Postan were well read. They gave much time to organisations which promoted and nurtured their subject, notably the Economic History Society. Scholars now are sometimes reluctant to become involved in such voluntary organisations because of the time they consume, but service given to a learned society enriches the lives of everyone involved, as contacts are made and ideas exchanged.

Which of them made the greatest contribution? That is a question of taste and temperament, so to some extent an answer depends on subjective preferences. Postan was the most incisive and scientific. He had a brilliant explanatory model into which the whole of history could be fitted: this reader, for a time, was totally convinced. His method was clear and yielded impressive results, depending on defining a problem, assembling the relevant facts and devising a solution. The result was satisfying because the sources were scrutinised critically and the figures were manipulated with skill. In contrast, Tawney's approach depended on surveying a wide range of disparate evidence and completing a formidable amount of reading, often using literary sources rather than the administrative records favoured by Postan. From these pamphlets, sermons and statutes connections could be made between economics, religion and politics. The results were rarely simple, but they were full of interest, empathy and thoughtful comparisons. Tawney's synthesis convinces the reader because it admits that in past societies, just as in our own, life could be complex and contradictory.

Chapter 2

Rural industry and the peasant agrarian economy: a study of the iron industry in medieval England

Alexandra Sapoznik

The Postan thesis

Few ideas have been more important to the study of medieval agrarian history, and medieval economic history more broadly, than the Postan thesis. First discussed at length in his highly influential chapter 'A medieval agrarian society in its prime' in the *Cambridge economic history of Europe*, published in 1966, and articulated with greater clarity in his 1972 work *Essays on medieval agriculture and general problems of the medieval economy*, the Postan thesis laid out a powerful argument for the settlement of land, its use and ultimately its depletion in the late thirteenth and early fourteenth centuries.[1] Simply put, Postan argued that, given the choice, people would first settle the most fertile and easy to cultivate land. As the population expanded, especially over the thirteenth century, more land was needed. The need for more arable land resulted in two simultaneous types of expansion, both of which were ultimately unsustainable. One was taking in new land that had previously lain uncultivated. Because the best land had been taken in the first waves of settlement, this new land was of lesser quality than that which was already under cultivation. Thus a growing section of the population was increasingly reliant upon holdings of land unsuited, or at least not best suited, to arable agriculture. Alongside this expansion of arable, land holdings in established settlements were fragmented to support a greater number of people. Thus the proportion of smallholding peasants increased over the period. Under such pressure, Postan argued, land use became more intense and yields began to fall by the end of the thirteenth century. Matters were made worse by what Postan considered to be a chronic lack of manure due to the conversion of pastures to arable in order to make room for more cereal cultivation. By the second decade of the fourteenth century the system was stretched so thin that there was no slack with which to cope in years

1 M.M. Postan, 'A medieval agrarian society in its prime', in M.M. Postan (ed.), *The Cambridge economic history of Europe, vol. I* (Cambridge, 1966), pp. 548–632; M.M. Postan, *The medieval economy and society: an economic history of Britain, 1100–1500* (London, 1972), pp. 62–72.

of poor harvests.[2] Now, in Postan's famous phrase, 'the marginal character of marginal lands was bound to assert itself, and the honeymoon of high yields was succeeded by long periods of reckoning, when poorer lands, no longer new, punished the men who tilled them with failing crops and with murrain of sheep and cattle'.[3] The breaking point came in the form of three years of spectacularly bad weather from 1314 to 1316 in which harvests failed, causing the Great Famine of 1315–17, during which period it is estimated that up to 10 per cent of the population of England died.[4]

Postan's thesis has been subject to numerous criticisms and qualifications in the decades since it was first promulgated, but subsequent research regarding the expansion of settlement, if not its later desertion, has broadly supported Postan's emphasis on expansion to more difficult terrain, such as upland areas, coastal marshes and regions of very heavy or very thin soils, particularly over the thirteenth century.[5] Yet, as Mark Bailey and others have noted, the assumption that this land was economically marginal overlooks the multiplicity of uses to which land could be put in the medieval period.[6] Postan was careful to note that his emphasis on the primary role of agriculture in the medieval economy did not imply that 'industrial and commercial activities were wholly insignificant and played little part in shaping the economic geography of the country'.[7] Yet the lack of sources with which to quantify domestic trade and levels of industrial production in England meant that he had little evidence with which to reflect further upon the ways in which rural

2 Ibid. Postan's assessment was based on Titow's research on the Winchester estates, which shows declining yields in the early fourteenth century: J. Titow, *Winchester yields: a study in medieval agricultural productivity* (Cambridge, 1972).

3 M.M. Postan, 'Economic foundations of medieval society', in *Essays on English agriculture* (Cambridge, 1973), p. 14.

4 I. Kershaw, 'The Great Famine and agrarian crisis in England 1315–1322', *Past & Present*, 59 (1973), pp. 3–50; M.M. Postan and J. Titow, 'Heriots and prices on Winchester manors', *Economic History Review*, 11 (1959), pp. 392–411; B. Harvey, 'Introduction: the crisis of the early fourteenth century', in B. Campbell (ed.), *Before the Black Death: studies in the 'crisis' of the early fourteenth century* (Manchester, 1991), pp. 1–24.

5 For critiques see, for example, B.M.S. Campbell and M. Overton, 'A new perspective on medieval and early modern agriculture: six centuries of Norfolk farming c.1250–c.1850', *Past & Present*, 141 (1993), pp. 38–105; G. Clark, 'The economics of exhaustion, the Postan thesis, and the agricultural revolution', *Journal of Economic History*, 52 (1992), pp. 61–84. For the expansion of settlement see the relevant chapters in H.E. Hallam (ed.), *The agrarian history of England and Wales. Volume II: 1042–1350* (Cambridge, 1988).

6 M. Bailey, *A marginal economy? East Anglian breckland in the later Middle Ages* (Cambridge, 1989). It must be noted that the long-standing assumption that waste land was economically marginal has been largely discredited, particularly for upland areas, where wastes were important resources for pastoral husbandry and for a range of agricultural and non-agricultural activities. See, for example, A.J.L. Winchester, *The harvest of the hills: rural life in northern England and the Scottish Borders, 1400–1700* (Edinburgh, 2000) and H.S.A. Fox, *Dartmoor's alluring uplands: transhumance and pastoral management in the Middle Ages* (Exeter, 2011).

7 Postan, *Medieval economy*, p. 183.

industry might complicate patterns of settlement and land use across wide spans of space and time.

This lack of written evidence is particularly frustrating with regard to the iron industry, which, unlike the mining of lead and especially tin, left very little trace in the documents of the period. Iron was used to make agricultural and domestic implements crucial to the livelihood of the population and the expansion of the economy. As Bartholomew Anglicus wrote in the mid-thirteenth-century encyclopaedia *De proprietatibus rerum*, 'well nigh no handiwork is wrought without iron: no field is eared without iron, neither tilling craft used, nor building builded without iron'.[8] Iron tools included ploughshares and coulters, spade shoes, hoes, axes, weeding hooks, horseshoes, nails and, importantly, the shears with which sheep were shorn to produce the wool which was of such famous quality and importance to England's export economy. Iron parts were fundamental to making medieval agricultural tools more effective, increasing efficiency and productivity. Indeed, the French historian Georges Duby considered the proliferation of rural forges to be 'one of the most reliable indexes of the improvement of peasant tools'.[9] It is no surprise, then, that court rolls indicate the universal presence of smiths on manors across England by at least the later thirteenth century. Although Postan famously noted the 'inertia of medieval agricultural technology', there can be no doubt that the increasing expansion of settlement and intensification of agriculture upon which his thesis rested would not have been possible without iron implements with which to clear and cultivate the land.[10] Consequently, as demand for arable increased, so too did demand for iron.

The improvement of peasant tools through the use of iron was a vital factor in enhancing the ability of peasants to use their land more intensively, which became particularly important over the thirteenth century as the number of smallholders increased and pressure on peasant land became ever more acute. It has recently been argued the application of small-scale, labour-intensive technologies, such as hand cultivation using iron-shod spades, was a crucial component of peasant agriculture and was driven by the need to increase land productivity on small holdings.[11] Thus, in addition to a growing number of ploughs with iron shares and coulters, a large proportion of the iron in medieval England must have been consumed as components for hand tools.[12] This in turn was a function of population pressure

8 R. Steele, *Mediaeval lore from Bartholomaeus Anglicus* (London, 1907), p. 40.

9 G. Duby, *Rural economy and country life in the medieval West*, trans. C. Postan (Philadelphia, 1968), p. 108.

10 Postan, *Medieval economy*, p. 44.

11 J. Myrdal and A. Sapoznik, 'Spade cultivation and intensification of land use 1000–1300: written sources, archaeology and images', *Ruralia X* (forthcoming).

12 It has been estimated that ploughs and ards required only a third to half as much iron as did the hand tools necessary for cereal cultivation. Comet considered the increased use of the plough during the Carolingian period to have been a response to iron shortage: G. Comet, 'Technology and agricultural expansion in the Middle Ages: the example of France north of the Loire', in G. Astill and J. Langdon (eds), *Medieval farming and technology: the impact of agricultural change in northwest Europe* (New York, 1997), p. 27. For a list of hand tools used in medieval agriculture see

on land and declining holding sizes, factors crucial to understanding the medieval economy and so clearly demonstrated in the work of Postan, Jan Titow and many others.[13] Given the economic pressure under which most peasants were operating over the thirteenth and early fourteenth centuries, it seems likely that demand for modest amounts of cheap iron encouraged small-scale production across the country, even in places far away from the main iron-producing regions. Moreover, the iron losses incurred from the friction involved in using medieval tools were significant and meant that implements needed constant repair and replacement.[14] Consideration of iron production, therefore, offers an opportunity to explore the relationship between landscape, small-scale industry and the technological developments that facilitated the intensification of peasant agriculture in the high medieval period.

The iron industry in England

Iron has been mined in England for over 2,500 years.[15] Unlike lead and tin, which are confined to relatively small areas, iron is found in almost every region of England, although the quality and quantity of the ore varies across the country.[16] Iron carbonate, soft and easy to smelt, is found in the Weald of Kent and Sussex and along the Jurassic ridge in the midland counties of Oxfordshire, Northamptonshire and Lincolnshire. Harder haematite, from which steel can be made, is found in Cumberland and Furness (Lancashire), while in the Forest of Dean (Gloucestershire) limonite is the principal iron ore. Bog iron, too, could be found in England, on the northern moors where the acidic soils reacted with iron-bearing water to precipitate out iron compounds. The iron produced through the processing of haematite and limonite was of higher quality than that taken from bogs or the Weald, and although the latter was an important site of iron-working over the Middle Ages, the greatest sources of iron ore were the Forest of Dean – which was of such high quality that it was transported all the way to London – parts of the Midlands and south Yorkshire, and, to the north, in Cumberland, Durham and Northumberland.[17] The iron mined

J. Langdon, 'Agricultural equipment', in G. Astill and A. Grant (eds), *The countryside of medieval England* (Oxford, 1988), p. 96.

13 Classically, J.Z. Titow, 'Some evidence of the 13th century population increase', *Economic History Review*, 14 (1961), pp. 218–24; see also J. Hatcher and M. Bailey, *Modelling the Middle Ages* (Oxford, 2001), especially pp. 44–9.

14 Karlsson calculated from experiments using medieval forging techniques that wear on ploughs in Uppland, Sweden over the high Middle Ages would have amounted to 100g per hectare (8.72 ounces per acre): C. Karlsson, 'Förlorat järn – det medeltida jordbrukets behov och förbrukning av järn och stål' (unpublished PhD thesis), Swedish University of Agricultural Sciences, 2015, p. 5.

15 For what follows see J. Geddes, 'Iron', in J. Blair and N. Ramsey (eds), *English medieval industries* (London, 1991).

16 In England, lead is found in parts of Yorkshire, Durham, Derbyshire, the Mendip Hills (Somerset) and south Devon; tin is found only in Devon and Cornwall.

17 Geddes, 'Iron', p. 167; D.W. Crossley, 'Wealden iron', in H.F. Cleese and D.W. Crossley (eds), *The iron industry of the Weald* (Leicester, 1988), p. 103.

in England was of varying quality, for the most part suited to everyday items such as agricultural implements and industrial tools, rather than expensive luxury items – although the almost-constant campaigns against the Welsh, Scots, and French over the thirteenth and early fourteenth centuries also drove iron consumption.[18] Indeed, it has been estimated that 500,000 crossbow bolts were purchased from the Forest of Dean alone between 1223 and 1297.[19] The existence of iron ore was not the only factor which determined the level of iron production in various regions of England. Iron-working required a tremendous amount of fuel, and so the main sites of iron production were in, or very near, large tracts of woodland. The growth of the iron industry, therefore, also stimulated and fed off of growth in the ancillary charcoal-burning industry. Because of the constant use of heat and fire, a steady source of water was also necessary for both charcoal and iron production.

Where the ore was close to the surface, bell pits were dug. The collapsed remains of these pits still mark the landscape in places such as the Weald and are a clear topographical indication of pre-modern mining activity (Figure 2.1). As the name suggests, bell pits were narrow – about 5 feet in diameter – and circular at the top. Miners then dug down to the iron deposit and worked out at the bottom until the seam was depleted, the mine started to collapse or the ventilation became too poor, often at a depth of about 12 feet. These pits, which were common in Yorkshire, Lancashire and the Weald, were typically between 7 and 20 feet deep, and contrast with trenches dug in the Forest of Dean, some of which reached depths of more than 40 feet.[20] Once the ore or ironstone was extracted the slag was melted off. First, the iron ore was washed before being roasted to make it break into smaller pieces more easily. The roasted ore was then crushed before being layered with charcoal in hearths into which bellows blew strong draughts to raise the temperature to 1,200 °C, the point at which slag melts. Slowly, the iron formed a mass in the hearth called a 'bloom', which was then further refined through a process of repeatedly reheating at temperatures reaching 1,400 °C and hammering the bloom to knock off remaining slag before forming it into bars which were then chopped into pieces and sold.[21]

Two points regarding land use will be clear from this brief description of iron production. First, it was intensely exploitative of the land and its resources. Second, it occurred largely in places not known for their highly productive arable agriculture. The iron industry, then, offers a glimpse of the complicated ways in which the landscape and its use were managed and controlled in order to meet the needs

---

18 Generally, very high quality iron was imported: Gascon and Breton iron was used for the late thirteenth-century improvements to St Stephen's chapel, Westminster; Spanish iron for the early fourteenth-century improvements to Canterbury Cathedral; Swedish iron for hardening the edges of weapons for war: Geddes,'Iron', p. 168.

19 C.E. Hart, *The free miners* (Gloucester, 1953) p. 49 cited in J. Birrell, 'Peasant craftsmen in the medieval forest', *Agricultural History Review*, 17 (1969), p. 100.

20 J.G. McDonnell, 'An account of the iron industry in upper Ryedale and Bilsdale, c.1150–1650', *Ryedale Historian*, 6 (1972), p. 25.

21 A comprehensive description is given in Geddes, 'Iron', p. 170; also J.G. McDonnell, 'Iron industry', pp. 26–8.

Figure 2.1 The remains of medieval iron workings, now in modern arable fields, near Elmley, West Yorkshire. Cambridge University Collection of Aerial Photography (CUCAP) NB008.

of various stakeholders. Those lands which might at first glance be considered 'marginal' in terms of agricultural productivity were nonetheless vitally important to arable cultivation.

One of the biggest obstacles to understanding iron production in England during the Middle Ages is that the industry was largely unregulated and, therefore, largely undocumented. Iron production is rarely mentioned in manorial documents, although it does appear occasionally. For example, the accounts for the Durham Priory manor of Muggleswick from the turn of the fourteenth century record that an average of just over 372 stones of iron were produced there annually and sent to Durham or to the Priory's non-iron-producing manors.[22] On the whole, iron for specific items ordered directly by a king or lord tend to be better documented. For example, the Weald was a favoured large-scale supplier of iron for the king, judging by the 8,000 horseshoes and 20,000 nails Henry III ordered the archbishop of Canterbury to supply in 1242, and the 30,000 horseshoes and 60,000 nails he ordered as purveyance from the sheriff of Sussex in 1253.[23] In 1359 Kent and Sussex smiths were to forge 500 steel arrowheads to supply the king's army in France, suggesting that the Wealden iron industry was not entirely confined to everyday items.[24] But, apart from a scattering of entries in royal and manorial accounts, it is difficult to know from where the greater part of the medieval population – the peasantry – acquired their iron. Lords held rights to minerals and wood on their lands, but tenants could pay for licences to mine, work a forge or burn charcoal. Once this licence was paid the industry disappears from the written record, and in many places even this documentation is lacking. For example, the exceptionally informative court rolls from Wakefield (West Yorkshire) note that in June 1316 John, son of Robert, 'began to work and burn in the great wood of Wakefield' and would pay 14s a week 'for his forge'.[25] How many people were working with him cannot be known, although the high price for renting the forge suggests that this could have been a major operation. On the other hand, there is no written documentation of iron-working at Stanley Grange (Derbyshire) in the Middle Ages, yet excavation of a modern open-cast mine has revealed eight medieval furnaces, one possibly wind-powered, burnt slag and scatters of pottery, including cooking vessels.[26] Archaeomagnetic dating indicates that iron was produced at this site between 1220 and 1315. Again, how many people were working at this site and how long they spent there is unknown. Similarly, no written evidence survives to indicate iron-working at Hemsworth and Baildon (Yorkshire), although archaeological evidence has revealed an extensive industry there.[27] On the other hand, iron finds, particularly large finds such as ploughshares and even spade irons, are surprisingly uncommon, despite their presumable ubiquity in the English countryside.[28] This may have been because larger iron pieces were re-formed by

22 R.H. Britnell (ed.), *Durham priory manorial accounts, 1277–1310* (Woodbridge, 2014), pp. lvii–lxi. I am grateful to Alex Brown for this citation. In the fifteenth and early sixteenth centuries Muggleswick was a centre of local trade in iron: M. Threlfall-Holmes, 'Late medieval iron production and trade in the north-east', *Archaeologia Aeliana*, 5th ser., 27 (1999), pp. 109–23.

23 H.F. Cleese and D.W. Crossley, *The iron industry of the Weald* (Leicester, 1988), p. 88.

24 Crossley,'Wealden iron', p. 104.

25 J. Lister (ed.), *Court rolls of the manor of Wakefield, vol. 3* (Leeds, 1917), p. 146 (hereafter *WCR*).

26 P. Beswick and K. Challis, 'Pottery from the medieval iron smelting site at Stanley Grange, Derbyshire', *Derbyshire Archaeological Journal*, 124 (2004), pp. 69–85.

27 M.L. Faull and S.A. Moorhouse, *West Yorkshire: an archaeological survey to A.D. 1500, vol. 3* (Wakefield, 1981), p. 776.

28 A comprehensive list of iron finds is in I.H. Goodall, *Ironwork in medieval Britain* (Wakefield, 2011).

local smiths and used for a variety of purposes.[29] This in itself is clear evidence of how valuable iron was to medieval peasants, and archaeological excavation of iron production sites is, therefore, vitally important to understanding the scale of the iron industry in England.

Some light may be shed on the iron industry by comparison with the better-documented lead and tin mining. Evidence from these industries shows that many workers were involved in metal production only part-time, and that they also had arable and livestock holdings.[30] The extent to which a household was engaged in industry or agriculture was no doubt related both to the size of the metal-working sector in the region and the number of people seeking – or competing for – employment in the industry. Manorial records show that over the late thirteenth and early fourteenth centuries agricultural wage rates fell as the market became saturated with those looking for work. A similar mechanism appears to have been at work in some areas of metal production. Tinners' wages are notoriously difficult to calculate, but the increase in the number of tinners and the consequent decline in tin output per person from 1288 to 1301 suggests a surfeit of labour and consequent poverty in ways not entirely dissimilar to that found in the agrarian sector.[31] Lack of similar taxation and regulation means that the iron-mining industry left no similar records, but it seems probable that iron workers, who were subject to the same broad economic conditions as tinners, also felt a downward pull on their income. Thus it is unlikely that many people found iron production to be viable as a full-time occupation and it is important, therefore, to note that miners, charcoal burners and others involved in iron production were not far removed from settlements and communities. An example of the close relationship between settlement and industrial activity is to be found near Parrock (Sussex), where fieldwalking has uncovered five smelting sites with slag and late medieval pottery very near a settlement that was deserted around the turn of the sixteenth century. At Parrock it appears that iron mining attracted settlement, and both industry and settlement expanded together over the thirteenth and fourteenth centuries but declined and contracted thereafter. The subsequent abandonment of Parrock appears to have been due in large part to changes in the iron industry in the sixteenth century.[32]

---

29 Although Karlsson has cast doubt on the efficiency of re-using iron by drawing attention to the losses involved in re-forming iron: C. Karlsson, 'Förlorat järn'.

30 I. Blanchard, 'The miner and the agricultural community in late medieval England', *Agricultural History Review*, 20 (1972), pp. 93–106; J. Hatcher, *Rural society in the Duchy of Cornwall, 1300–1500* (Cambridge, 1970).

31 The number of tinners presenting tin for coinage in Devon rose from 300 in 1288 to 440 in 1301, while the amount of tin presented for coinage fell from 98,052lb to 53,000lb, so that the amount of tin per tinner fell from 327lb to 145lb. In Cornwall the number of tinners rose from about 2,000 in the early fourteenth century to about 5,000 by the end of the century: J. Hatcher, *English tin production and trade before 1550* (Oxford, 1973), pp. 65, 67, 84; H.P.R. Finberg, *Tavistock Abbey: a study in the social and economic history of Devon* (Cambridge, 1951), p. 187.

32 C.F. Tebbutt, 'An abandoned medieval industrial site at Parrock, Hartfield', *Sussex Archaeological Collection*, 113 (1975), pp. 146–50.

Because the dating of materials is often problematic, the relationship between settlements and industrial sites is difficult to ascertain from the archaeological record. Nonetheless, excavations in Bourn (Cambridgeshire) and Braggington (Shropshire) have revealed evidence of iron-working within medieval crofts.[33] More interesting, perhaps, are the areas where industrial activity and agriculture overlapped, possibly coming into conflict, as land use shifted according to wider changes in the economic and physical environment. The court rolls of the manor of Wakefield reveal clues regarding the tensions between different types of land use and the very close proximity in which different activities could sometimes take place. So many iron pits were dug in the New Park of Wakefield in 1331 that an inquest found that 19 mines had not been backfilled, an important part of a licence to mine, and certainly important in the lord's hunting grounds, where they posed a risk to both rider and deer.[34] Although large-scale iron mining was clearly happening in the New Park, much smaller workings were also prevalent. For example, at Gawthorpe near Ossett in 1332 Hugh Sonman paid 12d for a licence to dig a pit to burn iron ore on one selion of land, and Richard, son of John, paid 18d for a licence to dig an iron mine 'at the head of three selions'.[35]

It is clear from these entries that arable agriculture and industrial activity occurred next to each other. Just as iron mining was undertaken in areas with ready supplies of wood for charcoal because transporting charcoal was difficult and cost inefficient, small-scale coal mining may have been more likely to take place close to settlements because the high bulk and low cost value made long-distance trade in mineral coal similarly inefficient.[36] Numerous instances of fines regarding digging for coal in the western part of Wakefield manor are further evidence of conflicting land use. In 1311 Nicholas Bately was amerced for 'digging coal underground on Henry de Walda's land, causing his soil and fences to fall in', while in 1316 in Dewsbury Ralph the Colier and William Cokewald – the names are themselves suggestive – were amerced 12d each 'for opening the King's highway in Dewsbury, in digging for coals, because it was to the injury of all travellers'.[37] That year William de Collay of Crigglestone was also fined 12d 'for digging coal on the lord's land and selling it', as was Margery Carpenter of Crigglestone for 'doing the same on villein land, 6d'.[38] The short-term nature of coal mining is clear from the agreement William le Templer made in June 1329, when he paid for a licence to take a pit in Wyverumthorpe in the Ryedale district

---

33 D. Baxter, *Medieval Bourn: a Cambridgeshire village in the later Middle Ages* (Cambridge, 2008), p. 123; M. Beresford and J.G. Hurst (eds), *Deserted medieval villages* (London, 1971), p. 140.

34 Faull and Moorhouse, *West Yorkshire*, p. 778; four tenants were fined for this offence: S. Moorhouse, 'The medieval parks of Yorkshire: function, contents and chronology', in R. Liddiard (ed.), *The medieval park: new perspectives* (Macclesfield, 2007), p. 123. I am grateful to James Bowen for this reference.

35 Faull and Moorhouse, *West Yorkshire*, p. 781.

36 E. Miller and J. Hatcher, *Medieval England: towns, commerce and crafts, 1086–1348* (London, 1995), p. 152.

37 *WCR vol. 3*, p. 124.

38 Ibid., p. 126.

of North Yorkshire on the condition that he would refill it by the following Michaelmas.[39] Coal mining would become this region's greatest industry in the modern period, and these early accounts indicate how prevalent the activity already was in the Middle Ages. Although this coal may have been used for domestic fires, it was very possibly meant for the iron forges, although not the smelting hearths, which were operating on the manor. The fuel-intensive nature of iron production, therefore, offered employment opportunities to a number of enterprising tenants of the manor, bringing them into conflict with others who wished to use the same land in different ways.[40]

Fieldwalking, excavations and aerial surveys have revealed that places such as Fineshade in Rockingham Forest (Northamptonshire), the site of a large industrial complex with no associated medieval settlement, were very rare. Far more typical of iron-working, as with other extractive industries, was close proximity to settlements, and, indeed, bloomeries were often worked within the bounds of arable fields in forest villages.[41] Thus in regions where it was possible, land was used for a multiplicity of purposes and overlapping and concomitant types of land use were common. In the thickly wooded Weald, thousands of acres were cleared between the eleventh and fourteenth centuries. As the population grew, particularly in the late thirteenth and early fourteenth centuries, settlement expanded onto the higher and hillier land of the High Weald.[42] This land was difficult to cultivate, although the prevalence of small, enclosed fields associated with dispersed settlements demonstrates that arable agriculture was undertaken there. But this remained a heavily wooded region, and the concentration of iron-working in the higher regions of the Weald indicates the close relationship between agricultural settlement and industry in this region.[43] As population pushed settlement higher in the search for new land to cultivate, the inhabitants of these new hamlets and villages also took advantage of woodland resources, again demonstrating the intrinsic importance of industry to arable agriculture and the dependency of each sector on the other. Indeed, by increasing the amount of iron available for agricultural implements, mining not only drew settlers to new regions but also facilitated the cultivation of the difficult land once they were there.

Charcoal-burning

Iron-working and charcoal-burning were key aspects of woodland industry and, as demand for iron grew, so too did the need for nearby charcoal production. It is estimated that 12 lbs of charcoal were needed to produce 1 lb of iron, and that for every ton of iron produced two acres of woodland were burned.[44] In some regions the

---

39 J. Lister (ed.), *Court rolls of the manor of Wakefield, vol. 4* (Leeds, 1930), p. 150.

40 Peasant coal miners are also noted in Cannock Forest: Birrell, 'Peasant craftsmen', p. 101.

41 G. Foard, 'Medieval woodland, agriculture and industry in Rockingham Forest, Northamptonshire', *Medieval Archaeology*, 45 (2001), pp. 76–7.

42 P.F. Brandon, 'South-eastern England', in H.E. Hallam (ed.), *The agrarian history of England and Wales. Volume II: 1042–1350* (Cambridge, 1988), pp. 184–9.

43 Crossley, 'Wealden iron', p. 95.

44 Geddes, 'Iron', p. 100; Crossley, 'Wealden iron', p. 95.

cost of charcoal could account for up to 50 per cent of the cost of producing iron.[45] The scale of charcoal-burning is difficult to quantify because the industry was largely undocumented and produced very little archaeological evidence. Wood was turned into charcoal by creating a slow-burning stack encased in a thick layer of soil onto which water was periodically thrown in order to keep the temperature down.[46] The stack burned for several days before being doused and carefully dismantled and allowed to cool completely. The charcoal was then put into sacks and transported to the iron ore. Charcoal-burning necessarily depleted woodland, even if only temporarily, and charcoal burners were constantly moving through woodlands and forests. Their transitory presence is evidenced by patches of very black earth or layers of charcoal ash, although these remains are very difficult to date. Documentary evidence gives some indication of the possible scale of the industry, as when Henry III's Regarders found 2,290 charcoal hearths in the Forest of Dean (Gloucestershire) in 1282. Not all of these were in current use, but the Regarders noted that tree stools, from which new shoots would grow, were also being destroyed. Extensive charcoal-burning apparently continued in the Forest after the inquest, and charcoal burners were again found to be damaging underwood and impeding new tree growth in 1326.[47] The Forest of Dean was the centre of high-quality iron production in the Middle Ages, so it is unsurprising that large numbers of charcoal burners were at work there. However, Foard's aerial survey of Rockingham Forest (Northamptonshire) found 600 'intensely black' patches of soil, indicating probable sites of charcoal hearths, in an area of ten and a half square miles.[48] Although not all of these were medieval, the number of potential hearth sites does suggest widespread charcoal-burning in the forest before the eighteenth century, and two hearths found in the Great Park at Brigstock have been positively dated to the medieval period. The quality of the charcoal suggests that the wood used was selected from similarly sized pieces, indicating coppiced woodland.[49] Charcoal-burning was probably a part-time occupation, and in the 1330s at Inglewood Forest (Cumberland) licences were purchased by the half or whole season in both summer and winter.[50] It is interesting to note that, even in the Forest of Dean, where iron production was a major industry, charcoal burners were often also smiths, and that, in addition to their industrial activity, they also held arable land.[51]

---

45 Foard, 'Medieval woodland', p. 82; R.F. Tylecote, *The prehistory of metallurgy in the British Isles* (London, 1986), p. 189.

46 This description of charcoal-burning is taken from J. Bond, 'Medieval charcoal-burning in England', *Ruralia VI* (Turnhout, 2001).

47 Bond, 'Medieval charcoal-burning', p. 279.

48 Foard, 'Medieval woodland', p. 86.

49 Ibid., p. 87; charcoal evidence also suggests the use of managed woodland at Rievaulx and Bilsdale: J. Wheeler, 'The environmental impact of iron-working on the woodlands of Rievaulx and Bilsdale, North York Moors, UK, c.1132–1647', in M. Atherden and T. Milsom (eds), *Yorkshire landscapes past and present* (York, 2008), pp. 61–7.

50 Birrell, 'Peasant craftsmen', p. 96.

51 Ibid., pp. 98–9.

The ways in which woods were managed in the face of rising demand for fuel may also be indicative of settlement patterns and pressure on resources. The charcoal recovered from the late medieval lead-smelting site at Linch Clough (Derbyshire) indicates that woodland there was not managed; rather, the analysis of tree rings suggests the slow growth typical of trees left to mature naturally in a difficult environment. The Linch Clough charcoal indicates a declining number of species used for fuel over a very long period, and it is possible that continued industrial activity at the site may have been responsible for some loss of tree diversity and clearance of woodland, although this must also be seen in the context of long-term climate change, among other factors.[52] But the lack of woodland management, even over the later period, may also suggest a relative lack of pressure on resources there compared with other regions of the country. In the West Riding of Yorkshire, for example, it has been argued that place-names indicating medieval coppicing may be used as evidence for iron-working and charcoal-burning, while the soaring price of wood for fuel is thought to have led to greater instances of coppicing in the Kentish Weald between the mid-thirteenth and the mid-fourteenth century.[53] This wood was used for domestic fires and as fuel for industrial hearths, in addition to acting as wood pasture for livestock.

Demand for woodland resources may be seen as a result of population growth applying pressure in a number of different, but intrinsically related, ways. Iron was needed for agricultural implements and, as population pushed arable agriculture into regions which had to be cleared of wood or walled and drained, implements with iron pieces – spade shoes, axe and mattock heads, billhooks and so on – were required. Once the land was cleared, more tools were necessary, including ploughshares and coulters. This iron was produced using charcoal burned in woods and forests, even as arable was expanding into these places. Balancing these different and competing needs in such a high-pressure environment necessitated careful woodland management. It has even been argued that the continued existence of woodland in the face of land hunger was due to the pressing need for charcoal and iron.[54]

Although iron production was naturally concentrated in forests and heavily wooded regions, it was not confined to these regions alone. Fieldwalking in the much less densely wooded Bourn Valley (Cambridgeshire) has revealed pits dug to access the ironstone found in small quantities on the Lower Greensands, while heaps of iron slag in the Densett Valley are further testament to small-scale iron production in this region.[55] Again, the dating of this material is difficult, although, as noted above, evidence of iron-working has been found in medieval crofts in Bourn. Ancillary evidence for iron production is perhaps also found in names of furlongs, such as 'Redreis' and 'Redherthe', in the open fields of Bourn and in patches of red

52 B. Bevan, R. Doonan and R. Gale, 'Medieval rural lead working: excavations at Linch Clough, Upper Derwent Valley, 2000–2001', *Derbyshire Archaeological Society*, 124 (2004), pp. 131, 135.

53 Faull and Moorhouse, *West Yorkshire*, p. 785; M. Mate, 'The economy of Kent, 1200–1500: an age of expansion, 1200–1348', in S. Sweetinburgh (ed.), *Later medieval Kent, 1220–1540* (Woodbridge, 2010), p. 3.

54 Ibid., p. 94.

55 Baxter, *Bourn*, pp. 120–30.

earth and burnt clay, suggesting hearth sites in the fields.[56] The iron production in this region, which appears to have been widely dispersed, suggests that even small-scale involvement in the industry in a region not typically associated with mining could be considered worthwhile. Thus, even the low-quality seams of iron ore found at Upper Ryedale (Yorkshire) were exploited. Archaeological evidence indicates that this ore was worked on small sites, and slag heaps and hearth remains indicate the highly itinerant nature of the industry there.[57] Similarly, scattered and small-scale iron-workings dating from the early fourteenth century are evident in coastal parts of north-east Yorkshire, again indicating highly specialised or localised production.[58]

Conclusion

Overall, archaeological, topographic and written evidence suggests that the iron industry was dominated by small temporary workings which, although most intensive in forests, parks and the Weald of Kent and Sussex, were established across the country in every region where iron ore could be found and charcoal burned. The seasonal nature of mining and the small size of most workings suggest that, as with the better-documented lead and tin industries, most of the people involved were also engaged in other, probably agricultural, by-employments. The close proximity of iron production to arable agriculture in some places is a clear indication that iron production could be very closely associated with long-established and successful agricultural settlements. But it is also likely that the relationship between iron mining and settlement acted in the opposite direction, making hitherto unexploited land attractive for agriculture and, consequently, in some regions, settlement.

The production of iron was time and labour intensive, for the ore had to be mined, roasted, crushed, smelted and refined before being sold to the smith. The employment opportunities provided by mining probably attracted people looking to supplement their income. Many of these people needed either further provisioning or land to support themselves. Thus mining could also open the way for the establishment of permanent settlements, and in fact, of an earlier period, Duby considered iron workers and charcoal burners to be important first colonisers, whose clearances of woodland areas encouraged permanent settlements and the laying out of arable fields.[59] Indeed, Bryan Waites has argued that parts of north-east Yorkshire were settled during the thirteenth century in precisely the way described by Duby. Here the land had not lain completely unused, but its use as extensive pasture did not necessitate or encourage permanent settlement. As the area was developed for mining, settlements were established and many who came took advantage of the landscape to raise cattle herds as well as to work the ironstone.[60] Perhaps something

56 Ibid., p. 122; see also D. Baxter, 'Roman tumuli or medieval industry? Moulton Hills, Bourn, reconsidered', *Proceedings of the Cambridge Antiquarian Society*, 95 (2006), pp. 49–56.

57 McDonnell, 'The iron industry', p. 34.

58 B. Waites, 'Medieval iron workings in northeast Yorkshire', *Geography*, 49 (1964), p. 41.

59 Duby, *Rural economy*, p. 78.

60 Waites, 'Medieval iron workings', p. 42.

of this type of movement of settlement is seen at Chellington (Bedfordshire), where archaeological evidence of early medieval iron production has been found in later medieval arable fields.[61] Many of the people involved in the industry were probably 'miner–farmers' of the type that existed in lead mining into the nineteenth century.[62] These iron workers were very much tied to permanent settlements, their household income being derived from industrial, arable and pastoral activities. This mixture of employment sustained settlement in regions where arable agriculture was difficult or secondary to other pursuits. This suggests that settlement patterns in some regions were the result of a capillary-like action, iron mining drawing settlement to difficult terrain and leading to the establishment and sustenance of permanent settlements. Thus, in addition to population pressure compelling settlement on less productive land to extend arable cultivation, as argued by Postan, patterns of settlement ought also to be seen as reflecting the whole range of rural activities available to colonisers of the medieval English countryside.

The foregoing discussion of medieval iron production has focused on the relationship between landscape, land use and settlement patterns within the context of economic pressure to expand arable production and intensify agricultural practices. The factors which led to the expansion of arable agriculture put pressure on other types of land use, not only through further encroachment by the plough but also through the expansion of industries necessary to support arable cultivation. While the amount of iron needed for the tools used to clear and cultivate the land increased alongside population, it is less clear how, and to what extent, these needs were met. In some places demand for iron led miners to clear land and establish new settlements. But growing demand for iron also encouraged the proliferation of small-scale and itinerant mining operations, even in regions where ore was hard won, of poor quality or far from trading centres. Mining and charcoal-burning also brought some of those involved into conflict with people who wished to put the same land to different uses, highlighting the multiplicity of ways in which the land and its resources could be managed, controlled and exploited. This 'economic balance of profitability' no doubt varied from region to region and even among different groups within settlements, depending on a wide range of environmental and household factors.[63] The local factors which affected the scale and organisation of iron production adds a further layer of complexity to our understanding of land use in the high and late medieval periods. Postan emphasised the very great pressure on arable land by the end of the thirteenth century, but the drive to greater agricultural output also placed increasing pressure on woodland, as charcoal was needed for iron production. This iron production was itself driven by demand for the agricultural implements needed to cultivate the land more intensively – a process in turn necessitated by the increasing proportion of smallholding peasants, an aspect of medieval society of which Postan was acutely aware.

In this, the importance of the small-scale iron worker should not be underestimated; but neither should that of the small-scale peasant, for whom much of his iron was

61 A. Brown and C. Taylor, 'Chellington field survey', *Bedfordshire Archaeology*, 23 (1999), pp. 98–110.

62 See Blanchard, 'The miner and the agricultural community'.

63 Foard, 'Medieval woodland', p. 94.

ultimately destined. Indeed, in some instances they may have been the same person. At the heart of the matter lies not only expansion but also the intensification of land use, as more people had less land from which to earn their livelihood. Recent research has highlighted the possibility of high peasant yields, the result of peasant cultivators using their land more intensively and caring for it more assiduously than their lords.[64] Iron was fundamental to agricultural technology, making tools more efficient and, ultimately, more productive. It seems likely that a good deal of iron production was driven by the need to supply the countryside not only with ploughshares and coulters, but also with the small and relatively cheap components of hand tools. A clearer understanding of the agricultural technology which peasants used on their land will not only help to explain arable agriculture but also provide a clearer framework for understanding the increasing demand for iron. Reconfiguring landscape as taskscape highlights the multiplicity of interactions between people and their environment, emphasising important relationships between the economic activities pursued and how these changed over time.[65]

The small-scale and dispersed nature of the iron industry means that its organisation is largely unknown. As noted throughout this discussion, frustratingly little evidence survives – if it ever existed – regarding the people involved in iron production in England, and perhaps the miners themselves are the least documented of all. It is highly unlikely that these miners were involved in the production process from start to finish, and perhaps the fuel and blowing required to create the intense heat necessary for the initial roasting and subsequent refining of the iron was too costly for many. Perhaps some miners were involved in the initial roasting, but no further. How the iron industry was organised, even in the later Middle Ages, before the iron was sold on by merchants in towns and to manorial lords remains to be discovered. This is yet another aspect of rural trade, vitally important and yet under-recorded in this period of commercialisation, about which so little is known. If we are to start to build a picture of the size of iron-workings and the extent of sites across the country, we must take into consideration developments in archaeology. Improved dating techniques will no doubt lead to a more precise understanding of the chronology of iron production, an aspect particularly important when thinking about settlement patterns and land use. Further research into iron production within the broader context of agricultural expansion and intensification will no doubt increase our understanding of the economic geography of medieval England and the impact of small-scale agriculture and industry on the medieval economy.

---

64 Sapoznik and Myrdal, 'Spade cultivation'; A. Sapoznik, 'The productivity of peasant agriculture: Oakington, Cambridgeshire, 1360–99', *Economic History Review*, 66 (2013), pp. 518–44; D. Stone, 'The consumption of field crops in late medieval England', in C.M. Woolgar, D. Serjeantson and T. Waldron (eds), *Food in medieval England: diet and nutrition* (Oxford, 2006), p. 21; D. Stone, *Decision-making in medieval agriculture* (Oxford, 2005), pp. 269–71.

65 For the concept of taskscapes see T. Ingold, 'The temporality of the landscape', *World Archaeology*, 25 (1993), pp. 152–74. Here the term is used to emphasise economic activities, although Ingold's concept encompasses all dwelling activities.

Chapter 3

English agrarian structures in a European context, 1300–1925

John Broad

European travellers to England in the later eighteenth century described the countryside they found in very different terms from their own. It was not so much the agricultural innovation in crops and livestock as different systems of land management. In particular, the large farms across the south and east, which they linked (generally incorrectly) to the parliamentary enclosure movement, and the enclosed fields of the Midlands, which eliminated customary open-field agriculture, sparked their imaginations. They also found considerably larger farms than in most parts of Europe, and a class of cultivators, 'farmers', running them who were often tenants rather than owners of the land, and on legally enforceable contracts rather than feudal tenures. The tenant farmer sank his (occasionally her) capital into the business of farming rather than the ownership of land. Wealthy tenant farmers might own some land, but did not necessarily farm it themselves. Above all, the large tenant farmer in England was perceived as the dominant cultivating group, contrasted with owner–proprietor peasants across the remainder of Europe. Their farms dominated the farmed acreage and farming output in the country, particularly in the east, though the numbers of small farmers were much greater.

Across Europe Enlightenment agronomists and agrarian reformers debated, and to a limited extent enacted, land reforms that copied the English 'model', but increasingly either adapted or rejected it as incompatible with local conditions.[1] Nevertheless, the stereotype of an English rural world, with its tripartite economy of landlords, large tenant farmers and a virtually landless agricultural workforce, continued to dominate. In the nineteenth century, political agendas distorted the picture. In England, urban predominance after 1851 pushed the rural economy into the background, and the word peasant held increasingly negative connotations, but in France the stereotype of the peasant became the backbone of French national identity, with the image of the sower (*La semeuse*) appearing continuously on French stamps and coins for more than a century. The divergent imagery is starker than the reality of developments in agriculture and rural society in the two countries.[2]

---

1 John Broad, *A common agricultural heritage? Revising French and British rural divergence* (British Agricultural History Society, 2009).

2 B.J.P. van Bavel, R.W. Hoyle and S. Brakensiek, *Social relations: property and power* (Turnhout, 2010); J.V. Beckett, 'The peasant in England: a case of terminological confusion?', *Agricultural History Review*, 32 (1984), pp. 113–23.

Nevertheless, there do seem to be some continuing marked differences in the structures of English rural society that set it apart. Recent transnational studies of European rural society undertaken under the aegis of the CORN (Comparative Rural History of the North Sea Area) and COST (European Cooperation in Science and Technology) projects have compared landholding, tenures and other aspects of rural society across the EU area.[3] In different parts of Europe over the course of the last millennium local reactions to fairly similar economic conditions but varying social and political structures show that similar outcomes could evolve at a distance. For instance, from the later Middle Ages large tenant farms evolved in the Guelder valley of the Netherlands that were comparable with parallel developments in England. However, in other parts of the Netherlands, such as inland Flanders, which had advanced agricultural techniques, agrarian structures differed, agriculture remained labour-intensive and leaseholds were largely absent.[4] Large leasehold farms did not come to dominate tenure systems across most parts of continental Europe in the seventeenth, eighteenth or even nineteenth centuries, although there were large capitalist farms in most countries. There were plenty of them in France, but the percentage of the total agricultural area held in large farms was much lower than in England.

Feudal and post-feudal proprietorship

This chapter will provide a survey of the relationship between rural families and their rights over land in England over a long period in terms of both land ownership and the size of farming units. The subject was judiciously surveyed by Hoyle and Dyer, but their approach was descriptive and made few comments on how or why the situation evolved. I want to suggest why England developed a different landownership profile from its neighbours. Possibly as early as 1700, and certainly by the mid-nineteenth century, ownership of around 70 per cent of the English land surface was concentrated among the 'great landowners' – a loosely constructed and permeable elite who did not generally cultivate the land themselves, and increasingly spent only a small part of the year in the countryside.[5] The typical great landowner of the 1870s had an estate within 100 miles of London, a sporting estate (often vast in acreage but agriculturally poor) in Scotland, Wales, Ireland or the English uplands, and a London house. From another perspective, relatively few farmers cultivated their own land, and even fewer worked *only* their own land. Given that, 500–600 years earlier, England had a social pattern and feudal institutions similar to those in northern France (with whom they often shared rulers), how did England come to be perceived as strikingly different by the mid-eighteenth century? Why, when the word 'paysan' was put on a

3 B.J.P. van Bavel and P.C.M Hoppenbrouwers (eds), *Landholding and land transfer in the North Sea area (late Middle Ages–19th Century)* (Turnhout, 2004); van Bavel et al., *Social relations*.

4 B.J.P. van Bavel and P.R. Schofield, *The development of leasehold in northwestern Europe, c.1200–1600* (Turnhout, 2008); E.A. Wrigley, 'Urban growth in early modern England: food, fuel and transport', *Past & Present*, 225 (2014), pp. 79–112.

5 F.M.L. Thompson, 'The social distribution of landed property in England since the 16th century', *Economic History Review*, 19 (1966), pp. 505–17.

political and social pedestal in nineteenth-century France, had the word 'peasant' in England developed entirely negative connotations and become a term of denigration, and did this represent a profoundly different agrarian environment?

This account says little about the expropriation of peasant land by great lords that played a major part in Tawney's interpretation of long-term agrarian change and was central to the Brenner debate over 20 years ago.[6] This is not to deny that it ever happened, but it occurred mainly in the fifteenth and early sixteenth centuries, when the English population was low, land was cheap and plentiful, and people could easily find land elsewhere. It was never more than locally socially explosive in other periods. Nor will I say much about rural protest movements, because although these occurred in every century from the fourteenth to the nineteenth – from the Peasants' Revolt (1381) to Captain Swing (1830–31) and the Revolt of the Field in the early 1870s – they appear to have done little to slow, let alone stop, the long-term processes that were at work.[7] Peasant insurrection was rarely central to significant political movements or regional revolts. Generally the interests of the larger cultivators and elite landowners were united against smallholders and farm labourers; they closed ranks.[8]

The medieval peasant farmer in England shared many attributes with his counterpart in France and north-west Europe. Within the prevailing feudal system most English land was held by farmers/peasants from a manorial lord who administered his manor at the manor court – specifically a Court Baron. There was undoubtedly an element of population pressure, as hypothesised by Postan, in the considerable agrarian traumas of the first half of the fourteenth century, but they were significantly worsened by very bad weather conditions and harvests and by severe animal disease. After the Black Death the tenant increasingly paid for his land with money rather than with labour services or payments in kind and, although these had not completely disappeared even in the seventeenth century, they became rarer and marginal. Peasants' capacity to pay money rents in itself tells us about the degree of market involvement and monetary exchanges in the English rural economy.[9] Equally, in the century of the Black Death there is plentiful evidence of a developing market in rural land, including the buying and selling of land held in feudal tenures. There was also, particularly in eastern England, a significant

---

6 R.H. Tawney, *The agrarian problem in the sixteenth century* (London, 1912); T.H. Aston and C.H.E. Philpin, *The Brenner debate: agrarian class structure and economic development in pre-industrial Europe* (Cambridge, 1985); R.W. Hoyle,'Tenure and the land market in early modern England: or a late contribution to the Brenner debate', *Economic History Review*, 43 (1990), pp. 1–20.

7 The most recent overview, C.J. Griffin, *Protest, politics and work in rural England, 1700–1850* (Basingstoke, 2014), takes a very different approach.

8 There were exceptions in very specific local circumstances. For instance, in those parts of East Anglia where the foldcourse system existed, it was in the landlord's interest to maintain open-field agriculture and exploit sheep keeping directly on a manor where the larger tenants might be adversely affected and therefore favour enclosure. See J.C. Whittle, 'Lords and tenants in Kett's Rebellion 1549', *Past & Present*, 207 (2010), pp. 3–52.

9 C. Dyer, *An age of transition? Economy and society in England in the later Middle Ages* (Oxford, 2005); R.H. Britnell, *The commercialisation of English society, 1000–1500* (Cambridge, 1993).

proportion of peasant land held in long-standing tenures free of strong manorial control (freehold and socage tenure).

Money and markets permitted a peasant land market to flourish in England, but two factors were at least as important in shaping it. One was derived from the unitary and centralised nature of English legal and taxation systems. A basic tenet of the English taxation system was that, when land was taxed, the nobility were taxed on a par with the peasantry. There was no concept, as there was in France and many continental countries, of 'noble' land that was exempt from taxation even if sold. English land was taxed indiscriminately.[10] The second was the legal framework for inter-generational property transfers. Custom had a well-established place in English rural society, but it developed differently from manor to manor. Its importance was strengthened as manor courts recorded their transactions from the late thirteenth century, but custom was nevertheless less important than other factors in transmitting village land. In England, the individual's testament (will) over-rode custom in the disposal of land. The peasant in possession had the right both to dispose of property in his/her lifetime and, through a properly witnessed written will, to decide who should receive property, including landed property, after death. What is apparent in English rural society is that custom was largely a residual force, taking effect only when no provision had been made by other means. This was an important contributory factor in enabling country people to adjust farm size by purchase or sale, or to choose a trade, and to move from place to place with relatively little restraint in the later Middle Ages.[11]

This legal position had a significant effect on the relationship between families and the land. The will over-rode customary rights to feudal land. Custom decided only how that land would be divided between children in its absence. In addition, custom was so varied that these residual rights did not always divide the land at all, or in the same way. In some places it went to the eldest son (or if no sons, the daughter), in others it was divided equally between sons, and in a few places it went to the youngest son (so-called Borough English custom). These legal rights became particularly significant in conjunction with the developing 'European Marriage Pattern' that came to prevail over much of north-west Europe by the early modern period, in which marriage was usually delayed until the couple could be economically self-sufficient (typically in their mid-twenties) and coincided with the creation of a new household with a separately managed farm or a non-agricultural means of sustenance.[12] Marriage became a second important inter-generational property transfer point, when parents might give the couple land or moveable property such as livestock to help them begin a successful farming enterprise. For this reason early modern wills often show married

---

10 One exception might be noted: the double taxation of Roman Catholics under the Land Tax legislation from the 1690s onwards.

11 This is a basic tenet underlying A. Macfarlane, *The origins of English individualism: the family, property and social transition* (Oxford, 1978) and, more recently, Jane Whittle, 'Individualism and the family–land bond: a reassessment of land transfer patterns among the English peasantry, c.1270–1580', *Past & Present*, 160 (1998), pp. 25–63.

12 J. Hajnal, 'European marriage patterns in perspective', in D.V. Glass and D.E.C. Eversley (eds), *Population in history: essays in historical demography* (London, 1965), pp. 101–43.

children receiving less from their parents than young and unmarried children. They had already received their share of their parents' property.

The legal framework and distinctive family patterns and dynamics which gave the individual high autonomy in the disposal of all types of property were combined in the later Middle Ages with developed markets in agricultural products. One factor fostering market orientation was the rising demand for wool even when food product prices were depressed. It helped develop an active land market at a time when opportunities in non-agricultural employment in the countryside were growing. Individuals seem increasingly to have used land (freehold or otherwise) as a store of wealth as much as a place to grow food for the family. Occupational diversity was increasing fast as rural by-employments developed in textiles, mining and metal-working, or, to a lesser extent, in service industries.[13]

Copyhold tenure and proprietorship in England

From the sixteenth century onwards legal changes (particularly the Statutes of Uses 1536 and Wills 1540) consolidated practice nationally. Peasant feudal customary tenures had evolved into 'copyholds' – tenure by copy of court roll – in the later Middle Ages.[14] Although customary tenure varied widely, it is possible to distinguish three basic types: copyhold of inheritance, copyhold for lives and tenant right. Copyhold of inheritance was the most stable. Here the copyhold rights were in the hands of one named individual. Traditionally the copyholder of inheritance paid fixed rent to the lord of the manor, which, with the inflation of the sixteenth and seventeenth centuries, increasingly became a small, even nominal, charge. More importantly, the payment to the manorial lord at death (herriot) or transfer was a small and fixed multiple of the rent, and increasingly negligible. Numerous court cases, mainly in the sixteenth century, sought to clarify whether rents and fines could be raised 'arbitrarily' by the lord of the manor or were controlled by custom. By the eighteenth century, those copyholds of inheritance where fines were fixed were so strongly entrenched in the law that they were treated almost as if they were freehold when determining the price of land at sale. The profits of the manor court in manors with copyhold of inheritance were small: manorial courts in such manors often met infrequently, or even ceased in the eighteenth and nineteenth centuries. Where in the late medieval period they had regulated agricultural life, particularly common rights, increasingly they became mainly registers of property transactions.

---

13 The importance of industry in the countryside was classically delineated by J. Thirsk, 'Industries in the countryside', in F.J. Fisher (ed.), *Essays in the economic and social history of Tudor and Stuart England* (Cambridge, 1961). This is substantially updated and a quantitative measure provided of the shift to industrial employment by L. Shaw-Taylor and T. Wrigley, 'Occupational structure and population change', in R. Floud, J. Humphries and P. Johnson (eds), *The Cambridge economic history of modern Britain: vol. 1* (Cambridge, 2014), ch. 2.

14 This sparsely documented process is cogently discussed by M. Bailey, 'The transformation of customary tenures in southern England, c.1350 to c.1500', *Agricultural History Review*, 62 (2014), pp. 210–30.

Copyholds for lives differed in important ways. Firstly, each copyhold normally had three names attached to it. These names ('lives') were traditionally those of the cultivator, his wife and their eldest son. The copyhold gave security of tenure as long as one of the three 'lives' was alive. When the last 'life' died the copyhold reverted to the lord of the manor, who could grant it to a completely different family (usually for a considerable cash sum) or, alternatively, change the tenancy to a lease or absorb the land into his park or demesne. Unlike the copyhold of inheritance, where the nature of peasants' rights made the land rights almost as good as freehold and the land eventually became the copyholder's freehold, the copyhold for lives ultimately reverted to the lord of the manor.

However, the peasant could normally change any or all of the three names who were the 'lives' on the copyhold. To do this he needed to pay a cash sum – 'fine' – to the manorial court, which by the later seventeenth century was a customary multiple of the market rent for the land, adjusted for the age of the new 'life'. Tables were published setting out precisely what these fines should be from the early seventeenth century.[15] The lord had a continuing interest in supervising copyholds and derived a greater income from manors with copyholds for life. The peasant's right to change the 'lives' on the copyhold was used in many ways. If the named child died, a brother or sister would replace it. If the wife died and remarriage followed, the new wife might be added, or, alternatively, the adding of a son or daughter's spouse in advance of the wedding could be part of the marriage contract. Equally, 'lives' might be used to obtain loans on the security of the copyhold, with the lender added as a name for the duration of the liability and, if the property was sold to outsiders, the buyers' names would be inserted. There are virtually no examples of customary restrictions on who might become a 'life' on a copyhold for lives. By the eighteenth century, manorial courts were also prepared to accept reversionary transfers of land, taking forward the tenancy for even longer periods.[16]

The third form of copyhold, tenant right, is more similar to copyhold of inheritance than to copyhold for lives. The main difference was that if the tenant sold the land, or if the tenant died and his son (or daughter) took over the copyhold, the lord of the manor had the right to a considerably larger cash sum 'fine' than on a copyhold of inheritance.[17]

Richard Hoyle's researches into Chancery and other court cases where the nature of copyhold custom was challenged and adjudicated in the sixteenth and

15 The first was probably T. Clay, *Briefe, easie, and necessary tables for the valuation of leases. Together with a chorologicall discourse*, 2nd impr., corrected (London, 1622).

16 C.G.A. Clay, 'Lifeleasehold in the western counties of England, 1650–1750', *Agricultural History Review*, 29 (1981), pp. 83–96.

17 R.W. Hoyle, 'An ancient and laudable custom: the definition and development of tenant right in north-western England in the sixteenth century', *Past & Present*, 116 (1987), pp. 24–55; R.W. Hoyle, 'Lords, tenants and tenant right in the sixteenth century: four studies', *Northern History*, 20 (1984), pp. 38–63; J.S. Holt, 'The financial rewards of winning the battle for secure customary tenure', in J.C. Whittle (ed.), *Landlords and tenants in Britain, 1440–1660: Tawney's agrarian problem revisited* (Woodbridge, 2013), pp. 133–49.

seventeenth centuries show strong evidence of the regional concentration of the three main copyhold forms. He has mapped cases showing that copyhold of inheritance was dominant in eastern England and copyhold for lives in the south-west up as far as Gloucestershire, Worcestershire, Hereford and Wiltshire, while tenant right was concentrated in the north-west. The court cases where the type of copyhold was contested were in 'border' areas such as West Sussex, Berkshire, Leicestershire, Warwickshire, north Worcestershire and Herefordshire.

The type of copyhold was an important influence on the long-term development of peasant tenures locally. However, a further aspect of rural land tenure with a marked contrast between England, France and parts of north-west Europe is ultimately about the nature of land use rights. In England, it became established in the early modern period that ultimately the woods, common pastures and wastes within any manor belonged to the lord of the manor. It was *his* (or *her*) manor court which regulated their use, ascertaining what use rights peasant farmers had over the land. There is an interesting contrast with the way in which tenures developed in northern France in the twelfth and thirteenth centuries, where manorial/feudal lords granted charters to village landholders that allowed considerable autonomy, while custom in England meant that property rights took a different trajectory.[18] At a later stage the difference was reinforced when, after the French Revolution, the common woodland in French villages became community property.[19]

This meant that if the lord of the manor wanted to measure and survey manorial lands, perhaps before enclosing all or some part of them, the copyholders could claim use rights, and contest these (often successfully) in the royal courts, but in the long run the lord of the manor could usually buy out their interest in the land or compensate (not always adequately or fairly) with other land that had no common rights over it. This was the main long-term process by which farming families lost common rights on a manor. Where the lord of the manor tried to eliminate such rights by claiming they were not customary, and where tenants contested this in the sixteenth and seventeenth centuries, the Royal Courts did support tenant claims if the tenants could provide good evidence, but if not they were likely to back the lord of the manor's position.

This gave manorial lords, largely members of the aristocracy and gentry, an incentive to treat their rural estates as a potential source of improved income. For the farming community the absence of pre-defined paths of land inheritance resulted in a fluid land market and allowed them to grow and shrink their holdings. The gentry and aristocracy were subject to the same laws (the Statutes of Uses and Wills), but many became consciously dynastic in their ambitions and sought to find ways to keep land within the family and to direct very precisely which heir (usually a single individual) would receive most of the lands and income. By the later seventeenth century their lawyers had devised watertight means of setting up trusts for elite land which meant

18 J. Birrell,'Manorial custumals reconsidered', *Past & Present*, 224 (2014), pp. 3–37.

19 N. Vivier and A. Corbin, *Propriété collective et identité communale: les biens communaux en France 1750–1914* (Paris, 1998).

that the person in possession of the land could not normally dictate who inherited it.[20] This explains one aspect of how and why the great landowners came to accumulate about 70 per cent of the land surface of England by the mid-nineteenth century. As a group they continued to keep the bulk of their wealth in land not just as an income source but for the local influence it gave them and the political leverage it provided when ownership of land was key to the right to vote.

The other side of their involvement in rural society was their attitude to the land and to copyhold tenures. The great inflation of the period 1530–1660 helped copyhold farmers with fixed low rents by reducing the real value of the dues they paid in the manorial court to a very small percentage of their market rental. Fifty years ago, Lawrence Stone's book *The Crisis of the Aristocracy* (1965) showed how the landed elite found their income slipping by the 1580s and sought to correct this by more scientific surveys and valuations of their land and by better estate management.[21] The two instruments they chiefly used to increase their landed income were enclosure – both the 'approvement' of waste and the enclosure of open fields – and the changing of tenures to increase their income.[22] Ideally, they wanted to move farming families from feudal tenures to modern leases, usually running for less than 21 years, with rents that reflected the economic value of the land.[23] Where local farming families embraced enclosure and cooperated with the landlord this was easy. It happened surprisingly often, and the significant proportion of enclosure that took place in the sixteenth and seventeenth centuries was done with the agreement of tenants, even where it meant that their tenancies changed. This is not to deny that there was considerable pressure to agree to the changes. In some cases, particularly in areas of copyholds for lives, tenants were tempted with leasing agreements that followed a formula not unlike their copyholds, promising security on the land for the longer of three lives or 99 years. The tenant was effectively offered fixed rents for himself and his children for the foreseeable future, further ahead than customary tenure took account of in the past. However, in the long term the land reverted to the landlord, who could then change the terms of the lease as he wished.

The challenge on every manor was different, and the potential for improving the value to the landlord depended on the numbers of tenants and the quality of the land, particularly its potential quality if shifted into more valuable pasture. Landlords concentrated on those villages where enclosure and/or tenurial change could most

---

20 The most comprehensive account is H.J. Habakkuk, *Marriage, debt, and the estates system: English landownership, 1650–1950* (Oxford, 1994).

21 L. Stone, *The crisis of the aristocracy: 1558–1641* (Oxford, 1965), ch. 5.

22 W. Shannon, 'Approvement and improvement in the lowland wastes of early modern Lancashire', in R.W. Hoyle (ed.), *Custom, improvement and the landscape in early modern Britain* (Farnham, 2011), pp. 175–202; John Broad, 'The Verneys as enclosing landlords, 1600–1800', in J. Chartres and D. Hey (eds), *English rural society, 1500–1800: essays in honour of Joan Thirsk* (Cambridge, 1990), pp. 27–53.

23 For the development of leasehold see especially J.C. Whittle, 'Leasehold tenure in England c.1300–c.1600: its form and incidence', in B.J.P. van Bavel and P.R. Schofield (eds), *The development of leasehold in northwestern Europe, c.1200–1600* (Abingdon, 2007), pp. 139–54.

easily be undertaken. Where the opportunity cost was too high, one alternative strategy was simply to sell the manorial rights to the peasants. This was what happened at Wigston Magna in Leicestershire, the subject of the seminal village study carried out by W.G. Hoskins in the 1950s. It turned Wigston into a community of freeholders who regulated their open fields on a communal basis. The same technique was more frequently found in northern England, particularly in upland Yorkshire under tenant right, creating parishes and townships with many freeholder smallholdings where the land was relatively cheap.[24]

French and Hoyle have undertaken two important studies of how the peasant land market operated in copyhold villages and townships using sophisticated database techniques that input all transactions in the manor court over a long period, allowing a calculation of the potential rental income to the lord of the manor in every year and a 'virtual' annual rental of tenants. One study refers to Slaidburn, a Pennine township in which tenant right operated. The second covered the village of Earls Colne in Essex, earlier studied by Alan Macfarlane in his analysis of Ralph Josselin's seventeenth-century diary, where copyhold of inheritance prevailed.[25] They confirm the very active nature of the land market, particularly in the period before 1650, and the important part played by outsiders. However, they also show that much of the buying and selling of land involved relatively small plots. These transactions do not seem to be connected with increasing (or shrinking) the size of the farm so much as adjusting family wealth. Increasingly, village landownership reflected not the size of the peasant's farm but their store of wealth.

There is no equivalent study of a manor under copyhold for lives in which the farmer paid small annual rents to the lord of the manor plus additional payments on the death of one of the three lives or when bringing a new 'name' into the copyhold.[26] On a group of Wiltshire manors the earl of Pembroke maintained a very conservative regime and made little attempt to alter tenures on his estate until late in the nineteenth century. New copyholds were still issued after 1850 and the manorial court was retained until the twentieth century.[27] Wylye was one such manor belonging to the earl of Pembroke and has been analysed in detail because excellent records were kept. A full survey of the manor made in 1632 was consistently annotated with the changes of 'lives', and this makes it possible to see how often each piece of land changed hands

24 W.G. Hoskins, *The Midland peasant: the economic and social history of a Leicestershire village* (1957); H.R. French and R.W. Hoyle, 'The land market of a Pennine manor: Slaidburn, 1650–1780', *Continuity and Change*, 14 (1999), pp. 349–83.

25 H.R. French and R.W. Hoyle, 'English individualism refuted and reasserted: the land market of Earls Colne (Essex), 1550–1750', *Economic History Review*, 56 (2003), pp. 595–622; H.R. French and R.W. Hoyle, *The character of English rural society: Earls Colne, 1550–1750* (Manchester, 2007).

26 The general situation for copyholds for lives is well discussed by Clay, 'Lifeleasehold'.

27 The 1632 survey was transcribed for publication by E. Kerridge: *Surveys of the manors of Philip, First Earl of Pembroke and Montgomery, 1631–2*, Wiltshire Archaeological and Natural History Society Records Branch, 9 (Devizes, 1953). He did not include any of the later annotations, and it is from these and the later follow-on surveys that this data has been taken and the analysis done: Wilts. RO Herbert papers 2057/S5, 2057/S27, 2057/S106.

and whether it stayed within the family or was sold to relatives, or to outsiders, over more than 250 years. Table 3.1 follows the trajectory of 37 holdings over this period, indicating the type of transaction on each occasion. Tenurial change at Wylye began only after 1750, and was not completed before the abolition of copyhold (Table 3.2).

Table 3.1
Property transactions in Wylye, Wiltshire 1632–1850

	Holding sold	*Exchange of lives*	*Regrant of copy/lease*	*Grant of lease for lives*	*Lifehold (copy or lease) ended*	*Total transactions in period*
1632–50	13	14	0	0	0	26
1651–75	4	19	0	0	0	23
1676–1700	10	14	2	0	0	26
1701–25	3	33	3	0	0	39
1726–1750	2	20	5	0	0	27
1751–1775	4	28	2	2	1	37
1776–1800	3	28	1	2	6	40
1801–25	1	9	1	4	6	21
1826–59	1	2	1	2	3	9

Table 3.2
Tenurial changes and cottage lettings in Wylye 1632–1925

	Copyhold to Leasehold for lives	*Lifehold to lease for years/year to year tenancies*	*Cottages first let*
1632–50			8
1651–75			0
1676–1700			3
1701–25			6
1726–50			4
1751–75	3		1
1776–1800	2	5	1
1801–25	6	5	
1826–50		3	
1851–75		3	
1876–1900		5	
1900–1918		5	

An active land market existed over the whole period, with sales concentrated in the seventeenth century and exchanges for lives predominant in the eighteenth, partly because the lives were used for mortgages and reversionary purposes. Only three of the 37 holdings had the same copyholder family over 200 years, but by the eighteenth century several families formed a core of village landowners and had concentrated considerable amounts of copyhold land, though the 37 copyhold tenancies remained separately identifiable in the manorial records. The data from Wylye reinforces the findings of French and Hoyle for the other types of copyhold in general terms, though the basic difference – that the land was more likely to revert ultimately to the lord of the manor – remained.

Farming and landownership

This chapter suggests that the conjuncture of legal and family structures with good market integration and a money economy integrated English peasant farmers into a wider land market at a relatively early stage, and that most families with a stake in the land were at ease in that market, making decisions based on current needs and future planning. Land, however, was not just a resource for growing crops and raising animals – it was a store of wealth and a reserve for a rainy day. Peasant farmers bought and sold small plots of land among themselves, a commonplace process by the early fourteenth century, but also interacted with the landed elite and with town dwellers seeking investment in rural land.[28] This was evident at Wylye and a central finding in French and Hoyle's studies of the land market in Slaidburn and Earls Colne.[29]

How, then, did the English peasant, defined as the owner of heritable freeholder or copyholder rights who directly farmed that land, disappear? When was his hold on the land weakened, and by what mechanisms? There were opportunities for landowners to seize peasant rights, mainly before the sixteenth century, when land was under-occupied and potential tenants could pick and choose. In the sixteenth and early seventeenth centuries the main targets were woodland and common pasture, over which copyholders had traditional rights at particular times of the year and for particular purposes but which were not in constant, intensive use. There are examples of the Crown removing significant land rights from peasants in the fenlands of eastern England in the early seventeenth century to provide those who invested in expensive drainage with a return on their investment. Yet, as recent studies have shown, the peasants affected by the process were ambiguous in their attitude. It destroyed a particular way of life, but made the land they still worked much more productive.[30]

Overall, however, it seems that the process by which peasant farmers became detached from the land was a gradual one driven by a variety of forces. One was

---

28 D. Noy, 'Winslow in 1341: the *Nonarum Inquisitiones* and the reliability of medieval tax self-assessment', *Records of Bucks*, 55 (2015) pp. 137–46.

29 French and Hoyle,'The land market', pp. 349–83.

30 K. Lindley, *Fenland riots and the English revolution* (1982); J. Bowring, 'Between the Corporation and Captain Flood: the Fens and drainage after 1663', in R.W. Hoyle (ed.), *Custom, improvement and the landscape in early modern Britain* (Farnham, 2011), pp. 235–62.

the opportunities for non-agricultural work in both industrial and service sectors in the countryside or in towns, which grew rapidly in the seventeenth and eighteenth centuries. This was a positive alternative for those who struggled on smaller and medium-sized farms, and it was these smaller farms that most obviously disappeared over time. Even in parts of the country which did not see a major growth in rural industries, the economy became monetised and farmers, small and large, both bought and sold in the market. By the late eighteenth century Arthur Young contrasted the English countryside with his observations on Ireland: 'the poor in England have so little to do with it [the land] that they subsist almost entirely by purchase of their necessaries'.[31]

The squeeze on copyhold and freehold holdings of between 15 and 60 acres (6 to 24 hectares) has been observed in a variety of village studies at different periods between the early seventeenth and late eighteenth centuries. The process was complex and gradual. In difficult years, a farmer might mortgage his property to tide his family over or more positively to invest in farm buildings or even more land. If things went wrong, he might be forced to sell, or forfeit his land to the lender. The need to provide for children setting up their own farms on marriage, or even dowries for daughters among the wealthier farmers, could lead to sales. There were three groups of people who might have an interest in rural agricultural land in the seventeenth and eighteenth centuries, and they obtained more land in different but overlapping ways.[32]

The buyers were the great landowners; urban and rural professionals and tradespeople; and successful larger farmers. They manipulated manorial rights, made outright purchases or lent on mortgage. The farming community was most likely to be buying or selling small plots as inter-generational transactions or because a family member had migrated to another village or a town. One considerable group of copyhold owners in the countryside were people who had inherited copyholds only after they had moved elsewhere and settled permanently. They were probably more likely to let out their land than to move back to the village. This was a long-term process that eroded the small landowner to a degree, the small landowner as working farmer to an even greater extent. There were regional differences, and in some parts of the north and west farming landowners were an important continuing presence of considerable influence, but for much of the country they became a residual feature of power in the countryside.

It is generally reckoned that by 1870 two-thirds of the English land surface was in the hands of 'great' landowners, in estates that were primarily let out to farmers for rent. The surveys that form the basis for this estimate work landowner by landowner rather than parish by parish, and based their results on the income landowners derived rather than acreage. After 1870 the great landowners continued to erode copyhold tenure and modernise estate management, but suffered significant income loss as rents fell with cereal prices, upon which they began to diversify their wealth

31 A. Young, *A tour in Ireland: with general observations on the present state of that kingdom. Made in the years 1776, 1777, and 1778. and brought down to the end of 1779* (Dublin, 1780), pp. 2, 87.

32 This is explored in more detail in J. Broad, 'The fate of the Midland yeoman: tenants, copyholders, and freeholders as farmers in north Buckinghamshire, 1620–1800', *Continuity and Change*, 14 (1999), pp. 325–47.

by investing in industry, shares and more urban property. There was a great shift out of land by the great landowners between 1885 and 1900, and again between 1919 and 1925. In that period they sold perhaps as much as a quarter of their rural landholdings, retaining good agricultural land and good hunting, shooting and fishing land. Ironically, as a debate began on the disappearance of the English peasantry, a significant proportion of the people who invested in rural land were wealthy tenant farmers. Between 1919 and 1925 tenant farmers bought half the land sold by the great landowners.[33] Indeed, Paul Brassley, in discussing the European phenomenon of land reform in the first quarter of the twentieth century, has argued that this was as dramatic a shift as state-orchestrated reforms in other parts of Europe.[34]

The same period saw the end of English tenurial feudalism. Land reform in the 1920s saw the abolition of copyhold, which was due to take place in 1926. However, with customary English gradualism, this only meant that no new copyholds could be created. Existing copyholds were subject to a negotiated surrender. Much was done in the 1920s and 1930s, but such negotiations were still going on in the 1960s and 1970s – and may still continue today. There are still manorial courts with vestigial rights in parts of the country.[35] The title of lord of the manor can still be bought and sold and, in a few places, for a year or so yet, the manor court may still regulate small communal spaces.

Proprietorship, tenancy and farm size

If land in communities with relatively dispersed property rights was used flexibly as a store of wealth, what relationship did ownership have to the farming enterprises in the village? One way of looking at the situation by the end of the eighteenth century is to compare the evidence of ownership and tenancies in the 1798 Land Tax assessments with information from estate sources such as manor court rolls. Looking first at tenancies in Wylye, shown in Table 3.3, we find that 95.9 per cent of the village land was held in just six farms.[36] Sub-letting of copyholds had taken place on a large scale. Even more interestingly, only one of the six farmers, William Potticary, had a farm that was mainly his own land, while Edward Fricker was farming *none* of his own land. He owned copyholds but let them out for others to farm, while his own income

---

33 J.V. Beckett and M.E. Turner, 'End of the old order? F.M.L. Thompson, the land question, and the burden of ownership in England, c.1880–c.1925', *Agricultural History Review*, 55 (2007), pp. 269–88; F.M.L. Thompson, 'The land market, 1880–1925: a reappraisal reappraised', *Agricultural History Review*, 55 (2007), pp. 289–300.

34 P. Brassley, 'Land reform and reallocation in interwar Europe', in R. Congost and R. Santos (eds), *Contexts of property in Europe: the social embeddedness of property rights in land in historical perspective* (Turnhout, 2010), pp. 149–51.

35 This was the subject of Michael Turner's Leverhulme Trust Emeritus Professorial Fellowship (October 2012–September 2014) – a project on the end of manorial tenure in England, 1841–1951, some findings from which were presented to the British Agricultural History Society conference in Spring 2013.

36 The National Archives (TNA), IR23/95.

was derived from his lease of the tithes. Comparison with landownership patterns in the same 1798 Land Tax assessment shows that, in Wylye, farming tenancies had concentrated the land far more than proprietorship. Thus, while six tenants occupied more than 95 per cent of landed wealth, the six largest landowners were proprietors of only 74 per cent of the land by wealth. It took 14 of the 22 landowners to pass the 95 per cent threshold.

Table 3.3
Tenants at Wylye in the 1798 Land Tax assessment and their share of the land

Tenant	*Percentage*	*Rough acreage equivalent*	*% Owner-occupied*
Edward Fricker	19.3%	300.4	0.0%*
John Lock(e)	17.6%	274.1	36.6%
George Patient	30.7%	477.1	55.9%
John Perrior	14.1%	218.6	49.7%
William Potticary	9.6%	149.0	92.1%
Stephen Titt	4.5%	70.6	18.7%
All six	95.9%		

* Edward Fricker held a copyhold but let it out.

Wylye, like the other types of copyhold manors studied by French and Hoyle, had an active land market, but it was not related directly to the size of farms. We need to move away from the idea that a typical farmer in England in the seventeenth and eighteenth centuries built an agricultural enterprise around his or her own freehold or copyhold land. Many farmers rented pieces of land from different landlords and, as at Wylye, let out their own property to someone else. A farm at any one time could be a patchwork of freehold, leasehold and copyhold land, together with short-term leasing of pasture for a few weeks, or even by the day.

A similar analysis of the Earls Colne Land Tax assessment for 1798 produces a different profile without significantly changing the overall findings.[37] Farms were considerably smaller, and while the largest farmer held over 20 per cent of the parish, and the second largest almost 10 per cent, the largest six held only 54 per cent, and it took 50 of the 83 tenants to account for 95 per cent of the land. Even more interesting was the way in which property holders in Earls Colne held a portfolio of both owned and tenanted land. The traditional stereotype of the 'owner occupier' as someone occupying only the land he owned, was a negligible feature of the parish profile. Only two small owners, Isaac Rice, paying 60p, and Frances Ruffel, £2.50 out of a total assessment of £266.30, were of this type. But 37 (35 per cent) of the 104 names found in the Earls Colne assessment were both owners and occupiers. These 37 owned almost 45 per cent of Earl's Colne's land, and were tenants to almost 73 per cent. While those who owned more than they occupied were tenants to relatively little,

37 TNA, IR23/27.

those who occupied more than they owned paid £196 tax on the tenanted land and £42 for the land they owned. A substantial proportion of Earl's Colne's taxpayers were both owners and tenants within their own parish.

This analysis of Earl's Colne in 1798 is part of a wider study of Lexden hundred in Essex and it is, therefore, possible to track landholding rights across the hundred. Out of 66 proprietors (28 per cent) in Earls Colne, 19 owned land in the 15 other parishes in the same hundred, while, perhaps more surprisingly, 23 of the 83 tenants (27 per cent) were in the same position. Furthermore, Earls Colne's profile was very similar to that in most of the other parishes in Lexden hundred. We can generalise that in that part of Essex, where land was relatively widely dispersed compared with many other parts of the country, a significant proportion of landholders were simultaneously proprietors and tenants and did not confine themselves to a single parish in either respect, but were spread across several villages, not necessarily adjoining ones. Only 4 of the 15 parishes did not have a tenant who also rented land in Earl's Colne.[38]

The data presented here suggests that the 'English model' that was so influential in Europe in the century after 1750 was not as simple as it has often been thought. The large farms that were central to the idea were often made up of a combination of different tenures, sometimes held from different landlords. The process is usually seen as substantially landlord driven, taking place primarily on the well-managed estates of the elite. Classically, there were model farms built by the great landowners and leased as a piece, but these were far from the norm.[39] Large farms run either by tenant farmers or owner-occupiers could be found right across the country, from Northumberland to Hampshire, Wiltshire and Dorset. By the later eighteenth century, when anything over 150 acres (60 hectares) was considered a large agricultural unit over most of Europe, it is not surprising that foreign observers of England were amazed by the much larger farms they found. The French aristocrat La Rochefoucauld toured eastern England with Arthur Young in 1784, finding farms of up to 3,000 acres (1,200 hectares) – 20 times this size. Norfolk had many: at Ringham near Castle Acre the main farm was over 3,000 acres, with some fields more than three miles from the main farmstead, requiring 14 farm servants and 30 regular labourers, using 70 horses; at Massingham, the largest farm was 900 acres, occupying two-thirds of the parish, and in the district all the farms were 'large – about seven hundred or eight hundred acres'; at Dunton the farmer held 1,600 acres 'all linked up', while at Barsham Mr Morley farmed 1,400 acres; the largest enterprise Rochefoucauld described was at South Creake, where Mr Glover rented 3,000 acres from Lord Townsend but also 'runs another farm as large that he owns'.[40] Rochefoucauld found plenty of farms of more than 500 acres in Suffolk and north Essex as well, frequently quoting in terms of rent per year of between £200 and £800, which at that time was roughly 10s per acre on

38 The data for this analysis was provided by Richard Hoyle as part of a project the author is engaged in with Richard Hoyle and Leigh Shaw Taylor to analyse the 1798 Land Tax nationally.

39 S.W. Martins, *English model farm: building the agricultural ideal, 1700–1914* (English Heritage, 2002).

40 François Armand Frédéric La Rochefoucauld and J. Marchand, *A Frenchman in England, 1784* (Cambridge, 1933), pp. 215, 221, 228, 231, 233.

good arable land, meaning farms of 400 to 1,600 acres.[41] Examples in other parts of the country include the enormous enterprise run by the Culleys that was managed as a whole across land in Durham, Northumberland and Yorkshire.[42]

Precisely when these large-scale enterprises became relatively common is unclear. We know that enterprises of over 500 acres were not unusual by the sixteenth and early seventeenth century, when sheep farming for wool was profitable, often associated with late medieval 'lost villages'. Some such villages can be found operating as single units in areas such as Leicestershire, Lincolnshire and Buckinghamshire. A classic example is the 886-acre parish of Creslow, just north of Aylesbury in Buckinghamshire, long denuded of a village and certainly run as a single livestock farm in the Restoration period by the goldsmith banker, Edward Backwell.[43]

The mid-eighteenth century may have seen an acceleration of the expansion of farm sizes, particularly on arable-based enterprises, and it was also the point at which literate society became conscious of it. In 1766 the *Gazetteer and New Daily Advertiser*, a London newspaper, ran an article by 'Britannicus' advocating large farms and setting out to refute the arguments against them. He was particularly keen on the labour efficiency of these larger units, and on a better understanding of markets and their higher productivity.[44] A good example where the process of landlord-initiated farm enlargement can be documented between 1730 and 1800 is on the duke of Bedford's Stratton Park estate near Micheldever on 5,000 acres of the north Hampshire chalklands. In 1755 there was an acute shortage of tenants for the nine farms covering about 1,100 acres (an average of just over 100 acres each). Some consolidation had taken place, and there were certainly farms of 400 acres of arable, with an additional 50 per cent formed by common downland pasture rights. However, in the 18 years before the estate was sold off in 1800 most of the parishes covered by it were enclosed, and the sale catalogue describes 11 large leased units ranging from 400 to 1,100 acres. Large Hampshire farms were found not only on major aristocratic estates. James Edwards leased Manor Farm in Silkstead from 1739 to 1760 and farmed 560 enclosed acres, together with sole grazing rights on 238 acres of Silkstead down.[45]

---

41 Ibid., pp. 160, 170, 172.

42 M. Culley, G. Culley and A. Orde, *Matthew and George Culley: farming letters, 1798–1804*, Surtees Society (Woodbridge, 2006); M. Culley, G. Culley and A. Orde, *Matthew and George Culley: travel journals and letters, 1765–1798* (Oxford, 2002). For the development of large farms in the north-east see P. Brassley, *The agricultural economy of Northumberland and Durham in the period 1640–1750* (London, 1985) and, more recently, R. O'Donnell,'The creation of ring-fenced farms: some observations from eighteenth- and nineteenth-century Northumberland', *Agricultural History Review*, 63 (2015), pp. 39–59.

43 The Royal Bank of Scotland archives, EB1/1–9. Backwell used his bank ledgers as estate and building accounts. Those for Creslow are predominantly composed of purchases and sales of livestock and livestock produce.

44 *Gazatteer and New Daily Advertiser*, 15 November 1766.

45 I am grateful to Gavin Bowie's work on demesne flocks on the southern chalklands for drawing my attention to this material in Hampshire RO R4/6048 /6051 /6063; R4/6011. 2M37/338.

Large farms were not necessarily purely a feature of enclosed villages. Although there had been some piecemeal enclosure at Wylye the process was not completed until the 1850s but the farms were already large in 1798, while the estate rental for 1863 shows one farm of 554 acres.[46] The open-field chalkland village of Ashwell in north Hertfordshire, with productive barley-growing land, had many copyholds, but the farm accounts of one farm around 1800 show that it consisted of 500 acres 50 years before enclosure.[47] Large farms may have been more prominent in arable eastern England, but not exclusively so, and the idea that smaller farms were primarily market orientated is well conveyed in an advertisement carried in the *Taunton Courier* in 1816 which described a 216-acre tenancy as 'truly eligible for a capitalist, who wishes to farm on a small scale'.[48]

What was central to the 'English model' was that farmers seized the business opportunities available in a well-integrated food market. They could take better advantage of it if their capital was invested in livestock primarily, but also in farm buildings, and in new equipment and techniques, rather than in the land. As they gained confidence in their ability to work this system in a very secure legal and political framework, the ownership of land became increasingly separated from its exploitation. To buy a large farm was increasingly difficult. The great landowners continued to invest in land, their timescale was long-term and they were prepared to pay premium prices for good farms. The dynastic imperative looked generations ahead, not years. They could afford to wait while copyholders and freeholders in their neighbourhood bought and sold land, taking the opportunities to buy when they arose rather than seeking expropriation.

Being a substantial tenant farmer was to run a sizeable business. The overall turnover of farmers on leasehold tenancies was not rapid, and on average a farmer might move farm once or twice in his lifetime. This looks like a slow rate, but it was sufficient to see the surnames of families come and go in village lists over time, perhaps more so in the seventeenth and eighteenth centuries than in the nineteenth, particularly in southern England. Stead's study of tenant turnover uses a variety of sources, including data on turnover generated by himself, Broad and Wade Martins. It analysed tenant turnover in different parts of the country and indicated significant turnover rates in the period 1650–1850, with families rarely remaining more than a generation on the same farm, and a mean tenancy length of less than 15 years. In late seventeenth-century Middle Claydon, Buckinghamshire, less than half the tenants remained over one eight-year period, though in other periods it was as high as 70 per cent, while on the Holkham estates in Norfolk in the late eighteenth and early nineteenth centuries survival rates over a 40-year period only once exceeded 20 per cent.[49]

---

46 Wiltshire RO 2057/S186.

47 TNA, IR23/33/213 shows that eight farmers in Ashwell, Herts., held farms ranging roughly from 100 to 470 acres in 1798.

48 *Taunton Courier*, 16 February 1816 quoted in [10, p. 19].

49 D.R. Stead, 'The mobility of English tenant farmers, c.1700–1850', *Agricultural History Review*, 51 (2003), pp. 173–89.

The part played by parliamentary enclosure in separating the peasant farmer from the land was a great cry at the end of the nineteenth century, and is still a popular myth. Large farms existed in seventeenth-century England, and not only in enclosed parishes. Enclosure was not a precondition for establishing large and efficient farm enterprises, but it did aid that process. Parliamentary enclosure is important because it was so well documented compared with earlier episodes, even though it enclosed only a minority of the land, and a parliamentary act was often used to facilitate enclosure because it enabled landowners to over-ride the opposition of many small landowners. Before the use of acts, the enclosing landowner needed the consent of all those with land rights. Parliamentary enclosure was possible provided the owners of 70 per cent of the land area involved agreed. Even if a huge majority of landowners owned a quarter of the land they could be over-ruled by one, or by a handful of landowners, who dominated the village. This was the element of friction surrounding parliamentary enclosure. Furthermore, in a point made recently by Richard Hoyle, the kind of enclosure that created conflict over the whole period 1500–1850 was largely confined to a narrow belt of open-field England 50–150 miles from London running from Salisbury plain to the Humber, areas on the margins of competing in the London food market. Elsewhere, enclosure was largely a procedure undertaken by mutual consent. Conflict was particularly pronounced in places where the small landowner's access to limited communal waste was threatened. In many cases these small landowners sold up even before the enclosure took place. Both Turner for Buckinghamshire and Neeson in Northamptonshire have demonstrated this process and how small landowner turnover was much higher in enclosing villages than in their open-field neighbours.[50] Parliamentary enclosure has been strongly associated with peasant immiseration fundamentally because the same open-field areas most subject to it were suffering from a combination of rapid natural population growth from higher fertility in the later eighteenth century and the collapse of non-agricultural employment, together with the painful food-price inflation of the Revolutionary war period. Enclosure undoubtedly aggravated rural immiseration, but there were greater forces at work.

The nineteenth and twentieth centuries saw the triumph of large farms. England remains a country where large farms occupy a high percentage of the land area – over 50 per cent. However, there is a statistical paradox, and the numbers of small farmers, smallholders, allotment holders and market gardeners has remained high. Chevet demonstrated that the number of small farming enterprises, which he defined as less than five acres or two hectares, in England in the 1880s was extremely large, proportionately not much lower than in France.[51] Some part of this probably comprised small semi-urban plots, but other smaller units represent a reaction to the collapse of world cereal prices after 1870, which led to a gradual diversification in agricultural

50 M.E. Turner, 'Parliamentary enclosure and landownership change in Buckinghamshire', *Economic History Review*, 28 (1975), pp. 565–81; J.M. Neeson, *Commoners: common right, enclosure and social change in England, 1700–1820* (Cambridge, 1996), ch. 8.

51 J.M. Chevet, 'Reconsidering a rural myth: peasant France and capitalist Britain', in J. Broad (ed.), *A common agricultural heritage? Revising French and British rural divergence* (British Agricultural History Society, 2009), pp. 37–54.

production fostered by higher real wages and a demand for greater diversity in diet. In England there was a huge expansion in allotments available to farm labourers. For example, in the 69 villages around Tysoe in Warwickshire analysed by Joseph Ashby, available allotment land rose almost fourfold between 1850 and 1890, with enough for every family in the area to have half an acre.[52] Ironically, this was also the time when the debate on the disappearance of the peasantry began, perhaps because, as Flora Thompson's *Lark Rise to Candleford* eloquently shows, the railway and the bicycle, combined with urbanisation even in rural counties, were altering rural culture significantly. Today, while there are areas where small dairy farms of less than 100 acres (40 hectares) survive, while smallholdings, market gardens and specialist agricultural enterprises can be quite small, and while 'average' farm sizes may seem small, the percentage of agricultural land held in large farming units remains high.

Conclusion

English agrarian structures differed both in the ways in which land ownership was perceived among non-elite proprietors and in the relationship between 'ownership' and the farming of land. The market in land was made use of from the fourteenth century, and possibly before, by small owners who were adjusting their investment in land rather than expanding their holdings in good agricultural times.[53] Weak manorial rules directing inheritance and the over-riding power of the will to determine inter-generational transfers allowed great flexibility in land transfer both during a person's lifetime and after death. This was even true in the restricted system of copyhold for lives, as shown on the Pembroke estates. However, the end of large-scale Crown land confiscations after the sixteenth century and the acceptance of legal instruments such as the strict settlement allowed the elite to reduce any individual inheritor's right to decide how much land was transferred at death. This provided a mechanism for large landowners to take over a high proportion of freehold land by 1650, certainly 70 per cent by 1870, at a time when most elite assets were invested in land, and the market for small land parcels was buoyant. This was overwhelmingly a long-term process of small accretions, though aristocratic bankruptcies such as those of Earl Verney in 1783 and the duke of Buckingham in 1847–8 occasionally brought large blocks of land onto the market.[54]

---

52 J. Ashby and B. King, 'Statistics of some Midland villages', *The Economic Journal*, 3 (1893), pp. 1–22; for a modern take on this see J. Broad, 'La dynamique du pouvoir dans les villages anglais du XIXe siecle: logement et protection sociale', in L. Brassart, J.-P. Jessenne and N. Vivier (eds), *Clochemerle, Ou, République Villageoise? La Conduite Municipale Des Affaires Villageoises En Europe Du XVIIIe Au XXe Siècle* (Villeneuve d'Ascq, 2012), pp. 123–37.

53 See, for instance, D. Noy, 'Winslow in 1341: the *Nonarum Inquisitiones* and the reliability of medieval tax self-assessment', *Records of Bucks*, 55 (2015), pp. 137–46.

54 J.V. Beckett, *The rise and fall of the Grenvilles: the dukes of Buckingham and Chandos, 1710 to 1921* (Manchester, 1994); J. Broad, *Transforming English rural society: the Verneys and the Claydons, 1600–1820* (Cambridge, 2004).

In parallel, the early sophistication of English markets for food and animal products powerfully driven by the extraordinary relative size of London as an urban centre encouraged farmers to produce for sale and to plough profits into upgrading buildings and inputs, or increasing the area leased rather than buying additional land for production. The lease as a contract for land use that was effectively determinable by the tenant provided the means for rapidly adjusting land area to capital availability. The 21-year lease of eighteenth-century improvement fame was relatively unimportant, though it could be an encouragement to tenant investment. The single system of law and taxation reduced transaction costs, as did low market dues and restrictions and good transport links. This combination of incentives for market production and competition for labour in a society where non-agricultural occupations in both the secondary and tertiary sectors were rising fast were at the heart of the rise of the large tenanted farm, producing improved output per acre with markedly less labour.

This account of the roots of rural tenurial change over 600 years has concentrated on how the majority of the land was owned and farmed, not how the majority of rural dwellers, who were increasingly excluded from both ownership and farm tenancies and who either worked small farms or smallholdings, found other modes of employment in the countryside or moved into towns. These substantial market-orientated farms took up a rising percentage of available land over time, and by the early nineteenth century predominated. Their importance reflected their willingness, driven by market forces and prices, to adapt techniques and crops to produce more from the land, partly by raising yields but also by bringing more land into cultivation by a reduction in fallows. Equally important was their impact on the structure of rural life, as from the seventeenth century they began to use farm labour more efficiently and employ more horses.[55] The timing of this is imprecise, but reflected both the need to produce efficiently to compete (especially when prices were falling) and the rise of rural non-agricultural employment. These features encapsulate the essence of the tripartite rural social division into landowners, capitalist tenant farmers and a rural proletariat that so fascinated visitors from Europe.

---

55 R.C. Allen, 'The growth of labor productivity in early modern English agriculture', *Explorations in Economic History*, 25 (1988), pp. 117–46; L. Shaw-Taylor, 'The rise of agrarian capitalism and the decline of family farming in England', *Economic History Review*, 65 (2012), pp. 26–60; L. Shaw-Taylor, 'Family farms and capitalist farms in mid nineteenth-century England', *Agricultural History Review*, 53 (2005), pp. 158–91.

Part II: Land and mobility

Chapter 4

Farming the Kentish marshlands: continuity and change in the late Middle Ages[1]

Sheila Sweetinburgh

In 1463 Thomas Wodman of Ivychurch in Romney Marsh took stock of his life, family and farm as he composed his last will and testament.[2] He was a substantial peasant farmer, probably at the higher end of the group characterised by Dyer as husbandmen (customary yardlanders in the Midlands), but Thomas did not give himself such a socioeconomic designation.[3] Rather, his status can be gleaned from his desired place of burial – in St Katherine's chancel chapel of his parish church – and the instigation of a temporary chantry, the latter financed from the sale of some of his land. Thomas was fortunate in that he had a wife and two adult sons, whereas among his neighbours and more broadly across the region, the likelihood of familial continuity was less sure.

Details concerning his landholding, goods and chattels similarly offer insights about his position and interests as a peasant farmer in the Kentish marshlands. Like many men of a similar rank in the county his property portfolio comprised numerous parcellated landholdings of various sizes from different landlords, often including lands in several parishes, a legacy of the particular and complex tenurial arrangements found in Kent. Within the parish of Ivychurch he held land from at least two manors. In some cases this meant the lands abutted or at least were close by, but whether this applied to Thomas' holdings is not clear from the sources; yet it probably did apply to the 22 acres of land belonging to his principal messuage. Thomas held this particular holding from the court of Wyk, whereas his six acres from Aldington manor placed him in the lordship of the archbishop of Canterbury. The full extent of his landholding is uncertain but, in addition to a further 3.5 acres in Ivychurch, his will mentions unspecified lands in Ivychurch and the neighbouring parish of Brookland.

1 I would like to thank Dr Mark Gardiner for his transcriptions of several documents relating to Denge Marsh; Andrew Butcher for his assessment on the Hundred of Newchurch and other work on the Romney Marshes; the Romney Marsh Research Trust for various grants that aided my research on the region in the past; and Canterbury Archaeological Trust for use of my survey of the documentary sources for the Thanet Earth site.

2 Kent History Library Centre, Maidstone (hereafter KHLC): PRC/32/2, f. 136.

3 C. Dyer, 'The agrarian problem, 1440–1520', in J. Whittle (ed.), *Landlords and tenants in Britain, 1440–1660* (Woodbridge, 2013), pp. 23–4.

Nor may this have been his entire holding, because the division of these unspecified lands between his two sons may indicate that each was already farming away from their father's main messuage. Such an apparent amalgam of lands is again typical of the region's prosperous peasant farmers and for Thomas allowed him to provide his wife with an annuity of £1 from the rent of his primary holding. Furthermore, his house was sufficiently large that she could be given the hall to live in without seemingly inconveniencing the sub-tenant, and the provider of the annuity.

Even though relatively few of his goods and chattels are mentioned in Thomas' will, his bequest of his pewter and brass, to be split equally between his two sons, with his wife to receive the rest of his household goods, does again place him within the more prosperous peasantry. Moreover, employment of a charter of enfeoffment for his lands and tenements in Ivychurch and Brookland would imply he was a man of some standing locally, as would his choice of feoffees, who were also substantial farmers. Following a mixed farming strategy was not unusual in the region, and Thomas grew wheat and barley as well as keeping cows and other livestock.[4] The presence of cows may imply a dairy herd, but he was presumably also rearing cattle for the meat trade, even if he sold them as steers to local butcher–graziers rather than fattening them himself.[5] Interestingly, he does not mention sheep, although this does not mean that they were absent from his farm, as they could have contributed both to his dairy and livestock-rearing enterprises as well as providing a valuable wool clip.

This biographical snapshot underlines many of the features at work in the late medieval Kentish marshlands and, as Dyer has illustrated using Robert Parman of Suffolk, Roger Heritage of Warwickshire and, in more detail, John, Heritage's son, such case studies can highlight ideas about lived experience rather than solely concentrating on social structural issues in rural history.[6] Among the features seen in Wodman's will are matters of tenure, landholding, inheritance and agricultural practice, as well as ideas about consumerism and commercialisation. These are explored here to see how, in Tawney's terms, husbandmen such as Wodman in the post-Black Death era had taken advantage of practices such as the 'redivision and reallotment' of land leading to 'the improvement in the condition of the peasantry': a 'gradual' process that was generally welcomed because the 'balance between their tentative individualism and the rule of communal custom [was] preserved by the action of the manorial court'.[7] Furthermore, and towards the end, this chapter returns

4 J. Thirsk, 'Kent's farming regions 1500–1700', in T. Lawson and D. Killingray (eds), *An historical atlas of Kent* (Chichester, 2004), p. 72.

5 Such men were often based in neighbouring towns: S. Sweetinburgh, 'Hythe's butcher-graziers: their role in town and country in late medieval Kent', in C. Dyer, A. Hopper, E. Lord and N. Tringham (eds), *New directions in local history since Hoskins* (Hatfield, 2011), pp. 98–113.

6 C. Dyer, 'A Suffolk farmer in the fifteenth century', *Agricultural History Review*, 55 (2007), pp. 1–22; C. Dyer, 'Were there any capitalists in fifteenth-century England?', in J. Kermode (ed.), *Enterprise and individuals in fifteenth-century England* (Stroud, 1991), pp. 1–24; C. Dyer, *A country merchant, 1495–1520: trading and farming at the end of the Middle Ages* (Oxford, 2012).

7 R.H. Tawney, *The agrarian problem in the sixteenth century* (London, 1912), p. 172.

to Wodman's family to examine whether the experiences of his sons demonstrate or at least show nascent signs of what Tawney called 'the plight of the husbandman'. For this was, as Dyer notes, one of the key issues which exercised Tawney in the *Agrarian Problem*, a concern reflecting that of several influential early sixteenth-century writers.[8] According to his analysis, it was conditions in the sixteenth-century countryside that adversely affected these fifteenth-century farmers, their more aggressive and acquisitive neighbours and, even more importantly, 'outsiders' becoming, in his phrase, successors to these 'petty capitalists' of the fifteenth century.[9] Among the causes of the husbandman's plight and that of his poorer fellow peasants, Tawney highlighted the conflict between public good and private interest, subsistence versus commercial priorities, the struggle for the commons, the leasing of demesnes and the activities of outsiders.[10]

Tawney's majestic survey of rural society across the medieval and early modern divide maintains its relevance within modern scholarship, but a couple of caveats would seem worthwhile. Firstly, even though Tawney drew on manorial and other sources from a large part of England, he frequently turned his attention to the Midlands and other regions that have often been characterised as 'traditional': those places where, before the Black Death, different 'classes' of villein held all or part of a standard holding within an open-field system, had rights in common meadow and waste and were generally burdened by heavy labour services on the demesne.[11] Moreover, while acknowledging that other systems did exist in medieval England, his primary point of contrast was East Anglia, which, although useful, is insufficient because, as Bailey, Whittle and Yates among others have shown, regional variation requires far greater detailed consideration in any analysis of peasant society.[12] Because, although there are some similarities between Kent and East Anglia, especially the importance of partible inheritance, Kent remains, as Campbell noted, a 'most remarkable medieval

---

8 Dyer, 'Agrarian problem', p. 23.

9 Tawney, *Agrarian problem*, pp. 138, 179, 184–5.

10 Ibid., pp. 179, 182, 184.

11 Ibid., p. 55; P.R. Schofield, *Peasant and community in medieval England 1200–1500* (Basingstoke, 2003), p. 135.

12 East Anglia: M. Bailey, 'The form, function and evolution of irregular field systems in Suffolk, c.1300–c.1550', *Agricultural History Review*, 57 (2009), pp. 15–36; M. Bailey, 'Beyond the Midland field system: the determinants of common rights over the arable in medieval England', *Agricultural History Review*, 58 (2010), pp. 153–71; J.C. Whittle and M. Yates, '"*Pays réel* or *pays légal*?" Contrasting patterns of land tenure and social structure in eastern Norfolk and western Berkshire, 1450–1600', *Agricultural History Review*, 48 (2000), pp. 1–26. Other regions: R.H. Britnell, 'Fields, farms and sun-division in a moorland region, 1100–1400', *Agricultural History Review*, 52 (2004), pp. 20–37; M. Yates, 'Change and continuities in rural society from the later Middle Ages to the sixteenth century: the contribution of west Berkshire', *Economic History Review*, 52 (1999), pp. 617–37. See also E. Miller (ed.), *The agrarian history of England and Wales Volume III: 1348–1500.* (Cambridge, 1991); J. Thirsk (ed.), *The agrarian history of England and Wales. Volume IV: 1500–1640.* (Cambridge, 1967), for the relevant regional sections; and eadem, *Agricultural regions and agrarian history in England, 1500–1750* (Basingstoke, 1987).

English county'.[13] In addition, Tawney very rarely mentions Kent at all, and, although understandable in terms of early twentieth-century scholarship, the particular nature of certain features regarding the county's peasantry, as discussed below, needs to be taken into account.[14] At this point it is probably also worth noting that Bailey, in his new survey on the decline of serfdom in England, similarly barely refers to the situation in Kent.[15] Yet some recent research has been conducted on the Kentish peasantry and, even though Mate's work on manorial tenants in medieval Sussex and Kent is probably more widely known, Draper has published quite extensively on the Romney Marshes in particular.[16]

Secondly, as Dyer and others have suggested, many of Tawney's ideas remain pertinent, but more recent scholarship has shifted its focus somewhat to investigate areas such as internal conflict within the village rather than the role of outsiders; the inter-relationship between rural and urban society, including migration; changes in settlement patterns and the role of pragmatic neglect of buildings; and the constitution and function of the peasant land market, taking account of the relative value placed on the family–land bond.[17] Some of these issues regarding cause

---

13 B.M.S. Campbell, 'Agriculture in Kent in the high Middle Ages', in S. Sweetinburgh (ed.), *Later medieval Kent, 1220–1540* (Woodbridge, 2010), p. 50. For those seeking a county-wide summary of settlement and land use, see G. Draper, '"Land and marsh": settlement, colonization and consolidation, c. 800–1220', in S. Sweetinburgh (ed.), *Early medieval Kent, 800–1220* (forthcoming).

14 Tawney, *Agrarian problem*, pp. 8, 36, 153, 167.

15 M. Bailey, *The decline of serfdom in late medieval England* (Woodbridge, 2014), pp. 49, 80, 98.

16 M. Mate, 'The farming out of manors: a new look at the evidence from Canterbury Cathedral priory', *Journal of Medieval History*, 9 (1983), pp. 331–43; eadem, 'Labour and labour services on the estates of Canterbury Cathedral priory in the fourteenth century', *Southern History*, 7 (1985), pp. 55–68; eadem, 'Tenant farming and farmers: Kent and Sussex', in E. Miller (ed.), *The agrarian history of England and Wales. Volume III: 1348–1500.* (Cambridge, 1991), pp. 680–703; eadem, 'Farming practice and techniques: Kent and Sussex', in E. Miller (ed.), *The agrarian history of England and Wales. Volume III: 1348–1500.* (Cambridge, 1991), pp. 268–85; eadem, 'The economy of Kent, 1200–1500', in S. Sweetinburgh (ed.), *Later medieval Kent, 1220–1540* (Woodbridge, 2010), pp. 1–24. J. Eddison and G. Draper, 'A landscape of medieval reclamation: Walland Marsh, Kent', *Landscape History*, 19, pp. 75–88; G. Draper, 'The farmers of Canterbury Cathedral priory and All Souls College on Romney Marsh *c.*1443–1545', in J. Eddison, M. Gardiner and A. Long (eds), *Romney Marsh: environmental change and human occupation in a coastal lowland* (Oxford, 1998), pp. 109–28; eadem, 'Small fields and wet land: inheritance practices and the transmission of real property in the Romney Marshes c.1150–1390', *Landscapes*, 6 (2005), pp. 18–45. Recently Draper has worked on the north Kent marshlands: eadem, 'Hoo marshland field systems', English Heritage unpublished report no. 6384 (2013); F. Meddens and G. Draper, 'Out on a limb: insights into Grange, a small member of the cinque ports confederation', *Archaeologia Cantiana*, 135 (2014), pp. 19–32.

17 Dyer, 'Agrarian problem', pp. 33–4. For example; P.D.A. Harvey (ed.), *The peasant land market in England* (Oxford, 1984); R.M. Smith (ed.), *Land, kinship and life-cycle* (Cambridge, 1984); Z. Razi 'The myth of the immutable English family', *Past & Present*, 140 (1991), pp. 3–44; L.R. Poos, *A rural society after the Black Death: Essex, 1350–1525* (Cambridge, 1991); C. Dyer, 'The English medieval

and effect in respect to the growth of commercial agriculture are applicable to the study of the Kentish marshlands, not least because, as Tawney himself had noted, enclosure rather than open-field agriculture had become the norm much earlier in Kent, leading among other matters to potentially greater individualism and a more developed commercialism in terms of producing for the market.[18] Not that the Kentish peasantry were unaware of the need to work collectively at times regarding issues such as reclamation and the maintenance of sea walls or during negotiations with their manorial lords, but their use of custom should be seen against a backdrop of light labour services compared with those imposed upon their open-field counterparts in the Midlands.[19] Consequently, to facilitate a greater appreciation of the regional distinctiveness of medieval England this chapter will consider continuity and change by examining first the period prior to the Black Death before turning to the later Middle Ages. The areas under consideration (Figure 4.1) are the northern marshes (totalling c.47,000 acres), those of north-east Kent (c.17,500 acres) and the largest expanse: the southern marshes of Romney, Walland and Denge, with the associated Rother Levels, covering almost 51,000 acres.[20] For the purposes of this chapter published

village community and its decline', *Journal of British Studies*, 33 (1994), pp. 407–29; J. Whittle, 'Individualism and the family–land bond: a reassessment of land transfer patterns among the English peasantry c.1270–1580', *Past & Present*, 160 (1998), pp. 25–63; P.V. Hargreaves, 'Seignorial reaction and peasant responses: Worcester priory and its peasants after the Black Death', *Midland History*, 24 (1999), pp. 53–78; Schofield, *Peasant and community*; R. Jones and M. Page, *Medieval villages in an English landscape: beginnings and ends* (Bollington, 2006); C. Dyer (ed.), *The self-contained village? The social history of rural communities 1250–1900* (Hatfield, 2007); B. Dodds and R.H. Britnell (eds), *Agriculture and rural society after the Black Death: common themes and regional variations* (Hatfield, 2008); C. Dyer and R. Jones (eds), *Deserted villages revisited* (Hatfield, 2010); M. Bailey and S. Rigby (eds), *Town and countryside in the age of the Black Death* (Woodbridge, 2012).

18 Tawney, *Agrarian problem*, p. 153.

19 A. Gross and A.F. Butcher, 'Adaptation and investment in the age of great storms: agricultural policy on the manors of the principal lords of the Romney Marshes and the marshland fringe c.1250–1320', in J. Eddison (ed.) *Romney Marsh: the debatable ground* (Oxford, 1995), pp. 107–17; Canterbury Cathedral Archives and Library, Canterbury (hereafter CCAL): DCc/Register P, ff. 45v–47; W. Dugdale, *The history of imbanking and draining of divers fens and marshes both in foreign parts and this kingdom and of the improvement thereby* (1662), pp. 38, 39. I would like to thank Andrew Butcher for drawing my attention to an undated petition in French by the poor tenants of Leysdown on the Isle of Sheppey, addressed to their lord the prior of Christ Church, where they refer to the desire to have the same customs as their ancestors had enjoyed; CCAL: DCc/ChAnt/L/360.

20 A.M. Everitt, *Continuity and colonization: the evolution of Kentish settlement* (Leicester, 1986), p. 57. Reeves and Williamson's figure for the Romney Marshes and the adjoining Rother and Pett levels is 74,500 acres; idem, 'Marshes', in J. Thirsk (ed.), *The English rural landscape* (Oxford, 2000), p. 151. See also M. Gardiner, 'South-east England: forms and diversity in medieval rural settlement', in N. Christie and P. Stamper (eds), *Medieval rural settlement: Britain and Ireland, AD 800–1600* (Oxford, 2012), pp. 104, 108.

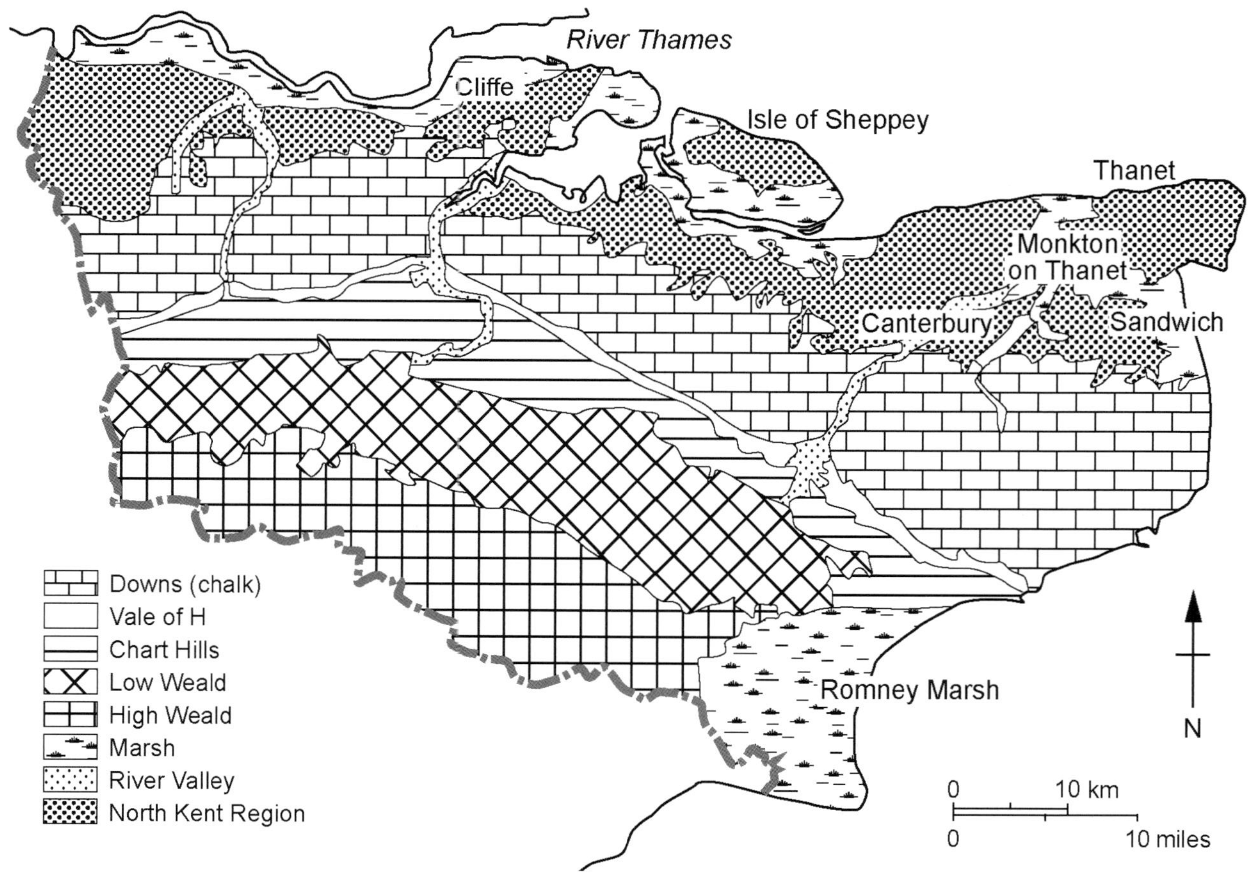

Figure 4.1 Map showing the marshlands of Kent.

and unpublished materials will be used in conjunction with further research for the Romney Marshes and other marshlands, especially the Christ Church Priory manors of Cliffe and Monkton that included such holdings.

Before the Black Death: landholding, settlement patterns and farming practices

During the medieval period, even though numerous laymen were manorial landlords in Kent, their individual manors were often small and instead the county's largest estates were in the hands of the Church.[21] This is particularly applicable to the marshlands, the principal lords being the archbishop of Canterbury, his subordinate at Rochester, and the ancient Benedictine houses of Christ Church Priory, St Augustine's Abbey, Rochester Cathedral Priory and the post-Conquest abbey at Battle, as well as certain smaller monasteries, several hospitals and, later, Oxford and Cambridge colleges.[22] These ecclesiastical manors varied considerably in terms of their size, form and composition, including the balance between demesne and tenant acreage. For example, Christ Church's largest manor on the Romney Marshes was Appledore (c.1,148 acres), which comprised 903 acres of tenant land scattered over three parishes, in addition to the demesne. In contrast, the priory's manor of Agney, with the associated manor of Orgarswick, was about two-thirds demesne land in a total of c.365 acres.[23] Different again was Battle Abbey's great manor of Wye, where the tenant land in Denge Marsh extended over a sizeable block in the large parish of Lydd, with a few small areas of land in the neighbouring parish of Broomhill. Although not to the same degree, the balance between demesne and tenant land, as well as the distribution of these lands, also varied on the northern marshes.[24]

The most widespread forms of tenure under which land was held differed considerably compared with the situation in the champion country of the Midlands.[25] As Witney, among others, has described in detail, there were five principal classes of tenancy in Kent, although even as early as the end of the thirteenth century the distinctions among some of them were becoming less clear owing to overlap.[26] In addition, although also subject to rent, the 'new lands' were established on reclaimed marshes after the Conquest and especially in the late twelfth and thirteenth centuries. Many were held by charter between the ecclesiastical lord and the tenant with his co-parceners, the agreement providing a right to reclaim a specified area as well

21 Campbell,'Agriculture', p. 29.

22 These colleges include All Souls College and Magdalen College, Oxford and St John's College, Cambridge.

23 On the nature of the manors: Andrew Butcher, personal communication.

24 Reeves and Williamson,'Marshes', p. 156; P. Morgan (ed.), *Domesday: Kent* (Chichester, 1983), pp. 3:6, 5:110.

25 Schofield, *Peasant and community*, pp. 22–4.

26 CCAL: U15/24/28; *The survey of Archbishop Pecham's Kentish manors 1283–85*, tr. and ed. with an intro. K. Witney (Maidstone, 2000), pp. lii–liii. See also Du Boulay's assessment, which remains a useful starting point: F.R.H. Du Boulay, *The lordship of Canterbury* (London, 1966), esp. ch. 4.

as requiring continued maintenance of designated sea defences, but otherwise stipulating only a 'fixed' rent, suit of court and the payment of reliefs.[27] Consequently, it is important to note that in Kent almost 'six times as much tenant land was held freehold as was contained in servile tenures'.[28] Leaving aside those lands held by military tenure, principally the knight's fee that was free of manorial services, the most significant and numerous tenancies were the freeholds or gavel lands.[29] These 'were held not by gift but by independent and immemorial right' and, as such, could be sold freely and were held by money rent – *gavel*, which had been set at 1d per acre. This fossilised rent was of considerable concern to the great landlords, who at times contrived to extract another payment called *mala*, as well as rents in kind: hens, eggs, salt and plough-shares.[30] The level of manorial services required was generally light, the main constituents being a limited amount of ploughing and reaping, along with some carriage of goods, whether by packhorse or cart.

Rather than designating the gavel lands under a system of yardlands or family holdings, they were allocated within a fiscal unit known as the *sulung/swyllyng/suling* on which services were imposed and fulfilled collectively by the relevant tenants.[31] The *sulungs* of the archiepiscopal estates varied between about 160 and 200 fiscal acres in size, and a comparable scale was employed by Canterbury's religious houses.[32] They were named predominantly after a tenant rather than topographically, which means that they are generally impossible to place in the landscape. How far they had originally been intended to be family holdings, or perhaps, more probably, the holding of the principal tenant and his associates, remains difficult to ascertain.[33]

By the late thirteenth century, and probably earlier, the *sulungs* had been sub-divided and become fragmented as peasants held small plots in a number of these larger holdings, and sometimes even more than one plot in the same named *sulung*. Such division was the result of partible inheritance (the equal division among all surviving sons or, in the absence of any legitimate male offspring, daughters), the land market and sub-letting. An example is the case of John Baker of Sarre, who held

---

27 Witney, *Pecham*, pp. lxvi–lxx. For example, in Appledore marsh: CCAL: DCc/ChAnt/A/123.

28 Witney, *Pecham*, p. lxxii.

29 The implications of this can be seen in the IPMs from the thirteenth century: among Thomas de Normavile's holdings were 16 acres of partible marsh in Oxenal held of the abbot of St Augustine's and other marshland of the priors of Horton and Bilsington: *Calendar of Inquisitions Post Mortem*, vol. ii (1–19 Edward I), no. 479.

30 Witney, *Pecham*, p. lv.

31 Derived from the Anglo-Saxon term for a plough: *sulh*; Witney, *Pecham*, p. lii. This and the yoke were the units employed in the Domesday Book for Kent and their nominal acreage bore little relation to the physical arable acreage; R. Eales, 'Introduction', *The Kent Domesday* (London, 1992), pp. 12, 19.

32 Witney, *Pecham*, p. 380; S. Campbell, 'Some aspects of the social and economic history of the manor of Adisham, c.1200–the Dissolution', (MPhil thesis, University of Kent, Canterbury, 1981), p. 267.

33 A.R. Baker, 'Some fields and farms in medieval Kent', *Archaeologia Cantiana*, 80 (1965), p. 164; Draper, 'Settlement'.

half an acre from the land of Mathew le Man within the *sulung* of Adam of Updown.[34] As a result of these processes of division there were at least 100 landholders who had a share in this 200-acre *sulung* in the 1280s. Moreover, the tiny size of some of these holdings can be seen in the same *sulung*, where the heirs of Simon Hubert had only one virgate (a quarter of an acre).[35] Additionally, even though other tenant land should not have been subject to the same influences, in reality it meant that across the county individual holdings were a complex patchwork and individual tenements might include parcels of free and unfree land.[36]

One of the reasons for such fragmentation was the increase in population during the twelfth and thirteenth centuries. Nevertheless, it was not the only factor and the presence of an active peasant land market was significant because it created an inherently fluid system.[37] Peasants might sell all or part of their often small acreage, sometimes through poverty, so becoming more impoverished in the longer term, although by-employment opportunities, such as part-time or seasonal work outside agriculture, might mitigate against their impecunious circumstances, but Mate believed that these had declined considerably by the early fourteenth century.[38] Conversely, however, such sales did offer opportunities for the more prosperous to increase their overall acreage through the acquisition of these same small plots. Those seeking to engage in land transactions were aided not only by limited tenurial restrictions, but also by the form of the open-field system in Kent. Unlike the great open fields of the Midlands, where strip farming was the dominant system, the large Kentish fields were generally divided into small unenclosed blocks held by various peasant landholders who could farm them with a considerable degree of personal freedom.[39] This contrast is important for, even if some peasants chose to collaborate with their neighbours, they were not bound by what Tawney called the 'common routine of cultivation' based on 'the customary routine of village husbandry'; rather, potentially, if their circumstances allowed, they could respond to market forces.[40]

---

34 Witney, *Pecham*, p. 75.

35 Ibid., pp. 75, 381. The term in this case referred to a measure of land rather than a fiscal unit (a quarter of a yoke).

36 Ibid., p. lxxii. Yet S. Campbell believes the land transactions she saw in the Adisham courts concerned only gavel land; eadem, 'Some aspects of social history', p. 261.

37 The transfer of customary land between tenants was accepted by manorial lords provided the transfer was recorded in the manorial court rolls, fealty was sworn and a relief was paid by the incoming tenant.

38 Mate, 'Economy of Kent', pp. 6, 9–10. Keibek and Shaw-Taylor believe historians have seriously over-estimated the incidence of by-employment using early modern inventories, yet the potential was presumably present in the medieval countryside; S.A.J. Keibek and L. Shaw-Taylor, 'Early modern rural by-employments: a re-examination of the probate inventory evidence', *Agricultural History Review*, 61 (2013), pp. 244–6, 248, 278.

39 Campbell, 'Agriculture', p. 26; Draper, 'Settlement'. The likelihood of co-aration was discussed by Baker, and, similarly, private arrangements about the grazing of livestock: Baker, 'Fields and farms', pp. 167–9.

40 Tawney, *Agrarian problem*, pp. 71, 106.

This extremely high population density within the Kentish marshlands, which seems to have reached its peak before 1250 on the Romney Marshes, presumably meant that some tenants suffered poverty at certain times during their lives, albeit on average these southern marshland families were moderately affluent and generally wealthier than their Thanet counterparts.[41] The 1334/5 lay subsidy figures calculated by hundred show that, whereas individual payments on Romney Marsh and its borders averaged 4s (albeit there was some variation over the area), such payments in the area of the Wantsum Channel were 3s 3d; however, those for central north Kent exceeded those of the Romney Marshes, being 4s 5½d.[42] The range of individual assessments within the Hundred of Ringlo (Wantsum Channel area) also varied, but it is worth noting that the lowest assessment of 1s is higher than that of some other hundreds, perhaps indicative of differing tenurial arrangements and, more particularly, the land quality.[43]

In addition to the impact on the peasantry, the county's tenurial conditions affected the management of the demesne land because, rather than relying on the tenants to perform the necessary works involved in running the estates, the sergeants or reeves had to hire specialists as well as agricultural labourers.[44] Such opportunities meant that certain tenants could survive, or even prosper, on a smaller holding or total acreage than in some other parts of England where, even though some *famuli* were used, there were still fewer opportunities for paid agrarian employment.[45] Consequently, taking all of these issues together, in addition to a probable greater stratification of the peasantry compared with the Midlands, commercialism was also a factor in rural Kent. However, this is not to dismiss the idea of custom as the governing principle of agrarian practices, but instead to see it as the mechanism whereby the community took on outside forces, whether this was the sea or their lords.[46] It is

---

41 A. Reeves, 'Romney Marsh: the fieldwalking evidence', in J. Eddison (ed.), *Romney Marsh: the debatable ground* (Oxford, 1995), pp. 89–90. Campbell, 'Agriculture', p. 27; Reeves and Williamson, 'Marshes', pp. 155–7; Mate, 'Economy of Kent', pp. 7–9. For one recent assessment of the necessary acreage required for peasant self-sufficiency, see H. Kitsikopoulos, 'Standards of living and capital formation in pre-plague England: a peasant budget model', *Economic History Review*, 53 (2000), pp. 237–61.

42 H. Hanley and C. Chalklin (eds), 'The Kent lay subsidy roll of 1334/5', in *Documents illustrative of medieval Kentish society*, Kent Records Series 18 (Maidstone, 1964), pp. 66, 68–9, 71–6; Mate, 'Economy of Kent', p. 10.

43 Hanley and Chalklin, 'Lay subsidy', pp. 71–6. CCAL: DCc/Register C, ff. 128v–9, custumal of Monkton. Whitney, *Pecham*, pp. 69–73, customs and services of Reculver manor. *Black book of St Augustine*, pt 1, 25–9, custumal of Minster.

44 In 1317/18, for example, 22 *famuli* are listed: CCAL: DCc/BedelsRolls/Monkton/49.

45 The heavy reliance on *famuli* and casual labour to farm the demesne lands did provide opportunities for some of these peasants: Campbell, 'Agriculture', p. 27.

46 Customs relating to the maintenance of sea defences on Romney Marsh were seen as 'ancient and approved' by the thirteenth century: Reeves and Williamson, 'Marshes', p. 161; a fourteenth-century copy of the customs of Romney Marsh survives: CCAL: DCc/Register P, ff. 46–7. Their governing principles continued to be employed into the early modern period: S. Hipkin, 'The

perhaps no coincidence, therefore, that there are numerous incidents of resistance and revolt involving the Kentish peasantry during the medieval period, as in 1318, when 600 local men attacked the St Augustine's Abbey manors on Thanet. They were said to have 'by unlawful conspiracy, in oath and writing among them, made collections and assessed divers tallages among themselves', such collective action mirroring the employment of custom.[47]

So what effect did such matters of tenure, landholding and the market have on local settlement patterns in the marshlands? Romney Marsh was characterised by a landscape of scattered farmsteads, where small enclosures with buildings (farmsteads and ancillary buildings) were more often sited against a roadway on slightly higher ground.[48] However, there were some settlements situated at manorial centres, allowing easy access, in particular, for those working on the demesne land. Some of these had become villages or, where marketing facilities were available, small towns.[49] On the northern and north-eastern marshlands these were predominantly located on higher ground, their liminal position between the marshes and the adjoining '*pays*' aiding the transference of goods and people.[50] For example, the churchyard was favoured as a place of business at Monkton: two peasants from Monkton intended that Adam de Wode should pay annually what he owed when they met in the local churchyard.[51]

Along the northern fringe of the southern marshes there was, to a degree, a similar relationship between the marshes and the surrounding uplands in the form of a ring of towns and villages from the Cinque Ports of Hythe in the east to Rye and Winchelsea in the west. Other market towns that provided a gateway to the interior were Appledore and the Wealden town of Tenterden. However, the far greater expanse of the southern marshlands necessitated manorial and marketing foci across the region

structure of land occupation in the Level of Romney Marsh during the late 16th and early 17th centuries', in J. Eddison, M. Gardiner and A. Long (eds), *Romney Marsh: environmental change in a coastal lowland* (Oxford, 1998), pp. 156–61.

47 *William Thorne's chronicle of St Augustine's Abbey Canterbury*, tr. and ed. A.H. Davis (Oxford, 1934), pp. 432–3.

48 Reeves, 'Romney Marsh', p. 90; L. Barber and G. Priestly-Bell, *Medieval adaptation, settlement and economy of a coastal wetland: the evidence from around Lydd, Romney Marsh, Kent* (Oxford, 2008), pp. 286–8.

49 There is a considerable literature on such towns, including M. Bailey, *Medieval Suffolk: an economic and social history, 1200–1500* (Woodbridge, 2007), chs. 6, 7; C. Dyer, *Making a living in the Middle Ages: the people of Britain 850–1520* (London, 2002), ch. 5, 6; C. Dyer, 'Small towns, 1270–1540', in D.M. Palliser (ed.), *Cambridge urban history of Britain, 600–1540*, vol. I (Cambridge, 2000), pp. 505–37; M. Kowaleski, *Local markets and regional trade in medieval Exeter* (Cambridge, 1995); K. Giles and C. Dyer (eds), *Town and country in the Middle Ages: contrasts, contacts and interconnections, 1100–1500* (Leeds, 2005); P. Schofield, 'Access to credit in the early fourteenth-century English countryside', in P.R. Schofield and N.J. Mayhew (eds), *Credit and debt in medieval England c.1180–c.1350* (Oxford, 2002), pp. 106–26.

50 Everitt, *Continuity*, pp. 66–8; Reeves and Williamson, 'Marshes', p. 156; Draper, 'Settlement'.

51 CCAL: DCc/ChAnt/M/168.

and particularly in the earlier-reclaimed area of Romney Marsh.[52] These varied in size and complexity, ranging from villages such as Midley, Snave and Ivychurch to the Cinque Ports of Romney and Lydd.[53]

Another characteristic was the use of seasonal settlements linked to other forms of employment such as fishing of various kinds: for example, the cabins on the gravel foreshore at Dungeness or, also on the southern marshes, the coastal salt workings at Belgar.[54] The use of seasonal settlements was similarly present in south Devon, where examples include the coastal cellars at Starcross, although there is insufficient evidence from Kent to test the apparent link that Fox saw between the size of agricultural holdings and the occupation of these cellars.[55] However, in some cases coastal settlements developed to become notable commercial centres, those in north Kent, such as Cliffe and Chatham, aided by the proximity to London for water-borne trade, whereas others remained small and remote.[56]

The form and layout of the peasant messuages or farmsteads is exceedingly difficult to ascertain from the documentary sources, not least because wills hardly survive at all in Kent from before the fifteenth century.[57] The Kentish charter evidence is often equally unhelpful, but there are a very few rare exceptions: an inquisition, taken in 1304, indicates a mix of domestic and agricultural buildings, including hall, kitchen (which may have been detached) and barn. Furthermore, the damage sustained at this Monkton farmstead included the removal of windows, doors, benches and the hall roof.[58] In addition, the two miscreants were said to have cut down trees, which may imply some sort of shelter break around the holding, a feature also found on the Romney Marshes.[59] Although the beadles' rolls refer only to buildings which formed part of the manorial complex, they do highlight the diversity of agricultural buildings.[60]

---

52 Reeves and Williamson, 'Marshes', p. 155.

53 For studies on Lydd and New Romney: S. Dimmock, 'Class and the social transformation of a late medieval small town: Lydd c.1450–1550', (PhD thesis, University of Kent, Canterbury, 1998); S. Dimmock, *The origin of capitalism in England, 1400–1600* (Leiden, 2013); G. Draper and F. Meddens, *The sea and the marsh: the medieval cinque port of New Romney* (London, 2009).

54 M. Gardiner, 'A seasonal fishermen's settlement at Dungeness, Kent', *Medieval Settlement Research Group Annual Report*, 11 (1996), pp. 18–20; E. Vollans, 'Medieval salt-making and the inning of tidal marshes at Belgar, Lydd', in J. Eddison and C. Green (eds), *Romney Marsh: the debatable ground* (Oxford, 1995), pp. 118–26. See also Reeves and Williamson, 'Marshes', pp. 163–4.

55 H.S.A. Fox, *The evolution of the fishing village: landscape and society along the south Devon coast, 1086–1550* (Oxford, 2001), pp. 118–21.

56 G. Draper, 'Timber and iron: natural resources for the late medieval shipbuilding industry in Kent', in S. Sweetinburgh (ed.), *Later medieval Kent, 1220–1540* (Woodbridge, 2010), pp. 71–3.

57 There are some court rolls from Kent that predate the Black Death but they offer little useful information in this regard: Baker, 'Fields and farms', p. 158. Hence the value of archaeology, including fieldwalking (see above).

58 CCAL: DCc/ChAnt/M/191.

59 A. Reeves, 'The testimony of trees', *Romney Marsh Irregular*, 24 (2004), pp. 21–4.

60 M. Adams, 'History of the demesne farm at Appledore from contemporary building records', *Archaeologia Cantiana*, 112 (1993), pp. 283–98.

Moreover, there is some archaeological and documentary evidence that indicates peasant brewing and baking in these regions.[61]

Even though most marshland households were probably involved in some form of by-employment, the primary economic activity among the peasantry would have been agriculture. Documentary evidence for peasant agriculture before the Black Death is exceedingly limited, yet Ben Dodds' work on tithes provides useful insights.[62] In his study of the rectory at Monkton, among other rectories, he concluded that there were considerable similarities between the agrarian practices carried out on the demesnes and by the peasantry.[63] By bringing together Dodds' conclusions and Campbell's assessment of the demesne accounts for thirteenth- and fourteenth-century Kent, it is feasible that the marshland farmers around Thanet followed an agrarian system based on intensive mixed farming with cattle and sheep.[64] As Campbell has noted, the key features of this system as employed on the demesnes were the close integration of arable and livestock production: the cropped land providing fodder and seasonal grazing for the animals, the latter in turn supplying draught power and manure to the arable.[65]

Moreover, using evidence from the Hundred of Newchurch in Romney Marsh, Butcher found that almost all the taxed peasant households had pigs, while three-quarters owned sheep, but only small flocks – over 80 per cent had fewer than 21 animals.[66] Cattle were less common, not least because they require a larger acreage, but 58 per cent had at least one cow, most having a small herd. Far fewer kept oxen, but over 40 per cent had horses, including mares and foals. The arable is more problematic because the taxation records refer only to surpluses, but from these it seems that wheat and oats were the main cereals, while beans, vetches and hemp were also cultivated.[67] However, in some areas at least spring barley was grown, as seen in the Monkton charter evidence.[68] It seems likely, therefore, that all three cereals – namely wheat,

61 J. Rady, 'Archaeological excavation of the Thanet Earth site' (unpublished client report).

62 For an assessment of the value of tithes as indicators of peasant productivity see B. Dodds, 'Output and productivity: common themes and regional variation', in B. Dodds and R.H. Britnell (eds), *Agriculture and rural society after the Black Death: common themes and regional variations* (Hatfield, 2008), pp. 73–88.

63 B. Dodds, 'Demesne and tithe: peasant agriculture in the late Middle Ages', *Agricultural History Review*, 56 (2008), pp. 123–41.

64 For the county as a whole cattle were predominant, but on the marshes sheep were also important, including for milk production: Mate, 'Economy of Kent', p. 8; S. Sweetinburgh, 'Overcoming disaster? Farming practices on Christ Church Priory's marshland manors in the early 14th century', in M. Waller, E. Edwards and L. Barber, *Romney Marsh: persistence and change in a coastal lowland* (Sevenoaks, 2010), pp. 97–115.

65 Campbell, 'Agriculture', pp. 27–34.

66 A.F. Butcher and A. Gross, 'The history of Romney Marsh c.1150–1350', unpublished report, Romney Marsh Research Trust (1991), cited in Barber and Priestly-Bell, *Medieval adaptation*, p. 20.

67 A.F. Butcher, 'Peasant use of cannabis in the early fourteenth century' (unpublished paper, Canterbury, 2000).

68 CCAL: DCc/ChAnt/M/150.

barley and oats – were to be found on local tenant holdings, individual peasants to a degree aided by the composition of their dispersed small landholdings. Presumably the buildings on these peasant farmsteads reflected such agrarian practices, but how far this would have involved specialist structures is difficult to assess.

After the Black Death: continuity and change

Taking this as a starting point, the arrival of the Black Death and subsequent plague outbreaks did not immediately lead to significant changes in either how the land was farmed or by whom. Yet, in the longer term, considerable changes did occur regarding who farmed the demesne, as well as concerning peasant landholding, farming practices and settlement patterns. To a degree these have implications regarding Tawney's contention that the 'freer and more elastic economy' during the century after the Peasants' Revolt of 1381 was a time of 'increasing prosperity for the small cultivator'.[69] Nevertheless, what is far less pertinent is the stress on the decline of serfdom in the later fourteenth century, as recently reassessed by Bailey, thereby again highlighting the importance of regional difference and the particularity of conditions in Kent.[70]

Despite the early effects of the plague, there were still considerable numbers who could take on the small plots of their dead neighbours and kinsmen because population density had been so high in certain areas of all these marshland regions.[71] In part this was a reflection of considerable wage rises, particularly in the short term, for demesne workers, both seasonal labourers and the permanent, annually employed *famuli*.[72] Yet by the next generation this apparent similarity among the Monkton, Appledore and Cliffe manors when comparing the form and scale of the land market had gone.[73] While small plots continued to be transferred through inheritance and alienation at Appledore and Cliffe, the court rolls for Monkton refer to far larger acreages in addition to continuing to record some small land transfers, although it is unclear how much of this was marshland. For example, Joan apparently inherited four acres from her widowed mother in 1397, Joan and Simon atte Weye, her husband, paying the necessary relief, and the same day the Monkton beadle paid relief in the name of the heirs of John Stapelgate for 200 acres of land. John Broke acquired 74 acres from John Kynton at the same court, whereas Thomas Stenedy's new acquisition was only an acre and three roods.[74] Thus, even though a few had apparently managed to acquire large acreages, pointing towards greater commercialisation, the majority can

69 Tawney, *Agrarian problem*, p. 136.

70 Bailey, *Decline of serfdom*, pp. 98, 307–37.

71 CCAL: DCc/ChAnt/M/160.

72 M. Mate, 'Labour', pp. 59–61, 64–6.

73 On the problems of using court rolls comparably, although for a different topic, see E. McGibbon Smith, 'Court rolls as evidence for village society: Sutton-in-the-Isle in the fourteenth century', in M. Bailey and S. Rigby (eds), *Town and countryside in the age of the Black Death* (Turnhout, 2012), pp. 248–52, 267–71.

74 CCAL: U15/24/26.

probably still be seen within Tawney's rise of the husbandman.[75] Nonetheless, it must be remembered that the causes of such differences remain a complex mix of national economic, political and social factors, as well as more immediate local concerns such as personal circumstances, weather conditions, physical factors including flooding, demographic changes, farming prospects and price and wage levels.[76]

In contrast, the size of individual land transfers in the Cliffe court rolls remained relatively static throughout the fifteenth century and, even though the extant series of rolls is far from complete, the largest known single transaction between 1399 and 1483 did not exceed 30 acres.[77] Nor does there appear to have been an increase in the size of these transfers across the fifteenth century: of those recorded in the 1480s Thomas Spiriot's purchase of nine and a half acres and half a virgate from William Godfrey and William Burbage in 1483 constitutes the greatest acquisition.[78] Furthermore, the surviving records suggest that almost half of the land transactions between those of different surnames concerned plots of no more than an acre, and some were far smaller. In September 1412 John Trikeler and Richard May finally paid a relief of 8d for eight separate pieces of land, ranging in size between 4 acres and half a rood, acquired from Thomas Casteyln.[79] Nonetheless, the flexibility and widespread use of the land market by the local peasantry would seem to highlight the relationship between lord and tenant that must at times have caused severe problems for court officials, especially at the point of transfer, and may partly explain the frequency of distraint owing to non-attendance at court by the buyer.[80] Yet, even if the individual land transfers were small, certain individuals were apparently acquiring a number of parcels of land, sometimes at the same or consecutive courts. Among these was William Mersham, who in 1421 purchased a total of eight acres in four transactions, including an acre from William Gamelyn, a butcher.[81] However, there is no evidence to suggest that this resulted in the construction of substantial holdings by local husbandmen solely from the priory's tenant lands.[82]

Such a scenario is also evident at Appledore from the far more complete series of court rolls for the fifteenth century, where it is also possible to see differing levels of activity in the land market over time and perhaps a slight increase in the acreage of the average sale in the later fifteenth century.[83] Nevertheless, the Romney Marshes

---

75 Tawney, *Agrarian problem*, pp. 72, 80.

76 M. Mate, 'Tenant farming', pp. 680–703; eadem, 'Economy of Kent', pp. 11–15.

77 The transaction involved a messuage and 29 acres of land; CCAL: U15/13/40.

78 CCAL: U15/13/47.

79 CCAL: U15/13/24.

80 Where the land was transferred again before a relief had been paid a double relief was required, and further similar transfers might lead to a quintuple relief: S. Campbell, 'Manor of Adisham', p. 259.

81 CCAL: U15/13/26.

82 The largest *post mortem* transfer recorded in the extant rolls is for 10 acres: CCAL: U15/13/34.

83 S. Sweetinburgh, 'Land holding and the land market in a 15th century peasant community: Appledore, 1400–1470', in A. Long, S. Hipkin and H. Clarke (eds), *Romney Marsh: coastal and landscape change through the ages* (Oxford, 2002), pp. 144–9, 152.

present a complex picture because land was being leased to local men from the late fourteenth century onwards and certain local individuals in the fifteenth century did acquire substantial holdings that they later bequeathed to their offspring.[84] Thus, even if these holdings still comprised numerous, perhaps scattered plots, it does indicate the realisation that individual peasants could build up far larger holdings over time that might also include lands from different landlords, as Thomas Wodman had done. Another feature, apparently first seen in Monkton, that contrasts with the other marshland regions, was the change whereby some *sulungs* came into the hands of one individual rather than being held by several peasants: for example, the *Swyllyng* of Dene at Monkton that was inherited by Edmund Wykes on the death of his mother in 1422.[85] For some, this offered a means of leasing out part or all of these holdings, the *sulung* or similar becoming in effect a sub-manor.[86] In c.1420 John Stapulgate's 200 acres of land appears to have been farmed by his own 'tenants'.[87]

Not all those acquiring or building up such holdings were local peasants, however, but again there does seem to have been variation between and within the marshland regions. Taking the north-east area first, from the later fourteenth century there was a growing engagement in the Monkton land market by those from Canterbury and other Kentish towns and from outside the county. Slightly further south, the marshes in Sandwich's hinterland at Lydden, Worth and Ham attracted the interest of local townsmen, although these too were targeted by Canterbury citizens, who also acquired such lands in the Stour valley at Chislet and Westbere.[88] This was not a new phenomenon but was more noticeable, not least because at times such activities encompassed large acreages and thus may have mirrored features seen by Tawney, as well as indicating that no stigma of servitude was attached to such lands.[89] In general these new landholders were prosperous leading citizens, men such as John Roper of

84 Two brothers leased land in Appledore on a 99-year lease from Christ Church Priory in 1382: CCAL: DCc/ChAnt/A/114. On the manor of Denge Marsh, Thomas Robyn acquired over 70 acres (11 parcels of land) in early 1489 and a few months later a further 50 acres (six purchases); The National Archives (TNA), SC 2/180/61. See Barber and Priestly-Bell, *Medieval adaptation*, p. 22; Dimmock, 'Class and the social transformation', pp. 108–9.

85 Compared to Monkton, this broad change to much larger peasant holdings appears to have taken place about a century later; see Draper, 'Farmers of All Souls', pp. 109–28; M. Merry and C. Richardson, '"To fasten itt upon his successors, heirs and owners of that howse … so longe as the world standeth": family identity and Romney marshlands in early modern Kent', in A. Long, S. Hipkin and H. Clarke (eds), *Romney Marsh: coastal and landscape change through the ages* (Oxford, 2002), pp. 157–72; T.R. Bellinger and G. Draper, '"My boddye shall lye with my name engraven on it": remembering the Godfrey family of Lydd, Kent', in M. Waller, E. Edwards and L. Barber (eds), *Romney Marsh: persistence and change in a coastal lowland* (Sevenoaks, 2010), pp. 117–40.

86 Mate, 'Tenant farming', pp. 689–90.

87 CCAL: U15/24/23.

88 Among the Sandwich townsmen was Henry Cacherell, whose will, dated 1435, refers to lands in Worth and Eastry as well as to his urban property; KHLC: Sa/AC1, f. 25v.

89 Tawney, *Agrarian problem*, p. 179. Mate, 'Tenant farming', pp. 681, 688–9; Schofield, *Peasant and community*, pp. 58–9; Bailey, *Decline of serfdom*, p. 333.

Canterbury, who from the late fourteenth century were in a position to accumulate land from several manors in east Kent, but their gentry friends and kinsmen also continued to be involved.[90] Thus, as the *inquisitions post mortem* demonstrate, the role of the nobility throughout this period added a further layer to the complex issue of landholding in the marshes and certain individuals acquired sometimes substantial holdings that included knight's fees, as well as gavel and other customary land. For example, William Garwynton's (1409) holdings included a toft in Snargate and almost 300 acres in the marshland parishes of Snargate, Midley, Fairfield, Brookland, Ivychurch and Old Romney. These various parcels of gavel land were mostly held of the archiepiscopal manor of Aldington, but seven acres was in the Christ Church manor of Fairfield.[91] Such acquisitions could have considerable implications for the local peasantry, although ones not always detrimental because of the prevalence of sub-tenancies; Tawney's 'petty commercialism' offered some peasant farmers opportunities and flexibility.[92]

For the north Kent marshes perhaps even more significant were the activities of certain extremely wealthy London merchants and master craftsmen. As Brown describes, men from London, as well as from more local towns such as Rochester and Milton, might become heavily engaged in the purchase of such lands, although these rarely seem to have been inherited by the next generation.[93] The proximity of urban settlements on the Romney Marshes had always seen townsmen active in the rural land market, their households combining farming and other commercial activities. Nevertheless, the butcher–graziers seem to have taken particular advantage of the customary land market and demesne leases as they responded to the growth in demand for meat.[94] Moreover, as well as being active in the local market, these urban butchers were able to use their position to export livestock to Calais, which also meant many saw the commercial advantages of fattening the livestock themselves, thereby extending their profit margins and exerting more control over the industry.[95] Such butcher–graziers resided in several coastal towns, including New Romney, Lydd and Hythe.[96] However, a similar group was also active in Appledore and the southern Wealden towns, such as Tenterden, which may have supplied the shipbuilding labour force at neighbouring Smallhythe and workers in the growing Wealden cloth industry.[97]

---

90 CCAL: DCc/ChAnt/M/161, 180.

91 *Calendar of Inquisitions Post Mortem*, vol. xix (7–14 Henry IV), no. 774.

92 Tawney, *Agrarian problem*, p. 80. Mate, 'Tenant farming', pp. 689–90.

93 A. Brown, 'London and north-west Kent in the later Middle Ages: the development of a land market', *Archaeologia Cantiana*, 92 (1976), pp. 145, 150–55.

94 Among the butchers involved in the manorial land market of Appledore was John Hornbroke, who seems to have accumulated 50 acres, although his acquisitions do not indicate that he was adopting a deliberate strategy: CCAL: U15/10/21, 26; Sweetinburgh, 'Land holding', pp. 149–50.

95 M. Mate, *Trade and economic developments, 1450–1550: the experience of Kent, Surrey and Sussex* (Woodbridge, 2006), pp. 34–5, 83, 97–9.

96 A.F. Butcher, 'The origins of Romney freemen, 1433–1523', *Economic History Review*, 27 (1974), pp. 17, 18; Sweetinburgh, 'Hythe's butcher-graziers', pp. 98–113.

97 Mate, *Trade*, p. 96; Draper, 'Timber and iron', pp. 73–5; S. Dimmock, 'English small towns and the emergence of capitalist relations, c.1450–1550', *Urban History*, 28 (2001), pp. 11, 23.

Furthermore, the role of outsiders in the customary land market was not confined to individuals because, as elsewhere in the county, real estate was used to endow and support the new Oxford and Cambridge colleges. For example, 143.5 acres of land at Nicholas Courte, Birchington, was purchased in 1495 by the master of Queens' College, Cambridge.[98] In some cases 'moribund' hospital estates were acquired by college founders: the lands of St Stephen and St Thomas' hospital, New Romney, for instance, for Magdalen College, Oxford; but Archbishop Chichele's endowment of another Oxford college involved the acquisition of various manors, rents and lands.[99] Acting on Chichele's behalf, in the early decades of the fifteenth century several locally prominent individuals bought up numerous generally small plots in specific areas that were transferred through intermediaries as a means of circumnavigating the Statutes of Mortmain.[100] For these men their involvement often continued beyond the land market because the colleges, as absentee landlords, leased out their marshland holdings. Nor was leasing confined to the new foundations in the fifteenth century. The ecclesiastical landlords had been experiencing increasing difficulties directly farming their demesnes, leading instead to a general policy of leasing by about the 1420s and, in some cases, even earlier. As Draper has noted for the Romney Marshes, short-term leasing of up to 10 years predominated in the fifteenth century, especially after 1450, the lessees generally being prosperous local peasants.[101] Lower rents during the earlier decades of the century may indicate that demand was more limited; however, changing farming practices and growing competition among the husbandmen and yeomen for such lands thereafter fuelled rent rises. Even though lessors placed some restrictions on the way the demesne could be farmed, as well as stipulating drainage maintenance requirements, they remained considerable commercial opportunities, lessees having use of the manorial farmstead, equipment and livestock.[102] For example, in 1403 Richard and John Scot became the farmers of Monkton manor, including a new salt pan, and, in addition to certain grain-carting duties to the ferry at Sarre, they were expected to repair the sea wall.[103]

Turning to the agrarian practices employed by Thomas Wodman and his fellow farmers in the Kentish marshlands, some of whom were lessees as well as tenants, it appears that these prosperous members of the peasantry were generally engaged in mixed farming in this period, although again there were some differences between and within the three regions. In the area of the Wantsum Channel wheat remained the premier cash crop, but some barley was presumably also sold, perhaps most frequently as malt. Oats, for animal and human consumption, were grown, as were

98 CCAL: U15/24/23.

99 A.F. Butcher, 'The hospital of St Stephen and St Thomas, New Romney: the documentary sources', *Archaeologia Cantiana*, 96 (1980), pp. 17–26.

100 Draper, 'Farmers of All Souls', pp. 111, 113–18.

101 Ibid., pp. 116–20. Yet, as at Fairfield, such leases could vary between 1 and 99 years: CCAL: DCc/ChAnt/F/33, 34.

102 CCAL: U63/64610 (Agney); DCc/ChAnt/B/368 (Bericourt); DCc/ChAnt/M/165A (Monkton).

103 CCAL: DCc/ChAnt/M/165A.

peas and tares.[104] John Malyn, in the mid-fifteenth century, was using a horse-drawn plough, and the other livestock on his farm included at least 250 ewes and a small number of cattle, including cows.[105] Thus livestock were seemingly becoming more important as average holdings increased in size; however, as at Lydden, near Sandwich, sheep had yet to dominate the landscape.[106]

On the Romney Marshes, too, the mixed farming regime seen in the Hundred of Newchurch remained characteristic into the fifteenth century. Cereals and legumes continued to be grown on many of the leaseholds as well as on the customary holdings, and some extended their cropping to saffron and fruit, such as apples.[107] As before, the parcellated nature of landholding meant that individual farmers could largely adopt their own cropping and grazing regime, but co-operation among neighbours presumably occurred.[108] Thus, as the balance shifted towards livestock owing to increasing commercial opportunities, the numbers of both cattle and sheep expanded, as they did in north and north-east Kent. Sheep had been the dominant species for centuries on the north Kent marshes.[109] However, the drastic fall in wool prices, part of the mid-fifteenth-century slump, badly hit the marshland farmers in north Kent and the Romney Marshes.[110] Such difficulties may partly explain local differences in livestock preferences on the Romney marshlands: at Scotney the All Souls lessee seems to have valued sheep more highly, whereas John Honeywode seems to have devoted a greater part of his pasture, which included marshland at Boroughmarsh, to cattle.[111] Such individual farming practices, although presumably highly valued by those concerned, could be problematic. The court rolls provide evidence of neighbourly disputes and communal strife regarding poorly maintained

104 Mate saw little evidence regarding tenant cultivation of legumes, but she did note the desire to improve yields through marling and manuring: Mate, 'Tenant farming', p. 697.

105 CKS: PRC 32/2, f. 160.

106 CCAL: DCc/Bedels Rolls/Lydden/76. It is worth remembering that, broadly, stocking rates per acre are, and presumably were in the Middle Ages, far higher for sheep than for cattle. This has considerable implications concerning perceptions of their relative dominance in any given area. Although not directly comparable, in terms of cheese production from summer pasture Walter de Henley believed that one cow was equal to 10 ewes; D. Oschinsky (ed.), *Walter of Henley and other treatises on estate management and accounting* (Oxford, 1971), p. 179.

107 John Swanne had a saffron garden and Alice Elyott bequeathed to her son the house with its apple garden: KHLC: PRC 32/6, f. 12; PRC 32/6, f. 13.

108 Such as sharing equipment or grazing livestock collectively: Baker, 'Fields and farms', pp. 167–8.

109 Reeves and Williamson, 'Marshes', p. 156. For example, William Milett (1500) had considerable marshland holdings around Dartford and in neighbouring parishes, where he kept large numbers of sheep and some cattle and grew cereals on an unknown acreage: <http://www.kentarchaeology.org.uk/Research/Libr/Wills/Bk08/181.htm> (accessed 1 May 2014).

110 Mate, 'Economy of Kent', pp. 19–22.

111 Barber and Priestly-Bell, *Medieval adaptation*, pp. 21–2; Draper, 'Farmers of All Souls', p. 118. Sweetinburgh, 'Hythe's butcher-graziers', pp. 107–9.

animal enclosures and damage caused by stray livestock.[112] Notwithstanding such tensions inherent within any society, these became more damaging because of the activities of certain livestock farmers and butcher–graziers in the later fifteenth century. As Dimmock has shown, the employment of strategies such as engrossing, enclosure and intimidation of his poorer neighbours by Andrew Bate, a butcher–grazier from Lydd and Battle Abbey's farmer on Denge Marsh, could have a detrimental effect on the locality.[113] As a consequence of his activities some smallholders apparently left the area, while others relied on by-employment such as fishing, their wives perhaps spinning or brewing.[114] Even though Bate seems an extreme example, his activities seem characteristic of those Tawney called the 'great farmers', who, he believed, did not care about the land, seeing it only as a commodity to be exploited.[115] Such a view is endorsed by Dimmock, who considers the scenario at Lydd to be indicative of an 'emerging agrarian bourgeoisie' in the later fifteenth century whose capitalist strategies led to 'a striking degree of instability and social polarization'.[116]

Nevertheless, how far this move in the later fifteenth century towards larger holdings and competition for land, as well as changes in landholding and farming practices, led to displacement of groups within the peasantry and so affected settlement patterns remains difficult to quantify. Even if the following are indicative rather than quantifiable, they still offer an idea of the relative significance of continuity and change for the marshland peasantry at this time. In Monkton at the beginning of the fifteenth century the connections between families and land were disappearing within communal memory: at an inquiry the jurors were unable to say who rightly held the tenement and land lately held by Roger Ynkele.[117] Furthermore, at Appledore, Monkton and Cliffe, the court officials frequently paid reliefs on behalf of unnamed heirs, having called on these and similar persons to attend court over a considerable period. In addition, most of the land transfers recorded in these same rolls apparently did not include houses/dwellings. Yet small plots with a messuage did not disappear completely, although it seems increasingly unlikely that

112 Mate, 'Tenant farming', pp. 697–8. Similar disputes can also be seen in the Cliffe rolls: Robert Aleyn complained that Johanna Stourstrete had detained a steer worth 7s; one of Robert Fluk's ewes strayed onto the demesne; Fluk was also fined for not maintaining his ditch; and on several occasions the tenants complained that the miller Thomas Marchant was taking excessive tolls: CCAL: U15/13/24; U15/13/30; U15/13/38.

113 Andrew Ayllewyn, the town's vicar, also seems to have been a disruptive influence locally: Dimmock, 'English small towns', pp. 13–19. For comparable, if less disruptive, local influence, see Dyer's Robert Parman: Dyer, 'A Suffolk farmer', pp. 1–22.

114 Dimmock, 'English small towns', p. 10; S. Sweetinburgh, 'Strategies of inheritance among Kentish fishing communities in the later Middle Ages', *The History of the Family*, 11 (2006), pp. 96, 102; Barber and Priestly-Bell, *Medieval adaptation*, pp. 22, 23–4. Evidence of local peasant cloth production includes cases of washing woollen cloth illegally, a wool loom and spinning equipment: CCAL: U15/10/21, 43.

115 Tawney, *Agrarian problem*, pp. 179, 184.

116 Dimmock, 'English small towns', pp. 20–2.

117 CCAL: U15/24/27.

they comprised the sum total of an individual's holding, except for the poor.[118] It is possible that some dwellings became dilapidated or had done so at an earlier date, because very few tofts are mentioned in the rolls, perhaps reflecting the inability of court officials to punish offenders and a realisation that, financially, there were no incentives.[119] Consequently for those continuing to live and farm in the marshlands, the mix of nucleated settlements and scattered farmsteads probably did not change fundamentally. Yet some settlements did shrink, or even disappear, as at Midley and Eastbridge on Romney Marsh, and the distribution of farmsteads probably became far more scattered.[120] Nevertheless, the Lydd and Thanet Earth archaeological evidence mainly covers the loss of structures by the end of the thirteenth century, and Reeves' fieldwalking evidence is difficult to date precisely. In addition, fifteenth-century court rolls, rentals and charters continue to record the presence of numerous roads and trackways across the various marshlands, as well as abutting farmsteads, suggesting that some areas within the marshes and their associated uplands were still relatively densely populated.[121]

Conclusion

At this juncture it seems valuable to return to Thomas Wodman and his family to consider whether their history exemplifies conditions on the Kentish marshlands more generally. For among those continuing to farm in the Romney Marshes were Thomas Wodman's two sons, yet neither seems to have been able to build on their inheritance, nor perhaps even to match the standing of their father. Richard made bequests of 13.5 acres, his tenement and adjoining land and an unspecified acreage, as well as two cows and two pigs.[122] Consequently, he was probably part of the middling peasantry, for whom mixed farming remained a viable enterprise. Conversely, for some among this group, and particularly for the poorer peasantry, the necessity of by-employment to sustain their households had increased, and this scenario may have applied to William, Richard's brother, who only mentioned his house, a cow and four acres in his will.[123] Others in his peer group may have migrated to local towns, regional centres or London, while the proximity of the Weald to the southern marshlands may have offered more realistic alternatives at a time of expanding industrial employment

118 Mate believes higher wages allowed even the former landless peasants to acquire a smallholding by the mid-fifteenth century: eadem, 'Economy of Kent', p. 18.

119 As Dyer demonstrates, in some villages in the Midlands lords might seize their peasants' goods to pay for building repairs: C. Dyer, 'Villages in crisis: social dislocation, 1370–1520', in C. Dyer and R. Jones (eds), *Deserted villages revisited* (Hatfield, 2010), p. 38.

120 Reeves and Williamson, 'Marshes', p. 158.

121 An agreement drawn up between Christ Church and John Bengekyn of Sarre included a right of way marked by stones from John's house to the common way: CCAL: DCc/ChAnt/M/198.

122 KHLC: PRC/32/4, f. 74.

123 KHLC: PRC/32/3, f. 96.

– predominantly cloth production but also some ship-building.[124] Another significant factor in the disappearance of these peasant families was the failure to produce heirs, especially sons, and William and Richard Wodman were among such casualties. William, dying in 1486, did not mention any offspring in his will and even though his brother had four daughters the reversionary clause in his will suggests that he feared they would not reach adulthood.

Yet, compared with some other parts of the country, there seems to have been a greater emphasis on continuity rather than on change in terms of the farming practices of the late medieval yeomen and husbandmen in these marshlands. Overall there had been a reduction in the number of farmsteads by c.1500, especially those of the middling and poorer peasantry, but how far this was due primarily to increasing commercialisation on the part of men such as Tawney's sixteenth-century 'great farmers' remains a moot point. Mixed farming was still practised by many on the marshlands and even though livestock numbers had grown to take advantage of the prevailing markets, this development was not the exclusive preserve of the large-scale operators. Also, too, John Leland in the 1540s continued to see the southern marshlands as a 'mervelous rank grownd for fedyng of catel' instead of exclusively the preserve of Thomas More's men-devouring sheep, which he cited as the main culprits in poor country people's misfortune in his *Utopia*.[125] However, such changes were perhaps more a matter of degree than radical departures from the earlier period, although some of these marshland areas, such as Walland and Denge Marshes, do seem to have suffered greater depopulation owing to the increasing prevalence of sheep pastures.[126] As already seen, the potential for individualism had been far greater in Kent than in many other English regions, and this heritage offered further opportunities for some farmers, albeit sometimes to the detriment of others, leading, as Mate and Draper believe, to greater differentials between large and small farms in the early sixteenth century.[127]

Yet whether the late Middle Ages witnessed a significant growth in socio-political tension within these marshland communities compared with the earlier period, a topic Dyer identified as having received attention in recent scholarship, is difficult to assess from the surviving records.[128] For example, there seems to have been a considerable history of resistance to manorial lordship and other impositions, such as tithe payments in the Romney Marshes, that highlights both the longevity and

---

124 Dimmock, 'English small towns', p. 23; Mate, 'Economy of Kent', p. 24; M. Zell, *Industry in the countryside: Wealden society in the sixteenth century* (Cambridge, 1994).

125 L. Toulmin Smith (ed.), *The itinerary of John Leland*, IV (1909), p. 67; *Thomas More: Utopia*, tr. and ed. D. Baker-Smith (London, 2012), p. 33.

126 Bordering the Weald, Walland Marsh sheep farmers were well placed to supply wool to the burgeoning cloth industry, which in turn provided work for the displaced peasants who became an essential part of this circle of goods and people: M. Gardiner, 'Settlement change on Denge and Walland Marshes, 1400–1550', in J. Eddison, M. Gardiner and A. Long (eds), *Romney Marsh: environmental change and human occupation in a coastal lowland* (Oxford, 1998), pp. 140–1.

127 Mate, 'Economy of Kent', pp. 22–3; Draper, 'Farmers of All Souls', pp. 109–28.

128 Dyer, 'Agrarian problem', pp. 32–3.

value of custom, as well as ideas about social memory and communal action which continued well into the sixteenth century.[129] Consequently it is the contention here that, even though there were differences among and within the various marshes, rather than witnessing a change from an agrarian regime governed by custom to one driven by commercialism between c.1300 and c.1500, the nature of tenure on the Kentish marshlands, and perhaps the county more generally, meant that throughout the period farmers could personally take advantage of favourable conditions. Thus, even though there appear to have been certain shifts towards the end of the period, such as a greater consolidation of holdings and an emphasis on livestock due to marketing opportunities, Tawney's husbandmen in the Midlands were less well placed to survive economic problems on the eve of the Reformation than were their peers in the Kentish marshlands.[130]

---

129 P. Simpson, 'The continuum of resistance to tithe, c.1400–1600', in R. Lutton and E. Salter (eds), *Pieties in transition: religious practices and experiences, c.1400–1640* (Aldershot, 2007), pp. 98–100, 105, 106.

130 Mate, 'Economy of Kent', pp. 23–4.

Chapter 5

'The struggle for the commons': commons, custom and cottages in Shropshire during the sixteenth and seventeenth centuries

James P. Bowen

In *The Agrarian Problem in the Sixteenth Century*, first published in 1912, R.H. Tawney recognised the impact of agrarian change on the peasantry – by which he was referring to copyhold tenants – and outlined the 'struggle for the commons' and the implications it had for the development of the poor law in England. This chapter focuses on three interlinked themes explored by Tawney in Part II 'The transition to capitalist agriculture', Chapter II 'The reaction of the agrarian changes on the peasantry': namely commons, custom and cottages.[1] Illustrated with evidence from Shropshire, it examines the implications of enclosure and disputes over the loss of access to commons both arable and waste, emphasising the value of commons in the everyday lives of rural communities. It will be suggested that disputes over common rights and between neighbouring lords, rather than conflict between landlords and tenants – the picture originally presented by Tawney – characterised much of the opposition to the enclosure and improvement of commons.

Discussion highlights the use of commons resources by those with or without legal common rights who frequently legitimised their claims on the basis of custom or, alternatively, were granted commons access as part of an informal system of poor relief. Lords also sought to exploit manorial waste for commercial purposes by the leasing of rights to commons and their resources, whether for agricultural or industrial purposes. This, it will be argued, led to interactions between custom and commercialisation which intensified with the increased use of commons. Moreover, consideration will be given to the significance of statutes regarding cottages, poor relief and vagrancy in influencing the population distribution of rural England and the pattern of cottage building at a local and regional level; this was originally outlined by Tawney, but has subsequently received relatively little attention.

---

1 R.H. Tawney, *The agrarian problem in the sixteenth century* (London, 1912), pp. 231–80. For the background to the agrarian problem see L. Goldman, *The life of R.H. Tawney: socialism and history* (London, 2013), pp. 219–25.

The value of commons and common rights

Referring to 'the struggle for the commons', Tawney recognised the 'difficulty of appreciating the part which common rights played in English husbandry before the nineteenth century'.[2] 'The value of a common to commoners', accordingly, 'consisted precisely in the guarantee given them by custom that no one might use it except holders of tenements which time out of mind had a right thereto, and that no man might use it to a greater extent than the custom of the manor allowed.'[3] Furthermore, he remarked that, 'so far from being merely a luxury or a convenience', commons and common rights were 'really an integral and indispensable part of the system of agriculture, a linch pin, the removal of which brought the whole structure of village society tumbling down'.[4] Common land was essentially land over which those other than the owner or tenant had use-rights, referred to as common rights, on either a legal or a customary basis. Historically the commons provided pasture or grazing as well as a range of other common rights, including the right for swine to forage for acorns, beechmast and nuts (pannage), rights to take timber, firewood, bracken, fern and rushes (estovers), peat and turf (turbary), and fish (piscary), certain rights to take some or part of the soil, such as gravel or earth, and the right to wild animals.[5]

It was traditionally thought that common rights were of little importance owing to declining regulation and poor commons practices, alongside changes in open-field farming which meant that they were considered to be insignificant.[6] While estimating the precise economic value of common rights is clearly problematic, subsequent work by historians emerging from the history of enclosure, social history and new rural history has challenged this view.[7] There has been a tendency to focus on the geographical areas studied by Postan and Tawney – the commercialising arable-orientated agricultural regions of the Midlands, southern England and East Anglia. By comparison, our understanding of the enclosure process in regions with mixed economies that exhibited varied landscapes and predominantly pastoral farming economies, often supplemented with rural crafts and industries, is less developed. While Tawney did appreciate local and regional variation in terms of enclosure, tenure and manorial administration, he rather simplistically made a binary division of the farming economy between arable and

---

2 Ibid., p. 238.

3 Ibid.

4 Ibid., pp. 238–9.

5 J.M. Neeson, *Commoners: common right, enclosure and social change in England, 1700–1820* (Cambridge, 1996); D. Woodward, 'Straw, bracken and the Wicklow Whale: the exploitation of natural resources in England since 1500', *Past & Present*, 159 (1998), pp. 43–76.

6 J.D. Chambers and G.E. Mingay, *The agricultural revolution, 1750–1880* (London, 1966), p. 19.

7 Neeson, *Commoners;* J. Humphries, 'Enclosures, common rights, and women: the proletarianization of families in the late eighteenth and early nineteenth centuries', *Journal of Economic History*, 1 (1990), pp. 23–31; L. Shaw-Taylor, 'Labourers, cows, common rights and parliamentary enclosure: the evidence of contemporary comment c. 1760–1810', *Past & Present*, 171 (2001), pp. 95–126. L. Shaw-Taylor, M. De Moor and P. Warde (eds), *The management of common land in north west Europe* (Turnhout, 2002).

pasture, recognising the significance of 'the pastoral side of agriculture' in many parts of England during the sixteenth century, for which an 'abundance of pasture land was very essential'.[8] It was not until the works of W.G. Hoskins and, particularly, Joan Thirsk that the extent of regional difference in terms of landscape and farming regions was recognised, and how this was reflected in the pattern of enclosure.[9]

Woodland or wood-pasture areas such as Shropshire typically had a varied landscape character consisting of a mixture of pasture, woods, arable and heaths with a mixed settlement pattern taking the form of villages, small hamlets and scattered farmsteads.[10] Common rights were vital for pastoral and woodland communities given the limited availability of farming land, extensive commons providing grazing for commoners engaged in pastoral farming whose livestock were sold in nearby market towns. In addition to their agrarian function, various commons resources were increasingly utilised for rural crafts and industrial purposes, as remarked upon by contemporaries. This included the exploitation of timber, firewood and other wood resources, such as holly, bracken, fern, gorse and heather, while peat and turf were also valuable fuel sources. Richard Gough (1635–1723) and Samuel Garbet (1685–1756), writing about Myddle and Wem in north Shropshire in 1700 and around 1750 respectively, emphasised the importance of commons in providing pasture for livestock, timber and wood as well as other resources which were necessary for everyday life.[11]

During the sixteenth and seventeenth centuries – which includes 'Tawney's Century', the period 1540–1640 – agricultural specialisms emerged with the growth of a more commercialised economy. Shropshire became defined as a farming region of 'open pasture' primarily concerned with 'rearing and fattening and dairying in the north', with further sub-regions or '*pays*' delineated.[12] By the fifteenth century a commercial cattle and horse trade had developed between England and Wales.[13] Dairy farming grew in north Shropshire with the enclosure and improvement of waste and piecemeal

---

8 Tawney, *Agrarian problem*, p. 239.

9 W.G. Hoskins, 'Regional farming in England', *Agricultural History Review*, 2 (1954), pp. 3–11; J. Thirsk (ed.), *The agrarian history of England and Wales. Volume IV: 1500–1640* (Cambridge, 1967), pp. 1–112.

10 O. Rackham, *The history of the countryside: the classic history of Britain's landscape, flora and fauna* (London, 1986), pp. 4–5; B.K. Roberts and S. Wrathmell, *Region and place* (London, 2002).

11 R. Gough, *The history of Myddle*, ed. D.G. Hey (Harmondsworth, 1981). The reference for the original is Shropshire Archives, Shrewsbury (hereafter SA) 1525/1; S. Garbet, *The history of Wem and the following townships Edstaston, Cotton, Lowe and Ditches, Hortons, Newtown, Wolverley, Northwood, Tilly, Sleap, Aston, and Lacon* (Wem, 1818). The original papers of Samuel Garbet have recently been located by the author and deposited at SA 9043.

12 J. Thirsk, *England's agricultural regions and agrarian history, 1500–1750* (London, 1987), p. 28.

13 C. Skeel, 'The cattle trade between Wales and England from the fifteenth to the nineteenth centuries', *Transactions of the Royal Historical Society*, 4th Series, 9 (1926), pp. 135–58; P.R. Edwards, 'The horse trade of the Midlands', *Agricultural History Review*, 27 (1979), p. 91; S. Letters, *Online gazetteer of markets and fairs in England and Wales to 1516* [Shropshire], Centre for Metropolitan History, Institute of Historical Research, 2006, <http://www.history.ac.uk/cmh/gaz/gazweb2.html> (accessed 4 June 2015).

enclosure of common fields.[14] This enabled new farms to be created and existing holdings expanded, providing additional pasture. Elsewhere in Shropshire, for example on the eastern sandstone plain, there was extensive open-field cultivation along with sheep and cattle rearing.[15] The period saw the emergence of a prosperous class of yeoman farmers who kept large herds of cattle and dairy cows and flocks of sheep.

Enclosure, enclosing and improvement

Both Tawney and later Thirsk recognised that the enclosure process took a wide variety of forms, and adopted the term 'enclosing' to encompass different types and periods of enclosure.[16] This has been used to refer to the exchange of open-field strips into consolidated holdings, the enclosure and reallocation of fields by supposed agreement, piecemeal enclosure or encroachment on commons. It has also included the enclosure and improvement of wastes, engrossment – the amalgamation of tenancies – and lastly, large-scale depopulating enclosure which saw the conversion of arable to pasture in lowland, fielden mixed farming areas. Work by historians since has further refined our understanding of the enclosure process.[17] Given his Christian socialist ideological perspective, Tawney, moralising, portrayed the enclosure process as the result of the increasingly powerful position of lords over tenants, the former members of the gentry or aristocracy being far removed from the land and the latter involved in everyday agriculture. This view has recently been challenged, Whittle's research shedding light on the 'blurred boundaries' which existed, with economic and social relationships regarding rights to land being more complex than simply a matter of 'lords and tenants'.[18]

Shropshire has been viewed as a county of 'ancient', 'early' or 'old' enclosure that failed to develop the open-field systems which characterised the Midland counties.[19]

14 P.R. Edwards,'The development of dairy farming of the north Shropshire plain in the seventeenth century', *Midland History*, 4 (1977), pp. 175–90; P.R. Edwards,'The farming economy of north east Shropshire in the seventeenth century' (PhD thesis, University of Oxford, 1976).

15 J. Thirsk (ed.), *The agrarian history of England and Wales. Volume V: 1640–1750* (Cambridge, 1984), p. 131.

16 Tawney, *Agrarian problem*, pp. 9–10; J. Thirsk, 'Enclosing and engrossing', in J. Thirsk (ed.), *The agrarian history of England and Wales. Volume IV: 1500–1640* (Cambridge, 1967), pp. 200–55.

17 For two recent studies of enclosure see B. McDonagh, 'Negotiating enclosure in sixteenth-century Yorkshire: the South Cave dispute, 1530–1536', in J.C. Whittle (ed.), *Landlords and tenants in Britain, 1440–1660: Tawney's agrarian problem revisited* (Woodbridge, 2013), pp. 52–66; W.D. Shannon, 'Risks and rewards in wasteland enclosure: lowland Lancashire c.1500–1650', in J.C. Whittle (ed.), *Landlords and tenants in Britain, 1440–1660: Tawney's agrarian problem revisited* (Woodbridge, 2013), pp. 150–65.

18 J. Whittle,'Conclusions' in J.C. Whittle (ed.), *Landlords and tenants in Britain, 1440–1660: Tawney's agrarian problem revisited* (Woodbridge, 2013), pp. 216–21.

19 G.C. Baugh and R.C. Hill, '1750–1875', in G.C. Baugh (ed.), *VCH: Shropshire, vol. 4 agriculture* (Oxford, 1989), p. 171; J.R. Wordie, 'The chronology of English enclosure', *Economic History Review*, 36 (1983), p. 490.

Beginning in the fifteenth century, open fields in Shropshire were gradually enclosed, with the enclosure process quickening in the sixteenth and seventeenth centuries. Where common-field agriculture was practised in the sixteenth and seventeenth centuries stinting agreements were imposed which limited or restricted the number of livestock which could be pastured and apportioned depending upon the size of an individual's holding.[20] Regarding the common fields of Prees manor, north Shropshire, a pain or by-law compiled in John Worswick's book stated that 'no person was to put in any manner of their cattle into the fields but according to the quantity of his ground', namely one beast and a mare for every 'strick' of land that produced a bushel of grain.[21] Anyone who broke the order was to forfeit the pain of 6s 8d, 6d and 4d for each beast, sheep and swine respectively.[22] Similarly, at Linley, a hamlet in south Shropshire, tenants were not allowed to 'keep or put into any of the common fields there sown with corn or grain any beasts or cattle after the feast day of St John Baptist [29 August] until the Saturday after all the corn and grain shall been taken out'.[23] Furthermore, it was ordered that none of the tenants or inhabitants were to put into any of the fields more cattle, geese and swine 'than according to the rate and quantity of land which the same tenant shall have in the field' – one ox or cow for land producing two bushels of grain.[24] It was stipulated that no tenant or inhabitant was to 'wilfully or maliciously suffer his corn or grain to remain in the field any longer than necessary (12d)'.[25] Two officers were appointed by the court to estimate the 'rating of every man's lands in every such field'.[26] Stinting agreements also governed on the pasturing of livestock on common fields and pasture closes in the Weald Moors manors.[27]

These pains highlight the careful seasonal and quantitative regulation of the pasturing of livestock, thus providing a degree of equity between the members of the rural community. Attempts to enforce a stinting system suggest a contemporary awareness of the carrying capacity of land. However, it is hard to imagine that rural communities, faced with the fluctuating pressures of population increase, changes in the extent of arable cultivation and the commercialisation of the livestock trade, did not challenge the relationship between the number of grazing livestock and the availability of pasture.[28] Moreover, it is equally difficult to conceive that lords, presented with

---

20 P R. Edwards,'1540–1750', in G.C. Baugh (ed.), *VCH: Shropshire, vol. 4 agriculture* (Oxford, 1989), p. 121. For stinting see A.J.L. Winchester and E.A. Straughton,'Stints and suitability: managing stock levels on common land in England, c.1600–2006', *Agricultural History Review*, 58 (2010), pp. 30–48.

21 SA 3607/II/A/15 (14 April 1586). Strick: Strike a bushel measure. G.F. Jackson, *Shropshire word book: a glossary of archaic and provincial words* (London, 1879), p. 417.

22 SA 3607/II/A/15 (14 April 1586).

23 SA 1037/1/26 f. 23verso (31 March 1586).

24 Ibid.

25 Ibid.

26 Ibid.

27 Edwards,'1540–1750', p. 121.

28 C. Dyer,'The agrarian problem, 1440–1520', in J.C. Whittle (ed.), *Landlords and tenants in Britain, 1440–1660: Tawney's agrarian problem revisited* (Woodbridge, 2013), p. 32.

the chance to increase their income by taking advantage of the fines for the illegal pasturing of livestock, would ignore this opportunity. Nevertheless, the laying of such pains by manor courts is indicative of the strength of their authority and their role in codifying a body of evolving customary law, coinciding with a reassertion of manorial authority which peaked in the late sixteenth and early seventeenth centuries.[29]

At Lilleshall in east Shropshire tenants of William Leveson-Gower in the seventeenth century, recognising the potential benefits of enclosure, pointed out that their strips lay inconveniently dispersed and requested that they should be exchanged to 'lay their grounds together and to make each other's farms convenient to them'.[30] As Tawney outlined, much enclosure was carried out by tenants with a view to increasing arable cultivation and allowing more intensive use of pasture, and, as he wrote, there was in some counties 'a good deal of enclosure by the peasants themselves with a view to better arable cultivation or to the more successful keeping of stock'.[31] Glebe terriers similarly record the enclosure of open fields. For example at Highley in the Severn valley in 1625/6 it was recorded that parishioners all being freeholders exchanged and enclosed the common field lands 'for theyr more commodious use thereof', and at Shawbury in north Shropshire it was recorded in 1698 that 'Our Parish is all enclosed except the Heathes & usuall commons'.[32] When common fields were enclosed common rights were extinguished, marking the transfer from common to private property rights. It is likely that with the intensification and specialisation of farming systems in the seventeenth century, linked to a more commercially orientated economy, farmers began to rely on enclosed pasture closes rather than commons for livestock pasturing, although smallholders and cottagers continued to rely on them for their survival. Restrictions were also placed on the informal exploitation of resources of common arable, such as gleaning, the customary practice whereby fallen grains were gathered after harvest by commoners and the landless poor.[33] For example,

---

29 For by-laws see W. Ault, *Open-field farming in medieval England: a study of village by-laws* (London, 1972); A.J.L. Winchester, *The harvest of the hills: rural life in northern England and the Scottish Borders, 1400–1700* (Edinburgh, 2000), pp. 29–40, 45–8.

30 Staffordshire Record Office, Stafford D593/D/3/23/1.

31 Tawney, *Agrarian problem*, p. 405.

32 S. Watts (ed.), *The glebe terriers of Shropshire*, Part 1 (Abdon and Llanfair) (Keele, 2002), p. 122; S. Watts (ed.), *The glebe terriers of Shropshire*, Part 2 (Llanyblodwel to Wroxeter) (Keele, 2002), p. 81.

33 For gleaning see S. Hindle, *On the parish? The micro politics of poor relief in rural England c.1550–1750* (Oxford, 2009), p. 41; J. Humphries, 'Enclosures, common rights and women: the proletarianization of families in the late eighteenth and early nineteenth centuries', *Journal of Economic History*, 50 (1990), p. 38; P. King, 'Customary rights and women's earning: the importance of gleaning to the rural laboring poor', *Economic History Review*, 44 (1991), pp. 461–76; P. King, 'Gleaners, farmers and the failure of legal sanction in England 1750–1850', *Past & Present*, 125 (1989), pp. 116–50; P. King, 'Legal change, customary right and social conflict in late eighteenth century England: the origins of the great gleaning case of 1788', *Law and History Review*, 10 (1992), pp. 1–31; Neeson, *Commoners*, pp. 313–14; A. Wood, 'The place of custom in plebeian political culture: England, 1550–1800', *Social History*, 22 (1997), pp. 54–5.

at Cound the manor court laid a pain ordering that no tenant or his servants were to collect 'spicas' of grain after the harvest.[34]

By contrast, the enclosure of common waste in Shropshire was gradual, beginning with assarting in the mid- to late thirteenth century in response to population expansion and the efforts of lords to increase incomes from their estates.[35] The enclosure process continued through the early modern period and up to the nineteenth century.[36] Assarting and medieval enclosure had the effect of clearing areas of woodland which tended to be waste and dividing intercommoned areas, resulting in the creation of private enclosed fields and sometimes causing tension and dispute.[37] A survey of Cheswardine and Ellesmere manors in 1280 recorded the process of assarting, with 563.5 acres of land being recorded in the case of the latter.[38] Also in the medieval period large commons were divided between communities. For instance, in 1340 an agreement was made to divide the commons of Smethcott manor, four miles north of Church Stretton.[39] Examples of medieval enclosure, drainage and reclamation provide rich evidence in support of Postan's account of changes in land use and technology in *The Medieval Economy and Society: An Economic History of Britain, 1100–1500*, and for his claim that the sparse settlement pattern of Shropshire and neighbouring counties meant that there was a 'reserve of fairly good land', even where the soils were of a comparable quality to those of Wiltshire, Hampshire, Suffolk, Northamptonshire and Oxfordshire.[40]

Later sources are suggestive of an enclosure movement of the sixteenth and seventeenth centuries, which, in this part of England, saw the enclosure and improvement of common waste into more productive arable and pasture land. For example, John Norden's (1547–1625) survey of Oswestry lordship in 1602, commissioned by Thomas Lord Howard, records the piecemeal enclosure of wastes and forest and improvement through drainage, being 'fitt to be enclosed'.[41] Cartographic evidence such as a map of Cherrington township, c.1576, on the edge of the Weald Moors in north-east Shropshire, a low-lying fen or wetland intercommon

---

34 SA 5460/1/1.

35 T. Rowley, *The making of the English landscape: the Shropshire landscape* (London, 1972), pp. 150–72.

36 E. Miller (ed.), *The agrarian history of England and Wales. Volume III: 1348–1500* (Cambridge, 1991), p. 105; A.J. Kettle, '1300–1540', in G.C. Baugh (ed.), VCH: *Shropshire, vol. 4 agriculture* (Oxford, 1989), pp. 80–5.

37 C. Dyer, 'Conflict in the landscape: the enclosure movement in England, 1220–1349', *Landscape History*, 29 (2007), pp. 21–33.

38 W.K. Boyd (ed.), 'Extent of the manor of Cheswardine, and a moiety of the manor of Childs Ercall, 24 October, 1280', *Transactions of the Shropshire Archaeological and Historical Society*, 3rd Series, 8 (1908), pp. 364–7; W.K. Boyd (ed.), 'Extent of the manor of Ellesmere, 1280', *Transactions of the Shropshire Archaeological and Historical Society*, 23 (1899), pp. 252–9.

39 SA 2922.

40 M.M. Postan, *The medieval economy and society: an economic history of Britain, 1100–1500* (Harmondsworth, 1972), p. 24.

41 J. Slack, *The lordship of Oswestry, 1393–1607* (Shrewsbury, 1951). The reference for the original is: John Rylands University Library, Manchester Latin MS 274.

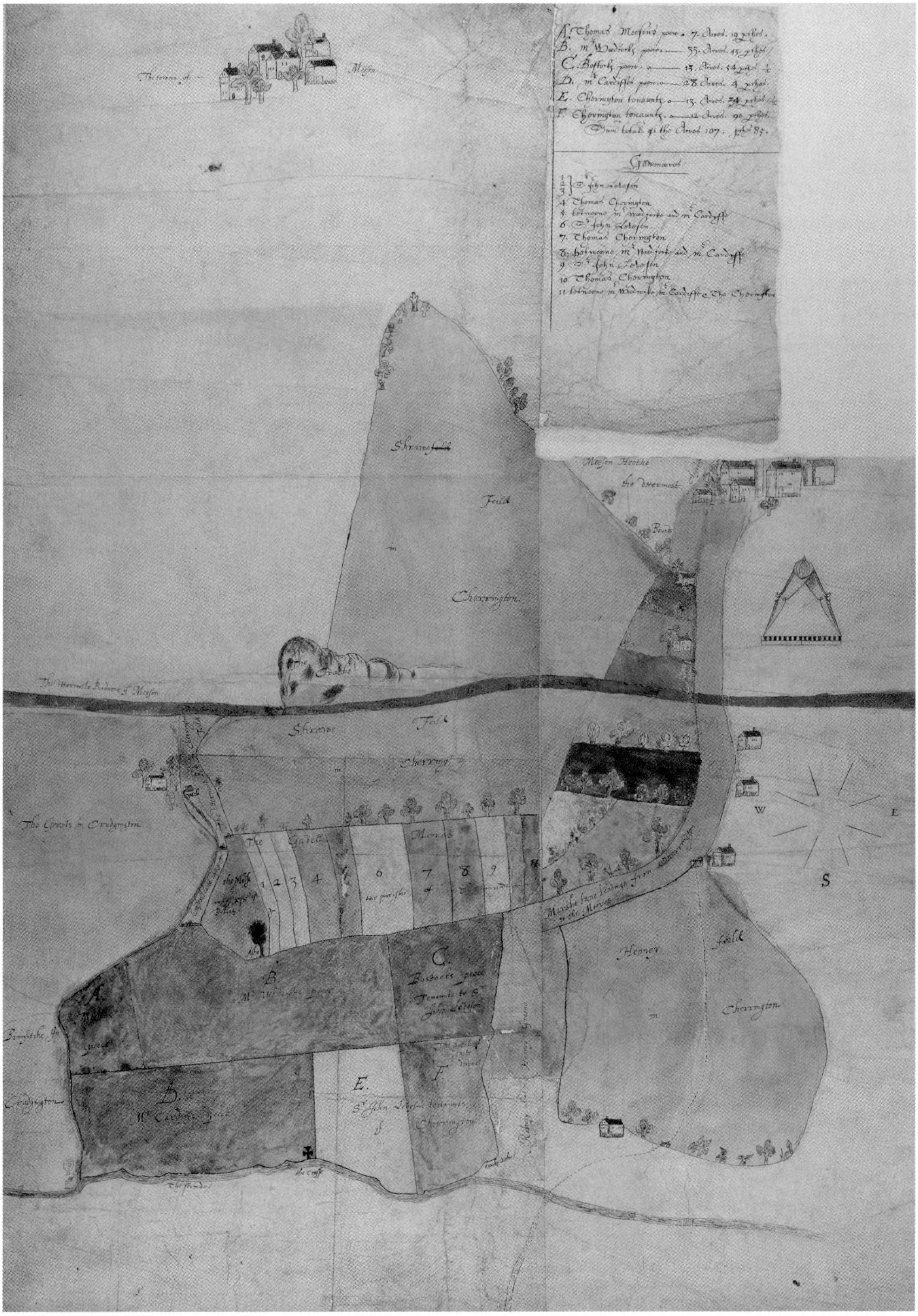

Figure 5.1 Map of Cherrington, a township on the edge of the Weald Moors, c.1576. Shropshire Archives, Shrewsbury 972/7/1/3.

upon which surrounding communities pastured their livestock, illustrates many of the characteristic features of agrarian landscape change during this period (Figure 5.1).[42] It shows the gradual or piecemeal enclosure of the open fields, the clearance and improvement of scrub, woodland and waste into large fields, and the benefit of drainage and reclamation (the 'strinde', a large drainage ditch, is marked) in bringing former waste into more intensive usage. Also annotated are the 'Kings highway' from Crudgington to Newport and a straker track funnelling onto the Weald Moors along which livestock would have been driven. While sufficient grazing remained, a system of intercommoning survived. Although areas of the moor appear to have been allocated to townships and communities at an early period, exact boundaries remained open, it being difficult to ascertain the extent to which areas of waste belonged to specific communities. This resulted in the need to define respective rights through establishing boundaries. As competition for resources increased, tension arose, often leading to disputes regarding the definition of boundaries between neighbouring communities.[43] Although manorial and township boundaries and, accordingly, property rights were increasingly defined by mere stones and topographical features such as ancient trees and ditches, as perambulations describe, disputes nevertheless occurred.[44]

This can be illustrated by a dispute that arose in 1698 in the south Shropshire hill country between the manors of Ratlinghope, known locally as 'Ratchop', and Church Stretton.[45] On 20 April 1698 a case was presented to the court of Ratlinghope, which stated that the wastes lying within the parish and manor of Church Stretton had always been considered as part of Ratlinghope manor. The ministers and churchwardens of Ratlinghope had frequently cut marks in the ground showing the first name of the manorial lord in the outermost boundaries of the parish, and some tenants had ploughed and sown the wastes without paying dues or money to Church Stretton manor.[46] Also, it was recorded that the cattle of Ratlinghope tenants had always accessed the 'great mountain forest or waste ground' of the Long Mynd, and that when their animals had become confused with those of Church Stretton tenants, they had been returned without any demand for payment of trespass. This implies that the practice known as 'overleap', whereby tenants of one manor paid a fee to a neighbouring lord of a manor into which their livestock had strayed was not enforced.[47] Furthermore, it was claimed that they had dug and carried away turf and ling (heather) – resources typically found in upland areas – from these wastes,

42 SA 972/7/1/3.

43 P.R. Edwards, 'Competition for land, common rights and drainage in the Weald moors (Shropshire): the Cherrington and Meeson disputes, 1576–1612', in R.W. Hoyle (ed.), *People, landscape and alternative agriculture: essays for Joan Thirsk* (Exeter, 2004), pp. 39–55.

44 N. Whyte, *Inhabiting the landscape: place, custom and memory, 1500–1800* (Oxford, 2009).

45 SA 93/25, 26.

46 Ibid.

47 Winchester, *Harvest*, pp. 78–9.

whereas the parishioners of Church Stretton had done so only 'stealthily'.[48] This case is interesting in that it records a dispute between two neighbouring manors abutting the Long Mynd, a large upland waste upon which the tenants of Ratlinghope claimed rights of pasture and turbary. As a former medieval forest subject to forest regulation, it was widely intercommoned by adjacent communities and was not the waste of a particular lord or community, providing an example of how layers of ownership and use-rights evolved over time.[49] Livestock frequently wandered across manorial boundaries on shared areas of common pasture in hill, woodland and wetland areas, and therefore in the late medieval and early modern periods communities sought to define their boundaries, ownership and property rights.

The majority of work by the present generation of early modern rural and social historians has explored examples of disputes over enclosure, or, as has been pointed out, what Tawney referred to as 'enclosing' and the loss of common rights. They have considered popular protest and riot with local and micro-historical analyses outlining the protracted legal and political complexities of enclosure disputes and highlighting the need to interpret them in their wider economic, social and political context.[50] The view put forward by Tawney and others – that disputes over enclosure were principally between lords and tenants – has been challenged, a body of research revealing that disputes in fact involved all levels of local societies, including the plebeian strata. In that sense our understanding has moved on considerably since Tawney was writing.

Instead, this period saw the power of lords diminish, while wealthier tenants sought to exclude a growing landless labouring population that were subjected to paying commercial 'rack' rents annually. Landowners, seeking to increase their income from tenanted lands, tried to convert tenures from copyholds which were the most prevalent form of tenure but offered a poor and fixed financial return, to leaseholds or copyholds at will. The latter form of tenure allowed for the raising of rents previously fixed on a customary basis. Newly enclosed land taken in from commons was generally leased from the outset. From the mid-sixteenth century lords began to issue shorter-term leases, typically for 21 years, although a more secure tenure was a lease for 99 years or three lives. Evidently clear parallels between the work of Tawney and more recent historians who have explored other regional settings can be identified.

As he pointed out, the amount of grazing land which villages had access to was dependent upon the local circumstances. While in some localities there was common waste for pasture, in others the lack of waste meant that tenants had to rely

48 SA 93/25, 26. For the so-called 'harvest of the hills' see Winchester, *Harvest*; H.S.A. Fox, *Dartmoor's alluring uplands: transhumance and pastoral management in the Middle Ages* (Exeter, 2011).

49 British Library, London, Royal MS.18.D.III.fol.87.

50 S. Hindle, 'Persuasion and protest in the Caddington common enclosure dispute 1635–1639', *Past & Present*, 158 (1998), pp. 37–78; S. Hipkin, '"Sitting on his penny rent": conflict and right of common in Faversham Blean, 1595–1610', *Rural History*, 11/1 (2000), pp. 1–35; H. Falvey, 'Crown policy and local economic context in the Berkhamsted common enclosure dispute, 1618–42', *Rural History*, 12 (2001), pp. 123–58; B. McDonagh, 'Subverting the ground: private property and public protest in the sixteenth-century Yorkshire Wolds', *Agricultural History Review*, 57 (2009), pp. 191–206; Whyte, *Inhabiting*, pp. 91–124.

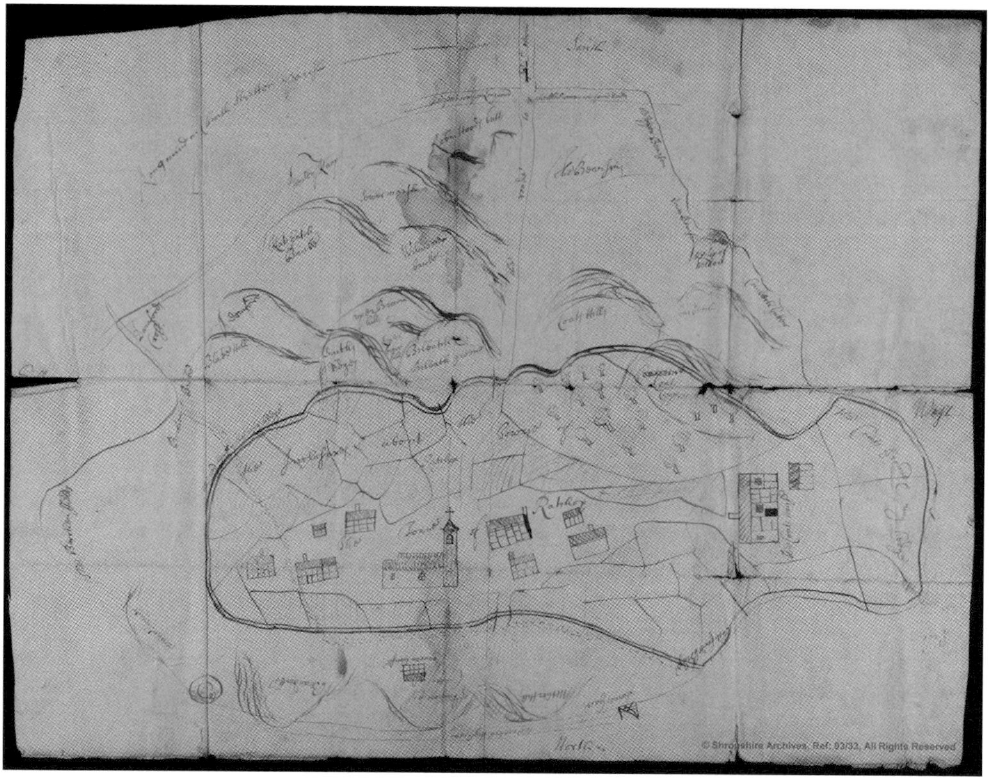

Figure 5.2 Map of the manor and parish of Ratlinghope (Ratchop), showing the Port way on Long Mynd, 1698. Shropshire Archives, Shrewsbury 933/33.

on the stubble which lay open after harvest where common fields remained. He also recognised that the management of the apportionment of grazing rights varied.[51] An impression emerges that in many Shropshire manors sufficient waste prevailed for the demands of rural communities until the sixteenth and seventeenth centuries. There were, however, exceptions, for instance in High Ercall manor on the edge of the Weald Moors, where the mixed farming economy allowed for cattle, sheep and arable production. Here waste had been 'reduced to a minimum', presumably because of strong lordship and the proximity of the common moors, although open fields survived until the end of the sixteenth century.[52]

It is, therefore, important to consider the variability in the extent of commons at a regional and national level and their relative importance in rural economies

51 Tawney, *Agrarian problem*, pp. 241–2.

52 M.C. Hill, 'The demesne and the waste: a study of medieval inclosure on the manor of High Ercall 1086–1399', *Transactions of the Shropshire Archaeological and Historical Society*, 62 (1979–80) (1984), p. 29.

– that is, whether they remained an agricultural asset. In upland environments of England and Wales, common wastes remained significant, forming a fundamental part of the agrarian system, with valley bottom land complemented by extensive rough hill pasture providing summer grazing.[53] In contrast, in lowland midland and southern England the relative significance of waste declined as enclosure and the intensification of farming systems reduced its value from an agricultural asset to a category of land that became almost exclusively associated with the landless poor.[54] The difference in the proportion of land constituting common land distinguishes the two predominant characteristic types of lowland and upland commons. There is, however, a further model of common land that needs to be taken into account, namely that of the woodland or wood-pasture countryside of lowland western England.[55] This is characterised by a greater extent of waste than in open-field champion areas and a more lowland pastorally orientated economy.

Custom versus commercialisation

Applying the approach of custom versus commercialisation to the history of commons offers an alternative perspective on how rural communities negotiated challenges to manorial custom, changes in land and property rights, competition over resources and the changing uses of commons. While the Statute of Merton allowed lords to enclose common waste as long as sufficient pasture remained for tenants, this did not mean, as Tawney rightly pointed out, that a lord could 'arbitrarily cut down rights of common to what he was pleased to think sufficient'.[56] As he wrote, 'The question "what is sufficient?" had to be answered by a jury' who had expert knowledge of both local customs and the agrarian functioning of the manor.[57] The customs of a manor varied between localities; it was, as E.P. Thompson notably observed, '*lex loci*'.[58] Moreover, the formulation of custom was important in articulating a community's sense of local identity. In the seventeenth century, Gough, in his 'Antiquities and Memories of the Parish of Myddle', described custom as 'a law or right, not written, which being established by long-use and the consent of our ancestors, hath been and is dayly practised', and, moreover, noted the apparent diversity between 'custome, prescription usage, and limitation, although they bee much of affinity, and often taken

53 Winchester, *Harvest*; Fox, *Alluring Uplands*.

54 Neeson, *Commoners*.

55 A.M. Everitt,'Common land', in J. Thirsk (ed.), *The English rural landscape* (Oxford, 2000), pp. 210–35; C. Dyer,'Woodlands and wood-pasture in western England', in J. Thirsk (ed.), *Rural England: an illustrated history of the landscape* (Oxford, 2002), pp. 97–121.

56 Tawney, *Agrarian problem*, p. 248. Statute of Merton (20 Hen. III); Statute of Westminster II (13 Edw. I).

57 Tawney, *Agrarian problem*, p. 248.

58 A. Wood, *The memory of the people: custom and popular senses of the past in early modern England* (Cambridge, 2013); E.P. Thompson, *Customs in common: studies in traditional popular culture* (London, 1991), pp. 97–184.

one for another'.[59] Tawney's idealised conception of custom shares many parallels with Gough's. Both viewed custom as a law or right which affected the population of England at large, while acknowledging the way that, at a local level, it influenced everyday life, having evolved over generations.

Historiographical developments, such as the work of Keith Wrightson, Steve Hindle and Andy Wood, have shaped historians' understanding of politics at a local, parochial level, showing how it was played out in the ordinary lives of rural communities.[60] Indeed, Wood had highlighted that, in defining custom, Tawney had the foresight to recognise that it 'formed part of popular politics' and 'changed over time, according to locally variable and historically specific conditions'.[61] The manor, as much as the parish, formed the basis of contemporaries' understandings of politics. Manorial courts sought to promote the interests of lords and the wider community in terms of entitlement to economic resources and to protect them from both those without common rights and overexploitation by those within communities.[62]

The case of Willaston Wood, which was originally part of Prees manor in north Shropshire but became separated, demonstrates how custom was articulated and the confusion that could arise over claims to lordship and access to resources.[63] The bounds of the manor were recorded at some point probably in the late sixteenth century; however, it was unclear whether the inhabitants of the manor had common rights in Willaston Wood.[64] Consequently, a case ensued between William Willaston and Rowland Hill over lordship and access to a 'parcel of waste ground called Willaston Wood'. Following a case at Westminster on 25 February 1658, witness depositions were taken at the market town of Whitchurch on 15 April 1658 to determine whether the inhabitants of Willaston had common rights in Willaston Wood.[65] William Goller, an 80-year-old husbandman of Great Ash, recorded that 'he did never know or hear of any other man to be lord or lawful owner of the lordship, manor or township of Willaston and of the waste ground aforesaid', and, furthermore, he noted cattle belonging to 'strangers', those from outside the manor, that were found pasturing in Willaston Wood were impounded in the lordship or township of Willaston and not elsewhere.[66] Thomas Pixley, a gentleman from Willaston aged 64, deposed that tenants of Willaston did 'fell, cut down, crop, lop and carry away at their wills and pleasures timber blocks, crops

59 Gough, *Myddle*, p. 64.

60 K. Wrightson, 'The politics of the parish in early modern England', in P. Griffiths, A. Fox and S. Hindle (eds), *The experience of authority in early modern England* (London, 1996), pp. 10–46; Hindle, *On the parish?*; Wood, *Memory of the people*.

61 Wood. *Memory of the people*, pp. 30–1.

62 C.J. Harrison, 'Manor courts and the governance of Tudor England', in C.W. Brooks and M. Lobban (eds), *Communities and courts in Britain, 1150–1900* (London, 1997), pp. 43–59; Winchester, *Harvest*; B. Waddell, 'Governing England through the manor courts, 1550–1850', *Historical Journal*, 55 (2012), pp. 279–315.

63 SA 731/1/8/2.

64 Ibid.

65 Ibid.

66 Ibid.

and underwoods out of the parcel of land in question'.[67] He went on, remarking that the inhabitants of Willaston and Moreton Say had at 'divers and sundry times met together within the deponents memory', and the inhabitants of Willaston had driven Willaston Wood and impounded all the strangers' cattle which they found pasturing there.[68]

In contrast to the evidence of the previous deponents, Allen Millington of Tilstock, a yeoman aged 77, recounted how the inhabitants of Willaston lordship had impounded 'strangers cattle', namely two heifers and a steer which were found depasturing in the wood, and the next day the cattle were brought to the lord of Prees manor as waifs and strays.[69] The deposition of George Chesters, a yeoman of Willaston aged 40, recalled how previously he had gone with his father to the disputed piece of waste ground, where he found Hill's team from Bletchley with a sled and servants cutting and loading wood. His father knocked down one of the oxen and with an axe broke their saw and drove the team and servants away.[70] Furthermore, the deposition of William Powell, a yeoman from Prees aged 77, described how when John Ryder of Bletchley had cut down a tree upon Willaston Wood, Master George Willaston called to his wife for breakfast and declared that Ryder was not to carry away the tree. After finishing his breakfast, he, along with John Chesters and others, went and fetched the tree, laying it upon Willaston land and converting it for his own use.[71] These plebeian witnesses, whose claims to custom were founded on social memory, implied that resources were increasingly contested and the source of potential conflict and dispute, not simply between lords and tenants but also between neighbouring lords, who encouraged individuals and communities to act in support of their claims.

Central to the transition between medieval and early modern England was custom, which persisted alongside the growing commercialisation of the agricultural and industrial sectors of the economy.[72] Contemporaries recognised the value of commons and the importance of custom since 'time out of mind', 'time immemorial' and 'in the memory of man' in defining entitlement, although the emergence of private property rights with enclosure and other forms of agrarian improvement reduced their ability to exercise such rights.[73] For example, in north Shropshire, tenants enjoyed generous common rights that were granted to the copyhold manors of the duke of Bridgewater, a court of survey of Wem manor dated 1564 presenting that the tenants and burgesses had 'time out of memory of man, free common of pasture' excluding spring time, with the exception of pannage in the lord's woods, namely Northwood, Cotton Wood and

67 Ibid.

68 Ibid.

69 Ibid.

70 Ibid.

71 Ibid.

72 For a recent volume on custom see R.W. Hoyle (ed.), *Custom, improvement and the landscape in early modern Britain* (Farnham, 2011).

73 A. Fox,'Custom, memory and the authority of writing', in P. Griffiths, A. Fox and S. Hindle (eds), *The experience of authority in early modern England* (London, 1996), pp. 97–8; A. Wood,'The place of custom in plebeian political culture: England, 1550–1800', *Social History*, 22 (1997), pp. 46–60; Whyte, *Inhabiting*.

Wem-Brockhurst.[74] They also had free common pasture in Wem Pool, 'until now of late', certain parcels of the wastes and woods having been enclosed.[75]

Describing the customs of Myddle lordship, Gough noted that, formerly, every housekeeper in the lordship had free pannage for swine in the lord's wood, paying 4d for the 'marking and tending of their swine'; however, this privilege had been lost as the woods had been felled.[76] Divlin Wood was cleared in the fifteenth century, the Holloway Hills and Brandwood in the early sixteenth century and, later, towards the end of the Civil War, Myddle Wood was cleared, it having been estimated that 240 acres were brought into cultivation by the felling of the latter.[77] Enclosure and the greater definition of individual private property rights marked a period of transition whereby customary rights of grazing, fuel and other resources which could have a commercial value were gradually replaced by formal legalised relationships. While manorial custom stipulated, for instance, that only those with legal common rights usually held by manorial tenants could exploit resources, lords frequently sought to increase their income by licensing encroachment, cottage building and the digging of peat and turves, selling timber and wood, and allowing the pasturing of livestock by those from outside the manor through agistment. In the peat mosses and moors of north Shropshire individuals took advantage of the common right of turbary by selling turves outside the lordship, contrary to custom and exceeding their entitlement. Furthermore, lords actively sought to derive an income, as at Myddle, where Gough noted that turves were 'sold att 8d a yard', and in the case of Tetchill Moor, where it was recorded that in the process of digging drainage ditches it was intended not to affect the turbary, as this was 'where the lord may make profit' by selling to 'strangers'.[78] It is apparent, as elsewhere in England, that tenants flouted the rule that turves were not to be sold outside each lordship, with amercements amounting, in practice, to licences for the digging of peat.[79] By the early eighteenth century much of the commons of Whixall, a township in north Shropshire, had been enclosed with the exception of a large peat moss from which, it was observed, 'most of the poor people in the neighbourhood' obtained their living by cutting and selling peat.[80]

Customary rights to grazing, fuel and other resources remained important throughout the sixteenth and seventeenth centuries and even into the eighteenth century. There was, however, a point of contest, as the gradual process of commercialisation put pressure on commons, contributing to the decline of effective communal management and eventually leading to overexploitation. This impacted negatively upon commoners and the rural poor, who had long held common rights on

---

74 'Customs relating to several copyhold and customary manors in the county of Salop', 15th–17th centuries, William Salt Library, Stafford, MS.352, 207; Garbet, *Wem*, pp. 108–41.

75 WSL MS.352, 207.

76 Gough, *Myddle*, p. 64.

77 Hey, *English rural community*, pp. 32–3, 63.

78 Gough, *Myddle*, p. 59; SA 212/92.

79 M. Bailey, *A marginal economy? East Anglian breckland in the later Middle Ages* (Cambridge, 1989), pp. 163–4; Winchester, *Harvest*, pp. 128–30.

80 SA 112/1/2376 Letter from John Dicken to the Honourable Richard Hill, 14 November 1719.

a legal or customary basis and relied on access to commons for their survival as part of an essentially traditional economy based on smallholding and the use of a wide range of resources.

Furthermore, the pressure upon commons was not confined to agricultural uses. During the sixteenth and seventeenth centuries early industrial development took place in Shropshire, particularly in the Severn Gorge and the east Shropshire coalfield, where coal mines and ironworks developed. This led to the leasing of mineral rights on commons and wastes and the construction of cottages for industrial workers which hampered the ability of those who had long held common rights to exercise them. This sometimes resulted in disputes, as at Broseley in 1605–7, where the colliers and industrial workers brought in by James Clifford, the lord of the manor, proceeded to enclose and build cottages upon Broseley Wood and Coal Pit Hill, leading to tension with freeholders and tenants, who felt that their common pasture rights were being hampered.[81] Analysis of a series of enclosure disputes that occurred in Shropshire has suggested that the main cause of tension was, in fact, ownership or boundary disputes between manorial lords, rather than necessarily the loss of customary rights.[82] Moreover, evidence from Shropshire has highlighted the apparent superficial legal connotations, with disputes reflecting not only past agrarian practice which can be linked to custom, but also the enclosure of waste for arable cultivation or more intensive pasture closes. Other contributory factors included overlapping patterns of lordship and rivalry between communities resulting from intercommoning and competition for fuel, minerals and resources associated with early industrial development.

Attempts at enclosure and improvement were motivated by increased profit for both lords and tenants, who it has been argued shared the risks of improvement.[83] This can be illustrated by the example of the enclosure of Tetchill Moor, in the manor and parish of Ellesmere, and nearby Kenwick Park, which has been examined by Sylvia Watts.[84] The reclamation of Tetchill Moor, which began around 1612, was completed by the early 1620s, the area being transformed from 'moss and moorish ground to fertile farmland'. This was contemporary with similar enclosure and improvement schemes in other parts of north Shropshire, for example in the parish of Myddle and in the lordship of Wem.[85] Tenants of the settlements of Tetchill, Lee and Kenwick, which bounded the moor, were supportive, recognising the potential benefits in allowing for the extension of arable cultivation and rich meadow land, thereby raising its profitability. However, this scheme did not go undisputed, as

---

81 The National Archives, Kew, London STAC 8/86/18.

82 J.P. Bowen, '"Before the breaking of the day, in a riotous manner and with great shouts and outcries": disputes over common land in Shropshire in the sixteenth and seventeenth centuries', *Rural History*, 26 (2015), pp. 133–59.

83 Shannon, 'Risks and rewards', p. 165.

84 S. Watts, 'From moss and moorish ground to fertile farmland: the early seventeenth century reclamation of Tetchill Moor', *Transactions of the Shropshire Archaeological and Historical Society*, 80 (2005), pp. 125–31. The reference for the original material, which is part of the Bridgewater Collection, is: SA 212/92.

85 Ibid.; Gough, *Myddle*, pp. 58–64; Garbet, *Wem*.

in 1622 it was reported that Edward Kynaston of Hordley, an 'odd humorous and conceited gent', intended to break open enclosures unless compensated for his loss of right of common pasture.[86] While part of the moor totalling 730 acres was enclosed and allotted to Kynaston, the dispute continued, with the agent George Gosse writing that he feared he would be aided by local Shropshire people who he described 'as dangerous swearing people'.[87] The outcome of the claim for common pasture is unknown, although it has been pointed out that a further claim was made in 1657 by the plaintiff's grandson, thus implying that it was unsuccessful.[88] In contrast, the later re-leasing of the Ellesmere estates in north Shropshire, which totalled 55 townships and included Tetchill Moor and Kenwick Park, provides an example of the way an absentee landowner sought to increase his estates' income prior to the Civil War by raising rents to correspond with upward trends in prices.[89]

In particular, Tawney recognised the grievance which small cultivators felt with regard to the loss of commons access, although, significantly, he questioned whether their 'outcry' was disproportionate.[90] But this assumes that common pasture rights were of little significance when clearly, in pastoral areas such as Shropshire, as well as in upland hill farming areas, they were. Even in arable areas where the farming system was orientated towards the growing of cereal crops for the market, commons were important, as they were generally smaller in extent and because they were vital to the maintenance of the arable holding via the manuring of fields by livestock.[91] While in the seventeenth century families with between 10 and 50 acres and generous common rights characterised rural communities, by the end of the early modern period there was a greater differentiation on the basis of wealth as the county became more commercialised, with the development of marketing centred on cattle and sheep production.[92] The loss of common pasture rights was thus detrimental to smaller landholders, who found themselves impoverished and destitute, losing access to land, whereas middling freeholders frequently gained, acquiring additional pasture. Given that farms in Shropshire were generally small, enclosure allowed for the expansion of holdings through engrossment – one form of 'enclosing' Tawney referred to – although, clearly, at the same time this was less beneficial for smallholders and cottagers.

This situation can be highlighted by the example of Highley, where developments in the late sixteenth century which brought about enclosure marked the passing of communal relations, the breakdown of kinship lines and the economic and social polarisation of the rural community on the basis of wealth.[93] The five- and six-acre

86 Ibid.

87 Ibid.

88 Ibid.

89 E. Hopkins, 'The re-leasing of the Ellesmere estates, 1637–1642', *Agricultural History Review*, 10 (1962), pp. 14–28.

90 Tawney, *Agrarian problem*, p. 239.

91 Ibid., p. 240.

92 J. Thirsk (ed.), *The agrarian history of England and Wales. Volume V: 1640–1750* (Cambridge, 1984), p. 149.

93 G. Nair, *Highley: the development of a community 1550–1880* (Oxford, 1988).

enclosures and common rights which cottagers lost as a consequence of the enclosure of Highley Wood in 1618 meant their holdings ceased to be viable, a trend which continued as new owners were not prepared to allocate land to accompany a cottage, meaning that families that combined smallholding with another occupation were basically landless.[94] Similarly, in Ruyton Eleven Towns manor in north Shropshire a series of articles of agreement made on 23 January 1608/9 specified that all the commons which lay open and not enclosed were to be 'enclosed and divided before Midsummer (24 June) next' into six equal parts (reserving 60 acres of the first sixth which was to be sold) with freeholders, copyholders and tenants having a rateable part according to the size of their tenements.[95]

By comparison, Tawney highlighted the strong position of freeholders, who were protected by the law and could enforce their rights, and this is evident in a seventeenth-century survey of the commons and wastes of Whitchurch, written by the agent of the duke of Bridgewater in a style similar to that of Norden.[96] The survey not only provides insight into the state of the manor's commons, but also alludes to their potential future uses and the absence of any freeholders and copyholders who might seek to oppose enclosure.[97] It reflects early modern attitudes towards agricultural improvement put forward in contemporary pamphlet literature and the benefits which, it was debated at the time, could be gained from enclosure. The view of the agent typifies that of contemporaries of the Commonwealth period, who saw waste as something that should be improved and brought into more intensive usage for the benefit of the common good, especially arable cultivation. For example, he wrote that the copyholders and other tenants of Whitchurch should be granted licence by the court to 'plough or till some part of the waste for the increase of corn or for sowing flax or hemp'.[98] Just as areas of fen, forest or moor came under increasing exploitation, comparable pressure was placed on areas of lowland heath, the enclosure of which became more frequent from the mid-seventeenth century, allowing for the temporary or permanent cultivation of rye, barley and wheat. Heathland enclosure was comparatively cheaper than the drainage and enclosure of wetland and woodland commons, but the soil tended to be less fertile. The agent speculated as to the improvement of the meres through drainage, writing that if they 'be laid dry there would be good meadow worth £20 or £30 per annum' – alternatively, he observed, an area of water could be beneficial as meadowland or for fishing, fowling and the breeding of swans. Another possible use suggested was a rabbit warren, while not infringing commoners' rights.[99] Evidently the motivation behind the survey was in seeking maximum profit for the lord, the agent suggesting ways of taking advantage of the considerable potential for further commercial exploitation,

---

94 Ibid., pp. 98–9.

95 SA 2171/91.

96 SA 212/60; Tawney, *Agrarian problem*, pp. 247–8. For example, see J. Norden, *The surveyor's dialogue (1618): a critical edition*, ed. M. Netzloff (Farnham, 2010).

97 SA 212/60; Thirsk, 'Enclosing and engrossing'.

98 SA 212/60.

99 Ibid.

noting the profit to be gained from fuel or turbary, iron, lead, coal, freestone, hard stone or slate, whetstones or chalk for lime, and whether there were any marl pits to improve the land.[100] It was also stated that tenants desired to enclose common to increase their tenements and the lord's revenue.[101] The agent referred to the absence of any 'freeholders and copyholders', indicating that he was aware that people who had common rights might seek to defend them by objecting to enclosure.[102] This description is thus testament to contemporary concerns about the commercial exploitation of commons, over which common rights pertained.

Commons, cottages and poor relief

Another aspect which Tawney discussed was the effects of agrarian change on the development of the poor relief system, which he wrote was 'not a medieval anachronism' but rather, he suggested, 'the outcome of conditions which seem to the men of the sixteenth century new and appalling', taking shape in Elizabeth I's reign (1558–1603).[103] Recent work has shown the wide range of sources of relief which existed before and after the onset of a national system of parish relief.[104] Indeed, prior to the 1662 Settlement and Removal Act, commonly known simply as the Act of Settlement or the Settlement Act, it was the 1589 and 1598 statutes regarding poor relief and the erection of cottages which influenced patterns of migration, settlement and vagrancy.[105] The terms of the statutes of 1598 and 1662 made specific reference to the movement of the poor to parishes where there was 'the best Stock, the largest Commons or Wastes to build Cottages, and the most Woods for them to burn and destroy'.[106] The lack of a formal definition of settlement meant that manorial and parochial officials were caught between providing relief for the maintenance of the poor and, concurrently, enforcing exclusivist policies relating to cottages and inmates with a view to maintaining the stability of rural communities. In fact, clause five of the 1598 Act for the Relief of the Poor allowed parishes to

---

100 Ibid.

101 Ibid.

102 Ibid.

103 Tawney, *Agrarian problem*, pp. 266–8, 270.

104 M. McIntosh, *Poor relief in England, 1350–1600* (Cambridge, 2012); M. McIntosh, *Poor relief and community in Hadleigh, Suffolk, 1547–1600* (Hatfield, 2013); C. Dyer, 'Poverty and its relief in late medieval England', *Past & Present*, 216 (2012), pp. 41–78; Hindle, *On the parish?*.

105 Vagrancy, e.g. Act against the Harbouring of Inmates 1 Eliz I, c.17 (1559); poor relief, e.g. An Act for the Relief of the Poor 39 Eliz I, c.3 (1598); An Act for the Relief of the Poor, 43 Eliz I, c.2 (1601); settlement, e.g. The Poor Relief Act 14 Car II, c.12 (1662), also known as the Settlement Act or the Settlement and Removal Act; and the regulation of cottage building, e.g. Act against the erecting and maintaining of cottages 31 Eliz I, c.7 (1589). This builds on a more general discussion of cottage and squatter settlement published in J.P. Bowen, 'Cottage and squatter settlement and encroachment on common waste in the sixteenth and seventeenth centuries: some evidence from Shropshire', *Local Population Studies*, 93 (2014), pp. 11–32.

106 An Act for the Better Relief of the Poor of this Kingdom (1662).

build 'convenyent Howses of dwelling' on common wastes for the poor with lords' agreement.[107] It also allowed parishes to place inmates or more than one family in a cottage or house in order to provide 'necessary places of habitation', regardless of the 1589 statute regulating cottage building which stipulated that cottages were to have a minimum of four acres of land allotted to them and placed restrictions on multiple occupancy.[108] This was further affirmed by clause four of the act of 1601, which stipulated that overseers could, with the lord of the manor's consent, build houses on wastes for the impotent poor.[109]

Significantly, Tawney recognised this legal mechanism, observing that the 'possibility of using the manorial waste to accommodate those who had no settled abode had occurred to statesmen as one expedient for meeting the problem of the infirm and destitute', although he also appreciated the potential problem inherent in this strategy given the scale of population movement, pointing out that the extent of labour mobility meant that it was 'impossible, even if it had been desirable, to reserve those unutilised territories for the maintenance' of the poor.[110] He further observed that, despite the protests of existing inhabitants, 'refugees from other villages swarm down upon them', so that the statute requiring four acres of land to be allocated to a cottage – a landholding deemed sufficient to maintain a household – could not be adhered to. Consequently, the issuing of licences for the erection of cottages became part of quarter session business.[111]

Analysis of the orders from the Shropshire quarter sessions for the licensing of cottage building supports the latter observation, although it appears to have been on a relatively small scale, with only one or two cottages being licensed at a time.[112] The geographical distribution of licensed cottage building shows a concentration of settlement in north Shropshire at Baschurch, Calverhall, Doddington near Whitchurch, Great Ash, Marchamley, Prees, Ruyton Eleven Towns, Stanton upon Hine Heath, Stanton Long, Wem and Whittington – parishes where there were extensive lowland heaths and lightly wooded commons.[113] There appears to have been licensed cottage building in the Severnside parishes of Alberbury and Great Ness to the north-west

107 An Act for the Relief of the Poor 39 Elizabeth I, c.3 (1598).

108 For the significance of 'An act against erecting and maintaining cottages', see D. Tankard, 'The regulation of cottage building in seventeenth-century Sussex', *Agricultural History Review*, 59 (2011), pp. 18–35.

109 An Act for the Relief of the Poor, 43 Elizabeth I, c.2 (1601).

110 Tawney, *Agrarian problem*, p. 277.

111 Ibid., pp. 277–8.

112 R. Lloyd Kenyon (ed.), *Abstracts of the orders of the Shropshire quarter sessions, vol. 1: 1638–1708* (Shrewsbury, 1908); O. Wakeman (ed.), *Abstracts of the orders of the Shropshire quarter sessions, vol. 2: 1709–1726* (Shrewsbury, 1908); R. Lloyd Kenyon (ed.), *Abstracts of the orders of the Shropshire quarter sessions, vol. 3: 1783–1839* (Shrewsbury, 1908).

113 Licences were granted for Baschurch (October 1687), Calverhall (Easter 1688), Doddington (July 1695), Great Ash (July 1693), Marchamley (October 1691), Myddle (October 1652), Prees (October 1695), Ruyton Eleven Towns (January 1690), Stanton upon Hine Heath (1658), Stanton Long (January 1704), Wem (October 1692) and Whittington (January 1696).

of Shrewsbury and Alveley to the south of Bridgnorth, and in south Shropshire at Brockton, Chetton, Easthope, Hope Bowdler, Kenley, Kings Nordley, Lydbury North and Munslow.[114] Cottages were erected upon commons, often for the poorer members of communities, with the consent of the lords of the manor. Identifiable is a clear chronology, with the licensing of cottage building taking place between 1652 and 1756. It is, however, probable that much informal unlicensed cottage building went unrecorded before and after 1662, despite the aforementioned legal statute.

Perceptively, Tawney made the link between the enclosure of commons and the impact this had in terms of the use of commons by the poor with regard to the resources they provided and also as a place on which to settle. Enclosure can, therefore, be seen to have been influential with regard to patterns of population movement and cottage settlement. The poor, he wrote, having lost their customary livelihood, proceeded to colonise 'in such number' that they could not be 'kept out', settling as squatters on the commons of unenclosed manors, which 'offered little or no obstacle to immigration'.[115] It is at a local level that the impact of cottage settlement on commons becomes most apparent. Again, Gough's account of Myddle is a useful source for examining the impact of cottage settlement, and a case study of Myddlewood provides insight into the process of enclosure and the way settlement affected the landscape.[116] The household economy of the inhabitants of the cottages described by Gough consisted of the grazing of a few livestock along with rural craft and industrial occupations. There appears to have been no attempt to enforce the act that each cottage should have four acres of land allotted to it at Myddle until the mid-seventeenth century, when population pressure increased.[117] Tawney observed the tendency for 'stern economists' in the seventeenth century to lament the ease with which permission to build cottages on the waste was obtained, thereby encouraging the 'existence of an improvident and idle class', which, he remarked, 'neither work for wages nor make good use of the land'.[118]

Following the 1662 Settlement Act, to be resident in a parish inhabitants were required to have been born in the parish, to have lived in the parish for 40 consecutive days without complaint, to have been hired for over a year and a day within the parish, to have held office in the parish, to rent a property worth £10 per year or pay the same in taxes, to have married into the parish, to be in receipt of poor relief in that parish previously, or to have a seven-year apprenticeship with a settled resident. Any incoming migration from outside the parish would have been subject to parochial control under the settlement laws. It is probable that there was a compromise between

---

114 Licences were granted for Alberbury (January 1653), Great Ness (October 1704), Alveley (October 1656), Brockton (October 1695, January 1704, April 1661), Chetton (April 1702), Easthope (October 1656), Hope Bowdler (Easter 1657), Kenley (April 1700), Kings Nordley (October 1695), Lydbury North (January 1695) and Munslow (Easter 1658, January 1659–60, April 1653 and January 1660–61).

115 Tawney, *Agrarian problem*, p. 277.

116 Gough, *Myddle*, p. 63.

117 Act against the erecting and maintaining of cottages 31 Eliz I, c.7 (1589).

118 Tawney, *Agrarian problem*, p. 278.

lords and larger tenants, as the wealthier in rural communities sought to avoid short-term increases in taxation by allowing the less wealthy access to commons which were of comparatively marginal importance to them. The price for smallholders, cottagers and the poor was relatively much higher, as the commons were more fundamental for their subsistence. Certainly, licensing cottage building on the commons implies that the lords put revenues above the existing property rights of their tenants, which meant that there was a greater burden on rural communities once the commons were overpopulated and degraded; hence later seventeenth- and eighteenth-century commentators were critical of cottagers and the rural poor.

The Tawneian approach

Collectively many of the changes that affected rural England, including the enclosure of commons, the engrossment of farms and commercialisation of the agricultural sector, population movement and the development of industry, contributed to the transition from 'feudalism to capitalism' with which Tawney was preoccupied. It is apparent that many of the themes which he explored in his *Agrarian Problem* still dominate current research. The examples discussed add to the picture of regional diversity in England, providing a discussion of enclosure in the context of the countryside of Shropshire and emphasising the variability in the extent and value of commons. Highlighting the usefulness of a local and regional approach, this chapter provides further evidence of the variety of experience which English rural society underwent in this transitional phase between the medieval and early modern periods and the significance of both custom and commercialisation. It is striking that the evidence presented, which builds on previous historians' findings, supports many of the assertions which Tawney originally made regarding commons, custom and cottages.

Aspects of this include the various forms of 'enclosing', or rather enclosure, increasing commercialisation with agricultural specialisation, the continued importance of custom, a more prominent role for law and legal redress and greater economic and social differentiation. The latter is starkly evidenced by the plight of cottagers and the rural poor, who settled on the commons because they provided a place to live in an increasingly enclosed countryside and offered a range of resources which could be readily exploited for agricultural, craft and industrial purposes. And yet he was not discussing Shropshire, which is significant, suggesting that it is possible to draw broad conclusions about pre-industrial rural society. In that sense there is still a need for such a Tawneian-style book and this volume, not only in revisiting his work, shows how his ideas were often played out in different regional settings. While, clearly, it is possible to identify weaknesses in his work, the vivid picture of 'the struggle for the commons' is one which broadly corresponds with findings from Shropshire and elsewhere in England and thus Tawney continues to inspire historians, who still seek to prove or disprove what he so admirably described over a century ago.

Part III: Custom and commerce

Chapter 6

The economics of shipwreck in late medieval Suffolk

Tom Johnson

This chapter examines a peculiar aspect of late medieval coastal economies: the resources gained from shipwrecks, and the ways in which these resources were distributed.[1] The first section contains some prefatory remarks on the socio-legal contexts for the administration of shipwreck and the nature of the mainly quantitative evidence used here. The main section of analysis focuses on two features of the local market in shipwreck: the values given to pieces of wreck and the people who tended to find them. In both cases, the market in second-hand goods received from shipwreck was strongly influenced by local social structures and legal processes. The conclusion considers how these features of the market were potentially affected by wider economic trends in late medieval England. Customary expectations and responsibilities shaped the way that shipwrecked goods were valued and distributed at the same time as much wider commercial pressures could affect the ways in which particular customs were articulated and claimed. An exploration of shipwrecks in late medieval Suffolk can thus help to demonstrate how transnational patterns of trade and exchange could influence the material culture and economies of local coastal communities.

Goods of all kinds that were found floating at sea, dragged up in nets or washed up on the shore were considered to be a royal prerogative right in England.[2] This included the animals that were known as 'royal fish': whales, porpoises and sturgeons. The writer of the thirteenth-century legal treatise called *Bracton* discussed shipwrecks and royal fish in the same passage, asserting that they were *res nullius* – the property of no one – while in the sea. When they are captured, they 'belong to the lord king because of his privilege or to those whom the king has granted such liberty'.[3] Indeed, it was comparatively rare in the fourteenth and fifteenth centuries for the Crown to make a claim upon shipwrecked goods, because by the end of the twelfth

---

1 The best account of small maritime communities in medieval England is H. Fox, *The evolution of the fishing village: landscape and society along the south Devon coast, 1086–1550* (Oxford, 2001).

2 In the Roman legal tradition the sovereign or state had no rights to goods lost (or gained) in shipwreck: see R. Melikan,'Shippers, salvors, and sovereigns: competing interests in the medieval law of shipwreck', *The Journal of Legal History*, 11 (1990), pp. 163–4.

3 S.E. Thorne (tr. and rev.), and G.E. Woodbine (ed.), *Bracton on the laws and customs of England*, 4 vols (Cambridge, MA, 1968–1977), ii, p. 339.

century the 'right of wreck' had been granted out to so many coastal landowners, whether individual lords or urban corporations.[4] Among the records surviving from East Anglia, for example, it is only at Kirkeley and Kessingland, near modern-day Lowestoft, which remained in royal hands, that we see shipwrecks reported for the benefit of the Crown.[5]

The majority of shipwrecks thus legally belonged to lords and municipalities; it was, however, more complicated than this. In the first place, the person who had owned the goods before they were wrecked had an interest in them. This idea had been the subject of the various royal proclamations governing the administration of wrecks since the late twelfth century.[6] It was codified in the first Statute of Westminster (1275), which established that if a man, dog, or cat escaped from the wrecked ship then it could not be adjudged, legally, as 'wreck'. The goods were to be kept for a year and a day, and any survivor could sue for what was his; the unstated implication is that, after this period of time, the goods would revert to the Crown or to the holder of the right of wreck.[7] Of course, this theoretical provision was difficult to apply in practice. It would be difficult for the salvager to know whether anyone – let alone a cat or dog – had escaped the particular shipwreck from which he was retrieving the fragments. This is not to say that it never happened. In the Suffolk fishing village of Walberswick, it was noted in a court of September 1436 that an anchor previously claimed as wreck in fact belonged to Thomas Fuller, who successfully claimed it back.[8] However, such cases were the exception rather than the rule. The vast majority of goods claimed as wreck in medieval England were unchallenged because the original owners were either dead or unable to track down their property.

The other legal interest in an item of shipwreck was that of the person who salvaged it. No royal proclamation or statute set this out in theory, but it is clear that throughout medieval England the lords and towns who held the right to wrecks allotted a share to the salvagers themselves. Generally this share was half of the assessed value of the particular item found. This is evidenced by a case from the Suffolk town of Orford: in 1461 John Carpenter 'found two ropes from wreck, worth 4d, of which 2d pertains to the finder'.[9] The other half went to the borough. In other places the fragmentation of lands might have ramifications for the distribution of wreck. At the court of the Norfolk

---

4 Melikan, 'Shippers, salvors, and sovereigns', p. 172.

5 Suffolk Record Office, Lowestoft, 194/B1/7–8.

6 In 1190 Richard I restricted the Crown's claim to take wreck; only in cases where neither the owner of the wrecked goods nor their heirs or siblings survived were goods to be called 'wreck' and forfeited to the Crown: H.T. Riley (ed.), *The annals of Roger de Hovedon*, 2 vols (London, 1853), ii, pp. 170–1. In 1236 Henry III granted that men who escaped shipwrecks would not lose their wrecked goods, and if any animal (*bestia*) escaped the ship, then the goods ought to be safeguarded for three months in case the owners returned to claim them; if they did not, then the king 'or person possessing the liberty [right] of wreck' should have them: *Calendar of charter rolls*, 6 vols (London, 1903–27), i, p. 220.

7 3 Edw. III, c. 4: *The statutes of the realm*, 11 vols (London, 1810–28), i, p. 28.

8 Suffolk Record Office, Ipswich (hereafter SROI), HA30/314/19d/1–21, m. 9r.

9 SROI, HD64/1/12, dorse.

village of Runton, for example, it was presented that a plank and a small piece of an anchor 'came from wreck of the sea to the land of the lord'. These items were worth 10d in total. A half part (5d) went to the lord of Beeston Hall. The other half was further divided. Three-fifths of this half (3d) went to the prior of Beeston. The other two fifths were divided unequally between the lord of the manor of Runton (1½d) and John de Plumsted, presumably the finder of the goods, who received the final halfpenny.[10] Such complicated divisions were unusual, though. In most cases the finder received a half-share and the holder of wreck-rights received the other half. The reason for this customary allocation is rarely made explicit in contemporary documentation, but on occasion scribes used a formula stating that the finder's half share was 'in reward for their labour'.[11] Exactly how this transaction was made is somewhat obscure, and will be discussed in more detail below.

Wreck rolls: reconstructing the market in shipwreck

This chapter focuses upon the 'wreck rolls' of Leiston Abbey.[12] While B. Schofield and Mark Bailey have examined this evidence before, here I build upon their analyses in two ways.[13] Firstly, the three rolls covering large parts of the fifteenth century have been repaired only very recently; while Schofield noted the existence of these later rolls, significant sections were illegible before conservation work was carried out in 2013.[14] Secondly, both Schofield and Bailey drew on these rich sources for anecdotal evidence about the everyday lives of rural maritime communities and the language and technology of seafaring. This chapter, by contrast, presents a quantitative analysis of the data in the almost continuous series of wreck rolls for the period 1377–1482. Such an analysis allows different kinds of insights into the mechanics of the shipwreck economy and the ways in which it was structured by legal procedures, custom and social status.

Leiston Abbey was a Premonstratensian house founded in the late twelfth century by Ranulf de Glanville, sometime chief justiciar to Henry I. Although the right of wreck was not specifically included in the list of legal privileges contained in their foundation charter, they claimed to have held the right 'for a long time' by the early thirteenth

10 Norfolk Record Office, WKC 2/166 398x7, m. 1r.

11 SROI, HA 30/369/390, m. 2r. This phrase was also used in a Chancery petition of May 1390 from merchants who had been shipwrecked and wished to reclaim the goods that had been salvaged: *Calendar of Patent Rolls*, 1389–1392, 74 vols (London, 1891–1986), p. 271.

12 The rolls, with their respective date ranges, are: SROI, HD 371/1 [1377–97]; HD 371/2 [1398–1409]; HD 1032/86 [1422–29]; HD 1032/87 [1432–35]; HD 1032/88 [1436–82].

13 See B. Schofield, 'Wreck rolls of Leiston Abbey', in J.C. Davies (ed.), *Studies presented to Sir Hilary Jenkinson* (London, 1957), pp. 361–71; M. Bailey, 'Coastal fishing off south east Suffolk in the century after the Black Death', *Proceedings of the Suffolk Institute of Archaeology and History*, 37 (1992), pp. 102–14.

14 I am very grateful to Bridget Hanley at the SROI for her assistance with this, and also to the conservators there for the repairing of the rolls.

century.[15] Later, during the *quo warranto* ('by what warrant') proceedings of the 1280s, the abbey successfully asserted its right to wreck on the basis that de Glanville, its founder, had exercised the same rights in the coastal properties he had granted them at Sizewell and Thorp.[16] The first evidence for the systematic administration of shipwrecks by Leiston Abbey, however, does not appear until the late fourteenth century. This evidence – the wreck rolls – records the business of a court called the Hethewardmote. The name of the court suggests some antiquity: 'moot' is an old word for a legal assembly; 'hithe' a now antiquated word for a port or landing stage. It is plausible, as Schofield suggested, that the name refers to an officer called the 'hitheward' – that is, the warden of the port.[17] In any case, it is likely that the first surviving rolls of the late fourteenth century simply represent the earliest extant records of a rather older institution.

The Hethewardmote was convened to regulate the legal business of the fishermen who lived in the vills of Sizewell and Thorp, coastal properties of Leiston Abbey. It did not deal exclusively with shipwrecks. The fishermen could sue interpersonal pleas of debt, detinue and broken covenant in this forum; in addition, criminal misdemeanours such as affrays were sometimes presented.[18] The vast majority of the Hethewardmote's business, however, was given over to the administration of shipwreck. The rolls are thus unusual in two ways. Firstly, most reports of shipwreck in late medieval England came within the context of other legal jurisdictions: manors, admiralty franchises and urban leet courts. The institutional focus of the Hethewardmote upon wreck presentments makes it unique among the surviving evidence from East Anglia. Secondly, the wreck rolls are unusual because they survive for nearly a century in complete sequence (the only large gap is the period between 1409 and 1421). In short, the uniformity of information provided and the range of time over which it is furnished make the wreck rolls an excellent source for quantitative analysis. By looking at trends in the collection, quantity and value of shipwreck over the late fourteenth and fifteenth centuries it is possible to speculate on both the endogenous and exogenous influences upon this peculiar kind of late medieval local economy.

What were the basic features of this economy? As noted above, it is actually quite difficult to know what kind of transaction we are dealing with when we look at a presentment of shipwreck. This entry from 1451 is typical: 'And that John Pope found one barrel, worth 2d, of which half pertains to the lord, etc'.[19] The name of the finder,

---

15 For the claim, see *Rotuli Hundredorum temp. Hen. II et Edw. I*, 2 vols (London, 1812–18), ii, p. 148. For the charter, see R. Mortimer (ed.), *Leiston Abbey cartulary and Butley Prior charters* (Ipswich, 1979), pp. 71–3 [no. 23].

16 *Placita de quo warranto temp. Edw. I., II., et III* (London, 1818), pp. 734–5.

17 Schofield,'Wreck rolls', p. 363.

18 For pleas of debt, see SROI, HD 371/2, mm. 1r, 2v; HD 1032/86, m. 1r. For pleas of detinue, see HD 1032/88, mm. 10v, 13v. For pleas of broken contract, see HD 371/1, mm. 1r, 4r, 9r [regarding an apprenticeship], 11r; HD 371/2, mm. 3r, 4r. For misdemeanours, see HD 371/2, m. 5v; HD 1032/86, m. 4v.

19 SROI, HD 1032/88, m. 8v: 'Et quod Johannes Pope similiter invenit I barell precij ijd unde medietas pertinet domino etc'.

the name of the object and the purported worth of the object are recorded. This worth was assessed by one of the two juries of the Hethewardmote (one each for the vills of Sizewell and Thorp). These juries were composed of all the men who had been shipmasters – that is, captains – in the previous year. The price they gave the wreck then appears in the margin of the roll. As in other kinds of court rolls, these values were added to other proceeds issuing from the court, such as fines for contumacy or disobedience, or fees for civil suits, at the foot of the membrane. The payment for wreck would thus appear to be a simple fine, paid or owed by the finder to the court official. If this analysis is correct, though, it raises a more interesting set of questions. For instance, how was the value of a shipwreck assessed? Does the price recorded in the rolls represent the amount of money the finder had already received for the wreck, or was it the price they could expect to receive if they chose to sell it?

These questions are difficult to answer, but there are some anecdotal hints in the rolls. It is likely that in most cases the object had not – indeed, perhaps could not – be sold until it had been presented to the Hethewardmote for valuation and registration. The evidence for this exists in negative form, in that people who concealed wrecks from the court were often said to have sold them. A particularly interesting example comes from 1479, when John Brandon – noted in the rolls as a 'stranger' to the communities of Sizewell and Thorp – was presented after he found 'a piece of timber worth 8d, and sold it to John Arnold [of Thorp] for 2d'.[20] Brandon was fined a shilling and John Arnold, a prominent local shipmaster who perhaps should have known better, was fined 4d. This example strongly suggests that the Hethewardmote set a price for found shipwrecks, rather than taxing sales that had already taken place; thus, it was the shipmaster–jurors who decided, collectively, how much a particular item was worth, rather than how much someone was willing to pay for it (although, of course, the latter consideration presumably influenced their valuations). This system had obvious benefits for the abbey. If there had been a free market in shipwreck as soon as it reached the shore, then it would have been more difficult to keep track of who had found what, how much they had sold it for and how to collect the fines owed.

The act of presenting an item of shipwreck to the Hethewardmote, then, was also an act of economic clarification. The finder lost half of the value of his wreck, it is true, but he gained a legitimate, fixed price should he choose to sell the goods he had found. This brings us to the second basic feature of the local shipwreck economy. As Bailey has remarked, 'if fishermen were consistently prepared to buy up all kinds of wrecked goods, then the clear assumption is that there was a ready "second-hand" market for their disposal'.[21] Did the mariners of Sizewell and Thorp pay to keep the things they found, or to sell them for a profit? This question cannot be answered directly, as the wreck rolls contain no information about what happened to the goods after they were reported. However, it is reasonable to speculate that, in most cases, the goods would have remained within the community of fishermen and mariners at Sizewell and Thorpe. As Figure 6.1 shows, the vast majority of goods found as shipwreck were related in some way to fishing, shipping and trade, and therefore

20 SROI, HD 1032/88, m. 17r.

21 Bailey, 'Coastal fishing', p. 108.

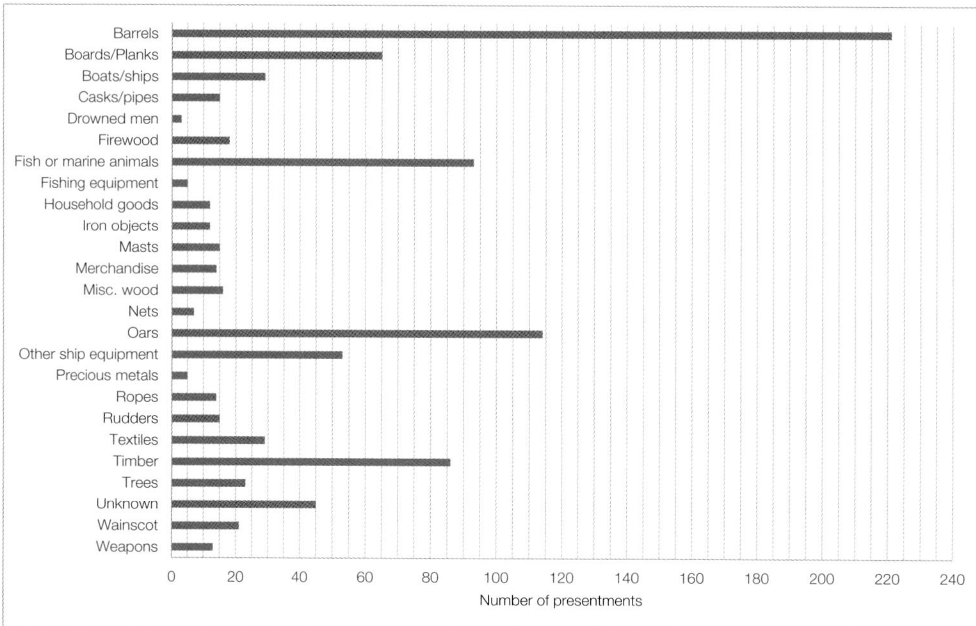

Figure 6.1 Wrecks presented to the Hethewardmote, 1377–1482.

would have been of use to locals. Bailey is therefore probably correct in assuming the existence of a second-hand market in shipwrecked goods.

A quantitative analysis of the data can provide a few more details about the dynamics of this market. There were nearly a thousand (943) individual presentments of wreck over a period of just over a century, giving an annual average of just over 11 objects. However, this average masks large fluctuations in the numbers of wreck presentments found from year to year, as can be seen in Figure 6.2.[22]

Alongside these fluctuations in the number of wrecks, the prices of wreck fluctuated over time as well: these price fluctuations can be seen in Figure 6.3, which shows the average price of wreck presentments in a given year in the period studied. Is there any correspondence between the two graphs, given the relationship of supply and demand? It might be expected that the greater number of wrecks found in a given year the lower the average price of a single item of wreck.

However, as can be see in Figure 6.4, which charts the prices and the number of wreck presentments together, there is rarely any correspondence between the

22 Note that I count presentments, not items of wreck found. There are three reasons for this. Firstly, the rolls are often unclear as to the numbers of items. The scribe might simply write vaguely of 'tablas' (planks) in some cases, whilst writing 'iij tablas' (three planks) in others. This data is therefore uneven across the set, and would produce distorted results. Secondly, the numbers that are given seem unreliable. It is unlikely that people always found bundles of *exactly* 20, 40 or 60 sticks of firewood, for example, but these tend to be the rounded-up numbers noted in the rolls.

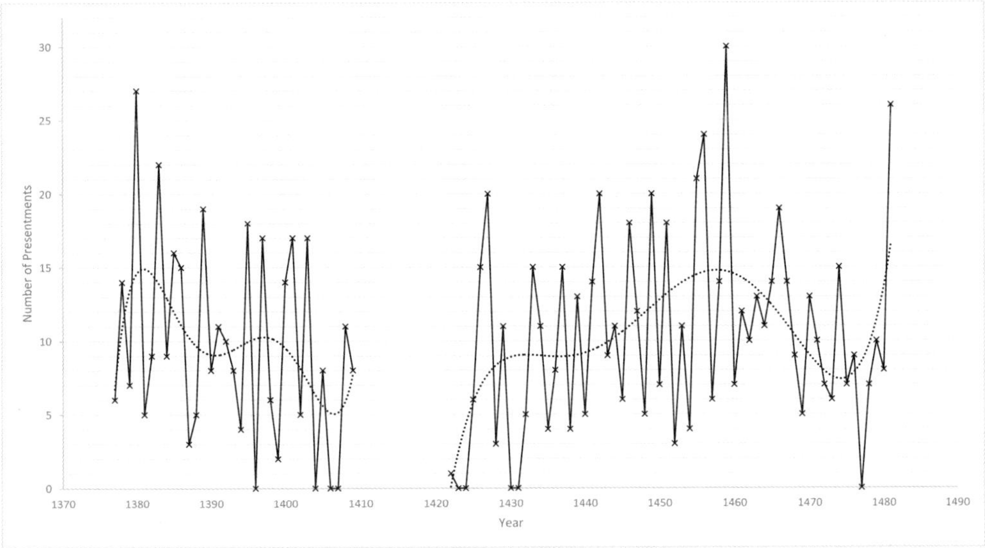

Figure 6.2 Number of wreck presentments, 1377–1482.

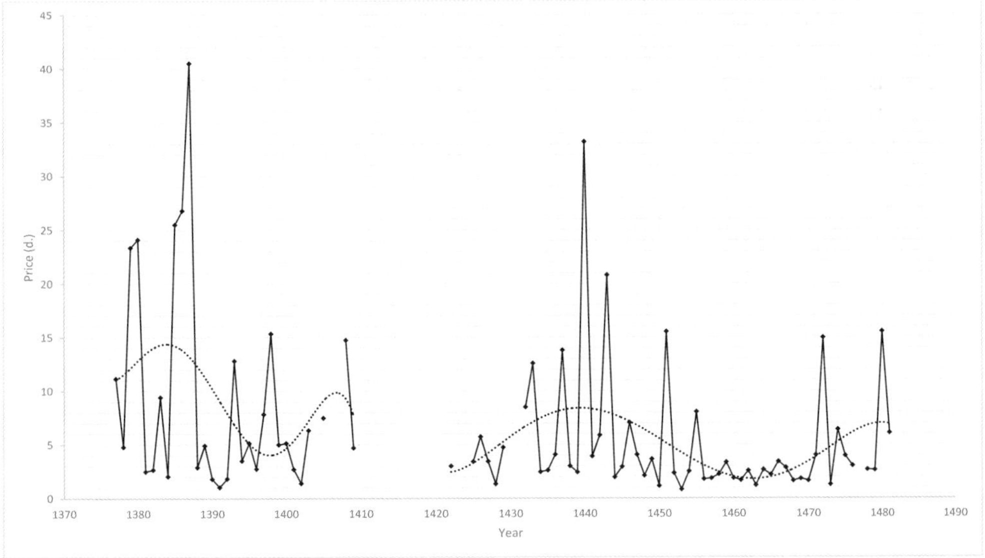

Figure 6.3 Average annual price of wreck presentments (in pence), 1377–1482.

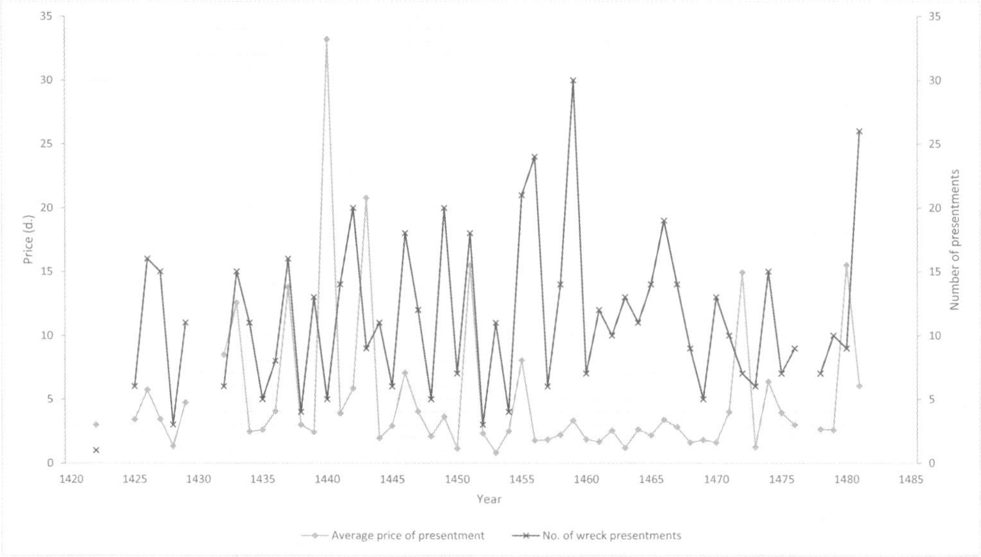

Figure 6.4 Number of presentments and average price of wreck finds (in pence), 1425–85.

number of wrecks presented and their average prices, demonstrating that there was no correlation between supply and demand. When the numbers of wreck increased, prices did not fall; when numbers decreased, prices did not rise. Indeed, there seems to be a slight correlation in the other direction. In general, Figure 6.4 shows that rising numbers of presentments saw increases in prices and falling numbers saw decreases in price. In 1459, the year in which the most number of wrecks were presented (30 wrecks), the average value increased from just over 2d in 1458 (which had seen 14 wrecks presented) to well over 3d. The following year, the number of wrecks dropped dramatically (7), and the value of those wrecks dropped under 2d.

This seems to be counterintuitive. Why would fewer wreck finds mean that prices fell? In answering this question it is important to remember that the wreck rolls do not represent a random sample: wreck presentments show things deliberately chosen by fishermen, picked out of the sea, taken to the relevant court official and paid for. In short, the presentments show only things that fishermen thought to be worth 'finding' in the first place. A fall in wreck presentments may mean that there were simply fewer things to collect (because the weather had been good, perhaps, or because the tides had taken wrecks elsewhere), but it may also mean that the materials available to collect as wreck were not thought to be worth the trouble. If not many things were found in a given year, this may well reflect a situation in which only low-value items (such as planks and driftwood) were available. Not every fisherman would have thought such detritus to be worth collecting. Therefore, the number of wreck presentments would fall and prices would remain low. By contrast, if a ship carrying a valuable cargo had been wrecked and its contents all washed up near the same settlement (or near a fleet of fishing vessels), then more people would attempt to collect more valuable items, sending up both the numbers and average prices of wreck presentments. There is a good anecdotal example of precisely this phenomenon: in 1438 the manor court for the coastal village of Wells on the north Norfolk coast reported that 2,245 planks called 'waynskot', 1,980 planks called 'tonole', 48 planks called 'firdelis' and some other pieces of broken wood, worth a total of £39 8s 4d, had washed up on the shore.[23] Although here the individual finders were not recorded in the rolls, the collection of such a large quantity of high-value wood suggests that it was very actively pursued and gathered by the local community. Overall, then, the price of shipwrecks was determined not merely by their availability but also in relation to the work of collecting them and having them valued in the Hethewardmote. The value of a shipwreck was always formulated in the shadow of the court.

However, there is another dimension to this phenomenon, because, of course, not all shipwrecked objects were identical. A boat found in 1398 was worth 12s, whereas an oar found the same year was worth 10d.[24] One was a valuable and comparatively rare object, the other was a rather cheap and common object. The two are not comparable in terms of their impact upon the local market and, therefore, it might be rather misleading to speak of the influence of supply and demand upon prices. What happens, then, if we chart the prices and quantities of similar or the same kinds of wreck objects? Although the data set is too fragmented to perform such an analysis in a systematic way, it is possible to look at this question in regard to the most common item found as wreck, the barrel. Rather than just looking at the number of presentments of barrels (which might include an indeterminate number of items), moreover, we can look at the actual individual numbers of barrels found between the years 1425 and 1481.[25]

Figure 6.5 compares the quantities of barrels and the average price per barrel between 1425 and 1481. As can be seen, there is no general correlation either way. Sometimes prices rose with quantities, and sometimes they fell. There was no relationship between supply and demand, but nor does there seem to have been a relationship between the value of the items and the aggregate decision-making of the fishermen–finders. For example, the spike in the graph for the years 1434–37 was caused by a glut of 40 beer barrels landing in the last of those years, worth an aggregate of 24s (or 6½d each). Freak incidents such as this did not affect the prices of barrels generally: six other barrels were found in that year, worth 6d each, and another (a 'half-barrel') worth 3d. This strongly suggests that barrels were not valued by finders in relation to their perception of a more general market in barrels. That is to say, barrels had an absolute value to the finder, who in collecting it made a calculated gamble that it would be assessed at a profitable price in the Hethewardmote. The market did not exert a direct force on the *prices* given to wrecks, but it may have

23 Arundel Castle, M878, m. 1r. The wainscot was worth 30s per hundred, or £33 11s 3d, the 'tonole' (probably barrels) were worth 2s per hundred, or 39s 5d, the fardels were worth a total of 48s, and the miscellaneous items made up the difference.

24 SROI, HD 371/2, m. 1r.

25 This is simply a fortuitous aspect of the data: in all but one case the precise number of barrels was given in the wreck rolls. The data from the earlier rolls (up to 1409) is patchy, with barrels not found so regularly; it has been omitted from the graph for convenience of interpretation.

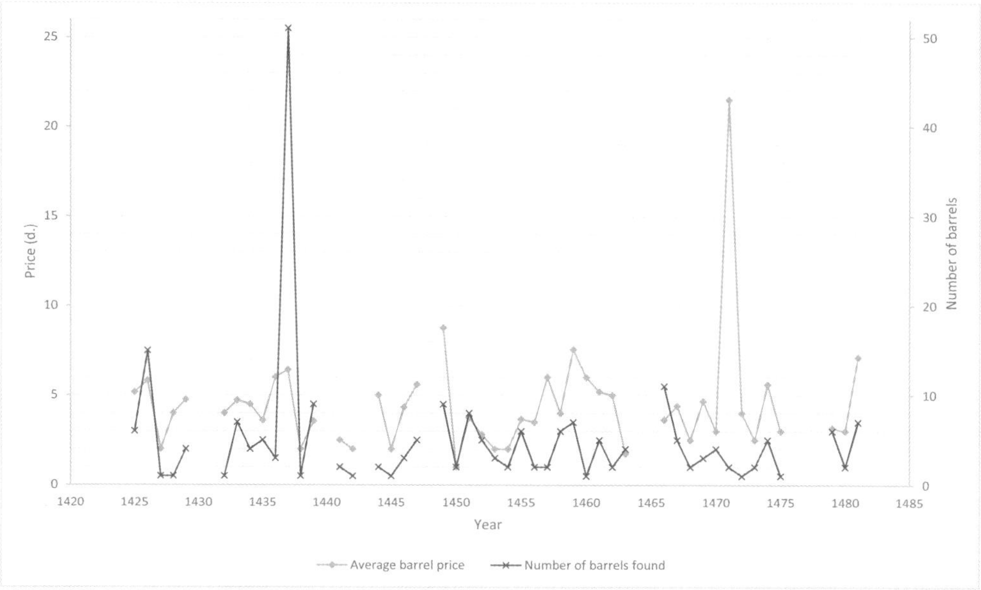

Figure 6.5 Number of barrels and average barrel price, 1425–85.

exerted an indirect force on *value* by influencing the decisions of finders about whether to pick up a particular piece of wreck if they intended to sell it.

Of course, this is not to say that prices were determined randomly. The Hethewardmote comprised two juries of shipmasters from Sizewell and Thorp. The lack of correlations in the data would seem to indicate that the jurors priced a particular piece of wreck on its own merits, rather than in terms of its relative value to other pieces of wreck. For these shipmasters, it seems, there was some absolute difference between a 'sixpence barrel' and a 'tuppence barrel'. For example, in 1451, when four barrels were presented at the Hethewardmote, one was worth 6d, two were worth 5d and one was worth 4d. These tiny gradations in price must have reflected keenly felt distinctions between the worth of the barrels. And, indeed, there is some anecdotal evidence in the rolls that the jury's valuations were based on such considerations. A barrel might be described as a 'beer-barrel' or 'half-a-barrel', a 'broken-barrel' or an 'empty-barrel'.[26] To men experienced in seafaring and fishing, such differences in size, quality and function (among other criteria) would have been important. While it is difficult, therefore, to access the full richness and scope of their maritime expertise, it is possible to discern some of its economic effects. Local knowledge, institutionalised through the Hethewardmote, exercised a decisive influence over value – certainly to a greater extent than the simple commercial forces of supply and demand.

26 Respectively: SROI, HD 1032/87, m. 2v; HD 1032/88, m. 17v; HD 371/1, m. 1r; HD 1032/86, m. 4v.

The finders of shipwreck

The men who were recorded as having found shipwrecks came from a relatively small segment of the coastal communities at Sizewell and Thorp.[27] In the course of the 105 years covered by the wreck rolls it has been possible to identify 446 distinct individuals who found wrecks. Such identification is subject to the normal cautions regarding the analysis of names in medieval court rolls, as spellings change year on year, and some sons have the same names as people we presume to be their fathers (although, fortunately, 'junior' and 'senior' were often used as personal descriptors). Yet, with no reliable estimate for the population over the same period, it is difficult to differentiate these 446 wreck-finders from the other inhabitants of Sizewell and Thorp.[28] One way around this problem is to draw on a rental compiled for Leiston Abbey in 1467, which names 100 people with holdings in the vills of Sizewell and Thorp (35 in Sizewell, 63 in Thorp and 2 in both).[29] There were undoubtedly many more people living in these busy fishing villages at this time. Women, outsiders and people described as servants appear sporadically in the wreck rolls, but not in the 1467 rental.[30] There was probably a significant minority of transient sailors, such as Iken Ducheman, who found wreck twice in 1466 and 1467 and then disappears from the rolls, or settled but landless foreign immigrants such as Henry Coupere, a Fleming listed in the 1483 alien subsidy for Suffolk, who first reported wreck at the Hethewardmote in 1470.[31] Although the calculation of estimates for medieval populations is infamously problematic, using the

---

27 On coastal populations more generally, see M. Kowaleski, 'The demography of maritime communities in late medieval England', in M. Bailey and S. Rigby (eds), *Town and countryside in the age of the Black Death: essays in honour of John Hatcher* (Turnhout, 2012), pp. 87–120.

28 While several manorial court rolls for Leiston survive from this period (SROI, HD1032/2–6), they are damaged and currently unfit for production. The Poll Tax returns of 1381 unfortunately cover Sizewell only and the relevant membrane is badly damaged (missing 130mm of text), yielding only 34 names. I was able to identify five of these as Sizewell shipmasters, all of whom paid the 2s rate of tax. See C. Fenwick (ed.), *The poll taxes of 1377, 1379 and 1381: Part 2, Lincolnshire–Westmorland* (Oxford, 2001), pp. 511–12.

29 Cambridge University Library, Vanneck Box 17, I/F/1, fos 54r–74r.

30 Thirteen women held land in Sizewell and Thorp, of whom four were described as widows: ibid. By comparison, only seven women found wreck, respectively: SROI, HD 371/1, m. 8v; HD 1032/87, m. 1v; HD 1032/88, mm. 6r, 10r, 12v, 14r, 15v. In the wreck rolls, three men were described as servants: Thomas Amys, 'Stephen' and William Beket, respectively: SROI, HD371/1, m. 10v, HD1032/86, m. 2v, HD1032/88, m. 17v. Another five men might be identified as outsiders because their surnames were written as 'de [place-name]', but of course this is not a reliable guide. Three canons from Leiston Abbey were also recorded as having found wreck: Walter Scham, Robert Greyve and John Brandon (SROI, HD 1032/88, mm. 11r, 17r).

31 For Iken Ducheman, see SROI, HD 1032/88, m. 14r–v. Henry Coupere found wreck in 1446 and 1470: SROI, HD 1032/88, mm. 6r, 13v; he appears, listed as an 'artifex', in the alien subsidy record at The National Archives, E 179/180/111, rot. 2r. (reference from the *England's Immigrants* database: <https://www.englandsimmigrants.com/person/17615>, accessed 4 August 2015).

standard fifteenth-century multiplier of four gives a population of around 400 people living in Sizewell and Thorp in 1467.[32]

Using this very rough estimate, it is possible to get a sense of the proportion of people who found shipwrecks in these communities. Looking at people who reported wreck in the five years either side of 1467, when the rental was made, we find 66 finders. This suggests that roughly 16.5 per cent of the total population of Sizewell and Thorp was engaged in wreck-reporting. As most shipwrecks seem to have been found out at sea, as Bailey argues, it is likely that the majority of the finders were themselves fishermen or sailors – thus this figure of 16.5 per cent probably represents the rough proportion of the population engaged in these occupations.[33] On the other hand, it is possible to calculate the proportion of wreck-finders who held lands locally: of the 66 people who found wreck in the years 1462–72, as many as 40 (60.6 per cent) were named in the rental of 1467. This correlation suggests that those who held land in Sizewell and Thorp were more likely to report wreck than their landless or transient peers; perhaps the pull of customary obligations exerted more pressure on those who owed rents, labour services and suit of court to Leiston Abbey.[34]

From the overall population of shipwreck-finders, who found more wrecks and who found the more valuable wrecks? The answer, in short, is that those who acted as shipmasters profited most from the shipwreck economy. This can be seen through a series of quantitative analyses. Of the 446 individual people who were named as finders over the whole period, 206 can be identified as shipmasters on the jury of the Hethewardmote. Just under half (46 per cent) of all finders had thus worked as shipmasters at some point. This may not seem an overwhelming proportion, but, to put it another way, of the 925 presentments of wreck 686 were found by shipmasters (74 per cent).[35] Considering that the fishing vessels at Sizewell and Thorp were manned by small crews – probably between five and ten men per boat – shipmasters were evidently claiming more than their share of wreck.[36] If wrecks had been

32 There is a good discussion of different population multipliers in P.J.P. Goldberg, 'Urban identity and the poll taxes of 1377, 1379 and 1381', *Economic History Review*, 43 (1990), pp. 212–13.

33 Bailey, 'Costal fishing', p. 107.

34 The vast majority of holdings in the 1467 rental carried obligations for autumn boon-works, although they were uniformly commuted at a rate of 2½d per acre. Following the wider pattern of landholding among the East Anglian peasantry, holdings were very small, people held both free and unfree land, and there seems to have been an active land market. Some rent was owed in kind: Henry Pottere (whose total annual rents came to 3s 6d) held an unfree pightell for which he paid 1d, a hen, and 10 sheep per year: Cambridge University Library, Vanneck Box 17, I/F/1, fo. 59r.

35 This slightly different total of 925 excludes those presentments when the finder was unnamed, their name was obscured in the manuscript, or in collective presentments (such as 'the whole village of Sizewell').

36 J. Middleton-Stewart, '"Down to the sea in ships": decline and fall on the Suffolk coast', in C. Rawcliffe, R. Virgoe and R. Wilson (eds), *Counties and communities: essays on East Anglian history presented to Hassell Smith* (Norwich, 1996), p. 74, suggests that Sizewell could accommodate boats of up to 10 tons. The coastal fishing fleet of Scarborough from this period comprised similar-

distributed randomly among the crews of these boats, then shipmasters would have claimed between 10 and 20 per cent of wrecks; in fact, on a year-by-year basis, 38 per cent of wrecks were found by men acting as shipmaster in the same year.[37] This broad trend held true for the value of the items they found, too: the sum total value of the wrecks found by the shipmasters was £37 3s 7d; the sum of the wrecks found by men who were never shipmasters was £10 15s 5d. Overall, then, it is clear that working as a shipmaster gave these men a decisive advantage over their peers in the 'finding' of wreck.

It is important to emphasise that shipmaster was not a solid occupational identity for an individual's whole life. As the 1467 rental makes clear, many of the fishermen of Sizewell and Thorp also held arable land, crofts and gardens, some of which were quite substantial.[38] William Brook, for example, held lands totalling 15 acres and 6 rods in size and paid a rent of 3s 9d. He was first recorded as a finder of wreck in 1429, when he was apparently just a regular member of crew; four years later, in 1433, he began working as a shipmaster. He subsequently acted as shipmaster in 1434, then continuously in the years between 1437 and 1447, and then twice more in 1450 and 1451.[39] His career was typical in this regard: those men who acted as shipmasters more than a couple of times tended to be active consecutively for around a decade before 'retiring'. If William Brook was also typical in terms of the holdings he managed to accumulate later in life, then it is possible that fishing and farming were not just complementary economic activities done in different seasons of the year (although they were certainly that), but also different stages in the life-cycles of the male inhabitants of coastal communities. As Maryanne Kowaleski has suggested, fishing may have been an activity predominantly performed by young men before they inherited land.[40] The shipmasters, then, as the group mostly likely to find shipwrecks, were also a distinct segment of the population in terms of their age and stage in life.

It still remains to be explained why they 'found' more wreck than their crew, however. There are probably a number of factors at work here. In the first place, the position of shipmaster carried with it a number of particular legal responsibilities. As Robin Ward has shown, a shipmaster's relations with the crew, his employer and the wider community were conditioned to some extent by maritime law.[41] Of course, the shipmasters of Sizewell and Thorp also operated within the particular legal framework of the Hethewardmote and the cluster of local expectations it enforced in relation to their rights and duties in the finding, reporting and valuing of shipwrecks.

sized boats, although larger offshore and deep-sea boats might be manned by crews of up to 30 men: see P. Heath, 'North Sea fishing in the fifteenth century', *Northern History*, 3 (1968), pp. 59–60.

37 This year-by-year figure is slightly lower than the aggregate of 46 per cent (above in text). This is because many men did not work as shipmasters in consecutive years, as discussed just below.

38 This was also noted by Bailey, 'Coastal fishing', p. 112.

39 SROI, HD1032/88, mm.

40 M. Kowaleski, 'The demography of maritime communities', p. 94.

41 See R. Ward, *The world of the medieval shipmaster: law, business and the sea, c.1350–c.1450* (Woodbridge, 2009), although the men he studied were engaged in trade rather than fishing.

It is possible that part of this cluster of unspoken customary assumptions gave shipmasters a superior claim to wrecks found at sea.[42] Furthermore, Bailey has shown that not all late medieval shipmasters owned their own boats, but were hired seasonally and contracted to hire crew and take a certain share of the catch.[43] In such a labour market, a shipmaster would have required 'initiative, courage, and physical strength', in Ward's phrase.[44] His local identity would also have been important within the local fishing communities at Sizewell and Thorp: a shipmaster had to have the necessary social contacts with shipowners to get hired in the first place, and he had to be dependable and diligent in order that he might be hired the following year. They thus look very much like the *fidedigni*, or 'trustworthy men' that Ian Forrest has identified in a number of other social contexts.[45] Shipmasters were at the forefront of the maritime community: the matrix of legal, social and professional characteristics possessed by these men seems to have translated into a superior claim on shipwreck.

Porpoises: custom or commercialisation?

I will now consider the ways in which the localised custom of the shipwreck economy was affected by external economic trends in late medieval England. This relationship can be perceived through an analysis of the royal fish presented to the Hethewardmote. As has been noted, the right to have 'royal fish' (sturgeons, whales and porpoises) was often granted and held in tandem with the right of wreck, entitling coastal landowners to take these marine animals when they were found by fishermen. At Sizewell and Thorp there is no definitive record of either a sturgeon or a whale being presented to the Hethewardmote, but there were 59 separate presentments of porpoises during the later fourteenth and fifteenth centuries.[46] These porpoises were subject to a peculiar local custom: rather than being given a monetary value by the jury, porpoises were normally handed over to the Abbey in exchange for a customary payment (four bushels, latterly a quarter) of wheat.[47]

---

42 Interestingly, the texts of maritime custom such as the Laws of Oléron do not mention how wreck found at sea ought to be dealt with. For a transcription of these laws, see T. Twiss (ed.), *The black book of the admiralty*, 4 vols (London, 1871–76), i, pp. 88–131. For an account of maritime custom in the North Sea more generally (which explicitly excludes wreck as part of the 'land law'), see E. Frankot, *Of laws of ships and shipmen: medieval maritime law and its practice in urban northern Europe* (Edinburgh, 2012).

43 Middleton-Stewart, 'Down to the sea in ships', p. 77.

44 Ward, *Medieval shipmaster*, p. 1.

45 See I. Forrest, *The detection of heresy in late medieval England* (Oxford, 2005), pp. 207–30; idem, 'The transformation of visitation in thirteenth-century England', *Past & Present*, 221 (2013), 3–38. His forthcoming project on *Trustworthy Men* will explore this intriguing subject further.

46 A 'great fish' (*magnum pissem*), worth 8s (96d), was found in 1389, and it is certainly possible that it was a sturgeon: SROI, HD 371/1, m. 11r.

47 I have not found evidence of this custom – which remains unnamed in the wreck rolls – being used elsewhere in late medieval East Anglia.

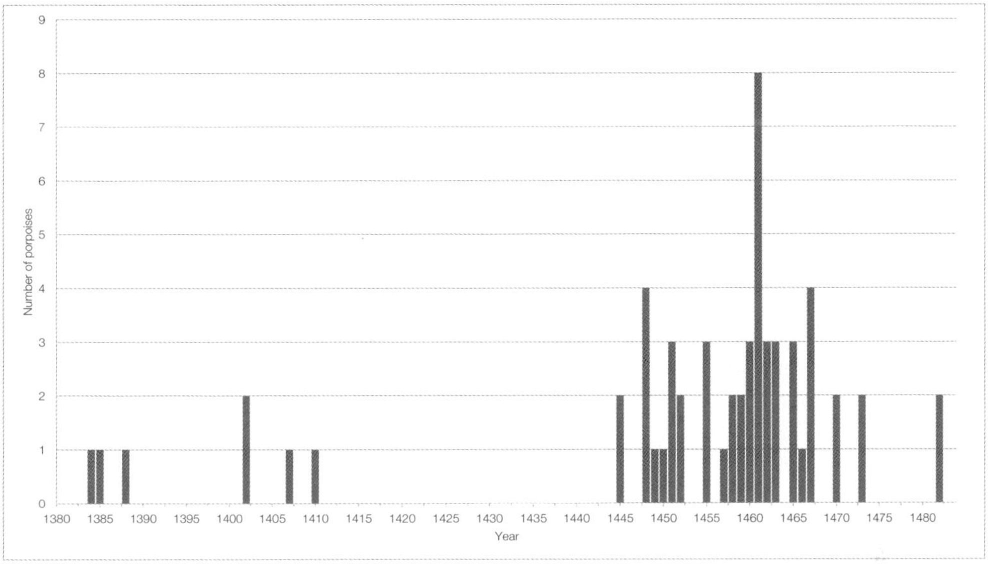

Figure 6.6 Number of porpoises captured, 1377–1482.

Looking at the numbers of porpoises captured in Figure 6.6, the most remarkable feature of the data is how the presentments cluster in the latter half of the fifteenth century. Of the 59 porpoises presented in the wreck rolls during the century c.1380–1480, just seven were caught before 1443. There are several possible – and not mutually exclusive – explanations for this highly visible trend. In the first place, this rise in the capture of porpoises coincided with the recession of the mid-fifteenth century.[48] As Postan himself did so much to show, there was a dramatic reduction in seaborne trade from the beginning of the 1440s, falling to a low in the late 1450s and early 1460s, before the 1470s saw the start of a recovery.[49] This general decline in trade seems to have affected the shipwreck economy at Sizewell and Thorp. As can be seen in Figure 6.2, the annual number of presentments seems to increase in the decades around 1450; perhaps the fishermen were looking for more economic opportunities during a time of slack trade. Yet as we see in Figure 6.3, the average value of wreck presentments stayed very low from the mid-1450s for over a decade. Moreover, the value of fish itself was in a gradual but stark decline over the course

---

48 See R.H. Britnell, 'The economic context', in A.J. Pollard (ed.), *The Wars of the Roses* (Basingstoke, 1995), pp. 41–65; J. Hatcher, 'The great slump of the mid-fifteenth century', in J. Hatcher and R.H. Britnell (eds), *Progress and problems in medieval England: essays in honour of Edward Miller* (Cambridge, 1996), pp. 237–72. See also the classic essay by M.M. Postan, 'The fifteenth century', *Economic History Review*, 9 (1939), pp. 160–67; A.R. Bridbury, *Economic growth: England in the later Middle Ages* (London, 1962).

49 See the tables for cloth, wool, wine and miscellaneous exports in M.M. Postan and E. Miller (eds), *The Cambridge economic history of Europe, vol. II: trade and industry in the Middle Ages* (Cambridge, 1987), p. 242.

of the fifteenth century as a whole, with the price of a thousand herring falling from an average of 16s 9d in 1375–99 (in Yarmouth) to just 4s 10d in 1475–99 (in Walberswick).[50] The increase in porpoise capture may thus represent the response of the fishing community to these rather dire wider economic trends: with the overall value of fish falling, and apparently fewer opportunities to claim high-value wreck objects, the fishermen may have attempted to capture more porpoises in order to augment their returns from fishing voyages.

Furthermore, the particular workings of the local customary exchange of porpoises for wheat at Sizewell and Thorp may also have prompted this increase in their capture during the middle of the fifteenth century. In the first place, there seems to have been a change in the formulation of the custom. From the early 1440s onwards the scribe began to note down where the porpoise was found, and this determined how much wheat it was exchanged for. If it was found on the land a porpoise was worth 4 bushels of wheat, but if it was found at sea it was worth a quarter of wheat (that is, twice as much). It is quite possible that this change – the reason for which, unsurprisingly, but unfortunately, is not recorded in the wreck rolls – prompted an increase in the numbers of porpoise captures. Nonetheless, such a change was probably related to wider monetary pressures. As is well known, the amount of money in circulation in England declined during the 1440s, and credit did not pick up the slack.[51] Recent research has shown, furthermore, that the contraction of money did not just affect bankers and merchants; local rural economies in late medieval England also saw a decline in the availability of credit.[52] The fact that the capture of porpoises increased so markedly from the 1440s onwards suggests that the men of Sizewell and Thorp felt the impact of this contraction in money supply and deliberately sought to capture these animals: unlike other wrecks, the porpoises did not incur a monetary fine, but could be exchanged directly for a commodity. When money and credit were restricted during the mid-fifteenth century, then, the fishermen seem to have creatively adapted a long-standing custom to their own advantage. Capturing porpoises allowed them to profit from a wreck without giving up scarce coinage to the lord.

And, indeed, on the three occasions – once in 1408 and twice in 1480 – when this customary exchange of wheat was not adhered to, it also seems to have benefited the fishermen.[53] Each time this cash exchange happened, the price of the porpoise was fixed at half a mark (80d), creating an expensive fine of 40d.[54] From the perspective

---

50 Bailey, 'Coastal fishing', p. 110. As he points out, this fall is probably exaggerated by artificially high prices recorded in Yarmouth, but the overall decline was nonetheless marked.

51 Hatcher, 'The great slump', p. 244.

52 See C. Briggs, 'The availability of credit in the English countryside, 1400–1480', *Agricultural History Review*, 56 (2008), p. 16 [Table 3]. Briggs stresses that monetary factors were not the sole cause of credit contraction, however, with institutional changes strongly affecting the data, taken from manorial courts.

53 SROI, HD 1032/88, m. 17v.

54 This price of 80d appears to have been a locally fixed value: it was noted down in 1446 when John Goodwyn failed to report the porpoises he captured to the Hethewardmote: SROI, HD1032/88, m. 6r.

of the fisherman who captured the porpoise, it would have been best to break from the customary exchange during years of low wheat prices. This was exactly what happened in 1480, when wheat prices were relatively low, at 69d per quart.[55] The fixed cash value of the porpoise, at 80d, was thus much higher than the equivalent price of the quart of wheat that the fishermen might have received in the customary exchange; in fact, there are reasons to suspect that a porpoise might have fetched an even larger sum. No index of porpoise prices has yet been compiled for the fifteenth century, but contemporary evidence from this region suggests that the market rate was rather higher than the fixed value of 80d that was used in the Hethewardmote: further up the coast at Easton Bavents a porpoise was valued at 9s 2d (110d); in 1478 a porpoise presented by the churchwardens of Walberswick was valued at 12s (144d).[56] John Baxter and John Pykbon, the men who paid cash fines in 1480, therefore received a valuable commodity for a very low fee, and would have been able to make a profit of at least a shilling if they sold the porpoises they had captured. Both men were from long-established families in the area, both served frequently as shipmasters in the Hethewardmote and both claimed substantial amounts of wreck: such considerations, perhaps, were what allowed them to override the normal custom for their own financial gain.

Conclusion

Quantitative analysis of the wreck rolls helps us to speculate on how the local economy in shipwreck at Sizewell and Thorp was connected to much wider economic trends and fluctuations in late medieval England. Undoubtedly the men of these fishing communities were affected in ways that were not recorded – let alone recorded systematically – by patterns of seaborne commerce, politics and piracy, monetary circulation, weather, wages and prices, and the diverse other features of complex medieval economies. And, indeed, at its root, the shipwreck economy was made possible by international maritime trade. The barrels, wainscots, cloths and other shipping material and commercial merchandise that washed ashore on this stretch of the Suffolk coast connected the men of Sizewell and Thorp to national and transnational trends, but this connection was mediated, crucially, through local custom, maritime expertise and local socio-economic structures. Of course, the wreck rolls are not nearly as reliable, nor as comprehensive, as the customs accounts favoured by Postan for analysis of England's trade, which he once described as *terra firma*.[57] Yet in the muddier waters of the wreck rolls we can see some of the

---

55 See the statistical supplement to D.L. Farmer, 'Prices and wages, 1350–1500', in E. Miller (ed.), *The agrarian history of England and Wales. Volume II* (Cambridge, 1991): Appendix D, p. 505.

56 See C. Richmond, *John Hopton: a fifteenth century Suffolk gentleman* (Cambridge, 1981), p. 145, and fn. 171.

57 M.M. Postan, 'English studies of the customs accounts', in M.M. Postan, *Medieval trade and finance* (Cambridge, 1973), p. 353 [first published in *Actes du Quatrième Internationale d'histoire maritime* (Paris, 1962)]. He was referring nostalgically to work such as the essays in E. Power and M.M. Postan (eds), *Studies in English trade in the fifteenth century* (London, 1933).

local effects of the dramatic economic structures described by Postan: as well as their susceptibility to quantitative analysis, the rolls have the 'smack of salt' that his wife and collaborator Eileen Power sought in her imaginings of the fifteenth-century maritime community.[58]

Overall, this chapter has outlined how the dynamics of the shipwreck economy were characterised by the interaction of local custom, maritime expertise and social structures with wider patterns of trade and commerce. In the first place, we saw how the monetary values given to objects issuing from shipwreck were not dependent on the economic logic of supply and demand; rather, valuation was made based upon the expertise of the shipmasters who made up the jury of the Hethewardmote. Secondly, we have seen that these same men were more likely than others to 'find' shipwreck – and more valuable shipwreck at that – not just because of some privilege inherent in the occupation of shipmaster, but because of the wider social qualities that these men possessed within the context of the local fishing communities at Sizewell and Thorp. And, thirdly, we have seen that the strong custom of the Hethewardmote regarding the exchange of porpoises for quantities of wheat in kind changed decisively in the middle of the fifteenth century, during a much wider downturn in the shipping and fishing industries in particular, and in the wider economy and its money supply more generally. Yet, as a means of obtaining wheat, and on the odd occasion as a way of selling the animals for profit, this superficially 'feudal' custom actually provided local fishermen with another financial opportunity. The commerce generated by shipwreck in these maritime communities was veiled in the language of custom, and customs themselves were creatively adapted in the crucible of economic change.

58 E. Power, *Medieval people* (London, 10th edn, 1963), p. 141.

Chapter 7

Custom and competition for woodland resources in early modern High and Low Furness, Lancashire

William D. Shannon

When Postan wrote of 'peripheral regions ... beyond the ancient core of English settlements', regions which 'were remote or inaccessible, or separated from the rest of the country by barriers, geographical or cultural or ethnic', he was not thinking specifically of the Furness district, yet the description fits.[1] Enclosed by the Lakeland Fells to the north and connected to Cumberland to the west and the rest of Lancashire to the east only by the dangerous tidal 'over sands' routes across the Kent and Leven Sands (now called Morecambe Bay), it seemed to Camden in 1586 to be a land that 'the sea hath after a sort violently rent apart from the rest' of the county.[2] As such, it was just the sort of 'desert place' which the monks of Savigny, and their successors the Cistercians, sought out.[3] In time, though, Furness Abbey became the richest monastery in Lancashire and indeed the second richest Cistercian abbey in England: yet, when the abbot surrendered the abbey on 9 April 1537, it was far from clear that Henry VIII had acquired as much of an asset as he might have hoped.[4]

In 1540, three years after the surrender, the lands of the abbey were attached to the Duchy of Lancaster, the private estate of the monarch which held lands in most counties, but particularly in Lancashire, Yorkshire and Lincolnshire.[5] In a well-wooded area such as Furness, the Duchy, as lord of the manor, may well have anticipated that there would be a respectable income to be had from timber sales. A lord, however, could only look to raising revenue from his woods once his tenants' customary rights had been satisfied: and therein lay the problem. 'Custom', as Hoyle has observed, 'served to limit a lord's income from his tenants'. The tenants of Furness Abbey, holding by that peculiarly northern form of tenure known as 'tenant right', which required the tenants

1 M.M. Postan, *The medieval economy and society* (Harmondsworth, 1975), pp. 23–4.

2 William Camden, *Britannia* (1586) (English translation from the original Latin, by Philemon Holland from the 1637 edn, p. 754).

3 J.C. Dickinson, *Furness Abbey* (London, 1987).

4 The National Archives (TNA), E322/91, Deed of Surrender, Furness Abbey, 9 April 1537; Christopher Haigh, *The last days of the Lancashire monasteries and the Pilgrimage of Grace* (Manchester, 1969), pp. 104–8.

5 Robert Somerville, *History of the Duchy of Lancaster, vol. 1 (1265–1603)* (London, 1953), p. 292.

to do military service on the borders against Scotland, had achieved for themselves not only what were in effect estates of inheritance with fixed rents and fines but also collective customary rights which significantly limited the lord's potential income.[6]

Although now part of the county of Cumbria, prior to 1974 the Furness peninsula was within the historic county of Lancashire, traditionally divided into the Furness Fells (or High Furness) and Low (or Plain) Furness. The latter was divided between the abbey's manor, centred on Dalton to the west and the manor of Muchland, while the Fells had been divided in 1160 between the abbey's lands, which stretched from Windermere to Coniston Water, and what was known as the Lancaster moiety, part of the barony of Ulverston, which stretched from the Westmorland border north of Coniston to Ulverston town itself, in which manor the abbey held a moiety.[7] All these lands came to the Crown in 1537, and thence to the Duchy of Lancaster.

Until the 1970s, the Furness peninsula was dominated by the mining and manufacture of iron, based upon rich deposits of haematite, which Furness Abbey had been ideally placed to exploit (Figure 7.1). [8] Whether the monks knew of these resources prior to settling there in 1123 is not known, but the fact that one of the three mines they subsequently operated was at a place called Orgrave, which means 'ore-pit' in Old English, suggests that the mine was there long before the monks.[9] The cartulary or Coucher Book of the abbey, in which copies of all charters and other important documents were kept, contains a quit claim to the abbey of all the rights which Roger of Orgrave had '*in tota mineria ferri in Campo de Orgrave*' (in all the iron mines in the field of Orgrave).[10] There is also a reference to Elliscales, where there was '*minam ferri ad unam astrum sustinendum*' (an iron mine for sustaining one hearth); while the possibility of a third mine is suggested at Marton.[11] In 1292, in a valuation for taxation purposes of the temporalities of the abbey, these iron mines were together worth £6 13s 4d, nearly twice the value of the monks' flocks and herds, and, indeed, over 40 per cent of the total value of their taxable possessions.[12]

Nevertheless, at the time of the Dissolution, the abbey does not seem to have been producing iron commercially; instead, abbey servants were making iron purely for internal consumption by the monks and their tenants.[13] The production method

6 R.W. Hoyle: 'Introduction: custom, improvement and anti-improvement', in R.W. Hoyle (ed.), *Custom, improvement and the landscape in early modern Britain* (Farnham, 2011), pp. 1–38: R.W. Hoyle, 'An ancient and laudable custom: definition and development of tenant right in north-western England in the sixteenth century', *Past & Present*, 116 (1987), pp. 24–55.

7 W. Farrer and J. Brownbill (eds), *Victoria County History of Lancashire, vol. VIII* (London, 1914), *passim*.

8 B.Young, 'Iron ore in Cumbria', in G. Brooks and C. Irwin (eds), *Master of them all: iron making in Cumbria* (Cumbrian Industrial Society, 2007), pp. 5–25.

9 E. Ekwall, *The place-names of Lancashire* (Manchester, 1922), p. 207.

10 Rev. J.C. Atkinson (ed.), *The Coucher Book of Furness Abbey*, vol. 1, part 1 (Chetham Society, 9, 1886) no. xii (3), p. 33: TNA, DL 42/3 Furness Abbey Coucher Book 1412, f. 89.

11 Atkinson, *Coucher Book*, vol. I, no. xiii (5), p. 38: no. xiv (3), p. 43.

12 J.C. Atkinson (ed.), *The Coucher Book of Furness Abbey*, part III (Chetham Society, 14, 1887), no. ccccviii, p. 633.

13 TNA, DL 4/25/13 Tenants of Furness vs Attorney General, 1583: Pleadings and Depositions.

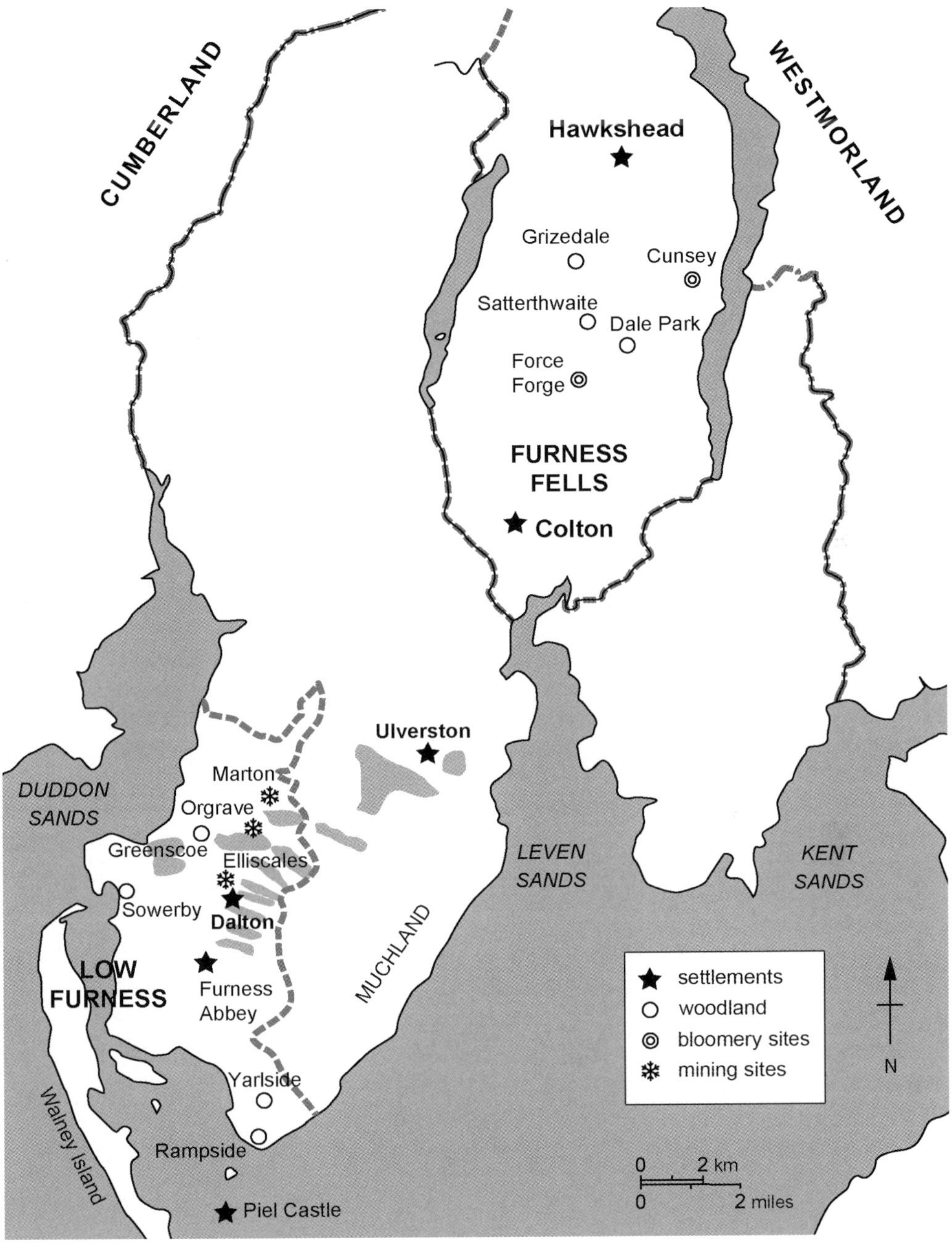

Figure 7.1 Map showing Low Furness and Furness Fells (High Furness).
The location of the main haematite ore-bodies are indicated (from Young, 'Iron Ore in Cumbria'). The outline is taken from Hennet's map of 1829, depicting the coastline before the extensive later land reclamation associated with the development of Barrow-in-Furness.

from earliest times had been the bloomery process, which involved converting the ore directly into wrought iron using a charcoal-fired hearth and employing muscle-powered bellows and hammers to produce a 'bloom' (an unworked mass of iron) which was taken elsewhere to be worked up by a blacksmith as required.[14] The bloomery required large quantities of charcoal, at the rate of around 120 sacks of charcoal per ton of iron produced; and, as charcoal rapidly turns to powder when shaken, it made sense to move the ore to the charcoal rather than vice versa.[15] In addition, as it took perhaps 40 tons of wood to make one ton of charcoal, charcoal production and hence iron production needed of necessity to be located in a well-wooded area.[16] Although the Coucher Book implied that iron in the medieval period had been produced and not just mined at Orgrave, by the time of the Dissolution it seems clear that the abbey's bloomeries were all located in Furness Fells. Almost certainly this was because, by the sixteenth century, the woods of Low Furness, long under pressure, were now reserved for things other than charcoal, as the following section will show.

Furness on the eve of the Dissolution

If we are to believe the claims made by tenants of the Duchy in a court case of 1583, a generation or so after the Dissolution – and that is a big 'if' – then the abbots had been generous landlords and their tenants had enjoyed significant benefits. In that court case, which will be discussed later, tenants came forward, one after the other, to swear that, for example, they had free education for their sons, with free school meals:

> Divers of the children of the sayd Tennantes had lib'tie to come to the scole in the said monasterie Where they were taught without any payment. And that this Deponent with diverse of the sones of the sayd Tenanntes, comynge to the same schole had meat & drinke for one meal a day in the sayd monasterie every day they came to the same Scole.[17]

Not only that, but if a son proved apt in learning, 'he was chosen to be mooncke beffore anye other or els to serve some other offyce within the said monasterie'.[18]

The tenants had paid their rents in kind, not cash, delivering grain and young animals to the abbey, and for entry fine had paid only a penny, known as God's

14 Alfred Fell, *The early iron industry of Furness and district* (Ulverston, 1908).

15 B.G. Awty, 'Force Forge in the seventeenth century', *Transactions of the Cumberland and Westmorland Antiquarian and Archaeological Society*, 51 (1979–80), pp. 97–112.

16 Around two-thirds of the cost of iron making in Cumbrian bloomery forges in the seventeenth century was the cost of charcoal: see B.G. Awty and C.B. Phillips,'The Cumbrian bloomery forge in the seventeenth century and forge equipment in the charcoal iron industry', *Newcomen Society Transactions*, 51 (1979–80), pp. 25–40.

17 TNA, DL 4/25/13 Tenants of Furness vs Attorney General, 1583: Pleadings and Depositions. See transcription, Thomas West, *The antiquities of Furness* (London 1774), Appendix VIII.

18 TNA, DL 1/31 W 17 24 Eliz, Bill, tenants of Low Furness vs John Brograve 1583.

Penny. The abbots at their own expense had repaired breaches to the sea walls of Walney Island, the low-lying island six miles long that was separated from the Furness peninsula by a narrow tidal channel, and which was in constant danger of being overwhelmed by the sea. The tenants had the right to take 'Sufficient Tymber trowse and tynsell' for the maintenance of the sea walls, as well as the usual 'botes' – hedgebote, haybote and ploughbote – and they also had liberty to cut gorse and bracken on the abbey's wastes for their livestock.[19] In return for delivering corn to the abbey they had drawn a weekly allowance of bread and ale and had been entitled to 'wurthinge' (dung) from the abbey stables, without which 'the same ground wold not have yelded any wheat' – but, most remarkably of all, they also had free iron.[20] Deponent after deponent claimed that they had used to receive an annual dole to be shared among themselves of eight or ten 'clots' or blooms of iron from the abbey's bloomeries, each weighing 14 stone. This adds up to not far short of a ton, which would have been worth £5 or more a year. However, it was not to be sold – it could only be used on their tenements 'for the mayntenance of their plowes and husbandrie'.[21] Assuming that the monks themselves also had certain requirements for iron, it is clear that there was fairly substantial, albeit non-commercial, production going on in the early sixteenth century; yet, at the time of the Dissolution, neither the abbot's own rental nor the *Valor Ecclesiasticus* nor the report of the Commissioners put any value on the mines as such.[22] On the other hand, the Commissioners regarded the woods of Low Furness as a considerable asset, with nearly 300 acres of fair oaks for timber.

By contrast, they reckoned the extensive woods of Furness Fells to have no value as timber, noting that those woods had been used by the abbots solely for the making of charcoal for the bloomeries:

> Also there is moche wood growing in Furneysfells in the mounteynes there, as Byrk, Holey, Asshe, Ellers, Lyng, lytell short Okes and other Underwood, but no tymber of any valewe, wherin the Abbotts of the same late Monastery have ben accustomed to have a Smythey, and sometyme two or thre, kepte for making of Yron to th'use of their Monastery.[23]

The Commissioners therefore decided to lease the woods of Furness Fells for £20 a year to two men who almost certainly, prior to the Dissolution, had been operating the bloomeries there as servants of the abbey:

---

19 TNA, DL 44/180 1568 Low Furness. 'Tymber' means wood of building quality, 'trowse' refers to brushwood, fallen boughs and the like, while 'tynsell' is smaller still, essentially hedge trimmings. The 'botes' refer to the rights for a tenant to take sufficient wood for necessary work on or repairs to hedges, fences and ploughs.

20 TNA, DL 4/25/13 1583: Deposition of John Richardson of Rampside.

21 Ibid.

22 SC 12/9/73 Furness Abbey Rent Roll, temp Henry VIII (c.1533): *Valor Ecclesiasticus tempore Henrici VIII*, vol. 5 (London 1825), pp. 269–70: SC 11/376 Survey of Possessions of Furness Abbey 1537.

23 SC 11/376 Survey, 1537.

> And so nowe the said Commissyoners have letten unto William Sandes and John Sawrey as moche of the said woodes, that is to saye of Byrkes, Ellers, Hasells, old rotten trees and other underwoods, as wyll maynteyne iij Smytheys, for the whiche they ar content and agreed to paye yerely to the Kinges Highnes, as long as hit shall please his grace they should occupy the same… xx^{li}.[24]

In leasing the woods in this way the Commissioners were, in effect, granting Sandys and Sawrey a monopoly on the making of iron in Furness.

The location of these smithies or bloomeries is not specified in the Commissioners' report, but a bill of 1549 informs us that Sandys and Sawrey had been operating smithies at Force Forge and Cunsey.[25] Both are located on fast-moving streams. At a later date water-powered smelting and refining took place on these sites, and it may be that even at this early date Sandys and Sawrey were employing water-powered bellows and hammers, in what are called bloomsmithies rather than bloomeries, suggesting a larger-scale, more commercial operation, one involving continuous production rather than the seasonal campaigns of the earlier bloomeries. Although this is only speculation, such operations would have involved a substantial increase in the demand for what were known as 'Colingwoddes' – wood from which charcoal was made. On the other hand, this may not have been the ideal time to invest in large-scale commercial iron-making, as the market was changing. England had recently become self-sufficient in iron as a result of a huge increase in domestic production based especially in the Weald and using the new finery process, which involved melting the ore before reworking it into bars.[26] By the 1560s, as finery production continued to expand, the price of iron fell and bloomeries and bloomsmithies went into decline. But the Furness producers nevertheless still had to find that 'wood rent' of £20 a year for the Duchy. However, before considering how that problem was to be resolved, it is necessary to review the 'rights' of the former abbey tenants in both Low and High Furness as they evolved and became fixed during the half century after the Dissolution, in particular with regard to how they impacted upon the Duchy's hopes of securing value from the former monastic woods.

The customs of Furness and the Duchy woodland surveys

An undated bill in the National Archives, probably from early 1557, tells of a serious tidal surge the previous December, affecting Walney Island and the adjacent coast, which had drowned cattle and washed away houses and barns, destroying the corn and hay therein.[27] This, we learn later, was despite the 'greate Somes of money [which] have been allowed by the Quenes ma[jes]tie and her Progenitors towards

24 Ibid.

25 TNA, DL 1/27/R8 3 Edw 6: transcribed in West, *Furness*, pp. 181–3.

26 P. King, 'The production and consumption of bar iron in early modern England and Wales', *Economic History Review*, 58 (2005), pp. 1–33.

27 TNA, DL1/40/W1 Bill, Walney Island, n.d. Philip & Mary (probably 1557).

the reparacon of the Walles and Bankes of the said Iland'.[28] The result was that the tenants had defaulted on their rents, but now they petitioned for a commission to survey the damage in the hope that their rents would be abated. It may be that the survey took place, but, as was the way with the Duchy Chamber, proceedings would have foundered with the death of Mary in November 1558, and would have required restarting under the new queen. However, in mid-1559 another event of significance for the tenants of Furness took place, with the appointment by the Duchy of John Braddyll as Surveyor of Woods in the North Parts.[29] The background to this appointment was a widespread concern dating back to the time of Henry VIII over what was perceived to be a very real problem regarding the survival of the woodlands of England, as a result of which the 1544 Bill for the Preservation of Woods had been passed.[30] Whether this 'Timber Famine' had any reality outside a few restricted areas in the south of England has been the subject of much debate among historians, with Rackham dismissive of what he saw as a myth.[31] Nevertheless, Hammersley, while accepting that there may have been no general crisis of timber supply, argued that in places there were indeed real shortages both of timber and of fuel, the main problem being the lack of any regional or national market in wood.[32] More recently, Warde has shown that governments across Europe at this time were starting to regulate woodland, even though evidence for a general, as opposed to localised, problem is lacking.[33] Nevertheless, as part of this international trend, as early as 1532 the Duchy of Lancaster had appointed its first Surveyor of Woods.[34] However, in 1559, presumably reflecting an ever growing concern about the supposed 'Timber Famine', the role was divided between two officers, split north and south of the Trent – and Braddyll, appointed to the northern post, was tasked specifically with 'the savegarde encrease mayntenance & good keeping' of the woods as well as 'the preservacyon and encrease of the springe of the same'.[35] In other words, his prime accountability was to ensure the sustainability of the Duchy's woods north of the Trent, for strategic national reasons.[36]

---

28 TNA, DL 6/12 Draft Decree. Low Furness, 6 Eliz (1564).

29 TNA, DL 42/33 Warrant appointing John Braddyll Surveyor of all woods beyond the water of Trent, 1559.

30 *The Bill for the Preservation of the Woods*, 35 Henry VIII, cap. XVII (1544).

31 O. Rackham, *The history of the countryside* (London, 1986), p. 91.

32 G. Hammersley, 'The Crown woods and their exploitation in the sixteenth and seventeenth centuries', *Bulletin of the Institute of Historical Research*, 30 (1957), pp. 136–61.

33 P. Warde, 'Fear of wood shortage and the reality of the woodland in Europe c.1450–1850', *History Workshop Journal*, 62 (2006), pp. 28–57. See also P. Warde and T. Williamson, 'Fuel supply and agriculture in post-medieval England', *Agricultural History Review*, 62 (2014), pp. 61–82.

34 Somerville, *Duchy of Lancaster*, pp. 310–11.

35 TNA, DL 42/23 Warrant appointing John Braddyll Surveyor in the North Parts 20 June 1559: contemporary copy in Lancashire Archives DDBR 8/1.

36 The greater part of the Duchy woodland in the North Parts was in Lancashire and Yorkshire, although others were in Staffordshire, Derbyshire, Cheshire, Cumberland and Northumberland.

The appointment of Braddyll led in 1559 to the first of a series of written surveys carried out for the Duchy between then and 1610, which together allow us considerable insight into the competition for resources within the Furness district, as parcel of the Duchy's woods. The 1559 survey was carried out between August and November, and Braddyll's report covers some woods in Cheshire (Halton Park) and a significant number in Yorkshire (including Knaresborough and Pontefract), as well as those within the bounds of the present counties of Cumbria (the former monastic lands of Low Furness, Furness Fells, Cartmel and Conishead) and Lancashire (the four forests of Quernmore, Wyresdale, Myerscough and Bowland).[37] The primary focus was upon the availability of building timber to meet the present and future needs of the Duchy and its tenants, as well as upon the availability of underwood to meet the needs of the tenants for fuel and for browse. Braddyll's work is detailed and thorough, and is clearly based upon personal visits to the woods concerned. His methodology, though, is not systematic enough to allow ready statistical analysis, while his style is somewhat discursive and his terminology not consistent. Nevertheless, we learn from the survey that there were in the whole district 5,876 acres of woodland, of which 69 per cent were in Furness Fells (Table 7.1). These, it should be noted, are local customary acres, not statute acres, so represent something like 5,000 hectares, or about half the size of the Forest of Dean – a very significant potential asset for the Duchy.

In Low Furness, Braddyll noted various woods which had belonged to the abbey since the time of Edward III.[38] The most significant of these was Sowerby Wood, containing 220 acres, wherein the underwoods were coppiced and enclosed, with 10 acres of two years' growth, 50 acres of six years, 60 acres of eight years, and 100 acres of 14 years' growth, clearly demonstrating current good woodland management, involving cropping on a regular rotation. Adding 200 acres at Rampside and a further 156 acres in some of the smaller woods gave 576 acres in all, a major asset for the Crown – at least potentially. However, it may well have been fear on the part of the tenants that the Duchy was surveying these woods intent upon extracting value that led them to press on with their petition, leading to a commission and then in 1564 to a decree in the Duchy court. This would seem to have been the outcome of negotiation rather than an imposition from above, and its key conclusions were that the tenants rather than the Crown should henceforth take full responsibility for repairs to the sea wall, while in return the Duchy confirmed the customs of Low Furness.[39]

The decree of 1564 recognised that the tenants either held their land by copy of court roll, according to the custom of the manor, or by the custom of tenant right.[40] The tenants were required collectively to provide three score men 'for the defence of the haven and castle callyd the Peele of Fowdraye [Piel Castle] or otherwise upon

37 TNA, DL 43/17/5 Survey of Woods (North Parts), 1559.

38 Atkinson, *Coucher Book*, no. lxiv (133b), p. 175: License by King Edward III to Furness to make parks in Ramesheved, Soureby, Ronheved, Grenescow, Hagg, Milnewood, Clayf et Fournes-fell.

39 TNA, DL 6/12 Draft Decree. Low Furness, 6 Eliz (1564).

40 Ibid.

Table 7.1
Survey of Duchy Woods in the North Parts, 1559

Lordship	*Wood*	*Customary Acres*	
Low Furness	Ramsyde	200	
	Sawerby	220	
	Bothparke	20	
	Rangldwoode	16	
	Grenescoughe	60	
	Dearparke	60	
	TOTAL Lowe Furneis		576
Furness Fells	Leggbarrowcragg	260	
	Hawkshedd	400	
	Elt[er]wat[er] | P[ar]ke | & Shelwarthe	600	
	Brathow	310	
	Soray	800	
	Ilchowse	12	
	Sat[er]thwaite	800	
	Daleparke	60	
	Graithwaite	60	
	Cunsoclose	80	
	Colton	180	
	Haverthwate	480	
	TOTAL Furneis Fells		4042
Cartmel	Cartmell		82
Conishead	Conyshed		4
Quernmore	Quernemore Parke		107
	Quernemore Foreste		145
Wyresdale	Wyresdale Foreste		75
Myerscough	Myrescough Park		76
	Myrescough Foreste		272
Leagram	Lathgrym Park		112
Bowland	Boland Foreste		341
Radholme	Radome Park		44
	GRAND TOTAL		5876

Note: The individual woods within the lordships are only shown for Low Furness and Furness Fells (names of woods are spelled as in the original document).

the Bordres againste Scotland'.[41] It then went on to fix and make certain the rents and fines of the burgages of the copyholders of the town of Dalton-in-Furness, which had been the main town belonging to the abbey (Figure 7.1), while the copyholders and customary tenants of Low Furness were to have all their necessary timber, housebote and ploughbote, with their fines of what used to be God's Penny now being fixed at two years' rent. Perhaps the key point, though, was that all customary tenants were now confirmed in their tenements, and any demise or lease which had been made by the Duchy Council for a term of years was declared 'frustrate voide and of none effecte'.[42] In a note on the last page, the clerk who drafted the decree made a reference to 'freehold', which he then corrected to read 'customary freeholde'. Such a term had no meaning in law, but well suggests the fact that these tenants, irrespective of what might have previously been the case, had now secured what were to all intents and purposes freeholds.

Not long after this decree – and perhaps not unrelated to it – Braddyll was again involved in a major woodland survey, this time as one of four commissioners appointed in June 1568. Unlike the earlier work, this survey was to be concerned solely with the woods of Low Furness (552 acres) and Furness Fells (4,090 acres), together with the manor of Borrowdale to the north, in the old county of Cumberland, and formerly part of the possessions of Furness Abbey, although not covered in the earlier survey (231 acres).[43] While their certificate says they visited each manor and surveyed and viewed all the woods, in fact the commissioners tell us they only did so as far 'as tyme wolde permitt', and it seems fairly clear that the data in their report comes largely from the sworn testimony of named tenants of the queen, rather than from the direct observations of the commissioners themselves.[44] A more significant difference from 1559, though, was the greater commercial edge to the survey, the commissioners now being required to ascertain exactly what rights the tenants claimed with a view to their reporting back on 'what woodes and underwoodes ... maye conveniently be spared and remaine to be used and disposed at our pleasure, Leavinge to our saide tenanntes ther according to their Lawfull right sufficient woodes'.[45]

The brief has thus moved significantly from an idealistic one of preservation and sustainability to a practical one of realising the potential asset value of the woods. The resultant report must have been something of a disappointment. In it, the commissioners acknowledged the tenants' rights in the woodland, noting that the recent incursion of the sea had required 300 trees, 'besyde trowse' to recover the situation. Given this, the commissioners concluded: 'Wee cannot perceive or otherwise see how any manner of wooddes within the said lordeshipe maye conveniently be

41 Ibid. Piel Castle had been built by the monks of Furness in the fourteenth century to protect their deep water harbour and so safeguard their possessions in Ireland and the Isle of Man. It was regarded as of particular strategic importance by the Tudors, as Lambert Simnel's expedition had landed there from Ireland in 1487, intent upon deposing Henry VII.

42 TNA, DL 6/12 Draft Decree. Low Furness, 6 Eliz (1564).

43 TNA, DL 44/180 Survey of Woods of Borrowdale, Low Furness and Furness Fells, 1568.

44 Ibid.

45 Ibid.

spared.' In other words, from the Duchy's perspective, money definitely did not grow on trees in these parts.

This must have been a matter of some considerable concern to the Duchy from a commercial standpoint. Yet soon its judicial arm again upheld the rights of the tenants of Low Furness in another decree.[46] The occasion for this was the fact that a certain Leonard Rawlinson had in 1561 been given a lease by the Duchy for 21 years for certain lands which had been parcel of the possessions of the abbey. Following the 1564 decree he had delivered up his lease, but the tenants of Low Furness had then collectively petitioned the Duchy Council to ensure the lease was not remade. The Council agreed this in a decree of 1573, noting that the tenants were required to maintain the sea walls at their own cost and to provide 60 men for the defence of Piel Castle and against Scotland. At the same time the Duchy again confirmed that the customs of tenant right should be upheld – although these were not in fact defined in this decree, other than that they should have all their necessary timber.

Perhaps this lack of clarity as to just what was covered by the phrase 'accordinge to the Lawe and custome used for coppiehouldes and tenenteright' contained in the earlier decree may have led, ten years later, to a further challenge being mounted, this time by John Brograve, who had been made Attorney General for the Duchy in 1580. The story has been dealt with at length by the first historian of Furness, the Jesuit Father Thomas West, who saw Brograve as committing 'an act of injustice and oppression to the country of Low Furness, and setting a precedent iniquitous, and ruinous to many other parts of the kingdom'; but this is to overstate the case.[47] Brograve had in 1582 'obtained a lease of the provisions that had been formerly paid to the late dissolved monastery'.[48] His lease was for 21 years and he had agreed to pay the Duchy £90 a year for it: but when he attempted to exercise his apparent rights under that lease the tenants objected and again appealed to the Duchy court.[49] In their petition they admitted that the abbot's tenants had paid the monastery provisions of calves, sheep, wheat, barley and oats, but countered with all the benefits that they had received from the monastery, including weekly hand-outs of bread and ale, not to mention all the iron needed for their implements, which benefits were said to have equalled or exceeded the value of the provisions. They further argued that the provisions had in any case been replaced with money rents and fines when Henry VIII took over the abbey's possessions. In reply, Brograve claimed that the benefits provided by the abbots were 'merely of benevolence and devotion towards their neighbours, which at their pleasure they lawfully might have withdrawn', and that neither King Henry nor his successors (nor, by implication Brograve himself) were obliged to make any recompense for these provisions.[50] He went on to claim that the decree of 1564 had in no way absolved the tenants from paying these provisions. The Duchy court reacted by setting up a commission to enquire 'concernynge dyvers

46 TNA, DL 6/21 Draft Decree Concerning the Customs of Low Furness, 1573.

47 West, *Furness*, pp. 122–9, Appendix VIII.

48 Ibid., p. 122.

49 TNA, DL 1/31 W 17 24 Eliz, Bill, tenants of Low Furness vs John Brograve 1583.

50 West, *Furness*, p. 128.

and sondrye rentes and services of all the Coppieholders and Customarye Tenantes called Tenante Righte'.[51] In their responses to the interrogatories, the deponents on behalf of both Brograve and the tenants largely told the same story as before, emphasising that their benefits had been granted by the abbots as of right, not of benevolence, in return for the provisions. These benefits, as well as the provisions, had since been set aside in return for money rents. In the face of this, the Duchy court found for the tenants against the Attorney General, and required Brograve to deliver up his lease to be cancelled.[52]

However, this still left obscure the details as to what exactly the customs of Furness were now, as opposed to what they might have been prior to the Dissolution: and so, in 1586, local juries charged with setting out those customs were set up in both High and Low Furness:[53]

> You shall sett downe indifferently suche Customs and orders as shalbe agreable with your Custome of late confirmed under Seale and shalbe for the wealth and commoditie aswell of your neighboures as your selves and the well governement of the same, So the same be not in any wise prediuciall nor hurtfull to her Majestie her highnes heires and successors.

In their verdicts, the formula used by the jury is interesting – 'our custome is, and it is also ordered and sett downe …'. This appears to suggest that the jury, while maintaining the fiction that these were all ancient customs, were in fact now making them permanent by the very act of writing them down. This reinforces a point made by Hoyle, Falvey and others that custom, which almost by definition is a matter of memory, unwritten and transmitted orally (and hence liable to change and evolve over time) was in this period increasingly contested, with both landlords and tenants coming to prefer the certainty of a written custumal.[54] The details of the now-agreed customs varied slightly between the two parts of Furness, but in both cases they were divided into two lists, '*pro regina*' and '*pro tenentibus*', and in both cases the focus was upon inheritance customs, showing very clearly that these were indeed estates of inheritance. There was, however, one major constraint: although tenants were free to sell their tenements, providing they informed the steward and providing the incomer paid the fine, they could not divide their properties because of the problems which that would present in terms of the obligation placed upon each tenant-right tenant from north Lancashire to Northumberland – namely to provide a man-at-arms for

---

51 TNA, DL 4/25/13, Commission, Interrogatories and Depositions, Furness, 1583.

52 TNA, DL 6/32 Draft Decree, Low Furness 1583.

53 TNA, DL 44/398 Verdict of the Jurors of Low Furness, 1586: TNA, DL 44/398 Verdict of the Jurors of High Furness, 1586.

54 Hoyle, 'Introduction', pp. 1–38; R.W. Hoyle, 'Cromwell v Taverner: landlords, copyholders and the struggle to control memory in mid-sixteenth-century Norfolk', pp. 39–64; Heather Falvey, 'The articulation, transmission and preservation of custom in the forest community of Duffield (Derbyshire)', pp. 65–100: all in R.W. Hoyle (ed.), *Custom, improvement and the landscape in early modern Britain* (Farnham, 2011).

service on the Borders when called upon.[55] In addition, the new custumals made it clear that the bailiff must deliver necessary timber to tenants, although the wording differed slightly, with the tenants of High Furness not being permitted to take timber without leave nor sell underwoods, while those in Low Furness did not so much have the right to necessary timber as the duty to maintain their houses in good repair: if they did not, they were to have no timber.

Soon after these customs had been clearly set down, yet another survey of the woods in the North Parts was undertaken, this time by Edward Braddyll, who had recently taken over from his father as Surveyor of Duchy Woods north of the Trent.[56] A copy of an order dated February 1579 in an Auditor's book records Edward's commission in very similar terms to that of his father 20 years earlier, again with the notional emphasis upon preservation of the woods.[57] But in his first survey everything was given a monetary value, the different types of underwoods at so much the acre, while oaks were valued at so much the tree. However, no totals were given, either by lordship or overall, and attempts to calculate them now are somewhat frustrated by the fact that, in some places at least, Braddyll seems to have used a count of six score to the hundred.[58] Nevertheless, what we see in more detail than ever before was just how little value the Duchy could obtain from its woods in Low Furness.

First, at Rampside, there were 200 acres of wood with 250 old oaks – but they 'hath bene topt from tyme to tyme, which Topps hath bene gyven away by the keaper thereof ... for Fyrewoode agaynste Crystmas'.[59] In the last eight years, 50 trees had been taken by the keeper for the tenants' use, while the underwoods were said to be worth nothing. At Sowerby the 220 acres contained 750 small (oak) saplings, meaning young trees not fully grown, suggesting a regime of coppicing without standards – but all were 'reserved for the repaire of the tenantes howses there by custome ... and for the mainetenance of the Sea bankes when nede requirethe'.[60] A number of smaller woods between them had a further 330 saplings plus underwood, again reserved as above.

There was to be a gap of nearly 20 years before these woods were next looked at, in a survey of 1608 which has been bound in the same volume as the 1587 survey.[61] This time the surveyor was one Leonard Houghton, and his work was clearly heavily based upon the earlier work. Coincidentally, the abbey manor of Furness had just been sold off, as was the moiety of Ulverston the following year, as part of James I's policy of disposing of Crown property.[62] Indeed, the new survey was itself

---

55 For Border Service, see A.J.L. Winchester, *The harvest of the hills: rural life in northern England and the Scottish Borders, 1400–1700* (Edinburgh, 2000), pp. 16–17.

56 TNA, DL 42/114 Survey of Woods 1587.

57 TNA, DL 42/46 Auditor's Enrolment Book, 24–29 Eliz 1. Cited in Somerville, *Duchy*, i, p. 311.

58 'CCl old smale scrud okes after the Raite of vi score to the hundrethe', TNA, DL 42/114, f. 4.

59 Ibid.

60 Ibid.

61 DL 42/114 Survey of Woods 1608.

62 There is a considerable literature on this subject, but note in particular R.W. Hoyle, 'Shearing the hog: the reform of the estates c.1598–1640', in R.W. Hoyle (ed.), *The estates of the English Crown 1558–1640* (Cambridge, 1992), pp. 204–62.

commissioned as part of the comprehensive review of all Crown woods ordered in December 1607, as part of what became known as 'The Great Survey', a planned enquiry into all aspects of Crown land and property, unfortunately never completed.[63] However, Houghton's work was nowhere near as thorough as that which had gone before. For some woods only the acreage is given, together with a brief description but no numbers of trees. Elsewhere, values were put on the trees or the underwoods, but this was not done systematically. What makes this survey different from the earlier ones, though, was the commentary, which reveals throughout the north of England a level of apparent depredation not previously reported – although this did not apply to Furness, where Houghton had little new to say. Nevertheless, taken as a whole, the report must have caused some consternation in the Duchy court, for yet another survey was commissioned less than 18 months later.[64]

This time the net was cast a little wider, aiming to ensure that no wood held of the Crown, whether 'by Lease, Coppie, or lives, Court-role or customary Tenaunte right', was excluded. Not only was every tenant of every wood named, but the number of timber trees, decayed trees and saplings was given, together with an average value for every tree, a total value for each wood and totals for each lordship, in both cases including the underwoods, valued by the load.[65] However, acreages were not given apart from in Low Furness, where, uniquely, detailed scale maps accompanied the written survey for four of these woods: Greenscoe, Sowerby (Figure 7.2), Yarlside and Rampside. The 1610 surveyors were Robert Treswell and Abraham Allen, the former of whom was the son of the well-known Tudor surveyor and map-maker Ralph Treswell (c.1540–1616/17).[66] Whether the original intention was to map all the woods or not is not known. It may be, rather, that a cartographically conscious commissioner surveyed Low Furness, while a less-conscious colleague did the other lordships: and the probability is that the author of the maps is Treswell. At this date Treswell was both Somerset Herald, a role he had occupied since 1597, and Surveyor General of Woods South of the Trent, a task which he went on from 1611 to share with the notable cartographer John Norden, the author of the *The Surveiors Dialogue*, with Treswell taking responsibility between Trent and Thames and Norden south of the Thames.[67] Why Treswell was asked to carry out the 1610 project for the Duchy, when he clearly had so much to do further south, is a mystery, but one possible explanation is that it reflected dissatisfaction in the Duchy over the quality of Houghton's 1608 work. Indeed, what is striking about Treswell and Allen's report, apart from the maps, is the significantly lower, but perhaps far more realistic, values put by them upon timber and other trees compared with Edward Braddyll's survey of 1587.

63 *VCH* vol. 8, pp. 312, 350; H. Lawrence, 'John Norden and his colleagues: surveyors of Crown lands', *The Cartographic Journal*, 22 (1985), pp. 54–6.

64 TNA, DL 43/17/12 Lancashire Woods 1610.

65 The survey has been summarised in considerable detail in *VCH*, vol. 2, pp. 449–53. See also R. Cunliffe Shaw, *The royal forest of Lancaster* (Preston, 1956), p. 73.

66 *ODNB*, Treswell, Ralph (c.1540–1616/17), painter-stainer and surveyor.

67 TNA, LR 2/1 Entry book of warrants etc. to Robert Treswell, surveyor general of woods south of the Trent, 1609–1630. See also Lawrence, 'John Norden and his colleagues', pp. 54–6.

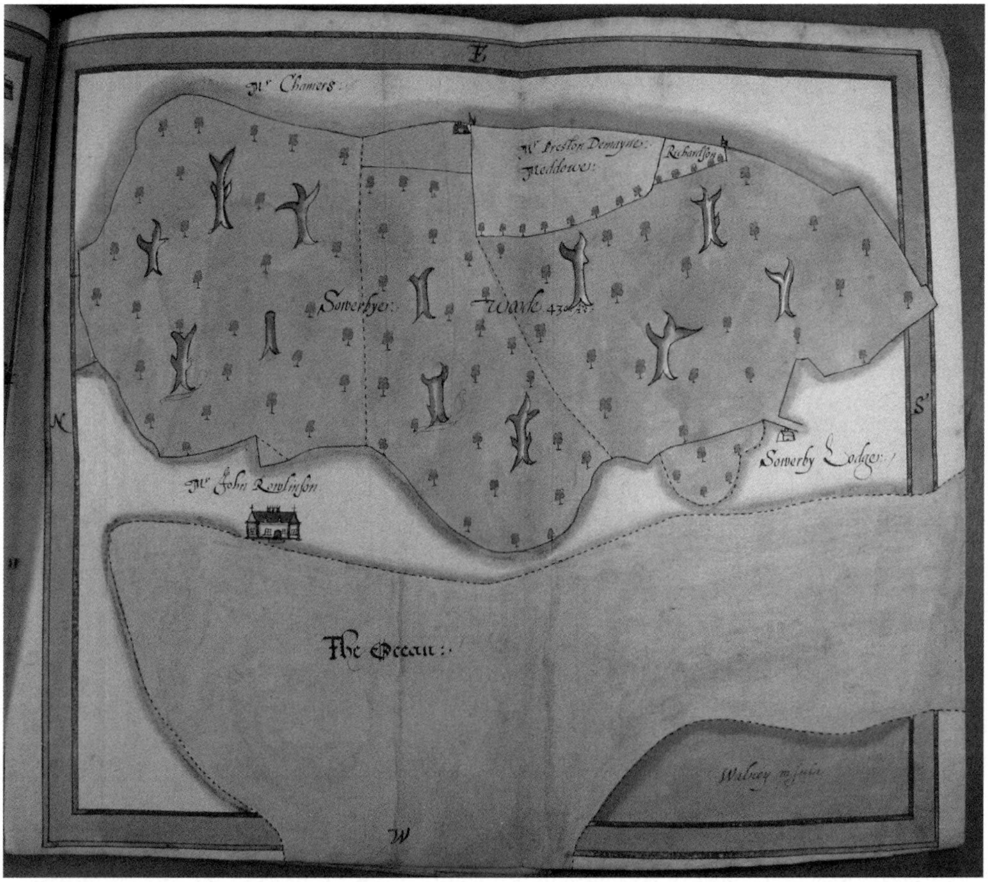

Figure 7.2 Sowerby Wood, from Survey of Lancashire Woods by Robert Treswell, 1610. The map shows an area of approximately 6 km^2. East is at the top, and the tip of Walney Island is shown at the bottom, separated from the mainland of Low Furness by the Walney Channel, here described as 'The Ocean'. There is no scale on this map, but the adjacent page, showing Greenscoe, has both a scale and a compass rose. Note that the large trees appear to be depicted as pollards, their branches having been lopped for fodder. TNA DL 43/17/12 reproduced with permission of the National Archives.

The summary for the whole of Low Furness showed that the woods were now assessed as being worth £232. There was just one problem, namely the by-now-settled customary rights of the tenants, by which they 'clayme by custome the benefit of the said woodes bothe for mainteyning the Island from over flowing of the sea. And also for the reperacons of necessary buildinges, house bootes and ploughe bootes'.[68] In effect, once again it would appear that the woods had no actual monetary value to

68 TNA, DL 43/17/12.

the Duchy – while, of course, the union of the crowns now meant that the Crown was not even getting military service in return any more.

Treswell and Allen's commission coincided with a change in attitude to the Crown estates, moving from exploitation to disposal. The resultant progress in land sales and disafforestation, as well as long leasing and copyhold enfranchisement, meant that, nationally, there was very little left by the time of the Civil War.[69] Nevertheless, an act of 1649 set out a programme to value all the remaining manors of the Crown and Duchy prior to selling them at a rate set at 13 times their annual value.[70] By 1656, 39 counties had been surveyed, including Lancashire, but these surveys add little to our knowledge of the Duchy's woods.[71] For Low Furness, the sole income which parliament, as successors to the Duchy, was getting from the woods was a 'greenhew' rent, a 2d customary payment per holding for the right to lop trees for browse for tenants' cattle, which added to a mere £1 14s 6d a year for the whole of the manor out of a total rental of over £1,000. No individual wood is named in the survey apart from Rampside, the herbage of which had been leased in 1584 for 31 years, and again in 1587 for a further 40 years to follow the 31.[72] There was said to be 'about eight years' of the lease remaining unexpired at the time of the survey and the wood, at that date held by 'Mr John Knype of Rampside (a Papist and under siquistration)', was described as being 'enclosed with a good hedg, and ... conteyneth ... forty Acres of brushy and scrubby ground', worth perhaps £12, to be sold after the expiry of the lease.[73]

Today, Rampside Wood has disappeared without trace into fields of pasture on the outskirts of Barrow-in-Furness, as has Yarlside, while Greenscoe Wood has largely been undermined by quarries. Only Sowerby Wood, which appears to have been understood from the sixteenth century to have been set aside in perpetuity to provide timber for the sea defences, remains a broadleaf wood, albeit fairly thinly planted.[74] Despite more than 100 years of surveys and valuations, the Duchy had found itself incapable of ever realising any significant return from its woods. In the competition for the woodland resources of Low Furness, custom – though not necessarily ancient custom – had been the clear winner.

Competition for resources in Elizabethan High Furness

The detail of the conflict in the Fells was a little different to that of Low Furness, but, despite the significantly greater acreage of woods, the outcome for the Duchy was broadly similar. Right from Braddyll's first survey of 1559 it had been claimed that

69 See Hoyle (ed.), *The estates of the English Crown*, especially chapter 9, Hoyle, 'Shearing the hog', pp. 204–62.

70 S.J. Madge, *The Domesday of Crown lands: a study of the legislation, surveys and sales of royal estates under the commonwealth* (London, 1938).

71 These surveys can be found in TNA, E 317.

72 TNA, E317 Lancs/14 Furness 1650.

73 Ibid.

74 Fell, *Iron industry of Furness*, pp. 121–2.

there was little or no value to be had by the Duchy, first because it was claimed that the 400 or so acres of underwood, young and old oaks at Coniston, Waterhead and Tarn Hows, were all needed for the smithies. Of the other woods in the Furness Fells, including 260 acres of underwood at Legbarrow Crag, 600 acres at Elterwater Park and Skelwith, 310 acres at Brathay and 800 acres within the bailiwick of Sawrey, there was said to be no building timber available, as such timber trees as there were 'growe in such Skarrs, Cragges & hills as no carriage can go'.[75] So Braddyll concluded that the only value that the Crown could obtain from all these woods was from charcoal. The problem was that exclusive rights to that charcoal had already in effect been given away to Sandys and Sawrey for a mere £20 a year. This problem may indeed have been noted somewhat earlier, as there is, on the fly-leaf opposite the title page of the rental of 1533, an undated and badly scrawled note to the effect that:

> the wudes of furnes fels had need to be well loked at (?) ther is iij smydis survaied to xx^{li} at [*sic*] thay tack no wudes bot suche as hathe byn acostomed as byrche oller the lop and falen wud and at [*sic*] …[illegible] bayle suffer not the wudes to be clossen.[76]

There is also a memo note on the rear end paper of the rental, in a different hand, which reads 'a remembrance for the Surveyor chyfe – Item for the woddes in Fourness Felles for Thomas Carus'.[77] Carus was made Vice-Chancellor of the Duchy in 1547 and appointed to a commission in 1550 to enquire into church lands, and both notes may date from around that time. However, he remained in office until 1571, so the surveyor referred to could be Braddyll. Whether or not that is the case, it suggests that the Duchy was already aware of the restrictions on the value of woods as reported in the rental, but was anxious to stress that the 'wood rent' applied only to woods for charcoal, and not to timber, should it ever be possible to get any out of the Fells.

However, it would appear that there was another problem, which has been variously interpreted by commentators, particularly those who have taken another Duchy decree at face value. The facts are that in 1565 commercial iron-making was banned in Furness Fells by a decree which, following hard on the heels of the Low Furness decree of 1564, similarly spelled out the customs of High Furness.[78] The reason given for the ban was that the queen's woods were 'sore decayed … by reason of certain iron smithies'.[79] This comment is of a piece with other legislation under Elizabeth which sought to restrict the operations of the iron industry, in the Weald and elsewhere, because of concern over its use of wood for charcoal.[80] However, it

75 TNA, DL 43/17/5.

76 TNA, SC 12/9/73 Furness Rent Roll, temp. Henry VIII (c.1533).

77 Ibid.

78 TNA, DL 5/13, ff. 705–709b, Decree as to the Customs of Furness Fells 1565; see also Fell, *Iron industry of Furness*, Appendix C.

79 TNA, DL 5/13, f. 705.

80 1 Eliz, c.15. An Act that Timber shall not be felled to make Coals for burning of Iron; 23 Eliz. C.5, An Act touching upon Iron Mills near unto the City of London and the River of Thames; 27 Eliz,

seems highly unlikely that more than 2,000 acres of underwood in High Furness could have been consumed in less than a generation since the Dissolution, and a more plausible explanation suggests itself. A key part of the new decree involved giving the tenants themselves licences to operate bloomeries, albeit once again on a non-commercial basis, providing they collectively paid the Duchy that 'wood rent' of £20 a year that Sandys and Sawrey had previously committed to pay. Reading between the lines, it would seem likely that, far from having exhausted the charcoal supply, the bloomeries may simply have ceased to be profitable as the market changed. Sandys and Sawrey were thus allowed to surrender their lease and the tenants in effect to buy it out, solving this problem for them. At the same time, this cleared the way for a new arrangement, of potentially greater value to the Duchy, whereby the tenants would still get their iron, provided they made it themselves – but they could now also start a commercial charcoal business, supplying the needs of a new market which was growing up to the north of the Fells, where German copper miners had been operating since the 1560s.[81] The Company of Mines Royal had been formed and the mine known as Goldscope, a corruption of '*Gottesgab*' (God's gift) had been opened, with a smelting works at Keswick which would soon have a considerable appetite for charcoal. The stumbling block was that the earl of Northumberland, who was the major landowner around Keswick, disputed the crown's rights to the minerals and, in the meantime, was refusing to supply charcoal to the Germans.[82] Braddyl's second woodland survey for the Duchy shows in detail how this was to be overcome.

As previously outlined, the 1568 survey, unlike that of 1559, focused upon how the Duchy might realise the potential asset value of its woods. As far as the woods of Furness Fells were concerned, in view of the access problems regarding timber, this meant exploiting the underwoods for charcoal. Braddyll informs us that, by now, the commercial bloom smithies had 'gone to utter Ruyne and Decaye'. However, as the tenants had sufficient wood for their own needs, they had agreed that they could commence delivering to the Mines Royal, each year for the next 20 years, 600 'Seames of Coles upon reasonable price' (a seam being a pack-horse load) to a place near the water of Windermere.[83] This deal, brokered by Braddyll, was ratified by a further Duchy decree in 1570 that stressed that this was a voluntary agreement on the part of the tenants, who would supply charcoal for which the Mines Royal

c.19 An Act for the Preservation of Timber in the Weilds of the Counties of Sussex, Surrey and Kent, and for the amendment of Highwayes decayed by Carriages to and from Iron Mines there. See also Hammersley, 'The crown woods'.

81 P. Fleming, *Lakeland's mining heritage: copper* <http://www.cumbria-industries.org.uk/copper.htm> (accessed 8 May 2014); R. Smith, S. Murphy and W. Allison, 'The lost German mines at Caldbeck', *Transactions of the Cumberland & Westmorland Antiquarian & Archaeological Society,* 3rd Series, 1 (2001), pp. 89–104.

82 J. Fisher Crosthwaite, 'The colony of German miners at Keswick', *Transactions of the Cumberland and Westmorland Antiquarian and Archaeological Society,* 6 (1881–2), pp. 344–54: *VCH*, vol. 2, p. 343.

83 TNA, DL 44/180 Survey of Woods within the manors of Borrowdale, Low Furness and Furness Fells, 1568.

would 'paye reasonably for the same and for the carriage therof'.[84] That carriage, incidentally, would have involved a boat-trip up Lake Windermere, followed by pack horse over Dunmail Raise (238 metres above sea level) to Keswick, a journey of some 30 kilometres, which was probably not ideal in terms of the quality of the charcoal delivered. What the Crown got out of this deal was its share of the output of the copper mines, which was set at one-fifteenth. What that was worth is hinted at in an account for the years 1586 to 1594, which shows that in those eight years alone some 500, 4 score and 12 quintalls of copper – nearly 40 tons – were delivered to the Tower of London as the queen's share from the smelting works at Keswick.[85] This may have seemed a good deal for the Crown at the time, but the downside was that the Duchy had effectively once again given up all rights to the produce of its woods in the Furness Fells.

The tenants, however, got far more from the decrees of 1565 and 1570 than just the profits from their charcoal business, as the former had laid down in some detail their rights under tenant-right, including fixed rents, a two-year entry fine and the right to 'cut and fall as well the said underwoodes as shredd top lopp cropp and bruse' the woods 'as often as they shall need and thinke mete', as well as sufficient wood and timber for their fuel and the needs of their tenements – housebote, hedgebote, ploughbote and the like. In return, they had collectively to supply 'forever' 40 horsemen for the defence of Piel Castle when required.[86] Finally, any lease for lives for the woods, or for any iron smithy, past or future, within Furness Fells, was declared 'frustrate voide and none effect'.[87]

At the next survey, that of Edward Braddyll in 1587, it was noted not only that the underwood throughout all Furness Fells was let by lease to the tenants, but also that they had received 'for the repair of theire howses and barnes vj^{C} $iiij^{xx}$ vj (686) timber trees sithens the xx^{th} year of her Ma'tie Reigne ... until the firste day of Julye in anno regin. Elizabethe ... xxix^{no} worthe iij^{s} $iiij^{d}$ the tree'.[88] Thus, while the tenants might be paying out £20 a year for the benefit of the underwoods, in less than nine years they had also received back £114 worth of timber under the custom of the manor. The only possible hint of any value for the Crown from these woods was a reference to Dale Park, where we are told that there were over a thousand young oaks fit for building – although these could not in fact be sold, as they were 'necessary to be preserved for the Queens Mills'.[89]

---

84 TNA, DL 6/18 Draft Decree: Furnes Felles a decre on coles to be delivered out of the woodes theare, 1570; see transcription in Fell, pp. 110–12.

85 TNA, LR 9/112 Account of Edward Braddyll, General Officer of the Mineral Works at Keswick, 1595.

86 The allocation of this number of men between Dalton and the various tenements had been fixed in an earlier agreement between the then abbot of Fumess and his tenants in Low Furness, 17 Hen VIII (1526): see West, *Furness*, pp. 96–8. This agreement had also confirmed their entry fines and the tenants' right to housebote etc.

87 TNA, DL 5/13, f. 709b.

88 TNA, DL 42/114.

89 TNA, DL 42/114 f. 6a

The survey of 1608 tended largely to repeat that of 1587, but that of 1610 provides us with far more detail, although, regrettably, it would seem that Treswell's less map-conscious colleague, Allen, carried out the work in High Furness, and so we have no equivalent for this district of Treswell's maps of Low Furness. The value of the woods to the Crown was assessed at over £700, more than three times that of Low Furness. Nevertheless, it must have been as clear to the Duchy Council here as it was for Low Furness that they were never going to be able to realise value from these woods other than by selling off the manors. And so the 'manor' of Colton, together with Satterthwaite, Grizedale and Dale Park, was duly sold in 1613, although the Duchy held on to the northern part of the Fells, known as the manor of Hawkshead, until after the Restoration.[90]

When the parliamentary surveyors came in 1650 they noted the 'Wood-Rent or Bloomesmithy rent', referred to the fact that much of the area had been sold in 1613, commented upon the reservation of timber for the tenants' necessary repairs and assessed the number of timber trees to be between 3,000 and 4,000, worth some £713 10s 0d – but concluded in the light of the tenants' rights that 'we do not positively certify concerning this timber as demisable'.[91] And so they sent with their survey 'a true copy of the rights and customs of the said tenants, that the trustees may judge whether the said woods are disposable by them or not'.[92] Which version this was is not clear, but it may well have been a copy of the 1565 bloomery decree which West reported in 1774 was in his day 'kept in the strong box in Coulton church'.[93] By 1650, incidentally, copper production by the Mines Royal, which, of course, had been the Crown's only source of profit from the woods of the Fells, had come to an end. On the other hand, there had been a return to commercial iron-making in the district, so the tenants would have been able to secure an alternative outlet for their charcoal production.

Custom and competition: discussion

The aim of this chapter has been to examine the competition for woodland resources in Furness between landlord and tenant from the Dissolution to the Commonwealth, in particular examining the relationship between custom and commercialisation. Hoyle has noted that,

> where manorial supervision grew lax, the tenants moved quickly to claim advantageous customs. It seems likely that this is a characteristic feature of manors which passed out of the control of well-managed monastic or episcopal estates into the hands of the Crown.[94]

---

90 *VCH*, vol. 8, p. 384: A.P. Brydson, *Some records of two lakeland townships (Blawith and Nibthwaite)* (London, c.1908), pp. 68–72.

91 E 317/Lancs/14 Furness 1650: See also transcription in West, *Furness*, pp. 170–84.

92 Ibid.

93 Colton, *Cumbria*, see Figure 1; West, *Furness*, Appendix IX.

94 Hoyle,'Introduction', p. 6.

Furness would appear to be just such a case, but possibly another characteristic feature of such manors was a well-organised tenantry, again as Hoyle and others, such as Morrin and Holt, have pointed out.[95] It is clear that from at least as early as the bill of c.1557 the tenants of Furness were able to act collectively and decisively. It may well be that the need for the abbey's tenants to organise themselves in such a way as to facilitate the provision of armed men for border service and to arrange the distribution of the annual doles of iron from the abbey had originally provided them in embryo with those institutions for collective action of which Elinor Ostrom has written.[96] Certainly by mid-century, the tenants of Furness appear to have met most if not all of Ostrom's seven 'design principles' for long-enduring Common Pool Resource institutions. Thus, when the wood rent was set at £20, to be allocated among the tenants of the Fells, it was determined that they should elect from among their number 24 men from Hawkshead and Colton to carry out the task.[97] We do not know the mechanism by which the 600 seams of charcoal a year were to be shared out among the producers after the 1568 agreement, nor do we know how the men of Low Furness allocated the work involved in repairing the sea walls of Walney when required. However, the active manorial courts at Dalton-in-Furness, for Low Furness, and at Colton and Hawkshead, for Furness Fells, some of whose records survive, would have provided the opportunity for the tenants to meet, discuss among themselves, organise and decide upon common action.[98] Whatever the means, they were certainly successful in taking on the might of the Duchy, acting collectively through a series of bills (petitions) which led to very favourable decrees for the tenants. These had the effect of registering 'custom' in such a way that the Duchy, when its policy changed from preservation to exploitation, found itself quite unable to get commercial value from its own woodlands other than by disposal.

All this is a far cry from the Tawneian view of a sixteenth century dominated by insecure tenants and rapacious landlords, a view which historians 100 years after the publication of *The agrarian problem* have, if not overturned, then at least significantly modified.[99] Today it is acknowledged that 'those who really lost out in sixteenth-century society were those who lacked customary tenures'.[100] Moreover, the Duchy's actions at this time seem to reflect the benevolent, if slightly amateurish, management of the Crown estates in general that came to an end with the death of Burghley in 1598.[101] In

---

95 J. Morrin, 'The transfer to leasehold on Durham Cathedral estate 1541–1626', pp. 117–32 and J.S. Holt, 'The financial rewards of winning the battle for secure customary tenure', pp. 133–49, both in J.C. Whittle (ed.), *Landlords and tenants in Britain, 1440–1660: Tawney's agrarian problem revisited* (Woodbridge, 2013).

96 E. Ostrom, *Governing the commons: the evolution of institutions for collective action* (Cambridge, 1990), p. 90.

97 TNA, DL 5/13.

98 TNA, DL 30/80/1083, 1084, 1085, 1086.

99 R.H. Tawney, *The agrarian problem of the sixteenth century* (London 1912); Whittle (ed.), *Landlords and tenants.*

100 Whittle, *Landlords and tenants*, p. 15.

101 Hoyle, 'Shearing the hog'.

this respect, we can see the Furness peninsula not as the remote, isolated, backward part of the country which it may at first appear to be, but at least as much a part of the mainstream history of agrarian England at this time – indeed, the industrial history too – as were Tawney's Midlands.

Although setting out to exploit its northern woods, the Duchy found itself torn between custom and commercialisation. In Low Furness, in accepting that it required its tenants to do the job that the abbots had once done by custom, and that it should grant them the timber to do so, it ensured that it could never itself take a profit from its woods in that district. At the same time in High Furness it was apparently prepared to ratify a new and favourable custumal for the sake of the relatively short-term advantage of securing a charcoal supply for the copper smelters of Keswick. For the tenants, custom and commercialism were not in conflict, and there seems little doubt that they could and did manipulate custom for commercial advantage; for the Duchy, it was a different matter. As Hoyle has pointed out, 'lords had every reason to want to escape from these customary relationships into market relationships'; yet in this case the problem was that the Duchy was more than just a lord.[102] While its officers might have wished to do away with custom, the Council, acting in its judicial role as the Chancery Court of the Duchy, a court of equity, clearly felt driven to do what was right by its tenants, even at a cost to itself. It is indeed a considerable tribute to the Duchy that it did not feel constrained to act purely in a self-interested way in this period at least, when the Duchy Chamber acted as a 'court of conscience'. But the result was that the competition for woodland resources between the Duchy and its tenants was clearly won by the tenants, albeit aided and abetted by the judicial arm of the Duchy itself.

102 Hoyle,'Introduction', p. 5.

Chapter 8

Custom, common right and commercialisation in the Forest of Dean, c.1605–40

Simon Sandall

> In that happy balance between the forces of custom and the forces of economic enterprise, custom is powerful, yet not so powerful that men cannot evade it when evasion is desired.[1]

Custom and common right in the Forest of Dean

Tawney's description of custom encouraged historians to explore the political nature of traditional practices in the context of tremendous social and economic change in many areas of England between the sixteenth and nineteenth centuries.[2] Much of this work has emphasised the power of custom in motivating and legitimating resistance to the loss of common rights through enclosure and the privatisation of material resources. It has also revealed the idealised and often fabricated nature of timeless practices that claimed the authority of antiquity through appeal to custom. This chapter explores these claims as they manifested themselves during

---

1 R.H. Tawney, *The agrarian problem in the sixteenth century* (London, 1912), p. 136.

2 S. Birtles, 'Common land, poor relief and enclosure: the use of manorial resources in fulfilling parish obligations, 1601–1834', *Past & Present*, 165 (1999); B. Bushaway, *By rite: custom, ceremony and community in England 1700–1880* (London, 1982); R. Houston, 'Custom in context: medieval and early modern Scotland and England', *Past & Present*, 211 (2011), pp. 35–76; R.W. Hoyle, 'An ancient and laudable custom: the definition and development of tenant right in north-western England in the sixteenth century', *Past & Present*, 116 (1987); P. King, 'Customary rights and women's earnings: the importance of gleaning to the rural labouring poor, 1750–1850', *Economic History Review*, 44 (1991); P. King, 'Legal change, customary right, and social conflict in late eighteenth century England: the origins of the great gleaning case of 1788', *Law and History Review*, 10 (1992); T. Stretton, 'Women, custom and equity in the court of requests', in J. Kermode and G. Walker (eds), *Women, crime and the courts in early modern England* (London, 1994); A. Wood, 'The place of custom in plebeian political culture: England, 1550–1800', *Social History*, 22 (1997); A. Wood, *The politics of social conflict: the Peak country, 1520–1770* (Cambridge, 1999), ch. 6; A. Wood, *The memory of the people: custom and popular senses of the past in early modern England* (Cambridge, 2013).

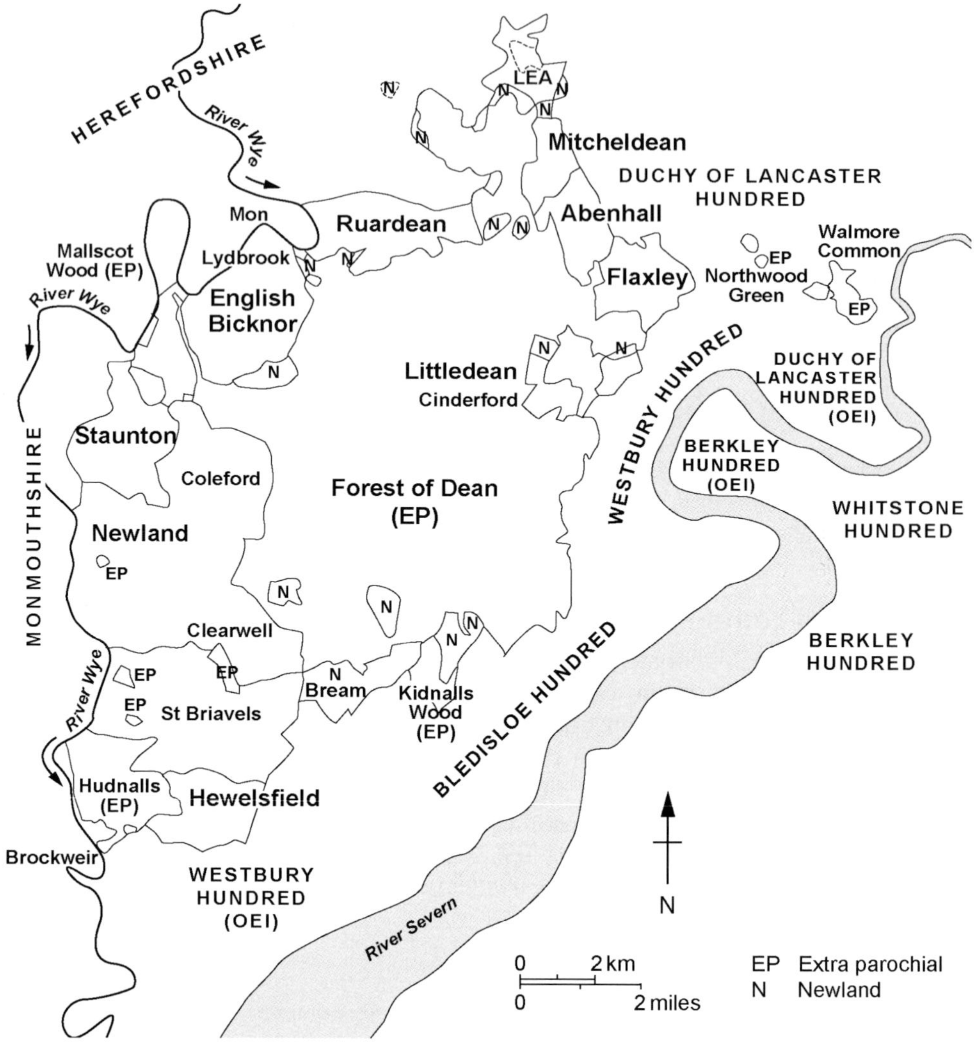

Figure 8.1 Map of the bounds of the Forest of Dean in the thirteenth and fourteenth centuries.

the seventeenth century in the Forest of Dean, Gloucestershire. This peripheral Crown estate became the subject of increased scrutiny from central government and potential external investors at the beginning of the seventeenth century on account of its rich mineral resources. Complex rights of access to these resources were intimately related to customary precedent, which was evidenced largely through orally transmitted traditions and the knowledge of local people. The obscure nature of these claims and occupational practices in the Forest of Dean during the seventeenth century is at the heart of this chapter, which particularly emphasises that these claims could be appropriated by those at all levels of the social, economic and political scale, not only the poor and vulnerable, who have often, understandably, been the primary focus of work in this area. The obscure world of custom, common right and tradition could also be deployed to aid rather than impede the commercialisation of local industry based on the exploitation of iron, wood and coal extracted from the forest.

The Forest of Dean lies in the west of Gloucestershire in the south-west of England, and its boundaries are roughly coterminous with the triangular area between the rivers Severn and Wye as they meet flowing south into the Bristol Channel. In legal terms, the name has often been taken to refer, more specifically, to the boundaries of St Briavels Hundred (see Figure 8.1), which correspond closely with the outline of the mineral basin which has been integral to this region's economy for many centuries.[3] The boundaries of the Forest, as an area governed by forest law and defining customary rights attached to residential status, have shifted several times since the twelfth and thirteenth centuries.[4] At its broadest interpretation, the Forest has been understood as all of the land between the two rivers and northwards into Herefordshire, thus including 33 parishes from both counties. These bounds were revised during the early fourteenth century, reducing the area to 14 Gloucestershire parishes and the extraparochial central Crown demesne lands which together constituted the Hundred of St Briavels.[5]

N.M. Herbert explains that, following the Dean Reafforestation Act of 1668, the region was reduced to the royal demesne lands which aligned broadly with the area of approximately 23,000 acres (9,308 hectares) that is currently understood to represent the Royal Forest of Dean.[6] Those that could claim residence and peculiar rights to common in the demesne lands of the forest and St Briavels Hundred were known locally as 'foresters'. This term was also used, in a more formal sense, to denote specific offices at various levels of forest administration. The Constable of St Briavels and his deputy headed this administrative system locally and claimed their authority from the Crown via the Justice of the Forest South of the Trent. Immediately below the Constable and his deputy were the foresters-of-fee, who each had charge of a designated area of forest known as a bailiwick, of which there were nine in the Forest of Dean during this period. Below each of the foresters-in-fee were one or more foresters. There were also several other specified offices, the verderers being most significant here as they held the court of attachment which regulated estovers and other uses within the forest. As Cyril Hart explains, 'the verderers were … elected in the county court by freeholders of the county under the supervision of the sheriff … their duty was to guard the vert and venison'.[7]

Describing the demographic and socio-economic transformations of the sixteenth century, Malcolm Gaskill noted a 'crucial outcome was that relationships

3 N.M. Herbert (ed.), *A history of the county of Gloucester: vol. V. Bledisloe Hundred, St Briavels Hundred, the Forest of Dean* (Oxford, 1996), pp. 285–9.

4 Ibid., p. 285.

5 Ibid.

6 Ibid.

7 C. Hart, *The verderers and forest laws of Dean* (Newton Abbot, 1971).

between high and low became based less on custom and oral tradition than on the wage-nexus and the market'.[8] This certainly characterises the experience of many in early modern England, as several regions, the Forest of Dean in particular, witnessed an assault on custom from the end of the sixteenth century. This clearly had a negative impact on the lives of many who depended on traditional common access to local resources. The early modern drive against custom has been broadly linked with the privatising impulses of capital investors, emblematised by processes of enclosure developing at different rates and with varying regional dynamics in early modern England.[9] Similarly, other work on this period highlights a move away from the vagaries of oral custom and tradition towards a more commercial world characterised by the specificity of the written record.[10] The malleability of custom and oral tradition could certainly accommodate collective or coincident usages on which many humbler people depended, while written property law lent itself to private and exclusive definitions of ownership.

We must be careful, however, not to construct a firm opposition between the social power of custom, on the one hand, and the economic logic of the market on the other. It would be misleading to think of custom simply as a timeless bulwark against the destructive impulses of innovation and privatisation, as it could also be deployed in the service of increasing commercialisation. As E.P. Thompson reminded us:

> In the eighteenth century custom was the rhetoric of legitimation for almost any usage, practice, or demanded right. Hence uncodified custom – and even codified – was in continual flux. So far from having the steady permanence suggested by the word 'tradition', custom was a field of change and of contest, an arena in which opposing interests made conflicting claims.[11]

This appears to have been equally true of the early seventeenth century. Using evidence from the Forest of Dean during this period, the following discussion considers the breadth of claims to rights of common in this field of contest that, in many cases, were far removed from the defence of a 'traditional' way of life. While emphasising the functional ambiguity of custom, this chapter suggests that associated claims to common right could be used or abused, precisely because of their obscurity, by local gentry to justify the exploitation of local resources.

---

8 M. Gaskill, *Crime and mentalities in early modern England* (Cambridge, 2000), p. 12.

9 J.M. Neeson, *Commoners: common right, enclosure and social change in England, 1700–1820* (Cambridge, 1996); C.E. Searle, 'Custom, class conflict and agrarian capitalism: the Cumbrian customary economy in the eighteenth century', *Past & Present*, 110 (1986), pp. 106–33.

10 A. Wood, 'Custom and the social organisation of writing in early modern England', *Transactions of the Royal Historical Society*, 6th Series, 9 (1999), pp. 257–69; A. Fox, 'Custom, memory and the authority of writing', in P. Griffiths, A. Fox and S. Hindle (eds), *The experience of authority in early modern England* (London, 1996), pp. 89–116, 110.

11 E.P. Thompson, 'Introduction: custom and culture', in E.P. Thompson, *Customs in common: studies in traditional popular culture* (New York, 1993), p. 6.

Increasing competition over forest resources

Speaking to parliament in May 1602, Lord Treasurer Buckhurst implored that 'it was fittest to have peace with Spain before we be too far spent, for he [Spain] hath a spring that yieldeth continual supply, his Indies, & we are like a standing water, which war will exhaust & make dry & barren'.[12] Explaining the likely impact of war on the rest of the English economy, Buckhurst's comments presaged the financial situation awaiting James I as he acceded to the throne in 1603. As a result of an early Jacobean drive to tighten the use of royal demesne lands through leasing assarts and granting mineral rights to private interests, many foresters were made to feel increasingly insecure over their common rights.

Post-conquest forest law had been upheld by the Justices in Eyre, a triennial circuit made by royal courts. Since the decline of these sessions in the fourteenth century, royal forests were increasingly managed through an array of swanimotes and local courts which operated under the influence of local gentry. Peter Large concludes that 'the progressive weakening of the Crown's administrative hold during the sixteenth century had effectively handed over the control of many royal forests to their inhabitants'.[13] This concern had an impact on perceptions of forests in England generally, but many legal records from Dean particularly reflect this shift away from the protection of Crown interests by the first half of the seventeenth century. This forms the context for the later discussion of the Eyre in 1634, when Charles I sought to find alternative methods of raising royal finance as he ruled without parliament.[14]

This was, of course, true of other forested areas, but the Forest of Dean was particularly valued as coal was to be found in abundance alongside other natural resources and, as is well attested, this commodity was becoming increasingly valuable from the mid-sixteenth century.[15] Despite the marginal location of the Forest, these plentiful mineral and timber resources ensured the economic significance of this region, which was to increase in the face, not only of burgeoning industrial enterprises, but also of the weapons and ship manufacture central to ongoing war efforts. Dean was therefore of crucial strategic importance to the sixteenth- and seventeenth-century English state. This period witnessed a two-pronged assault on forest custom from both changing Crown policies and novel opportunities for private projectors, several of whom were members of the local gentry. Under James I, 'searchers', men of no particular qualification, were sent to such marginal yet important regions

---

12 Roger Wilbraham, *The journal of Sir Roger Wilbraham, Solicitor-General in Ireland and Lord of Requests, for the years 1593–1616* <http://www.archive.org/stream/journalofsirroge00wilbrich> pp. 49–50 (accessed 28 January 2009).

13 P. Large, 'From swanimote to disafforestation: Feckenham Forest in the early seventeenth century', in R.W. Hoyle (ed.), *The estates of the English Crown, 1558–1640* (Cambridge, 1992), pp. 389–417, 389.

14 Tawney himself wrote of the 'revival of forest claims and the exaction of fines for knighthood, by which Charles tried to dispense with Parliamentary taxation'. Tawney, *Agrarian problem*, p. 391.

15 J.U. Nef, *The rise of the British coal industry* (Abingdon, 1966).

as forests and 'surrounded lands' to look for anomalous and obscure practices that might be 'rationalised' to improve revenue from these Crown estates. In many cases, commoners were required to compound for rights that they claimed had descended to them from time immemorial.[16] At the same time, local gentry were developing entrepreneurial tendencies and proposing schemes to privatise areas of Dean's woodlands. This chapter suggests that custom and traditional perceptions of rights could often aid as well as hinder this process of commercial development.

Free miners of the Forest of Dean claimed, and fiercely defended, a body of mining custom that sustained their industry. They seem to have operated with a remarkable level of autonomy compared with similar industries in England during the late medieval and early modern periods. Discussing the lead miners of the Mendip Hills, J.W. Gough confirms that proportions of extracted lead payable to the lord of this area in Somerset were increasing during the sixteenth century. This trend apparently reflected the nascent tendencies of a localised gentry-led capitalism.[17] Those who mined the Thievely lead field in Lancashire during the early seventeenth century also worked under conditions dictated by the 'lord of the soil'. R. Sharpe France suggests that the miners of this region looked enviously to the free-mining industry in Derbyshire's Peak country as a system which offered more desirable occupational terms.[18] Even this mining community, however, was subject to the scrutiny of local manorial lords through the 'lot and cope' system.[19] The Forest of Dean mining customs gave free miners access to essential material resources, such as timber for mine supports and valuable grazing land for livestock and working animals, and allowed them to sink pits wherever iron or coal was to be found within the boundaries of the Forest of Dean, more specifically the Hundred of St Briavels, which were closely aligned with the perimeters of these mineral fields. These customs, derived directly from the Crown and allowing a greater degree of occupational autonomy than many other mining operations in seventeenth-century England, were enforced by the miners' own Mine Law Court, which held a monopoly of jurisdiction over the industry.[20]

16 R.W. Hoyle,'"Shearing the hog": the reform of the estates, c.1598–1640', in R.W. Hoyle (ed.), *The estates of the English Crown, 1558–1640* (Cambridge, 1992), pp. 204–62; S. Sandall, *Custom and popular memory in the Forest of Dean, c.1550–1832* (Saarbrucken, 2013).

17 J.W. Gough, *The mines of Mendip* (New York, 1967), pp. 109–10.

18 R. Sharpe France (ed.), *The Thievely lead miners 1629–1635*, Lancashire and Cheshire Record Society 52 (Preston, 1947), pp. 1–2.

19 A. Wood, *The politics of social conflict: the Peak country, 1520–1770* (Cambridge, 1999), p. 121.

20 Sharpe France, *The Thievely lead miners*; C. Hart, *The industrial history of Dean; with an introduction to its industrial archaeology* (Newton Abbot, 1971); J. Langton, *Geographical change and industrial revolution: coalmining in south west Lancashire, 1590–1799* (Cambridge, 1979); J.A. Jaffe, *The struggle for market power: industrial relations in the British coal industry, 1800–1840* (Cambridge, 1991); C.C. Owen, *The Leicestershire and south Derbyshire coalfield 1200–1900* (Ashbourne, 1984); W. Ashworth, R.A. Church, M.W. Finn, J. Hatcher and B. Supple, *The history of the British coal industry* (Oxford, 1984–7); D. Levine and K. Wrightson, *The making of an industrial society: Whickham 1560–1765* (Oxford, 1991); A. Wood, *The politics of social conflict: the Peak country, 1520–1770* (Cambridge, 1999).

These free miners wielded great influence and provided leadership for action to resist perceived encroachments on traditional rights. This action invariably drew on local custom for legitimacy and to gain support.[21]

Another significant economic and cultural force in early modern Dean, one that also derived profits from local iron and coal reserves, were the industrial gentry of the Forest. They took an increasing interest in coal from the early seventeenth century but their pursuit of this and various types of wood was primarily to fuel their increasingly large-scale ironworks, which were blamed for excessive despoliation. This despoliation was to become a cause for complaints both from local inhabitants and from the Attorney General acting on behalf of the Crown. The Winter family represent a fairly typical example of this group of established local gentry with a significant investment in the rapidly growing local iron industry. The family first settled in the Forest during the 1560s, when prominent Elizabethan admiral Sir William Winter purchased the manor of Lydney towards the south-eastern edge of Dean and the Hundred of St Briavels. Following his death in 1589, his son Edward increased the family's property in the area and, by 1604, had acquired both the title of the Constable of the Castle of St Briavels and significant ironworks in the southern part of the Forest. These operations, particularly the smelting of ore, demanded vast amounts of charcoal. It is difficult to ascertain the exact size of his smelting and export operations, but Cyril Hart has estimated that, assuming a consumption rate of 150–300 acres of coppice per year, Winter's ironworks would have demanded approximately 3,000 acres of woodland.[22] This suggests that he was operating at the limits of his capabilities, a situation which meant that wood to be used for charcoal in his operations would have been a prized commodity. The ironmasters' thirst for the raw materials of the forest meant that they were often in direct conflict with other commoners and the mining community, as well as central government. There was a growing perception that this type of industrialisation was depriving the nation of ship timber for naval production at a time when it was felt to be crucial to the security of the realm. This will be explored in more depth, but the key point here is that, in these conflicts, we can observe custom and the notion of common rights as a point of contest between opposing parties. And it is also here that we can explore the creative interpretation of custom and obscure local practices in a way that aided, rather than impeded, processes of commercialisation during the early seventeenth century.

In 1606 Edward Winter complained to the Court of Star Chamber of violent action against his interests and employees in the Forest. This dispute was essentially rooted in conflicting interpretations of forest custom. Winter told the court that, as 'constable of St Brevells', he had a customary entitlement 'everye Wynter towards the provision of his house, One pitt of Coales to be Cutt, taken and Coaled yearlie in the said Forrest'.[23] Other foresters evidently disagreed as, according to Winter, on 14 December 1606 the defendants in the case attacked the two unfortunate labourers that had been

21 Sandall, *Custom and popular memory*, pp. 141–79.

22 C. Hart, *The Forest of Dean: new history 1550–1818* (Stroud, 1995), p. 4.

23 TNA, STAC8/303/7: the following material is taken from the records of Winter's star Chamber action against Whittington, Ayleway, Bond, Woorgan et al.

employed by him to 'make some foure or five loades of Coales' with wood taken from the Forest.[24] On the evening of the 14th, he claimed:

> Richard Whittington and Richard Ayleway gent Christopher Bond Richard Woorgan John Goughe Edward Rickard and George Reeve yeoman ... together with on Richard Katchmaye of late advanced to the Capteynshippe of one of the trained bands in that division of the Forrest ... in warlike and insolent manner marched with great shouts and braverye to the said cole pitt, and then and there most ryotouselye and forceblye in violent manner assaulted the said Nicholas Langley and Phillipe Langley his sonne beinge then and there in a little Cabbyn adioyning to the saide Colepitt.

While they 'did most stryke beate hurt and wounde the said Collyer and his sonne in dyvers p[ar]tes of their bodies', and threatened to kill them, Winter suggested that they had acted out of personal malice against him. This had apparently developed out of previous conflict as he had tried to do his duty in preventing them hunting to the detriment of the Forest. These defendants had all, he complained, 'Consult[ed] and Complott[ed] together to make [him] odious and hatefull to the common people'. While this is plausible, the anger of this crowd was clearly directed at what they saw as a contravention of Dean's mining custom, which restricted mining rights to free miners, although the defendants were mostly of higher status and had only indirect links to the industry.

Winter asserted that they had exploited the early seventeenth-century sensitivity over custom in the Forest in order to gain broader support from the 'vulgar sort'. He claimed that these defendants acted 'Well knoweinge that in the myndes of the vulgar sort (of that Countrye especially) there is not anything that leaves a deep[er] impression of hatred and malice' than a perceived threat to their 'freedomes and liberties'. Catchmay and the others, he said, had thus:

> slanderouslye and maliciouslye publishe[d] amongst theire neighbours that the quyet having and taking of the said Cole pitte and coals would prove the certeine and likeliest meanes to bereave them the said enhabitant[es] of their pretended customes and liberties within the saide Forrest, presuming upon this plausible suggestion that the common people woulde have tumultuouslie and Ryotouslie without further deliberation overthrowen and wasted the saide pitt.

While the crowd's target was evidently Winter's 'illegitimate' mining operation, this is not to entirely discount his particular version of events. Given the status of some defendants – Catchmay and Bond were from prominent gentry families – it is possible that they were highlighting a threat to forest custom to stifle the operations of a rival industrialist. Winter's testimony does imply that he was trying to trivialise or minimise the amount and type of wood that his workers had used in the production of his

24 It is presumed here that Winter referred to the process of making charcoal, which is more usually associated with generating the higher temperatures required for iron smelting.

'Coales'. He was keen to state that they had only 'caused certain olde stubbes of some decayed and weather broken beeches to be taken', and that these were due to him as a customary perquisite of his office, the key phrase appearing to be 'for the provision of his house', the implication being that this allowance was intended to be for his personal, domestic use rather than for profit.

Exchequer litigation of 1612 suggests another view of Winter's customary and purportedly domestic perquisites. Winter and other local wealthy inhabitants, including Thomas James, William Hall and William Kingston, were the subjects of a bill of complaint entered by Robert Treswell, Surveyor-General of Woods South of the Trent. They were accused of taking excessive amounts of wood from the Forest 'contrary to the laws of this Realme'.[25] As with his claims regarding the coal pit in 1606, Winter claimed that the 'said fee of 1 Oke & 1 beeche per year do of right belong to the office of warden & keeper of the said forest'. Treswell, however, was concerned that the 'wastes coppices springs woodes & underwoods' were being endangered by the defendants, who had apparently acted 'verry wastfully to the great wrong and disheritance of his ma[ies]tie & to the great decay waste & spoyle of his maiesties said forrest'. Winter's co-defendant, Thomas James, assured the court's commissioner that he had been impeached by Otho Nicholson, one of James' controversial searchers. He had made him compound for his existing right to take 'howsebote, plowbote, cartbote, hedgbote & firebote', traditional allowances of inferior-quality wood that could be gathered for use as each respective label suggests. James thus argued that the collection of wood was 'lawfull in regard of the custome & usage herin before alleadged'. He assured the commissioner that he had taken no more than was due apart from '4 Oakes' purchased from Charles Jones and William Brown, and these trees had been due to them for performance of their office as verderers of the forest.

The reply to Winter's answer was made by Sir Henry Hobart, Attorney General. Hobart confirmed the defendants' customary rights to 'howseboote, plougheboote, Cartboote, hedgeboote & fireboote', but claimed that Winter, particularly, had 'also taken other than those whereunto he pretendeth a title'. Hobart claimed that, since 1592, he and his deputies and servants had taken '500 Oakes … 300 Beeches … 40 Elmes … 100 & 3 score Ashes', together with '6000 loads of greate armes & boughs'. The problem here, then, was not simply that Winter and his employees had massively exceeded customary allowances but also that they had taken far higher-quality timber than 'boote' wood.

The constellation of perceptions and traditions associated with custom, and the way that these traditional uses were evidenced, offered a space for manipulation not only by the struggling miner and commoner but also by wealthier industrialising gentry. There are two immediately pertinent aspects to this type of evidence. Firstly, as in this case, the purported orality of customary law and perquisites meant that they were loosely regulated and accounted by comparison with modern bureaucratic standards. This pragmatic legal fiction could aid in accommodating coincident use rights but, here, this aspect of customary traditions apparently allowed Winter to shield

25 TNA, E112/82/310: the following material is taken from the Bills and Answers of the Exchequer dispute Treswell v Winter et al.

his abuses behind a vague claim to perquisites attached to his position as a forest officer. He and the other defendants were seemingly able to exploit this laxity in taking the large amounts of wood needed to fuel his rapidly expanding iron operations in the Forest of Dean. Responding to the Exchequer commissioner's request for information, in fact, co-defendant William Kingston bluntly asserted that the amount of 'divers trees cutt downe this defendant cannot p[re]cisely sett downe' and claimed that 'nether is it materiall'. It appears from these documents that the defendants, all of whom were local gentlemen, were attempting to use the indistinct nature of local custom to gain access to the large amounts of wood required by the burgeoning local iron industry in the Forest.

Secondly, we need to consider the ways in which custom in early modern England was evidenced by reference to the local landscape. I have previously argued that Dean's landscape operated as a 'memory palace' which literally stored information that was drawn upon in defence of local custom.[26] This material legal record was often recalled, alongside memories of working in the landscape, to establish continuity of rights and garner support for their defence when they were perceived to be under threat. The claim to custom then, just as it depended to a large degree on the oral recall of local inhabitants, depended on boundaries, markers and landscape features for their legitimation. Custom, as *lex loci*, attached to particular hundredal, manorial, parochial and other boundaries.[27] These boundaries were committed to popular memory through such collective rituals as the beating of the bounds and were, therefore, open to manipulation by parties attempting to exceed their customary entitlement because of the lack of written or cartographic record.

This certainly appears to have been at the core of allegations being levelled at Winter and the others. Treswell's original bill of complaint went to great lengths to refer to the names of various closes, hills, areas and landmarks that defined the space from which he asserted that they had 'felled, cut downe & carried away tenn thousand timber trees'.[28] He suggested that they had manipulated boundary markers to maximise their operations, claiming that 'Sir Edward Winter knight, William Kingston & Thomas James gent … the better to maintain their sayde uniust clayme have of late taken and removed the auncyent hedges meanes and boundaries of the same land[es] and premises'. Not only had they moved metes and bounds in this part of the Forest, but Treswell also complained that they had:

---

26 This approach to popular memory and the material environment has emerged with some force in recent historiography. For example, see D. Rollison, *The local origins of modern society: Gloucestershire 1500–1800* (London, 1992) N. Whyte, *Inhabiting the* landscape*: place, custom and memory, 1500–1800* (Oxford, 2009); N. Whyte, 'Landscape, memory and custom: parish identities c.1550–1700', *Social History*, 32 (2007), pp. 166–86; Wood, *Memory of the people*; A. Fox, *Oral and literate culture in England 1500–1700* (Oxford, 2000). For my work on the Forest of Dean more specifically, see Sandall, *Custom and popular memory*, pp. 81–97.

27 For a seminal treatment of this concept, see E.P. Thompson 'Custom, law and common right', in E.P. Thompson, *Customs in common: studies in traditional popular culture* (New York, 1993).

28 TNA, E112/82/310.

> gotten into their hands divers Records Court Rolls Rentalls accompts and Mynument[es] which ... manifest the true boundes of the same p[re]misses in the said Foreste and his ma[es]ties title in and to the said Land[es] tenem[en]t[es] and premises by meanes wherof they mean to obscure and suppresse the knowledge of his ma[ies]ties title thereunto.

According to Treswell, Winter and the other defendants acted deliberately and consciously to maintain the pretence of custom as an oral legal code as this allowed them to disguise their industrial despoliation of Dean's woodlands. In his testimony, Treswell then turned to traditional modes of legal memory in the absence of written evidence, suggesting that:

> There be yet living divers aged and auncyent men whose testimonie is requisite for the Manifesting of the same Land[es] where they bee and of his ma[ies]ties title to the premises, who yf they should be decease before they be examined might eterne to his ma[ies]ties great prejudice and hurte.[29]

The malleability of custom and the methods through which it was invoked in legal dispute thus lent themselves to use and abuse by those at all levels of the social, industrial and political scale. Treswell, on behalf of the Crown, emphasised the exigency of questioning older inhabitants of the Forest with a view to tackling Winter's efforts to exploit traditional legal cultures in furthering his commercial iron production and export.

This court action proceeded only to the initial bill of complaint and an exchange of answers but, in 1616, Treswell pushed a similar complaint against Winter to deposition. In reply, Winter resorted to the traditional defence of contested 'boote' rights through the spoken testimony of local inhabitants. The innovation here, of course, was that the Exchequer commissioners transcribed this oral evidence into written statements. Treswell alleged that Winter had been taking far more than his allowance of wood – in both quantity and quality – from his manors of Lidney, Aylberton, Allaston and Purton along the south-eastern edge of Dean, as well as from other areas such as St Briavels, Coleford and Newland that were further in towards the central wastes and demesne of the forest. Thomas Maddock, a 76-year-old gentleman of Tiddenham, told the court that 'by all the tyme of [his] remembrance', Edward Winter had taken 'ploughboote' and other forms of 'boote' from these lands since his inheritance upon the death of his father William Winter. Winter was supported in his claims by 23 other deponents, a group which mostly consisted of older gentry, yeomen and husbandmen. John Tanner, an 84-year-old yeoman of Flaxley, for instance, deposed that he had known the defendant since the death of his father William and that, for all of that time, Edward Winter had been in possession of these lands and the associated 'boote' rights. More direct questioning pushed this evidence further back into the world of orality and local custom. Asked how he came to this knowledge, John Hannys, a 53-year-old yeoman of 'the Lea', assured the commissioner that 'by the gen[er]all report and relac[i]on of ancient men inhabiting within the said forrest he hath credibly heard'.[30]

---

29 Ibid.

30 TNA, E143/14Jas1/Hil8.

It was not only the Crown that felt it was being deprived of its entitlement in this manner. In the same year, 1616, a similar dispute was played out between local gentry as traditional markers had apparently been manipulated in an attempt to increase the freehold land of two gentlemen, William Braine and William Meeke. Christopher Hawkins of Newnham, 'gent', alleged that they had similarly seized documentation of rights to land in Littledean, Westbury and Rodley. Having removed written evidence of these rights, he claimed, they had also:

> digged up and removed the mounds, meerestones, boundaries and other markes that should sett forth and manifest the certeyntie and contents of the same p[re] misses and having by the destroying and defaceing of the said mounds mere stones and bundaries intermingled the same with theire own lands adioining to the p[re]misses doe now clayme and geeve forth the same to be theire own free land.[31]

The defendants vigorously denied these accusations but, more broadly, the cases suggest that it was easier to exploit the indistinct nature of local custom once written evidence had been removed. In this sense legal action between Winter and the Crown, and that taken between members of the local gentry, demonstrate that custom was a force not only to defend the traditional occupations or subsistence strategies of the poor but also to assist the commercialising impulses of the rich in the Forest. This calls into question a tendency to associate increasing bureaucratisation with an emergent commercialism in early modern England, while aligning the oral defence of custom with the 'weapons of the weak'.[32] In this region at the start of the seventeenth century, at least, large capital interests seemed as keen to avoid the specificity of the written record in their exploitation of a vague unwritten notion of custom.

The Forest Eyre of 1634

Legal disputes between the Crown and the Winter family over levels of customary wood allowances were to continue into the next generation with Edward's son John. Sir John Winter pursued the family interest in the Forest of Dean iron works and, by all accounts, followed his father's example in exploiting the lax regulation of wood in the Forest. By the late 1620s he had established very substantial operations and had acquired a reputation for despoliation of large parts of the Forest to the detriment of other commoners and Crown interests. In a retrospective Exchequer case of 1668 that sought to establish rights to common as they had pertained before the civil wars, the plaintiff hoped 'to prove that the greatest spoyle & destruct[i]on that hath beene committed in the wood & timber of the said Forrest hath beene done and committed by S[i]r John Wintour'. The accusation was that Sir John had an established history of converting young trees into coal for his iron works and that these would have made 'very good shippetimber for his Ma[ies]tyes service'.[33]

31 TNA, E112/82/311.

32 J.C. Scott, *Weapons of the weak: everyday forms of peasant resistance* (New Haven, 2008).

33 TNA, E112/403/8.

Hart confirms that, in 1629, 'Winter succeeded in obtaining a share of the principal Dean iron industry "concession", tacked on to the end of the grant to Sir Basil Brooke and George Mynn (via the Earl of Pembroke).'[34] What followed was an aggressive expansion of his iron-work operations which appears to have been aimed at industrial domination within the forest. Accusations that he was taking more wood than was allowed under his grant began to issue from the usual quarters and there were constant allegations that the scale of his operations could not be supported by legitimate allowances as defined by his 'concession'.[35] In the context of Charles I's financial situation as he attempted to rule without Parliament, the proceeds of Crown estates were of no less importance to him than they had been to his father earlier in the century, as explained. The suspected abuses of Winter and others, such as Sir Basil Brooke and George Mynne, in similar situations lent themselves to an increasing conviction that the obscurity of local custom and industrial practices were depriving the Crown of much needed revenue. Added to this was the repeated charge that the despoliation of ship timber in royal forests was directly undermining naval capacity at a time of great national danger.

This was a hotly contested issue in early modern England and has, indeed, been a matter of debate between modern historians. Many works have addressed a perceived 'wood scarcity' in early modern Europe and advanced various theories about both the credibility of and the reasons behind this perceived ecological crisis.[36] At a continental level, the European 'wood scarcity' has received two broad strands of historiographical treatment. Those influenced by the post-Marxist materialist approach suggest that the perceived scarcity was an imagined crisis that was advanced by antagonists in an attempt to justify changes to the social order and traditional use rights. Environmental historians, contrastingly, have pointed to a real crisis engendered by ecological limitations in response to demographic expansion and economic mismanagement. Paul Warde suggests that, in an English context, two avenues of enquiry have dominated this debate since the publication of John Nef's work on the British coal industry.[37] The first concentrates on Nef's claim that wood

---

34 Hart, *The Forest of Dean*, p. 10.

35 TNA, E112/179/37.

36 B. Fritzboger, *A windfall for the magnates: the development of woodland ownership in Denmark c.1150–1850* (Odense, 2004); T. Kjaergaard, *The Danish revolution 1500–1800: an ecohistorical interpretation* (Cambridge, 1994); J. Dirkx, 'Wood-pasture in Dutch common woodlands and the deforestation of the Dutch landscape', in K. Kirby and C. Watkins (eds), *The ecological history of European forests* (Wallingford, 1998); O. Rackham, *Trees and woodland in the British landscape* (London, 1990); J. Sieglerschmidt, 'Social and economic landscapes', in S. Ogilvie (ed.), *Germany: a new social and economic history: vol. 2, 1630–1800* (London, 1996); J.L. van Zanden, 'Early modern economic growth: a survey of the European economy, 1500–1800', in M. Prak (ed.), *Early modern capitalism* (London, 2000); E.J.T. Collins, 'The coppice and underwood trades', in G.E. Mingay (ed.), *The agrarian history of England and Wales. Volume VI: 1750–1850* (Cambridge, 1989); R.G. Albion, *Forests and sea power: the timber problem of the royal navy, 1652–1862* (Cambridge, 1926).

37 P. Warde, 'Fear of wood shortage and the reality of the woodland in Europe, c.1450–1850', *History Workshop Journal*, 62 (2006), pp. 28–57; Nef, *British coal industry*.

scarcity stimulated a move towards the consumption of coal and, thus, represented a crucial step on the path to industrialisation. The other emphasises the 'importance of native timber to English maritime supremacy', the depletion of which stocks were accounted as the cost of naval domination but were nonetheless a cause for concern at various social and governmental levels.[38] Warde himself points to a more productive dialectic between 'imagined' and 'real' representations of an early modern European 'wood scarcity'. He highlights the influence of a complex array of ideological and material factors that impacted both perceptions and experience of different types of forest management and the novel demands being placed on existing stock. Exchequer litigation relating to the Forest of Dean during the seventeenth century is replete with claims that damaged woodland was undermining the king's navy and, by extension, the defence of the realm. This is not surprising because the Exchequer court was initially concerned only with matters relating to royal finances and, therefore, it was expedient to frame litigation in the context of protecting the interests of the Crown. Warde is sceptical of any claims of actual wood scarcity before the late eighteenth century, a point which suggests the rhetorical nature of these claims in seventeenth-century Dean. Industrialists in the forest, embroiled in disputes with other interested parties, appear to have appropriated concerns over a shortage of naval stock to emphasise the depredations of their competitors.

These pressures and the perception that obscure practices were shielding great abuses led to the decision to institute the Justice Seat in Eyre for the Forest in 1634. As suggested, this was evidently an attempt to reimpose medieval forest law on a valuable Crown estate that was felt to be slipping out of royal control. As with suspected abuses of custom and common rights, there was a growing perception on the part of central government that administration of the Forest was an unwieldy and complex system in which many officers had overlapping and indistinct responsibilities. This, it appeared, was working to the detriment of Crown finances and the exhaustive proceedings of the Eyre sought to penetrate this obscurity to claim rents and dues owed to the Crown while attempting to limit the large-scale despoliation of this valuable asset. The Eyre, lasting eight days, was held at Gloucester Castle in June 1634 before the Right Honourable Henry, earl of Holland, Lord Chief Justice in Eyre, assisted by Justice Jones, Baron Trevor and Sir John Bridgeman.[39] Charges presented ranged from illegal commoning to the erection of many encroaching cottages by the humbler of Dean's inhabitants. Sir John Finch's notes on the proceedings, however, show that the gravest charges of despoliation were levelled at Winter, Brooke and Mynne, as the dealings of these three industrial magnates formed the primary focus of the proceedings.[40]

In addition to the litigation surrounding Winter in the build-up to the Eyre, an Exchequer bill of 1633 suggests that both Brooke and Mynne were exploiting 'pretended' local custom and administrative obscurity to take wood that far exceeded

38 Warde, 'Fear of wood shortage', p. 32.

39 Notes of the proceedings of the Justice Seat in Eyre by Sir John Finch, Cambridge University Library (CUL), LL.4.7.

40 Finch's notes, CUL, LL.4.7.

the limits of their grant.[41] Finch's notes on the Eyre offer a more thorough assessment of the actual methods that these two entrepreneurial gentlemen deployed to avoid the scrutiny of Crown officers in the Forest. The list of charges paints a picture of manipulation and deception as the obscurity of traditional practices allowed them to stretch their permitted allotment of wood in every direction. Most blatantly, it was alleged, Brooke and Mynne had caused large quantities of cordwood to be taken into their pits without the presence of the king's officers and had thus deceived the Crown entirely in this case.[42] Similarly brazen was the misrepresentation of the quality of wood they were taking for their industrial use. According to Finch and the officials of the Eyre, Mynne and Brookes had been felling the best timber trees which were valued at 6s 8d per cord, but instead claimed that this wood consisted of logwood, windfalls and offals, for which they were only paying 3s 4d per cord. They also had a rather more alarming method of gaining access to the better sort of timber without paying full price in the form of large-scale environmental engineering. Finch claimed, and this seems to have been upheld, that they and their servants had been cutting glades into the lower levels of wooded hills which left the remaining trees, and the ground in which they grew, exposed to the elements. Deprived of this shelter, the ground became waterlogged and the strong winter winds had caused many 'goode timber trees' to fall. In this way, Mynne and Brookes were able to claim these trees as windfalls, which were legitimately encompassed in the terms of their grant. It was suggested that as many as 1,000 timber trees were lost this way in the course of one night.

Other measures were more subtle. Manipulation of wood measurements had a less dramatic yet no less harmful impact on Crown revenue, according to the officials of the Eyre. In one instance they had simply been cutting wood of a greater size than accorded with their 'bargaine with the king'. More regularly they had been making bundles of 23 cords together when each was supposed to consist of 20 and they had apparently discovered a way of making half cordwood instead of whole. This, allegedly, increased the size so that for every two whole cords Mynne and Brookes gained an extra quarter in volume. Aside from this, there was a long litany of other offences which included the destruction of woods which were home to eyries of hawks, paying other foresters to cut down wood to make 'coals' to serve their furnaces, and continuing to fell timber in direct contempt of a restraining order from the Lord Treasurer. They were also held responsible for the vast influx of cottagers and cabiners that had moved into the Forest to work for them and who had settled on the wastes and demesne lands, drawing their living by exploiting the easier access to common grazing and wood.[43]

41 E112/180/66.

42 By contrast with the very general term 'wood', 'cordwood' generally referred to shorter (usually up to four feet) cuts of wood to be used for firewood and other purposes, while 'timber' referred to larger planks and beams that had been prepared for construction.

43 'Cabiners' was a local term used to denote those that had moved into the forest seeking employment and had settled in the central wastes. The cabins were often called 'sun-ups' by way of reference to a purported custom that if a settler could erect a cabin by dawn on their first night then they would be allowed to remain.

This was, it was suggested, all to the great detriment of royal finances. Finally, they were accused of using their influence within the traditional community of the Forest of Dean in order to cover up the scale of these abuses. They had threatened to have officers thrown out of their jobs if they pried too keenly into their affairs. It was also alleged that, upon further investigation, most of the Forest of Dean's officers had turned out to be confederates and accomplices of Mynne and Brookes.

Winter stood accused of very similar misdeeds. Before these hearings he had denied using his influence and the vagaries of customary forest practices to enhance his industrial operations but, on witnessing the trial of Brookes and Mynne, he quickly had a change of heart. Finch tells us that:

> S[i]r John Winter had by graunte as assignee of the Earle of Pembrooke 2,500 Cords of wood a yeare at 6s 8d the Cord. S[i]r John Winter was p[re]sented and convicted for Cutting down and taking w[i]thin six years last past 60,700 Cords of wood to the value of 2,050 [pounds]. S[i]r John Winter was also indicted for the same Quantitie and on tuesday the __ of July pleaded *non Culpabilis*.[44]

When the king's counsel was prepared for trial, however, Finch tells us that:

> S[i]r John Winter considering his case to be like S[i]r Basil Brookes and Mr Mynnes Case in open Co[ur]te *relict verificacione* he confessed the Indictm[en]t soe the Co[ur]te gave Judgment against him according to his Confession [fining him] Twentye Thousand two hundred and thirty pounds.[45]

This massive fine obviously reflected the scale of abuse and the degree of profit that was to be drawn from this kind of manipulation and deceit. Brooke and his business partner Mynne were fined '£50,039 16s 8d'.[46]

These practices, as indicated by the degree of complicity on the part of Dean's officers, were evidently widespread during the 1620s and 1630s. In 1639 Attorney General Sir John Bankes entered a bill to the Exchequer court naming a long list of local gentlemen and other freeholders for similar abuses against the royal interest in the Forest of Dean. William Kingston, Edward Ball, William Morgan, Richard Machin, John Wilse, Katherine Rudge, Thomas Arram, William Gardner, Richard Morse thelder, Christopher Tucker, John Hardwicke, John Yearsely and Fortune Wood had all, it was claimed, entered lands 'unlawfully with horses, carts, wains, and axes' to remove ship timber in the guise of 'bootes' 'under their p[re]tended customs'.[47]

---

44 The specific date is left blank in Finch's text.

45 Notes of the proceedings of the Justice Seat in Eyre by Sir John Finch, CUL, LL.4.7.

46 CUL, LL.4.7; N. Herbert (ed.), *The Forest of Dean Eyre Roll, 1634*, Gloucestershire Records Series 26 (2012).

47 E112/182/196.

Conclusion: commercial appropriation of custom in the Forest of Dean

It is well established that the forests of England offered a refuge for many displaced labourers seeking to exploit the lax management of commons during the difficult years of the late sixteenth and early seventeenth centuries.[48] The case of the Forest of Dean during this period demonstrates that local gentry could also find commercial potential under the cover of obscure local custom and complex, often contradictory, administrative structures in exploiting the forest for their benefit. While geographically and culturally peripheral, the forest was strategically important to the English state. This was increasingly true from the latter part of the sixteenth century with growing coal consumption and the military need for wood, iron and other mineral resources, all of which the Forest of Dean had in abundance. Management of the forest depended on a multi-layered and obscure system of local officers whose private interest, it was often perceived, could conflict with their public duties to the detriment of royal coffers. To compound this, while land tenure and common grazing rights were tied to written documentation, a significant aspect of local access to resources was bound to the less distinct world of oral transmission in a number of ways. This obscure world of custom, it has been argued, allowed for the exploitation of forest resources not only by the poor but, on a larger scale, by many industrial interests in the Forest. This serves to undermine sharp distinctions between commerce, on the one hand, and the force of custom that could protect the poor against encroachments of capital interest on the other. Rather than simply being a force for resistance against innovation and for preserving the livings of the poor, it seems more appropriate, following Thompson, to conceive of custom as a field of force in which competing interests challenged for access to resources.

This chapter has explored increasing competition over forest resources at the beginning of the seventeenth century in the context of increased royal scrutiny and emerging industrial opportunities. This competition was between three major groups: royal grantees, local industrial gentry, and the free mining community who, it has been argued, represented Dean's commoners. Both the local gentry and the mining community, as forest residents, were engaged in the creative interpretation of custom that could both aid and impede commercial enterprise. Surviving records indicate that this was a regular occurrence during the period. The most dramatic example, however, was revealed in the cases of Sir Basil Brooke, George Mynne and Sir John Winter at the Justice Eyre of 1634, when all were handed down massive fines for concealment of wood consumption in ways that took advantage of custom and traditional practice in the seventeenth-century Forest of Dean. This is not to argue against the significance of custom for the study of popular politics – and, of course, this legal world constituted an immense resource for resisting encroachment on traditional ways of everyday life and forms of early industry. It is crucial, however,

48 J. Thirsk, *Economic policy and projects: the development of a consumer society in early modern England* (Oxford, 1978); J. Thirsk, 'Seventeenth-century agriculture and social change', *Agricultural History Review*, 18 (1970), pp.148–77.

not to idealise custom as an inert force that simply worked to resist privatisation and commercial interest as the seventeenth and eighteenth centuries progressed. Rather, the malleability in continuity that was the very essence of customary law and tradition was also open to appropriation by those higher up the economic and social scale, particularly those that dominated attempts to commercialise industrial production in the Forest.

Part IV: Accommodating change

Chapter 9

A money economy? Provisioning Durham Cathedral across the Dissolution, 1350–1600

A.T. Brown

> On the very eve of the dissolution of the monasteries we find a religious house in Northumberland reversing the movement which had been going on for two centuries in most parts of the country, and actually commuting money rents into payments in kind, on the ground that the tenants could not command the necessary coin. Such facts should warn us that England was far from being a single economic community, and that the effects of the cheap money penetrated into the more backward regions only very slowly indeed.[1]

Tawney's remarks relate to a dispute between the earl of Northumberland and his Tynemouthshire tenants in 1595, which came to a head when the earl's representative, Robert Delaval, demanded that his tenants pay their corn-rents by the Newcastle measure, while his tenants insisted they had always used the Winchester measure.[2] Such was the disturbance created by this argument that Robert's brother, Raphe, gave one of the tenants, 'being most busy, a bob of the lypps till he bled'.[3] Receiving little sympathy or perceived justice from their lord, the tenants took their petition to a higher authority, the earl of Huntingdon, lord lieutenant of the north. This led to lengthy depositions being taken from elderly tenants who recalled the initial change to payments in kind before the dissolution of the priory of Tynemouth, which had previously been their landlord. Edward Dinnand, a 100-year-old yeoman of Newcastle, for example, stated that he had been a servant to Prior Gardner when the tenants asked him to be allowed to pay their rents in corn: the prior did not wish it, but agreed for half the rent to be paid in corn; while Richard Cutter, an 80-year-old yeoman of Earsdon, similarly noted that the change to payments in kind had been for the benefit of the tenants, not for the profit of the priors, remarking that he 'hath harde his ancestors saie that

1 R.H. Tawney, *The agrarian problem in the sixteenth century* (London, 1912), p. 198.

2 The Newcastle measure was larger than the Winchester measure by two and a half pecks in every bushel of oats and barley and one peck in every bushel of wheat, and so paying their rents in the former would have greatly disadvantaged the tenants.

3 This dispute is retold at length, with summaries of the depositions, in H.H.E. Craster, *A history of Northumberland vol. VIII: the parish of Tynemouth* (London, 1907), pp. 231–6.

money was so scante then that coyned leather wente bargaininge betwene man and man'.[4] Tawney used examples like this to show how the survival of payments in kind into the sixteenth century 'supply a link between the vanishing subsistence cultivation [of medieval England], and the growing commercial economy'.[5]

Tawney and Postan were both aware of the caution required when discussing broad economic narratives such as the 'rise of a money economy' because of the regional diversity of medieval and early modern England. According to Postan, for example, the fifteenth century provides a 'good example of a declining money economy' as it was a 'period of declining trade [and] of growing self-sufficiency', except, of course, in the labour market, where 'labour services were being commuted and money payments were being substituted for labour dues'.[6] This perceived decline of the money economy was primarily because of the fifteenth-century recession and the associated shortage of silver bullion.[7] A shortage of silver has been seen as being particularly detrimental for many people in medieval England because it was the coinage of minor transactions, whereas gold tended to be the medium for international trade. Yet, between 1377 and 1483, the surviving mint accounts show that nearly £2.5 million of gold was struck, but only £430,000 of silver, providing considerable problems for everyday transactions during the fifteenth century.[8]

Payments in kind, however, imply neither 'a general retreat from monetised relationships between landlords and tenants' nor a decline in commercialisation.[9] In particular, Christopher Dyer has emphasised the commercial nature of the economy in the fifteenth century, showing how the new breed of demesne farmers engaged with markets on a considerable scale in terms of both selling their produce and employing labourers.[10] For example, because of the commercial advantages of selling barley many Norfolk landlords took part of their rent in barley, with John Paston II giving instructions in 1473 to 'make a goode bargeyn for my ferme barly in Fledge, so that I myght haue mony now at my beyng in Ingelond'.[11] Elizabeth Griffiths and Mark

---

4 Ibid., p. 233.

5 Tawney, *Agrarian problem*, p. 211.

6 M.M. Postan,'The rise of a money economy', *Economic History Review*, 14 (1944), p. 131. For more on the money economy, see J.L. Bolton, 'What is money? What is a money economy? When did a money economy emerge in medieval England?', in D. Wood (ed.), *Medieval money matters* (Oxford, 2004).

7 See, for example, J. Hatcher, 'The great slump of the mid-fifteenth century', in R.H. Britnell and J. Hatcher (eds), *Progress and problems in medieval England: essays in honour of Edward Miller* (Cambridge, 1996), pp. 237–72; for landlord–tenant relations see C. Dyer, 'A redistribution of incomes in fifteenth-century England?', *Past & Present*, 39 (1968), pp. 11–33.

8 N.J. Mayhew, 'Coinage and money in England, 1086–c.1500', in D. Wood (ed.), *Medieval money matters* (Oxford, 2004), p. 82.

9 R.H. Britnell, *The commercialisation of English society, 1000–1500* (Cambridge, 1993), p. 184.

10 See, for example, C. Dyer, 'Were there any capitalists in fifteenth-century England?', in J. Kermode (ed.), *Enterprise and individuals in fifteenth-century England* (Gloucester, 1991), pp. 1–24; C. Dyer, 'A Suffolk farmer in the fifteenth century', *Agricultural History Review*, 55 (2007), pp. 1–22.

11 R.H. Britnell, 'The Pastons and their Norfolk', *Agricultural History Review*, 36 (1988), p. 134.

Overton have connected these barley rents with share-farming and show how rents paid in kind continued as part of this form of commercial agriculture in early modern Norfolk.[12] Just how representative of the penetration of money into 'the more backward regions' of England were Tawney's observations based upon the experiences of these Tynemouthshire tenants, and did this represent a retreat into relative self-sufficiency by some tenants?

Certainly, there are other examples of tenants paying their rents in kind in the north of England during the fifteenth century, as seen not least in William Shannon's chapter in the current volume concerning Furness Abbey in Lancashire.[13] Studies by Richard Lomas and Miranda Threlfall-Holmes on the north-east of England have shown that many tenants on Durham Cathedral Priory's estate were also paying their rents in kind at the end of the fifteenth century in a manner similar to the nearby tenants at Tynemouth.[14] For example, Lomas estimated that in 1495/6 the Durham monks acquired 428 quarters of wheat, 733 quarters of barley, 311 quarters of oats, 199 sheep, 115 cattle, 104 items of poultry, 30,000 red herring, 8 barrels of white herring, 1,000 dogdraff, 306 bushels of salt and 235 ells of cloth through rents paid in kind – a staggering sum of goods which never reached a discernible market and were instead consumed by one of the largest households in the region.[15] This payment of rents in kind was neither a one-off nor a short-term expediency, and the surviving rent books make it clear that this system had become an established practice on the priory's estate by the end of the fifteenth century. Nor was this restricted to England, with Lies Vervaet similarly finding that many of the tenants of the St John's hospital of Bruges paid their rents in kind in late fifteenth-century Flanders.[16]

The provisioning of large Benedictine cathedrals has been the subject of a growing body of literature, with Threlfall-Holmes' work adding to that of Barbara Harvey on Westminster Abbey and Philip Slavin's more recent research on Norwich Priory, and yet these studies have not explored the changes in management and household requirements brought about by the Dissolution of the monasteries.[17] How did this transformation in the personnel, management and households of these

---

12 E. Griffiths and M. Overton, *Farming to halves: the hidden history of sharefarming in England from medieval to modern times* (Basingstoke, 2009), pp. 36–8.

13 W.D. Shannon,'Custom and competition for woodland resources in early modern High and Low Furness, Lancashire', Chapter 7 above.

14 R.A. Lomas, 'A priory and its tenants', in R.H. Britnell (ed.), *Daily life in the Middle Ages* (Stroud, 1998), pp. 119–20; M. Threlfall-Holmes, *Monks and markets: Durham Cathedral Priory, 1460–1520* (Oxford, 2005), pp. 138–61.

15 Dogdraff appear to have been a type of cod. Lomas,'A priory and its tenants', pp. 119–24.

16 L. Vervaet, 'Lease holding in late medieval Flanders: towards concentration and engrossment? The estates of the St John's Hospital of Bruges', in Frederic Aparisi and Vicent Royo (eds), *Beyond lords and peasants: rural elites and economic differentiation in pre-modern Europe* (Valencia, 2014), pp. 123–4.

17 P. Slavin, *Bread and ale for the brethren: the provisioning of Norwich Cathedral Priory, 1260–1536* (Hatfield, 2012); B. Harvey, *Living and dying in England, 1100–1540: the monastic experience* (Oxford, 1993); Threfall-Holmes, *Monks and markets*.

cathedrals affect their relationships with their tenants and the exploitation of their resources, and in the process change the surrounding economy? At Durham there was little discontinuity in the ownership of many of the priory's manors, while the last prior, Hugh Whitehead, was made the first dean of the new foundation.[18] Such was the continuity in the management of the cathedral that David Marcombe referred to 'the new cathedral as but old abbey writ large'.[19] And yet there were considerable changes in the management of their estate that are disguised by this administrative continuity, for there is no mention of the previous payment of rents in kind in the receiver's books, with tenants simply recorded as paying '*in curia*'. How far did this change from payments in kind to monetary rents in the sixteenth century affect local marketing networks, and why did this system originate in the first place? These changes in rent collection were also mirrored in the exploitation of their mineral resources, which had been kept in hand for much of the fourteenth and fifteenth centuries, but which were all leased out after the Dissolution. The lessees included notable Newcastle merchants such as Henry Anderson, who undoubtedly increased the commercial exploitation of these natural resources. The relationship between custom and commercialisation is a complicated one, often full of contradictions in this period, but the overall effect of these changes produced an increasing market orientation in different sections of the economy by the end of the sixteenth century.

Rent payments in kind

Durham Cathedral Priory housed between 60 and 80 brethren in the fifteenth century, up to 30 of whom could at any given time be residing in one of its nine cells: Finchale, Jarrow and Wearmouth in county Durham, Holy Island and Farne Island in Northumberland, Coldingham in Berwickshire, Lytham in Lancashire, Stamford in Lincolnshire and Durham College, Oxford.[20] There were also a number of servants and dependents of the priory who would similarly need providing for, with Threlfall-Holmes estimating that the monks possessed 'a household comprising of at least 140 members [who] had to be fed, clothed, and (for many of them at least) housed'.[21] She went on to show that in 1480/1 the monks of Durham Priory spent the following amounts on the principal provisions of the monastery: £364 2s 3d on grain; £215 2s 2d on meat; £128 11s 5d on fish; £44 7s 1d on spices; £62 3s on other food; £61 15s 2d on wine; £85 0s 5d on clothing; and £11 6s on fuel; with numerous other expenses, this came to a total of £1,877 3s 9d.[22] Undoubtedly, the priory was feeling

18 Although the priory did lose some lands, including those held by its dependent cells, much of the bursar's considerable lands were restored to the new foundation.

19 D. Marcombe,'The dean and chapter of Durham, 1558–1603' (PhD thesis, University of Durham, 1973), p. 6.

20 J. Hatcher, A.J. Piper and D. Stone, 'Monastic mortality: Durham Priory, 1395–1529', *Economic History Review*, 59 (2006), p. 668. Durham Cathedral lost Coldingham Priory in the fifteenth century.

21 Threlfall-Holmes, *Monks and markets*, p. 15.

22 Ibid., table 1.1.

considerable financial pressure in the fifteenth century given that in this same year the bursar's expected income was only £1,399 17s 8d, while annual arrears were £454 and cumulative arrears had reached the sum of £3,089.[23]

At Durham Priory many of these expenses were actually fictional account entries which, instead of being purchased from external markets, were supplied by their own tenants as payments in kind for their rent. Thus a tenant would appear as a supplier of the cathedral in the expenses section of their accounts even though they had not in fact sold any produce to the monastery, having instead paid their rents in kind.[24] The bursars' rent-books reveal that many of the cathedral's tenants were paying at least part of their rents in kind rather than in coin, although it is unclear when this form of payment originated on the priory's estate primarily because the bursar's rent-book of 1495/6 is the first surviving example of this detailed administration.[25] Was this payment of rents in kind a top-down imposition upon their tenants by the monks of Durham Priory as a way of provisioning the cathedral or did this system emerge in the fifteenth century because of the inability of the tenants to pay their rents in coin?

There are several indications that the requirements of the cathedral were indeed behind these payments in kind. Threlfall-Holmes has estimated that the priory attained over 95 per cent of its grain through rents paid in kind, as well as around half of its meat and fish, and various other resources that the monks needed.[26] It cannot be a happy coincidence that the priory sourced so much of its grain through this method, and this surely represented some kind of pre-arranged system of payment. Such a conclusion is confirmed by the rent-books, with grain payments often being very regular from all the tenants of an area in each year, only deviating by a few quarters of a certain grain as a tenant could not make the payment in that type. In Tawney's example from Tynemouth the tenants were paying a fixed corn-rent in lieu of coin, which actually had precedent on their lands, with tenants at Preston, for example, being required to pay corn-rents of five and a half quarters of barley-malt and one quarter of oats in 1294, compared with the four quarters of barley and two quarters of oats due in 1539.[27] At Durham the decision to pay rents in kind was not part of a fixed or customary due required of the tenants: all rents and goods were given a monetary

23 Durham Cathedral Muniments (DCM), Bursar's Account, 1480/1; for more details on Durham Priory's arrears see A.T. Brown, 'Surviving the mid-fifteenth-century recession: Durham Cathedral Priory, 1400–1520', *Northern History*, 47 (2010), pp. 209–31.

24 Threlfall-Holmes, *Monks and markets*, p. 137.

25 After a gap in the records of almost a century, the 1495/6 rent-book is the 'earliest example of this type of document to survive', though it was foreshadowed by a similar document for the communar's office for 1454 and the Bursar's Receipts Book of 1432; R.A. Lomas and A.J. Piper (eds), *Durham Cathedral Priory rentals, vol. I bursar's rentals*, Surtees Society 198 (1989), pp. 8–9 and pp. 129–32. However, Lomas has contended that payments in kind may have originated not long after the demesnes were originally leased out in the late fourteenth and early fifteenth centuries. See R. Lomas, 'The priory of Durham and its demesnes in the fourteenth and fifteenth centuries', *Economic History Review*, 31 (1978), pp. 343–4.

26 Threlfall-Holmes, *Monks and markets*, pp. 136–61.

27 Craster, *Northumberland vol. VIII*, p. 229.

value, while the amount and type of payment in kind could, and did, vary year upon year.[28] However, there was a regularity to these payments which at least suggests some top-down direction to how tenants paid in kind, as shown in Table 9.1.

Table 9.1
Payment of rents in kind by Hesilden tenants in 1495/6

Tenant	*Wheat*	*Barley*	*Oats*	*Coin*	*Other*
W. Twedall	8 quarters, 32s	8 quarters, 24s	4 quarters, 5s	9s 8d	4d; 2s 8d
W. Wilkynson	8 quarters, 32s	6 quarters, 18s		4s	1 turbett, 6s
John Calvert	8 quarters, 32s	8 quarters, 24s	4 quarters, 5s	6s	4 chickens, 16d
Robert Birden	8 quarters, 32s	5 quarters, 15s	4 quarters, 5s 4d	8s 10d; 12s 8d	
John Ranaldson	8 quarters, 32s	8 quarters, 24s	3 quarters, 4s 4d	13s 4d	2s 4d; 17d
T. Wilkynson	10 quarters, 40s	2 quarters, 6s		6s	4 piglets, 16d

Source: R.A. Lomas and A.J. Piper (eds), *Durham Cathedral Priory rentals, vol. I bursar's rentals*, Surtees Society 198 (1989), p. 156.

Moreover, this regularity of payments continued into the next generation of tenants, with Richard Calvert, for example, paying his rents in 1509/10 in ten quarters of wheat, seven quarters of barley and four quarters of oats, amounts very similar to those of his predecessor.[29] The variation between these payments is minimal and may just reflect the quality of the individual harvest, but the Calverts often met a quarter of their rental obligations in either several oxen or cows rather than in grain between these two dates, showing that these were not fixed corn rents and that the tenants had considerable flexibility in this system.[30]

Despite this seeming flexibility, however, tenants often met their rents in kind in a similar fashion to that of their neighbours in the same village, much as in Hesilden above, again suggesting a level of direction from the Durham monks. Figure 9.1 shows the regional variation of this in 1495/6, with tenants in the more fertile lowlands paying the majority of their rents in grain, while those townships on the Tyne and near Wearmouth paid the bulk of their rents in coin, with several villages near South Shields paying predominantly in fish. Durham tenants could, therefore, be paying vastly differing amounts of their rents in coin or in kind dependent upon their location, as shown in Table 9.2.

28 There was precedent for payment of rents in kind on Durham Priory's estate perhaps dating back into the fourteenth century but certainly from the middle of the fifteenth century. See Lomas, 'The priory of Durham', pp. 343–4.

29 Lomas and Piper (eds), *Durham Cathedral Priory rentals*, p. 156; DCM, Bursar's Book H, 1509/10, f. 167r.

30 In 1507/8 John Calvert paid part of his rents in one cow and one ox worth 16s 4d and, the year later, Richard Calvert paid in two oxen worth 16s 6d. See the bursar's books G–M for this variation.

Table 9.2

Payment methods by a selection of Durham Priory townships, 1495/6*

Harton		*Cowpen Bewley*			*Billingham*			*Hesilden*		
Type	*Value*	*Type*	*Amount*	*Value*	*Type*	*Amount*	*Value*	*Type*	*Amount*	*Value*
Coin	469s	Coin		128s 5d	Coin		128s 2d	Coin		60s 6d
Dogdraff**	40s	Wheat	35.5 qtrs	142s	Wheat	9.5 qtrs	39s	Wheat	50 qtrs	200s
Salmon	21s 3d	Salt	34.5 qtrs	119s 6d	Barley	71 qtrs	224s 6d	Barley	37 qtrs	111s
Cod	13s 8d	Horse	1	26s 7d	Sheep	25	33s 4d	Oats	16 qtrs	19s 8d
Herring	6s 8d	Pigs	2	4s 6d	Horse	1	11s	Turbot		6s
Casks	13s 4d				Pigs	15	19s 4d	Piglets	4	16d
								Chickens	4	12d
Coin	469s	Coin		128s 5d	Coin		128s 2d	Coin		60s 6d
Kind	94s 11d	Kind		292s 7d	Kind		327s 2d	Kind		339s

* Entries are blank or partial for numerous tenants and so these are not the total rents due from the townships, only those recorded as having paid (and how) by the time the rent-book was drawn up in 1495/6.

** dogdraff appear to have been a type of cod.

Source: R.A. Lomas and A.J. Piper (eds), *Durham Cathedral Priory rentals, vol. I bursar's rentals*, Surtees Society 198 (1989).

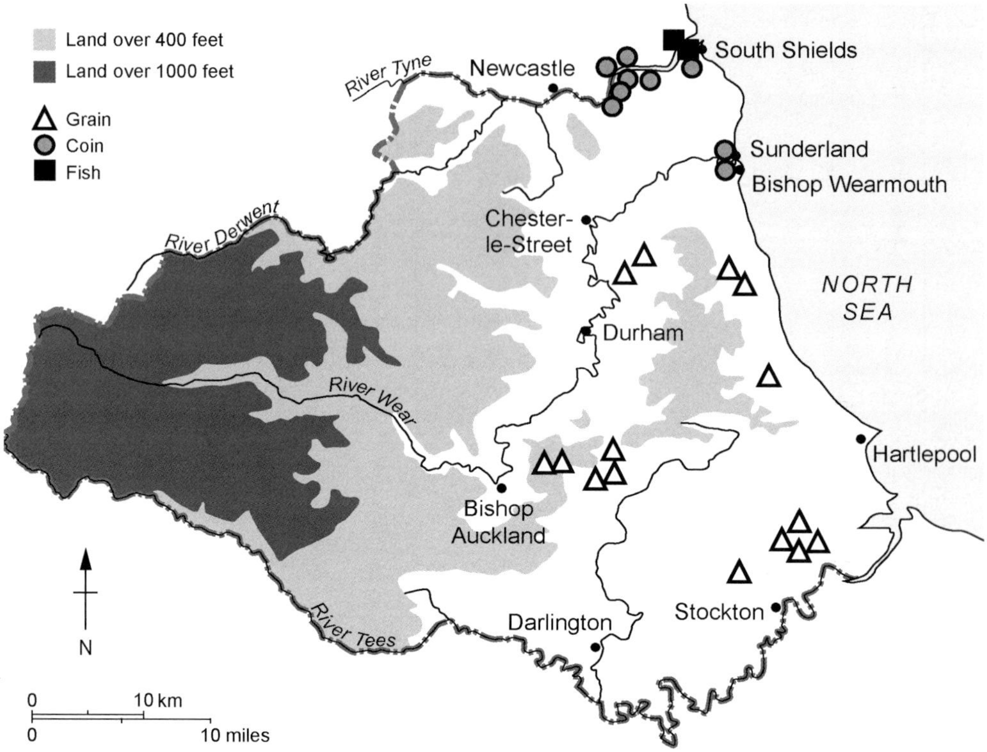

Figure 9.1 Map showing the payment methods of Durham Cathedral Priory tenants in 1495/6.

Payments in kind thus represented a much larger percentage of rental payments by certain tenants on the priory's estate than by others, perhaps reflecting the more developed commercial networks growing up around the river Tyne and the city of Newcastle compared to the predominantly rural south-east of the county.[31] As Table 9.2 shows, the tenants of Harton, a township near the coast and mouth of the Tyne, paid 80 per cent of their rents in coin and the remainder in fish, whereas tenants of Hesilden, in the east of the county, paid 85 per cent of their rents in kind, primarily in grain.[32] There were similar geographical variations to rent payments in kind on the estate of the St John's hospital of Bruges, where 'tenants in coastal Flanders tended to pay with cheese and butter, while the tenants of inland Flanders mostly brought animals to the hospital'.[33] Unlike at Durham, however, 'the importance of paying in kind did not differ that much between both regions' in late medieval Flanders, suggesting that there was perhaps more to the Durham story than simply the provisioning of the cathedral.

31 Harton was on the south bank of the Tyne; Cowpen Bewley and Billingham in the cluster of villages to the south-east of the region; and Hesilden to the east of Durham city.

32 Lomas and Piper (eds), *Durham Cathedral Priory rentals*, pp. 142–3, 156–7.

33 Vervaet, 'Lease holding in late medieval Flanders', pp. 123–4.

Threlfall-Holmes, for example, questioned whether this system was implemented because tenants were struggling to pay their rents in coin because of a severe shortage of small change in circulation, but concluded that this 'theory does not suffice to explain the widespread use of payments in kind found at Durham': firstly because 'the chronology is wrong',[34] the bullion famine being at its worst during the 1450s and 1460s, whereas Durham tenants were paying their rents in kind even in the early sixteenth century; and secondly because payments in kind were 'not the primary means by which the priory's tenants paid their rents', with 226 rents paid entirely in coin in 1495/6, 165 partially in coin and goods and 138 entirely with goods.[35] Similarly, Lomas questioned how far the tenants were meeting their rents in kind because of a shortage of coin, suggesting that although 'there are hints in the rent book that this was indeed the case' there were a considerable number of tenants paying entirely in coin, 'notably those in the Tyneside townships, where it would be difficult to argue that coin was more abundant or more easily come by than elsewhere in the region'.[36] However, given the close proximity of these villages to Newcastle, the major port city north of York, it seems much more likely that these tenants could find a market for their produce than elsewhere in the region, and that coin was perhaps more readily available there.

There are many other indications that this system of rent payments, if not originating because of a shortage of coin, was at the very least exacerbated by this problem. After all, the nearby tenants at Tynemouth were complaining that coin was 'so scante then that coyned leather wente bargaininge betwene man and man'.[37] In the above example from Hesilden, the Calverts did not always meet their rents in grain as, it seems, the Durham monks preferred, choosing instead to pay in cows or oxen – but, importantly, not coin. Indeed, although there was a regularity to many payments for the bulk of their rents, tenants were also paying in occasional items – a pig here and a few chickens there – rather than in coin, suggesting that tenants really were struggling to find money in the region. Although it might be expected that the presence of a mint in Durham would alleviate these problems in the immediate locality, the output from the mint declined rapidly in the late fourteenth century. Between 1351 and 1355 the average annual output of the Durham mint may have been as high as £30,000, which fell to £15,000 between 1355 and 1361.[38] By 1384, the mint's output was no more than £200, and between 1416 and 1460 the highest known annual output was only £292 16s. The Durham mint was not, therefore, in a position to alleviate any shortage of coin in the north-east.[39]

A comparison of these rents in kind with the tithe receipts of these villages would show how far their payments reflected the varying cropping patterns of the townships,

34 Threlfall-Holmes, *Monks and markets*, p. 144.

35 Ibid., p. 145.

36 Lomas,'A priory and its tenants', p. 124.

37 Craster, *Northumberland vol. VIII*, p. 233.

38 For estimates on the Durham mint, see M. Allen,'The Durham mint: the control, organisation, profits and output of an ecclesiastical mint' (PhD thesis, University of Durham, 1999), pp. 86–144, and M. Allen, *The Durham Mint* (London, 2003), pp. 64–76.

39 M. Allen, *Mints and money in medieval England* (Cambridge, 2012), p. 242.

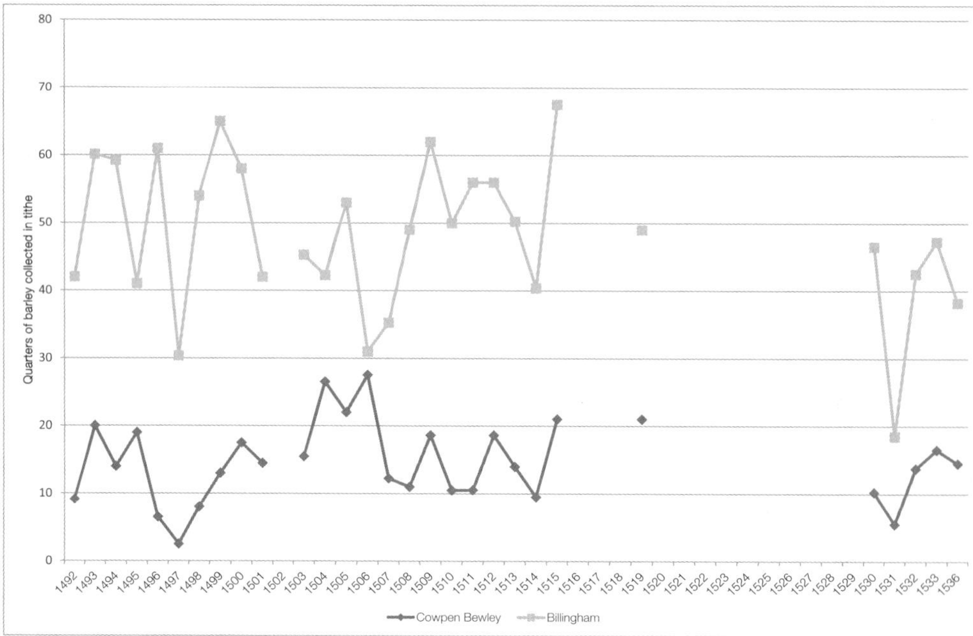

Figure 9.2 Quarters of barley collected in tithe for Billingham parish, 1490–1536.

but unfortunately the only tithes kept in hand by this date are for Billingham parish. However, this does enable comparisons to be made between the two nearby villages of Cowpen Bewley and Billingham for several years at the end of the fifteenth and the start of the sixteenth centuries. For example, in 1495/6 tenants of both villages met approximately 70 per cent of their rental obligations in kind, but did so in distinctly different commodities, with tenants at Cowpen Bewley paying predominantly in a combination of wheat and salt, whereas Billingham tenants paid the bulk of their rents in barley, a grain noticeably absent from the former's rent payments.[40] If we look at the tithe collected for barley from the two villages it quickly becomes apparent that the cropping patterns were indeed different, with an average of less than 15 quarters of barley collected in tithe from Cowpen Bewley, compared to the average of 48 quarters of barley collected from Billingham (Figure 9.2).

The differences in tithe between these two villages do not reflect their respective sizes; although Billingham had an estimated population of 570 people and Cowpen Bewley only 328, this does not account for the fact that the former produced three times as much barley as the latter.[41] Indeed, there is much greater parity in the tithe

40 Although in later years some tenants at Cowpen Bewley did meet a small proportion of their rental obligations in barley, this never approached the amounts paid by Billingham tenants in this grain.

41 T. Lomas, 'Land and people in south-east Durham in the later Middle Ages' (PhD thesis, University of Durham, 1976), p. 183.

of wheat between the two villages: an average of nearly 25 quarters for Cowpen Bewley compared with the 30 quarters for Billingham. Thus tenants at Billingham were growing considerably more barley than their neighbours at Cowpen Bewley, perhaps as a cash crop with which to pay their rents, an impression enhanced by the average of each grain collected in tithe from Billingham between 1490 and 1536: 29 quarters of oats; 30 quarters of wheat; 30 quarters of peas and beans; but 48 quarters of barley. Much of this extra production of barley was used to pay their rents. In 1495/6 this amounted to 71 quarters of barley, or 50 per cent of their payments recorded in the bursar's rent-book. By comparison, the tenants at Cowpen Bewley paid a substantial portion of their rents in salt, which had a long precedent on their holdings as a customary payment. For example, in 1296 Roger Barri took on a salt pan there for which he owed 30 measures of salt per annum, while in 1379 John Berwyk held a cottage, three acres of land and a salt pan, for which he owed 5s and one quarter of salt per annum.[42] Importantly, these ancient obligations were fixed payments of goods rather than a substitute for cash payments, which is what their fifteenth-century descendants were paying.

Durham Cathedral Priory was one of the largest households in the north-east of England, requiring substantial quantities of grain, meat, dairy produce and fish, much of which came from their own tenants. However, the dissolution of the monastery brought an end to this style of management, partly because of the different composition of personnel in the cathedral but also because of a more fragmented and individualistic approach to their lands. After the dissolution, Durham Cathedral had a dean, twelve prebendaries, twelve minor canons and various subsidiary officers, but the large communal household requirements of the cathedral were transformed. Not only did this lessen the provisioning requirements of the cathedral as a whole, but the individuals concerned were paid a considerable stipend and given lands out of the cathedral's estate with which to look after their own needs. The dean, for example, was allocated a wage of £266 13s 4d per annum; the twelve prebendaries shared a further £400 between them; and the twelve minor canons were paid £120. As a result of these changes rents no longer seem to have been paid in kind. There is no mention in the receiver's books of a comparable system to that of the bursar's books before the dissolution, despite the seeming similarities in the method of recording payments; payments were simply described as '*in curia*' after the dissolution, much akin to the '*ad primum turnum*' of the bursar's books, suggesting that rents were met in coin.[43] This was because the cathedral no longer needed to feed such a large household,

42 W.H.D. Longstaffe and J. Booth (eds), *Halmota Prioratus Dunelmensis. Extracts from the Halmote court of manor rolls of the prior and convent of Durham,* Surtees Society 82 (1886), pp. 2 and 155. There are some signs of this continuing after the dissolution when, for example, Robert Clifton paid £15 fine and six 'hives of salt' per annum in order to purchase the reversion of his lease during the 'lottery' system on the dean and chapter's lands. This is one of the few examples of any goods rather than cash being paid after the dissolution. Ibid., p. 242.

43 Jean Morrin also noted that 'there is no evidence of any rental payments in kind in the receivers books' after 1540. See J. Morrin, 'Merrington: land, landlord and tenants, 1541–1840: a study of the estate of the dean and chapter of Durham' (PhD thesis, University of Durham, 1997), p. 41.

while the dean and chapter had their own stipendiary wages out of the cathedral's income and their own lands, which could be worked directly by them or leased out. It also suggests that tenants could once again find coin in the regional economy.

Each prebendal stall had its own allocation of land, known as 'corpes lands', which could either be sub-let or worked directly.[44] Given the tendency for prebendaries to move between stalls it seems that these lands varied in value from a relatively early stage. For example, the dean was allocated the manor of Beaurepaire (Bearpark) and various other tracts of land; the second stall held half of Elvet Hall manor; and the seventh stall held Finchale manor. From the reign of Mary the dean and canons also divided the majority of tithes owed to the cathedral between themselves, which became known as their 'by-corpes', with the dean holding the valuable tithes of the rectories of Billingham and Merrington. Whether these lands were farmed directly by the dean and canons or sub-let at market rents, the dean and prebendaries were in effect self-sufficient with their own individual households. Gone was the common dormitory, for example, with each prebendary being given former monastic buildings in the cathedral close to live in.[45] The only real mention of a common table in the foundation statutes of the new cathedral relates to that of the 'minor canons, the deacon and subdeacon, and as many of the clerks as have not wives', who 'shall mess and feast in company in the common hall'.[46]

Unfortunately the majority of the individual accounts created by these prebendal estates within the new foundation do not survive until the eighteenth century, and so we cannot explore their administration or profitability. Marcombe did, however, suggest a valuation of these lands: half of Elvet Hall manor, for example, had a reserve rent of £8 6s 8d, but was valued at £150 later in the sixteenth century, and the manor of Finchale, with a rent of £9 18s 8d, was valued at £200.[47] Only a handful of the dean's accounts survive for this period, but these more than adequately reveal the value of these individual allotments to the canons. The tithe of the rectories of Billingham and Merrington brought in over 2,750 thraves of grain in 1591/2, showing that tithes were being collected in corn rather than leased out.[48] However, these were often sold by the dean rather than transported to the cathedral, with the tithes of Billingham rectory, compromised of Billingham, Wolviston and Bewley, fetching £183 18s 7d when sold in 1593/4.[49] By 1617/18 the dean had an estimated personal revenue of £1,130 per annum from his 'corpes' lands, his 'by-corpes' lands and his stipend and dividend, an income which was more than half the reserved rent of the property of the entire

---

44 P. Mussett, 'Lists of deans and major canons in Durham, 1541–1900' (Durham finding aid in the archives and special collections, 1974).

45 For more on the dissolution of Durham Cathedral see G. Moorhouse, *The last office: 1539 and the dissolution of a monastery* (London, 2008), p. 203.

46 A.H. Thompson (ed.), *The statutes of the cathedral church of Durham*, Surtees Society 143 (1929), p. 151.

47 Marcombe, 'Dean and chapter of Durham', p. 136.

48 During the fifteenth century many of the priory's tithes were leased out. See Ben Dodds, *Peasants and production in the medieval North-East: the evidence of tithes* (Woodbridge, 2007), p. 102.

49 DCM, H/DRA/7.

cathedral combined.[50] It is little wonder, then, that the dean and prebendaries were expected to provision their own individual households after the dissolution.

The arrangements concerning the dean and canons are made even more explicit in the foundation statutes dealing with the topic of hospitality and residences. The dean and every canon who had £40 or more a year from a source outside the cathedral was required to maintain a separate household and to provide hospitality. Residence was a period of three consecutive weeks each year, during which time a member of the chapter was to 'keep more sumptuous entertainment than they are wont at the other periods of the year, giving meat to the choir and inviting the citizens or strangers'.[51] Each canon of the cathedral was to have 'his separate dwelling and spend the night within the enclosure', with a common dividend which was divided between the 'canons in residence according to the number of days for which they have been resident'.[52] The chapter was required to reside throughout the year, with the exception of any periods spent away on royal or ecclesiastical business and an annual leave of 100 days for the dean and 80 days for a canon.[53] Hospitality was clearly an important obligation in the new foundation statutes, with the dean allocated an income of £40 1s 3d per annum and £8 4s 9d for a canon to aid in its provision, once again showing the divorce between the household requirements of the cathedral and the income of the individual canons after the dissolution.

The requirements of hospitality were not, however, a new or necessarily increased pressure upon the resources of Durham Cathedral. Prior to the dissolution the monks of Durham regularly used the nearby priory of Finchale as a rest-house, where they could withdraw from the larger monastic community in the city proper, but there were also shorter periods of relaxation allowed on the manor of Beaurepaire, just outside Durham. These priors' games, known as *ludi*, were normally held four times a year, at the feasts of the Purification, Easter, Saint John the Baptist and All Saints, and would last for at least two weeks at a time. These were well-supplied affairs, especially with meat: at one such gathering in the autumn of 1391 the prior and an unknown number of monks were supplied with five oxen or cattle, 22 sheep and seven pigs over the course of just 14 days.[54] Given the description of furniture at the manor in 1464, these occasions could also be large: in the great hall there was a wooden long settle, five dining tables with four trestles, four long forms and four stools for high table; and in an outer chamber there were five wooden forms, one long dining table with two trestles, a

---

50 This income was comprised of the following: £157 8s from Bearpark; £30 from Ravenflatt; £192 from Holme; £320 from the above tithes of the rectories of Billingham and Merrington; £266 13s 4d from his stipend and a further £114 10s 6d for his dividend, as well as £50 14s 4d from arrears. In total: £1,130. See the deanery accounts, DCM, H/DRA/10.

51 Thompson (ed.), *The statutes of the cathedral church of Durham*, pp. 108–15.

52 Ibid., p. 111.

53 P. Mussett, 'Hospitality residence at Durham Cathedral', *Transactions of the Architectural and Archaeological Society of Durham and Northumberland*, new series 6 (1982), pp. 67–70.

54 R.B. Dobson, *Durham Priory, 1400–1450* (Cambridge, 1973), pp. 97–9.

long settle, a chair and a stool.[55] Threlfall-Holmes has estimated that 'it would appear that the inhabitants of Durham Cathedral Priory consumed nearly four times as much meat as those of Westminster, and over 50 per cent more fish'; however, much of this extra consumption presumably occurred during the priors' *ludi*, for their accounts make little distinction between supplies for the main house and Beaurepaire, whereas the prior's allocation of meat was accounted for separately at Westminster, perhaps explaining at least some of this disparity.[56]

The transformation of Durham Cathedral undoubtedly had a significant impact upon local society, not just in terms of religious, political and social life but also in changing the way one of the largest households in the region was provisioned. The communal household needs of the monastery were replaced with a more independent and individual collection of canons who had their own lands and incomes out of the endowment of the cathedral with which they were to look after their own needs.[57] At no point did the system of rent payments in kind devolve into simple bartering during the fifteenth and early sixteenth centuries, and it is clear that the market value of goods was maintained wherever possible, with all animals and grains given a monetary, if perhaps slightly fictitious, value.[58] There were obvious benefits to the landowner and tenants alike in this arrangement, but a shortage of silver probably played a part in the geographical variations of payments in kind. A similar 'retreat' into payments in kind has been found in various arrangements across the country during the fifteenth century because of this lack of silver. Although on a much smaller scale than at Durham Priory, Dyer has noted the tendency for demesne farmers to pay off their debts in kind on the estates of the bishopric of Worcester in the 1450s and 1460s.[59] Such was the problem even in urban centres that an act of Edward IV of 1464 reiterated the need for carders, spinners, weavers and fullers to be paid 'lawful money for all their lawful wages', while Pamela Nightingale has shown that part of the reason for the relocation of the cloth industry into the countryside was because workers could be paid in kind

55 W. Greenwell, *Feodarium Prioratus Dunelmensis: a survey of the estates of the prior and convent of Durham compiled in the fifteenth century*, Surtees Society 58 (1871), pp. 190–1.

56 Threlfall-Holmes, *Monks and markets*, p. 51. Harvey, *Living and dying*, pp. 34–71. As explored by Harvey in her review of the book: Barbara Harvey,'Reviewed work: *Monks and markets: Durham Cathedral Priory, 1460–1520* by Miranda Threlfall-Holmes', *English Historical Review*, 120 (2005), pp. 1378–80.

57 For some of the tensions this could cause see Marcombe,'Dean and chapter of Durham', pp. 94–160, 242–69. The treasurer's expenses after the dissolution were primarily concerned with paying out stipends, salaries and dividends, and necessary repairs of the cathedral. See, for example, DCM, Treasurer's Books, L/BB/18.

58 Threlfall-Holmes has convincingly shown that prices did fluctuate and that the 'priory does not appear to have used its influence to insist upon goods when prices were high and cash when prices were low, and neither do the tenants seem to have been attempting the reverse'. Threlfall-Holmes, *Monks and markets*, pp. 160–1.

59 C. Dyer, *Lords and peasants in a changing society: the estates of the bishopric of Worcester, 680–1540* (Cambridge, 1980), p. 183.

more readily than in the towns.[60] In Chapter 6 above, Tom Johnson has also explored the innovative way fishermen dealt with a shortage of coinage in the 1450s and 1460s in a Suffolk coastal village.[61]

A.J. Pollard linked these problems in the north-east of England to the 1438–40 agrarian crisis, with the likes of Lord Fitzhugh receiving the rents of manors nearest Ravensworth 'directly to him, many in kind, to supply household needs', a practice which was still continuing in 1476/7. He went on to argue that 'such a hand to mouth arrangement' was 'surely a step backwards', while 'even a partial retreat from the market to a self-sufficient economy was likely to have had repercussions for local towns'.[62] It is not surprising that many tenants would struggle to find coin during the fifteenth century in county Durham, which, for much of this period, was 'a region of fields and moorlands, of villages, hamlets and lonely farmsteads'.[63] Despite describing Darlington as 'the best market town in the bishoprick, saving Durham', and Barnard Castle as 'a meatly praty toun, having a good market', the sixteenth-century antiquarian John Leland dismissed Bishop Auckland as 'of no estimation, yet there is a praty market of corne'; Wolsingham as at some time having 'a smaul market, now none'; and Chester-le-Street as 'chiefly one streat of very meane building yn length'.[64] The nearest market for many of Durham Priory's tenants in the predominantly agricultural south-east of the county lay at Stockton, although this was little more than a small port town in the fifteenth century: hardly a bustling urban entrepôt where tenants from the surrounding villages of Billingham, Cowpen Bewley and Wolviston could find coin or perhaps even sufficient buyers of grain.[65] Indeed, it is likely that the household requirements of Durham Priory hindered the development of these local marketing networks because its tenants sent so much of their produce straight to the cathedral rather than selling it in the immediate vicinity.

This episode reveals not only the under-commercialised nature of areas of the Durham countryside but also the considerable role a large seigniorial landowner could have on the development of marketing networks.[66] After the dissolution of the monastery tenants, especially those in the south-east of the region, would need to

---

60 D. Wood, *Medieval economic thought* (Cambridge, 2002), p. 80; P. Nightingale, 'Gold, credit, and mortality: distinguishing deflationary pressures on the late medieval English economy', *Economic History Review*, 63 (2010), p. 1092.

61 T. Johnson, 'The economics of shipwreck in late medieval Suffolk', Chapter 6 above.

62 A.J. Pollard, 'The north-eastern economy and the agrarian crisis of 1438–40', *Northern History*, 25 (1989), p. 102.

63 M. James, *Family, lineage and civil society: a study of society, politics and mentality in the Durham region, 1500–1640* (Oxford, 1974), p. 11.

64 L.T. Smith (ed.), *The itinerary of John Leland in or about the years 1535–1543, vol. I* (London, 1907), pp. 69–77.

65 For the population of Stockton see T. Lomas, 'Land and people in south-east Durham in the later Middle Ages' (PhD thesis, University of Durham, 1976), p. 183.

66 See the small number of market towns in S. Letters, *Online gazetteer of markets and fairs in England and Wales to 1516* <http://www.history.ac.uk/cmh/gaz/gazweb2.html> (last updated 15 July 2010).

sell their produce at local markets in a fashion which had not been happening for at least several generations. The nearby borough of Stockton, for example, had been granted a weekly market and annual fair by Bishop Bec in 1310, but this declined at some point after the Black Death. The notional revenue from the 104 burgage plots, common oven, shops, ferry, ships anchorages and perquisites of the court at Stockton came to a total of 113s 3d in 1443/4, but very little of this money was in fact being collected: arrears increased from £25 19s 1d in 1443/4 to £30 18s 4d in the following year, while high levels of decay were a constant burden throughout the fifteenth century.[67] The town's fortunes improved in the sixteenth century, however, and in 1602 Bishop Matthew reinstated the town's market charter, while in 1620 the fee for the anchorage of ships was sufficiently valuable to be disputed between the burgesses and the bishops of Durham.[68] Although broader trends in the regional economy help to explain the success and failure of this small market town, the need of local tenants undoubtedly played a role here, with the market falling into disuse when tenants circumvented the town and provisioned Durham Priory directly in the fifteenth century and experiencing renewed demand in the late sixteenth century.

Coal: household consumption and leases

Tawney's *Agrarian problem* is unfortunately lacking any real reference to, let alone sustained analysis of, the burgeoning coal industry in the sixteenth century or its early beginnings. Although he was aware of the growth in trade and industry, describing it as 'the most pregnant economic phenomenon of the period', he consciously confined himself to the 'study of agrarian conditions'.[69] The coal industry is similarly largely absent from Postan's *Medieval economy and society*, with his chapter dedicated to trade and industry focusing primarily on foreign trade and the wool industry. This is unfortunate because coal mining in this period produced, and in many ways was stimulated by, a range of agrarian problems: we cannot divorce the one from the other at this relatively early stage of its history. As Postan noted, 'burnable timber appeared to be very dear and presumably scarce' in arable regions already by the thirteenth century, which undoubtedly stimulated demand for coal, while custom played a significant role in the expansion of the coal industry in the sixteenth century, with copyholders at Whickham, for example, defending their rights to carry coal across their lands.[70] In his study of Norwich Priory, Slavin noted that the monks tended to use

67 Durham University Library, Archives and Special Collections (DUL, ASC), CCB B/73/2–3: bailiffs of the bailiwicks accounts. For the fortunes of other small market towns in the region see C.M. Newman,'Economy and society in north-eastern market towns: Darlington and Northallerton in the later Middle Ages', in C.D. Liddy and R.H. Britnell (eds), *North-east England in the later Middle Ages* (Woodbridge, 2005), pp. 127–40.

68 W. Page, *The Victoria History of the County of Durham, vol. III* (London, 1905), p. 354.

69 Tawney, *Agrarian problem*, p. viii.

70 M.M. Postan, *The medieval economy and society: an economic history of Britain in the Middle Ages* (London, 1972), p. 199. D. Levine and K. Wrightson, *The making of an industrial society: Whickham, 1560–1765* (Oxford, 1991), pp. 121–4.

wood and faggots from nearby woodlands, as well as charcoal for a smithy, but at Durham the overwhelming fuel of choice was coal.[71]

Already by 1310 the monks of Jarrow possessed two iron chimneys or grates, designed for the burning of coal in their hall.[72] The monks of Durham Priory owned a number of mines in the region from at least the late thirteenth century, most notably at Rainton, Fery and Aldin Grange, while their dependent cells often had their own coal mines, as at Finchale Priory and Jarrow.[73] The management of these mineral resources underwent significant changes with the dissolution of the monastery in a similar fashion to the system of payments in kind as the household requirements of the cathedral were transformed. In the Middle Ages these coal mines were organised towards the household consumption requirements of the Durham monks rather than large-scale commercial exploitation, although the monks did regularly sell surplus coal. It has often been argued that the position of the priory's mines, away from navigable rivers or the coast, provided the monks with 'no real opportunity to engage in large-scale capitalistic exploitation of coal-mining in the fifteenth century'.[74] However, given the financial success of the bishop of Durham's coal mines at Railey, a land-locked area near Bishop Auckland, access to water was not necessarily a prerequisite for successful coal mining in the fifteenth century, provided there was sufficient demand and few competitors in the region.[75]

The account rolls of the bursars contain numerous outlays for these mines, primarily from the fourteenth century onwards, that show the expenses of sinking new pits and repairing aqueducts, which were primarily borne by the house.[76] A dispute between Thomas Woodifield of Ferryhill and John Fossor, prior of Durham, survives from 1342, when the former was alleged to have diverted an underground watercourse so that a coal mine was flooded at Ferryhill, halting production at a cost to the prior of £100.[77] In the same

---

71 Slavin, *Bread and ale*, p. 143. In her work focusing on the provisioning of Durham Priory Threlfall-Holmes did not extensively explore the fuel needs of the cathedral.

72 J. Hatcher, *The history of the British coal industry. Vol. 1, before 1700: towards the age of coal* (Oxford, 1993), p. 410; J. Raine (ed.), *Inventories and account rolls of the Benedictine houses or cells of Jarrow and Monk-Wearmouth*, Surtees Society 29 (1854), p. 3.

73 For more on the coal-mining activities of the monks of Durham Priory and Finchale Priory see A.T. Brown, *Rural society and economic change in County Durham: recession and recovery, c.1400–1640* (Woodbridge, 2015), chapter 1.

74 Dobson, *Durham Priory*, p. 279.

75 See, for example, R.H. Britnell, 'The coal industry in the later Middle Ages: the bishop of Durham's estates', in M. Bailey and S.H. Rigby (eds), *Town and countryside in the age of the Black Death: essays in honour of John Hatcher* (Turnhout, 2012), pp. 439–72, and A.T. Brown, 'Estate management and institutional constraints in pre-industrial England: the ecclesiastical estates of Durham, c.1400–1640', *Economic History Review*, 67 (2014), pp. 699–719.

76 In 1351/2 '*in via aquatica minere de Rainton novo facienda*, £39 8s 2.5d'; in 1368/9 '*in expensis factis pro uno Watergate pro minera de Rainton* £8 17s 4d'; and again in 1375/6 '*in expensis factis circa aqueductus carbonum de Rainton*, £37 7s 2d'; while in 1397/8 they sank a new pit for coal at Aldingrange which cost £14 5s 6d: DCM, Bursar's Accounts, 1351/2, 1368/9, 1375/6, 1397/8.

77 DCM, Locelli IV: 35, 1342. An extensive online description and catalogue is available here: <http://reed.dur.ac.uk/xtf/view?docId=ead/dcd/dcdlocel.xml> (accessed 10 June 2014).

year the communar of Durham Priory accused several men of breaking into the nearby wood at Hett and mining the prior's coal at a cost to the monastery of £20.[78] The dangers of this early coal mining are well attested to, with a William Scot cutting coal in a mine at Whickham dying on 31 December 1328 because a stone the weight of a plough fell on him; while Gilbert, a coalminer at Thurstanton, died on 2 March 1329 after the rope he was using to climb out of the mine slipped out of his hands and he fell back into the pit.[79] There were even hidden dangers for passers-by, as Matilda Douf of Hett found out in the same year, when she was travelling by night and fell down an old coal mine and died.[80]

The coal mine accounts of Durham Priory survive for only the first half of the fifteenth century, but these do provide an in-depth view of their mining activities, as well as their relatively limited scope. For example, between 3 May 1443 and 6 December 1443 the monks of Durham Priory received £12 1s from their Rainton mines and £10 1d from Aldin Grange, besides the coal delivered to the monastery. In so doing, they built an aqueduct and sank new pits at Aldin Grange at a cost of 67s 7d; they allowed Bertram Gaythird £4 8d for digging and sinking a new pit at Rainton; and paid workmen £10, as well as 47s 10d for the workmen's ale and scoops and picks.[81] There are, however, references littered throughout the surviving accounting material which hint at their coal operations. Just prior to the dissolution the bursar can be seen excusing any rental receipts from the coal mines of Rainton because they were kept in hand, while the Durham household book provides a detailed view of this coal mining in the early sixteenth century.[82] In 1439/40, for example, the monks employed two hewers to work their Rainton mines for, on average, three to four days a week.[83] By 1531/2, however, they employed John Dawson and four others to work their mines, who were paid, altogether, 21d per day, although they tended to work only two days a week, highlighting the somewhat limited nature of coal exploitation by the monks.[84] The household book also discusses the various means of carrying coal to the monastery, categorised as those '*cum plaustris*' and '*cum equis*'. The former accounted for 119 cartloads and cost 69s 6d in 1531/2 and the latter cost £6 15s 6d.[85]

The dissolution of the cathedral affected not only the way in which Durham tenants paid their rents but also the manner in which the cathedral's coal resources were exploited. The previous focus upon the household consumption of the monks of Durham Priory had dominated the use of their coal reserves: even when the pit of Aldin Grange

---

78 DCM, Locelli IV: 38, 1342.

79 DCM, Locelli V: 33, 1329.

80 Ibid.

81 See, for example, DCM, Coal Mines, 1409/10–1452/3 and J.T. Fowler (ed.), *Extracts from the account rolls of the abbey of Durham. Vol. III*, Surtees Society 103 (1900), pp. 708–13.

82 DCM, Bursar's Account, 1536/7.

83 DCM, Bursar's Book F, ff. 25r–27r.

84 It is unclear which coal mines John Dawson and colleagues were working at: see J. Raine (ed.), *The Durham household book, or the accounts of the bursar of the monastery of Durham, 1530–4*, Surtees Society 18 (1844), pp. 87–8, 184–5.

85 Tenants were paid 6d each whether by cart or horse.

was leased out, for example, the lessee was obliged to supply all of the coal needs of the monastery and its tenants on the nearby manor of Beaurepaire.[86] Nef thought that the Church was overly conservative in its exploitation of its mineral resources and hindered the development of the industry because they held proportionally more coal than any other kind of property. He went on to argue that the transition away from ecclesiastical ownership of coal mines was important because the Church was 'not prepared to invest heavily in them', did not offer leases which would 'induce others to invest heavily in them' and 'was not entirely in harmony with the municipal trading class'.[87] However, even where coal mines continued in ecclesiastical ownership, there was a considerable change in their use during the sixteenth century, which, in Durham, shifted from the direct exploitation of these resources to their wholesale leasing out after the dissolution, as Table 9.3 shows.

Table 9.3
The lessees of Durham dean and chapter's coal mines after the dissolution

Coal mines	*Lessee*	*Rent**	*Date*
Rainton, Moorsley, Pittington and Moorlaw	Ralph Dalton and Thomas Whitehead	£20	1550
	William Sherwood	£22	1560, 1562
	Godfrey Tofte	£22	1568, 1588
	Hugh and Richard Wright	£22	1605
Fery, Hett and Spennymoor	Thomas Fery	£20	1562
	Godfrey Tofte	£20	1580
	John Heeth	£20	1591, 1594
	Hugh and Richard Wright	£20	1595
	Roger Kirby	£20	1628
Jarrow	Henry Anderson	£20	1575
	Henry Anderson	£3 6s 8d**	1595, 1599
	Henry Anderson	£1 6s 8d**	1601, 1606, 1613, 1618
	Leonard Carr	£1 6s 8d**	1628
Baxter Wood and Aldin Grange	Lionel Smith	£1	1545
	Cuthbert Lowson	£1	1585

* For the majority of these leases the rent given is per pit worked by the lessees.

** Lease includes a stipulation of £13 6s 8d per extra pit sunk by the lessee.

Source: Durham Cathedral Muniments Dean and Chapter Registers, 1–15.

86 J.U. Nef, *Rise of the British coal industry, vol. 1* (London, 1932), p. 139. For more on the north-east coal industry see J.B. Blake, 'The medieval coal trade of north-east England: some fourteenth century evidence', *Northern History*, 2 (1967), pp. 1–26; Hatcher, *History of the British coal industry*, pp. 70–96; Britnell,'The coal industry', pp. 439–72.

87 Nef, *Rise of the British coal industry*, p. 135.

The majority of these coal mines were close to Durham city and so of questionable value in the take-off of the coastal coal trade in the late sixteenth century. Beneficiaries of these mines include the likes of Thomas Whitehead and Ralph Dalton, presumably relatives of the first dean, Hugh Whitehead, and the seventh prebendary, Robert Dalton. However, the Jarrow mines clearly attracted the attention of more considerable interests because of their location, with Henry Anderson and then Leonard Carr leasing them out in this period. These were two of the wealthiest Newcastle merchants in the late sixteenth and early seventeenth centuries. Henry Anderson, in particular, came from a long line of Newcastle merchants who had been aldermen, mayors and MPs of Newcastle, and had a prominent role in securing the Grand Lease of the bishop of Durham's mines.[88] But, as the dean and chapter's registers show, he was also trying to benefit from the leasing out of other mines in the region. He was involved in another lease, along with Ralph Lever (a prebend) and Christopher Lewin, of the dean and chapter's coal mines and salt pans at Hayning for £20 per annum in the 1570s. The Elizabethan survey of 1580 described this as 'a lease hereof made about six years since to the men aforesaid, and now do not work coal there and therefore pay no rent, occupying also the salt pans without rent'.[89] Perhaps he deliberately acquired the lease to take the mine out of production, but if so it was an expensive proposition, for he is recorded as having paid £200 for the privilege of taking on the lease. The management of the cathedral's mineral resources once again reflects this transition from the communal needs of the monastery to the individual requirements of the canons, and with it saw the transference of the working of coal mines from the Durham monks to a range of different interest groups.

Custom and commercialisation

The dissolution of Durham cathedral produced relatively little administrative disruption. The last prior became the first dean; many of the former monks became prebendaries; the bursar's office was changed to that of the receiver and treasurer; and much of the priory's lands were restored to the new foundation. This continuity should not disguise the fact that there were considerable economic changes resulting from the organisational transformation occurring in the cathedral. The large communal household requirements of Durham Priory were replaced with the smaller, more individual needs of a group of canons who possessed their own lands and income from which they were expected to provide for their own households and their obligations of hospitality. This meant that the system of payments in kind that had predominated under the monks' supervision was largely unnecessary, and there are few, if any, signs that it continued for long after the dissolution. Similarly, the coal mines of the priory, kept in hand for much of the fourteenth and fifteenth centuries, were leased out after the dissolution, often on more commercial or generous terms

88 For more on the mining activities of the merchants of Newcastle, see A.T. Brown, *Rural society and economic change*, chapter 5.

89 Longstaffe and Booth (eds), *Halmota Prioratus Dunelmensis*, p. 197.

than they had been previously.[90] The combined effects of these changes increased the market participation of many of the cathedral's tenants, while the single large household of the monastery splintered into a group of prebendal estates, each with their own requirements and sources of provisions.

Bruce Campbell, whose considerable work upon the topic has shown the commercial influence of the market upon production and consumption, has noted that 'although much of what was produced was intended for the market, rather more was not' in the early fourteenth century.[91] Production decisions were generally influenced by prevailing local conditions, but disposal decisions 'were much more a matter of estate policy and therefore of institutional factors'. He went on to note that 'it was clearly not good enough merely to be in the right location. It was being in the right location and belonging to the right estate that made the difference.'[92] Even after the withdrawal from direct demesne management, these institutional factors played a key role in the marketing strategies of both landowners and tenants alike, and in the development of local marketing networks. Indeed, it is entirely possible that the original demesne structure of Durham Priory played a major role not only in the shape of the payment of rents in kind in the fifteenth century but also in the lack of large commercial centres in the south-east of the county. Bewley, for example, was 'by far the Priory's most important centre' and was its largest demesne, with around 700 sown acres, 22 ploughmen and 104 oxen in 1304/5, nearly twice that of any other priory demesne.[93] Much of this produce went towards feeding the Durham monks, just as the payments of grain did in the fifteenth century. If priory tenants at Cowpen Bewley so desired they hardly needed to engage with a local market besides purchasing the bare essentials in the early sixteenth century, whereas just a generation later they would have needed to sell substantial amounts of grain to meet their rents and entry fines. This, in turn, had a considerable impact upon local market towns such as Stockton, which were in decline in the fifteenth century but recovered from the mid-sixteenth century onwards.

Custom has often been described as offering tenants 'a considerable measure of protection from the full force of the market', but it could be a sword that cut both ways.[94] Custom did not always favour tenants in the English countryside, as Tawney's initial example from Tynemouth makes clear. Although custom protected the Tynemouth tenants in their legal dispute with the earl of Northumberland – they won their case and were allowed to continue paying their corn-rents with the Winchester rather than Newcastle measure – the existence of these customary payments in kind at the end

---

90 For example, the dean and chapter were to provide for the timber requirements of the pits, as well as providing access across their lands. Dean and Chapter Register 1, f. 158v; and Register 3, f. 95r.

91 B.M.S. Campbell, 'Matching supply to demand: crop production and disposal by English demesnes in the century of the Black Death', *Journal of Economic History*, 57 (1997), p. 829.

92 Ibid., p. 848.

93 R.H. Britnell (ed.), *Durham Priory manorial accounts, 1277–1310*, Surtees Society 218 (2014), pp. xlii–xlvi.

94 J. Hatcher,'English serfdom and villeinage: towards a reassessment', *Past & Present*, 90 (1981), pp. 24–5.

of the sixteenth century was to the detriment of these tenants. In his testamentary evidence Robert Helme, a 64-year-old yeoman, noted that when their landlord had been the priory of Tynemouth a bowl of bigg (barley) had been worth 12d but, by 1595, inflation had increased the price to 10s, and thus their corn-rents, which had been worth 20s, were now worth over £8: profit which found its way into the lord's coffers, to the detriment of his tenants. Indeed, one of the plaintiffs even recalled that Prior Gardner had said that 'you will repente it another daie', when agreeing to the corn-rents earlier in the century.[95] The tenants of Durham Priory were, therefore, fortunate that their rental payments in kind did not become fixed customary dues in the late fifteenth century, as this would have been to the disadvantage of their descendants.

Richard Hoyle has recently noted that 'custom served to limit a lord's income from his tenants' because 'the customary tenant's outgoings to his lord were relatively fixed', which 'brought substantial financial penalties to the landlord', especially in 'a society which was rapidly changing and undergoing price inflation'.[96] The tenants of these two northern monasteries paid their rents in kind just prior to the dissolution, but the continuation of this fixed customary practice on the Tynemouth estate shows that it was possible for tenants to lose out in an age of inflation directly as a result of custom: the more commercial, monetary rents owed by Durham tenants actually proved beneficial to them by the end of the sixteenth century.[97] The overall changes experienced by Durham cathedral in the sixteenth century and their consequences for the local economy reveal the important role institutional factors continued to play in the commercialisation of the English countryside and the effect a large landowner could have upon the development of regional markets.

95 Craster, *Northumberland vol. VIII*, p. 234.

96 R.W. Hoyle, 'Introduction: custom, improvement and anti-improvement', in R.W. Hoyle (ed.), *Custom, improvement and the landscape in early modern Britain* (Farnham, 2011), p. 4.

97 For the difficulties the dean and chapter faced in increasing these monetary rents in the sixteenth century see A.T. Brown, *Rural society and economic change*, chapter 2, and J. Morrin, 'The transfer to leasehold on Durham Cathedral estate, 1541–1626', in J.C. Whittle (ed.), *Landlords and tenants in Britain, 1440–1660: Tawney's agrarian problem revisited* (Woodbridge, 2013), pp. 117–32.

Chapter 10

Elizabethan entrepreneurs: three clothiers of the Frome Valley, 1550–1600

John Gaisford

At the accession of Elizabeth I in 1558, Wiltshire was one of England's most important manufacturing regions. Its main product was white woollen broadcloth, a durable, heavy-duty cloth used for coats and cloaks, which was made by village weavers, then 'fulled' at water mills to thicken the cloth and make it almost waterproof. Broadcloth production was regulated by statute: each Wiltshire cloth was required to be 'in length being thorough wet betwixt 26 and 28 yards and shall be seven quarters of the yard in breadth … and being well scoured thicked milled and fully dried shall weigh every piece 64 pounds'.[1] Metal seals were attached at the fulling mill to show that the cloths had been measured, weighed and checked for defects and that the aulnage (inspection) fee and Crown subsidy had both been paid.[2] The cloths were 'raw' or unfinished when they left Wiltshire. The majority were sold to London merchants, who shipped them to the Low Countries or Germany, where the cloths were dyed, shorn and pressed before being distributed throughout northern and central Europe. Others were finished in London and sold by domestic retailers, or exported to the Baltic or the Mediterranean.[3]

According to George Ramsay, the mid-twentieth-century historian of this trade, Wiltshire provided almost a quarter of all London's 'raw' cloth exports in the 1540s and had doubled its market share by 1606.[4] This was a business of national significance, which fuelled the import trade of London's merchants. 'Throughout the sixteenth century,' wrote Fisher, '[woollen] cloth was by far the most important commodity exported and by far the greater proportion of cloth went out through London'.[5] In the

1 5 & 6 Edward VI, c. 6 (1552).

2 The aulnage fee was ½d, the subsidy 4d per cloth, both payable to the county aulnager.

3 C.G.A. Clay, *Economic expansion and social change, England 1500–1700* (Cambridge, 1984), vol. 2, pp. 108–9. The finishing process involved raising the nap of the cloth with teasels and trimming it with shears to achieve a smooth surface, ready for folding and pressing.

4 G.D. Ramsay, *The Wiltshire woollen industry in the sixteenth and seventeenth centuries* (Oxford, 1943; rev. edn. 1965), pp. 65, 71.

5 F.J. Fisher, 'Commercial trends and policy in sixteenth century England', *Economic History Review*, 10 (1940), p. 96.

exchequer year 1559/60, London merchants paid nearly 93 per cent of the customs payable on cloth exports.[6] In 1564/5, when exports boomed following a year-long closure of the Antwerp market, cloth accounted for 78 per cent by value of all exports from London – £851,417 4s 6d out of a total £1,087, 866 15s 8d – and by the end of the reign cloth accounted for 'well over four-fifths of English exports'.[7] If Ramsay was correct, and Wiltshire by 1600 was supplying half of London's output, its products were generating nearly 40 per cent of England's export revenues.

The cloth was produced near the rivers used for washing and rinsing the wool and cloth and for powering the fulling mills. The main centres were made clear in 1576 by *An Act for the Toleration of Certain Clothiers in the counties of Wilts, Somerset and Gloucester to inhabit out of Townes Corporate*. The act notes that the clothiers of these counties have: 'at their great Costes and Charges planted themselves and their Dwelling Howses dispersedly throughowte the said Counties', and the first locations named are 'the Ryvers of Frome water, Kingswood water and the river Avon … and the branches of the said waters [which are] verie good and apt for clothinge'. It refers to 'the great number of Fulling Mylnes and other Workhouses thereunto adjoyning' and the 'greate multitude of poore People as Weavers, Tuckers, Spinsters and such like [who] have of long tyme heretofore and at this present do inhabite and dwell nere unto the said Places and Waters, by means of the great Clothmakinge there'.[8] The areas designated are in west Wiltshire and an adjacent strip of east Somerset, on both sides of the river Frome, which was often described as 'in Wiltshire' by Elizabethan exchequer officials; and at Kingswood, now in south Gloucestershire, but then a remote enclave of Wiltshire (Figure 10.1).[9]

With the growth of Wiltshire's market share, the west Wiltshire manufactory had become of particular interest to local magnates, exchequer officials and members of the Privy Council. John Thynne of Longleat (1513?–80), who acquired monastic lands in west Wiltshire while serving as steward to Protector Somerset, was surveyor of the Crown's Wiltshire properties (including Kingswood) during Elizabeth's reign and steadily extended his estate in the Frome Valley.[10] William Paulet, Lord Treasurer at Elizabeth's accession, had already acquired the former priory of Edington, just a few miles west of Longleat.[11] In 1567 Walter Mildmay, Paulet's *protegé* as Chancellor of

6 L. Stone, 'Elizabethan overseas trade', *Economic History Review*, 2 (1949), p. 39. The customs charge for exporting Wiltshire cloths was 1⅙ × 6s 8d, or 7s 11d per cloth: B.E. Supple, *Commercial crisis and change in England 1600–1642* (Cambridge, 1959), p. 275.

7 Stone, 'Overseas trade', pp. 37 and 45.

8 18 Elizabeth c. 16.

9 The National Archives (TNA), E159/361 Humphrey Yerbury of Beckington, John Whalley of Bath; TNA, E159/371 John Baylie of Beckington, Henry Davis (Davison?) of Norton St Philip, Gregory Style of Bath are all described as 'in Wiltshire'. Numerous other examples could be cited.

10 M. Girouard, 'Sir John Thynne (1512/3–80)', *ODNB*. Thynne was closely involved with London's overseas merchants: he married Thomas Gresham's sister Christian and held the office of Packer of Strangers' Goods.

11 R.B Pugh et al. (ed.), *The Victoria History of the County of Wiltshire* (hereafter *VCH Wiltshire*), 18 vols (London, 1953–2014), vol. 8 'Edington: Manors'.

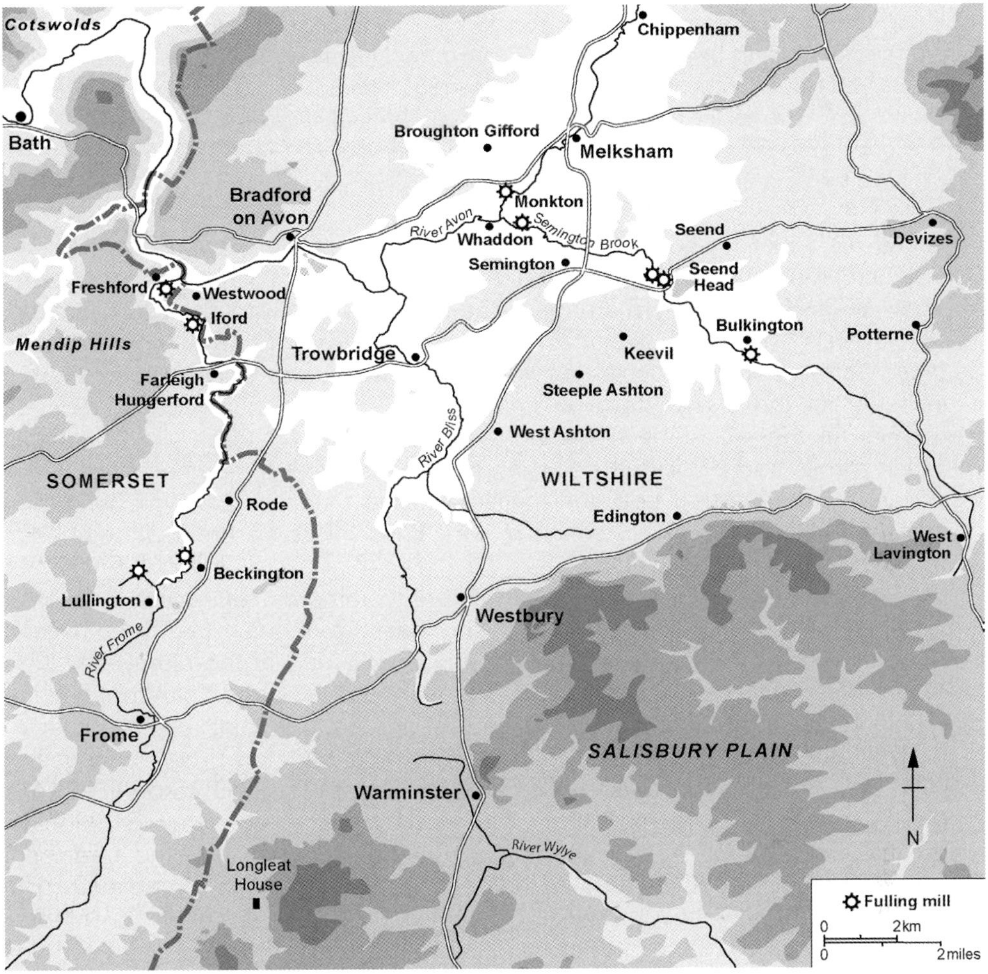

Figure 10.1 Map of the Frome Valley.

the Exchequer, encouraged his eldest son to marry a west Wiltshire heiress, Grace Sharington of Lacock.[12] In 1576 Mildmay's brother-in-law Francis Walsingham, Secretary of State and beneficiary of a valuable licence to export cloths free of customs duty, was granted the Hundred of Bradford and the reversion of the manor of Bradford-on-Avon, held meanwhile by the earl of Pembroke.[13]

The importance of west Wiltshire to the leading merchants of London can also be clearly demonstrated. John Stow recorded that:

> The number of merchants in London in the beginning of Queen Elizabeth, viz. when Alderman Lodge was mayor (which was Anno 1561), were in all 327.

12 L.L. Ford, 'Sir Walter Mildmay (1520/1–89)', *ODNB*.

13 TNA, SP 46/16 ff. 223–4; *VCH Wiltshire*, vol. 7 'Bradford Hundred', 'Bradford-on-Avon: Manors'.

> Whereof the Company of Mercers afforded 99. And these were the names of the chief, Sir Thomas Leigh, Sir Thomas Gresham, Mr Alderman Martin, Mr Alderman Baskerfield, Sir Rowland Hill, Vincent Randal, Lionel Duckett. Of the Grocers were 57. Whereof the chief were Sir John Lyon, Mr Alderman White, Mr Alderman Lodge, Lord Mayor, Mr Edward Jackman, Alderman. Of the Drapers 29. Whereof the chief were Sir William Chester, Mr Alderman Champion.[14]

Of these 13 'chief' mercers, grocers and drapers, all but Lyon, Randal and Champion can be shown to have had direct links with west Wiltshire as purchasers of cloth, as landowners, by marriage or as beneficiaries, witnesses or overseers of clothier wills.[15] During Elizabeth's reign such ties became ever more valuable because Crown policy favoured the wealthiest merchants. William Cecil thought it desirable for the export trade to pass into 'the hands of a fewer number of merchants, of those that be richer and that will deal and trade like merchants with their stocks and not with the exchange as all the young merchants do'.[16] The wealthiest merchants had both the motive and the means to cultivate long-term relationships with the leading clothiers in west Wiltshire, to secure their sources of supply and to shut out competition.

Yet, despite these indicators of a vibrant commerce, even the wealthiest Elizabethan clothiers of west Wiltshire and east Somerset have been almost invisible to economic historians. Tawney had no doubt that the cloth trade was the main driver of the sixteenth-century enclosure that absorbed him, but was far more interested in the effects than the causes and so took relatively little interest in the western counties, which he found 'relatively unaffected by the changes of our period'.[17] Postan, in contrast, traced the fortunes of the cloth trade from early medieval times to the sixteenth century, but from this macro-economic perspective found the 'new draperies' of East Anglia more noteworthy than the traditional broadcloths of the west.[18] Carus-Wilson's account of Wiltshire's medieval cloth economy did identify several wealthy clothiers, but ended at 1550. Mann's complementary study of the later period leaned heavily on Ramsay for its account

14 J. Stow, *A survey of the cities of London and Westminster*, ed. J. Strype (London, 1720), Book 5, p. 291.

15 Leigh as a 'very loving friend' of Robert Long, a west Wiltshire-born mercer: TNA, PROB 11/35/78; Gresham as a buyer of Wiltshire cloth: Mercer's Company *Thomas Gresham day book*; Martin, Baskerfield, Duckett and Jackman as brothers-in-law of Richard Lambert, a grocer with estates in Wiltshire and Gloucestershire: W.P.W. Phillimore (ed.), *Visitation of the county of Worcester made in the year 1569*, p. 102 and TNA, PROB 11/49/267; Hill as an overseer of Robert Long's will TNA, PROB 11/35/78; Lodge as a witness of Thomas Horton's will TNA, PROB 11/32/463; Chester as a beneficiary of Thomas Long, d.1562 TNA, PROB 11/46/130.

16 D.R Bisson, *The merchant adventurers of England: the company and the Crown, 1474–1564* (London, 1993), p. 98.

17 R.H. Tawney, *The agrarian problem in the sixteenth century* (London, 1912), pp. 195, 262–3.

18 M.M. Postan, *The medieval economy and society: an economic history of Britain in the Middle Ages* (London, 1975), p. 220.

of the Elizabethan era and, in Ramsay's view, 'not one of the clothiers whose activities lay at the base of the Wiltshire woollen industry during the sixteenth and seventeenth centuries could be considered worthy of mention in any text-book of English history during the period'.[19]

Ramsay's research was, however, hampered by the difficulty of accessing local archives.[20] There is no such problem today, but since the 1960s economic historians have moved on to other concerns and only local historians such as Ken Rogers and Colin Brett have continued the documentary research that enables individual clothiers to be linked to specific locations and activities in the Frome Valley.[21] Their findings have raised many questions about the conventional account of the late Tudor broadcloth manufactory. This chapter, therefore, will build on their work to outline the activity of three Elizabethan clothiers – Thomas Webb of Beckington in Somerset, his son-in-law Robert Webb of Kingswood and Beckington, and Edward Horton of Bradford-on-Avon in Wiltshire. It will demonstrate that, contrary to the prevailing narrative, the leading clothiers of the Frome Valley achieved unprecedented wealth and influence during the Elizabethan era, and thus are as worthy of attention as their merchant customers, who have been much more fully studied.[22] First, however, it will examine the historiographical context and the themes and debates which were generated in the 1960s by the successors of Tawney and Postan.

Entrepreneurs and 'industrialists'

Ramsay's monograph, published in 1943 and reissued with minimal revision in 1965, remains the standard source for the Tudor and early Stuart era.[23] But Ramsay viewed the first, not the second, half of the sixteenth century as the golden age for the Wiltshire cloth entrepreneurs.[24] In this he followed the seventeenth-century antiquarians Thomas Fuller (1608–61) and John Aubrey (1626–97). Fuller named among the Tudor 'worthies' of Wiltshire only the Henrician clothier William Stumpe of Malmesbury, who in the 1540s set up a large weaving workshop in disused buildings at Malmesbury Abbey and proposed (but never realised) an even more ambitious project to the corporation of Oxford, projected to employ as many as 2,000 cloth workers.[25] Aubrey

19 E. Carus-Wilson, 'The woollen industry before 1550' and J. de L. Mann, 'Textile industries since 1550', *VCH Wiltshire*, vol. 4, pp. 115–47, 148–82; Ramsay, *Wiltshire woollen industry*, p. 138.

20 Ibid., pp. 145–6.

21 C.J. Brett, *The manors of Norton St Philip and Hinton Charterhouse, 1535–1691*, Somerset Record Society 97 (2004); K.H. Rogers, *Wiltshire and Somerset woollen mills* (Edington, 1976).

22 See, for example, R. Grassby, *Kinship and capitalism: marriage, family and business in the English-speaking world* (Cambridge, 2001).

23 For the subsequent period J.de L. Mann, *The cloth industry in the west of England from 1640–1880* (Oxford, 1971) is much more detailed.

24 Ramsay, *Wiltshire woollen industry, p.* 65.

25 T. Fuller, *The history of the worthies of England*, ed. P.A. Nuttal (London, 1840), vol. 3, pp. 337–8; T.F.T. Baker, 'William Stumpe (by 1498–1552)', in S.T. Bindoff (ed.), *The history of parliament: the House of Commons 1509–1558* (*HoP*) (London, 1982).

noted as 'eminent clothiers' of the sixteenth century only the same William Stumpe and Robert Long of Steeple Ashton, whose will was proved in 1501.[26]

Stumpe's reputation has been swollen by academic controversy. Some economic historians have hailed him as an important innovator and seen his Malmesbury workshop as a milestone on the road to the factories of the nineteenth century. But when Nef argued that Tudor England had experienced an 'early industrial revolution', in which capitalist entrepreneurs had established large-scale centralised activities, he was forcefully rebutted by Coleman, who succeeded Postan as Professor of Economic History at Cambridge.[27] Coleman argued that most Tudor industry was in fact very small in scale, and later dismissed Stumpe as a 'boom-time freak' quite untypical of his period.[28] Nonetheless, in 1969 Stumpe was hailed by Gough in his history of entrepreneurs as 'the most authentic forerunner of the factory system'; and, as recently as 2008, François Crouzet cited Stumpe as an important example of an early industrialist.[29]

Stumpe has also been seen as an exemplar of what Brown described as the 'achievement norm' of Elizabethan entrepreneurs: the self-made man who strives to achieve social advancement into the landed gentry.[30] The son of a clothier of North Nibley, near Kingswood, Stumpe married into the aristocratic Berkeley family, major landowners in Gloucestershire and Somerset. Baker declared that his 'greatest achievement was to win for himself a place in the ranks of those who monopolised local government'.[31] Stumpe's eldest son James married a daughter of Edward Bayntun, a west Wiltshire magnate who served as vice-chamberlain to Henry VIII's queens.[32] Later in life James Stumpe married Bayntun's own widow and resided at William Paulet's estate at Edington.[33] Coleman shared Brown's view, remarking of rich clothiers that 'such men climbed the social scale by the money made in their business and married into the local gentry'.[34] Beier, however, observed in 1975 that 'the idea that successful entrepreneurs moved out of trade and industry into the landed classes has not ... been proven for a significant part of the entrepreneurial class', and Wrightson in

---

26 J. Aubrey, *The natural history of Wiltshire*, ed. J. Britton (London, 1847), pp. 112–13; TNA, PROB 11/13/90.

27 For J.U. Nef's theory and its critics see Clay, *Economic expansion*, vol. 2, pp. 65–6.

28 D.C. Coleman, 'Industrial growth and industrial revolutions', *Economica*, 23 (1956), pp. 1–22, especially pp. 13–16; D.C. Coleman, *Industry in Tudor and Stuart England* (London, 1975), pp. 11–12.

29 J.W. Gough, *The rise of the entrepreneur* (London, 1969), p. 36; F. Crouzet, *The first industrialists: the problem of origins* (Cambridge, 1985), p. 22.

30 This model, set out in R.H. Brown, 'The achievement norm and economic growth: the case of Elizabethan England', *Review of Social Economy*, 27 (1969), pp. 181–201 was summarised and criticised by A.L. Beier, 'Industrial growth and social mobility in England, 1540–1640', *The British Journal of Sociology*, 26 (1975), pp. 242–4.

31 Baker, 'William Stumpe'.

32 A. Wall, 'Bayntun Family (*per* 1508–1716)', *ODNB*.

33 T.F.T. Baker, 'Sir James Stumpe (by 1519–53)', *HoP 1509–58*.

34 D.C. Coleman, *The economy of England, 1450–1750* (Oxford, 1977), p. 77.

2002 was similarly tentative.[35] Yet so little work has been carried out on clothiers since the 1950s that the presumption of social ambition among entrepreneurs remains a core theme of the prevailing literature and one which will be tested against the careers of the three Elizabethan clothiers examined in this chapter.[36]

In 2015 only one Elizabethan clothier, Benedict Webb of Kingswood, has an entry in the *ODNB* (written by Joan Thirsk, who had been supervised by Tawney at the London School of Economics); but even that entry focuses less on Webb's activities as a clothier than on his production of rapeseed oil in the early seventeenth century.[37] Yet, as Moir first revealed, Benedict Webb was much more influential as a clothier than as an oil producer. The son of a Kingswood clothier, he was apprenticed to a London linen draper whom he served as a factor in Rouen and Paris during the 1580s. There he made a close study of French cloth, which he thought 'far more curious and better than ours'.[38] Back in England by 1589, he married the daughter of a Taunton merchant and experimented in Somerset with the production of two types of dyed and finished cloth.[39] One was a thin but hard-wearing 'perpetuana' or serge, often dark blue.[40] The other was a lightweight broadcloth in 'divers and sundry colours', which Webb created not by a combination of dyes but by blending dyed wool of different colours before spinning.[41] Early in the seventeenth century Webb's medley broadcloths were sold in Cheapside by the mercer William Stone, who named them Spanish cloths.[42] This innovation was rapidly adopted in the Frome Valley, but while Moir recorded that Webb had a brother named Robert she did not identify him as the clothier Robert Webb of Beckington.[43] In 1610 their niece Mary Browning married the Berkeley steward John Smyth of North Nibley in Gloucestershire (William Stumpe's birthplace). This constituted a move into the gentry, no doubt, but was probably motivated by commercial rather than social considerations, since Smyth was a Middle Temple lawyer who spent half the year in London, had extensive business interests of his own and was soon funding Benedict Webb's oil-seed operation.[44] The development of the Western broadcloth manufactory was accelerated by such kinship and marriage ties among entrepreneurs.

---

35 Beier, 'Industrial growth', p. 242; K. Wrightson, *Earthly necessities: economic lives in early modern Britain, 1470–1750* (London, 2002), pp. 200–1.

36 M. Zell, *Industry in the countryside: Wealden society in the sixteenth century* (Cambridge, 1994) is a notable exception. But few if any Kentish clothiers matched the prominence achieved in the Frome Valley.

37 J. Thirsk, 'Benedict Webb (1563–after 1626)', *ODNB*.

38 E. Moir, 'Benedict Webb, Clothier', *Economic History Review*, 10 (1957), pp. 256–7.

39 His father-in-law was Thomas Trowbridge: F.A. Crisp, *Abstracts of Somersetshire wills* (London, 1887–90), vol. 1, p. 23.

40 For the identification of perpetuana as serge see E.W.J. Kerridge, *Textile manufactures in early modern England* (Manchester, 1985), p. 118 and *OED*.

41 Moir, *Benedict Webb*, p. 257; Mann, *Cloth industry*, p. xv.

42 Mann, *Cloth industry*, p. xvii. Stone died in 1607: TNA, PROB 11/110/269.

43 This identification can be made from a 1597 document cited by Moir: TNA, C3/294/81.

44 A. Warmington, 'John Smyth (1567–1641)', *ODNB*. Mary Browning's mother was Christian Webb, sister of Robert and Benedict: J. Mclean and W.C. Heane (eds), *Visitation of the county of Gloucester, taken in the year 1623* (London, 1885), p. 32.

In a highly influential article, 'Industries in the countryside', however, Thirsk suggested drily that entrepreneurs had perhaps had too much attention.[45] She argued that factors other than individual enterprise were crucial for industrial success, notably that an adequate labour force was even more important than the local availability of raw materials or the ease of transport. The wool and the fuller's earth used in cloth-production could both be imported. Much of the Wiltshire cloth industry, she claimed, 'was concentrated in north-west Wiltshire [a dairying economy] where wool was among the least important products of the farm'.[46] A local port was not essential, she said, 'since the West Country cloth merchants in the Tudor period managed without undue inconvenience to carry their burdens by road to Blackwell Hall in London'.[47] And, pondering how families could dovetail the requirements of both cloth-making and farming, she concluded that this had been achieved in 'a region given over to the small pasture farms of cheese-making dairymen'.[48]

Thirsk's article, first published in 1961, has rightly been described as 'pioneering': it ranged across several industries in different parts of the country and emphasised regional variation more strongly than either Tawney or Postan; it was followed by numerous studies of local industries.[49] Thirsk's account of Wiltshire cloth-making, however, was based not on her own research but on another key work – volume 4 of the *Victoria History of the County of Wiltshire*, with essays on agriculture by Eric Kerridge (another former student of Tawney, who would soon become his most hostile critic) and on the textile industries by Eleanora Carus-Wilson and Julia de Lacy Mann.[50] Since then, a further 14 volumes of *VCH Wiltshire* have been published, providing a mass of new evidence with which to reassess Thirsk's argument. Over the decades it has become increasingly apparent that the most prosperous part of the Wiltshire manufactory was in the west, close to the sheep-runs of the Salisbury Plain and Mendips, to good supplies of fuller's earth and to the clean water of the Frome and its tributaries, rather than in the north-west of the county, and in an area of mixed farming rather than one specialised in dairying.[51]

It is timely, therefore, to reconsider the role and importance of the clothing entrepreneurs in the cross-border area of the Frome Valley. While *VCH Somerset* has not yet covered the eastern parts of the county, important archival work has nonetheless been published. The Somerset historian Colin Brett has identified many Henrician clothiers on both sides of the county boundary and the Wiltshire historian

---

45 J. Thirsk 'Industries in the countryside', in F.J. Fisher (ed.), *Essays in the economic and social history of Tudor and Stuart England* (Cambridge, 1961), pp. 70–88.

46 Ibid., p. 71.

47 Ibid., p. 72.

48 Ibid., p. 74.

49 G.F.R Spenceley, 'The origins of the English pillow-lace industry', *Agricultural History Review*, 21 (1973), p. 81.

50 E.W.J. Kerridge, *Agrarian problems in the sixteenth century and after* (London, 1969), p. 15.

51 Carus-Wilson, 'Woollen industry', section 7 detects strong growth in this area from the late fifteenth century, as London merchants bought increasing quantities of white (undyed) broadcloth for export to the Low Countries.

Figure 10.2 Photograph of Iford Mill House.

Ken Rogers has detailed many owners and tenants of fulling mills on the Frome.[52] Of the ten or more mills which operated between Beckington and Freshford, where the Frome joins the Bristol Avon, two stand out as of special interest: Clifford's Mill at Beckington in Somerset, owned in the Elizabethan era by Thomas and then Robert Webb; and Iford Mill, also just in Somerset, but used by Edward Horton of Westwood, on the Wiltshire side of the river (Figures 10.2 and 10.3).

Three clothiers of Fromewater

Thomas Webb became established at Clifford's Mill at Beckington during the 1540s, after an apprenticeship with Edward Langford of Witcombe Mill at Freshford.[53] His business evidently flourished, since in 1558 he was the second-highest-rated taxpayer

52 C.J. Brett, 'Thomas Kytson and the Somerset clothmen, 1529–1539', *Proceedings of the Somerset Archaeological and Natural History Society*, 143 (2001), pp. 29 56, and 'Thomas Kytson and Wiltshire clothmen, 1529–1539', *Wiltshire Archaeological and Natural History Society Magazine*, 97 (2004), pp. 35–62; Rogers, *Wiltshire and Somerset woollen mills*.

53 TNA, E134/20Eliz/East12.

Figure 10.3 Photograph of Iford Mill Bridge crossing the river Frome.

in Beckington, assessed at £20 in goods.[54] By 1566 he had generated enough free cash to acquire a moiety of manors and lands in Beckington, Rode and Westbury, the catchment area from which he drew his labour.[55] He was probably the Thomas Wobb (*sic*) who in 1568 sold a pack of broadcloths in London to the Hamburg factor Matthias Hoep for £53.[56] In 1569 he was described as 'gentleman' when mustered that year with armour including a pair of 'almain [German] rivets', a harquebus and a bow and sheaf of arrows.[57] Webb's lordship of Beckington included 'suit' of the fulling mills, requiring all his weaver and clothier tenants to have their cloths fulled at Clifford's Mill, as well as the advowson of the parish church, St George's, which he exercised in 1577.[58] In 1581 Webb was prominent enough to serve as high collector of the subsidy for much of east Somerset.[59]

---

54 A.J. Webb, *Two Tudor subsidy assessments for the county of Somerset: 1558 and 1581–2*, Somerset Record Society (SRS) 88 (Taunton, 2002), p. 7.

55 TNA, C 3/188/27.

56 R. Ehrenberg, *Hamburg und England im Zeitalter der Koenigin Elizabeth* (Jena, 1896), p. 274.

57 E. Green, *Certificates of musters, 1569*, SRS 20 (London, 1904), p. 319.

58 The right is included in the 1633 deed of sale by his great-grandson, another Robert: Gloucester Record Office D 2700/NR/12/2; Clergy of the Church of England Database.

59 Webb, *Tudor subsidy assessments*, pp. xviii, 47, 67.

Almost uniquely for this period, it is possible to estimate the profitability of Webb's enterprise, because in 1578 he was sued by a Crown informer, Peter Blackborrow of Frome, and witnesses were questioned about his activities. Commissioners at Frome took evidence from four weavers, a joiner and two tuckers who declared that Webb was commissioning about 20 cloths 'and more' a week which were worth about £5 each, suggesting an annual output of up to 1,000 cloths.[60] Operating at that scale, Webb can be compared even with the greater London merchants, few of whom exported more than 1,000 cloths annually.[61] His profit margin, which can be estimated at around 15 per cent (see Table 10.1), was probably as large as theirs; but, unlike most London merchants, the western clothiers of this period did not have to give credit. Their terms were cash on delivery, although they often left funds on deposit with their customers. The accumulation of retained profits, swelled further when loaned out on interest, would have made him a wealthy man over the course of a 40-year career, perhaps wealthier even than William Stumpe in the 1540s.

Table 10.1

Thomas Webb trading account, c.1575[62]

Income	
Sales revenue	£5,000
Third party fulling	£67
Variable costs	
Wool	£2,100
Oil	£350
Spinning	£875
Weaving	£700
Fuller's Earth	£5
Aulnage & subsidy	£19
Carriage to London	£92
Fixed costs	
Mill rent & repair	£50
Servants' wages	£24
NET ANNUAL PROFIT	£852 (17%)

60 TNA, E134/20Eliz/East12. The tucker Richard Jordan deposed that Webb had made 800 cloths worth £5 each in the past year. He may have bought others to resell.

61 A. Friis, *Alderman Cockayne's project and the cloth trade* (London, 1927), pp. 95–6, lists those who exported more than 1,000 at some time between 1606 and 1622.

62 J. Gaisford, 'Capital in the countryside: social change in west Wiltshire, 1530–1680' (PhD thesis, Birkbeck, University of London, 2014), Appendix 3.

But while Webb was generating substantial cash surpluses, his opportunities for expansion may have been limited. His fulling mill at Beckington was evidently at full capacity, since he had to place some work nearby at Lullington, where one of the witnesses was a fuller. Wool was becoming more difficult to source. In 1577 a group of Wiltshire clothiers deposed that 'the wool growing within this our shire is not sufficient for the draping and working of the inhabitants of our said shire by twenty thousand tods at the least yearly'.[63] Webb's land purchases, noted above, were probably made at least partly for sheep pasture, to provide some of his own wool and help keep his costs under control. Skilled labour may also have been tight, since Webb had at least three local rivals for the spinners and weavers of Beckington and many other competitors nearby, especially at Westbury and Frome. While we have no records of Webb's employees or apprentices, his total workforce must have run well into the hundreds. At his own premises, Webb would have employed a small group of men and boys to wash and sort his wool, which he then sent out to a much larger number of women spinners who worked in their own homes.[64] The yarn they produced was then taken to the weavers (always men), who also worked from home. Broadcloths took about two weeks to weave, so the production of 1,000 cloths a year would have involved at least 50 broadlooms, each with two weavers to throw the shuttle back and forth and a boy to spool the shuttle. At the fulling mill several more men would handle the washing, fulling, rinsing, stretching, drying and folding of the long heavy fabric. Mann estimated that at least 14 full-time workers or their equivalent were needed to support each loom, but contemporaries put the figure even higher, at 18 or 20.[65] Thus, the maintenance of Webb's output would require a labour force of between 700 and 1,000. To put this number into perspective, Ken Rogers has estimated that in 1576 the entire population of Trowbridge, one of the most important cloth towns in west Wiltshire, was only about 1,000.[66]

Thomas Webb had no son to continue his business, but around 1570 his daughter Elizabeth married Robert Webb of Kingswood, in the Gloucestershire Cotswolds, a brother of Benedict Webb (see Figure 10.4).[67] After Thomas Webb died in 1585 his widow Margaret lent £1,000 to Robert, whose subsequent activities reinforce the notion that conventional expansion may have become difficult on the Frome.[68] In 1589 he

---

63 TNA, SP 12/114/27.

64 For a detailed account of the spinners' role in the English cloth-making economy see C. Muldrew, 'Th'ancient Distaff and "Whirling Spindle": measuring the contribution of spinning to household incomes and the national economy in England, 1500–1770', *Economic History Review*, 65 (2012), pp. 498–526.

65 Mann, *Cloth industry*, p. 316.

66 K.H. Rogers, *The book of Trowbridge* (Buckingham, 1984), p. 39.

67 Their first son, Thomas, was baptised in September 1571 and buried in 1600: Somerset Record Office, Beckington Parish Registers. In 1611, the year of his death, Robert Webb wrote to his brother Benedict about the manor of Beckington during the wardship of Thomas's heir, another Robert: Birmingham City Archives MS 3549/146.

68 TNA, PROB 11/108/77.

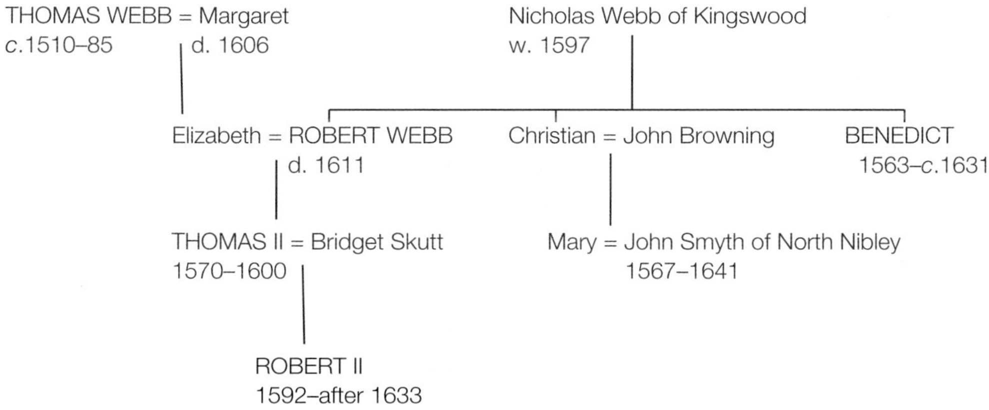

Figure 10.4 Families of Thomas and Robert Webb of Beckington, Somerset.

sold the manor of Rode and purchased property in Gloucestershire near Kingswood.[69] By 1593 he had acquired the lease of the aulnage for Wiltshire and Somerset, being responsible for measuring all cloth made in the region and collecting the Crown subsidy.[70] In 1595 he entered a partnership in London with the rising young Draper Thomas Hayes (later a lord mayor) and the Inner Temple lawyer Thomas Caesar, a servant of the privateer earl of Cumberland, to buy a half-share in the lease of the aulnage of new draperies throughout England.[71] In 1596 Webb bought the aulnage of old drapery for the cities of Bristol and Gloucester.[72] From 1597 to 1600 Webb and Caesar purchased, then sold, a valuable estate in Goodwood, West Sussex.[73] In 1600 they petitioned to lease from the Crown the right to export unlimited quantities of white cloths for a period of 21 years at a fixed annual payment of £2,000. This bid came to nothing following a counter-petition by the Merchant Adventurers, but the lease was granted the following year to Caesar's patron, the earl of Cumberland, and the original projectors may well have remained involved in its administration.[74]

Robert Webb's activities were far more ambitious than those of his father-in-law Thomas, and show how forcefully a well-connected entrepreneur with an appetite for risk could leverage the cash generated from steady sales of cloth. In the seller's market of the 1590s forging links with ambitious merchants such as Thomas Hayes

69 J. Collinson, *The history and antiquities of Somerset*, vol. 2 (Bath, 1791), p. 224; W. Page et al. (eds), *Victoria History of the County of Gloucester* (London, 1907–), vol. 11,'Westonbirt with Lasborough: manors and other estates'.

70 M.A.E. Green et al. (eds), *Calendar of state papers, domestic series, 1547–1704*, 92 vols (London, 1856–1924), *Elizabeth, 1591–4*, p. 312.

71 E.L.C.M.,'Thomas Caesar (1561–1610)', *HoP 1558–1603*.

72 R. Perry, 'The Gloucestershire woollen industry, 1100–1690', *Transactions of the Bristol and Gloucestershire Archaeological Society*, 66 (1945), p. 122.

73 West Sussex Record Office GOODWOOD/E736–743.

74 E.C.L.M.,'Thomas Caesar'.

would have been straightforward.[75] Webb's association with Caesar and Cumberland is more difficult to explain, but if not initiated by Hayes could have been mediated by Webb's kinsman John Smyth, the Berkeley steward, since Sir John Berkeley had been a captain in Cumberland's privateer fleet; or through connections with the Thynne family.[76] After Sir John Thynne's death in 1580, his widow Dorothy married Carew Ralegh, brother of Sir Walter and owner of the privateer *Barque Ralegh*, captained in 1591 by his step-son Henry Thynne.[77] Both Ralegh and Thynne must surely have known Cumberland. While other clothiers may have had access to such contacts, Webb's willingness to speculate is uncharacteristic of his clothier contemporaries. Initially at least he was probably motivated by the scarcity of local resources. But Webb's forays into the aulnage business, funded by cloth sales and property speculation, might best be described as 'vertical' expansion, an attempt to go over the heads of his clothier competitors and extract value from their output as well as his own.

By contrast, Edward Horton of Westwood developed his business 'horizontally', expanding it through a series of commercial alliances cemented by marriage. In 1549, soon after Thomas Webb had moved to Clifford's Mill in Beckington, Horton inherited £200 and a house and fulling mill in Bradford-on-Avon; in 1564 he inherited the leasehold manor of Westwood from his mother.[78] Horton was part of a substantial commercial network (see Figure 10.5). His elder brother William inherited the manor of Iford, with its fulling mill on the Frome.[79] His sister Maud married the clothier Christopher Baylie of Stowford on the Frome; another sister, Alice, married Thomas Yerbury of Trowbridge; a third, Mary, married Henry Long of Whaddon, who had acquired a large estate and fulling mill there in mid-century; and a fourth married a clothier in Newbury.[80] The influenza epidemic of 1557–9 left all three Wiltshire sisters widowed, and this family crisis was compounded in 1562 by the death of Henry Long's brother, Thomas Long of Trowbridge, leaving an estate of nine manors to Henry's fourth son Edward, whose name may indicate that he was Horton's godson.[81] In this desperate situation, Edward Horton of Westwood effectively became the patriarch of a clothing empire: uncle of the young heirs Henry Long II and Edward Long of Whaddon, Thomas Baylie of Stowford, William Yerbury of Trowbridge and John Yerbury of Bradford. Influence over their upbringing and their businesses seems to have enabled Horton to exert a form of economic hegemony over a large part of west Wiltshire and east Somerset.

75 Cloth exports were high for much of the decade: R. Davis, *English overseas trade, 1500–1700* (London, 1973), pp. 52–3.

76 K.R. Andrews, *Elizabethan privateering during the Spanish War, 1585–1603* (Cambridge, 1964), p. 267.

77 M. Booth, 'Carew Ralegh of Downton (c.1550–1626)', *HoP 1558–1603*; Andrews, *Elizabethan privateering*, p. 263.

78 TNA, PROB 11/32/463; *VCH Wiltshire*, vol. 11 'Westwood: Manors'.

79 *VCH Wiltshire*, vol. 11 'Westwood: Manors'.

80 E. Kite, 'Horton Wills', *Wiltshire Notes and Queries* (*WNQ*), 4 (1905), p. 170. For Alice, see Yerbury pedigree in W.H. Jones, *Bradford-on-Avon: a history and description* (Bradford-on-Avon, 1907), inserted after p. 200.

81 TNA, E 150/1001/11.

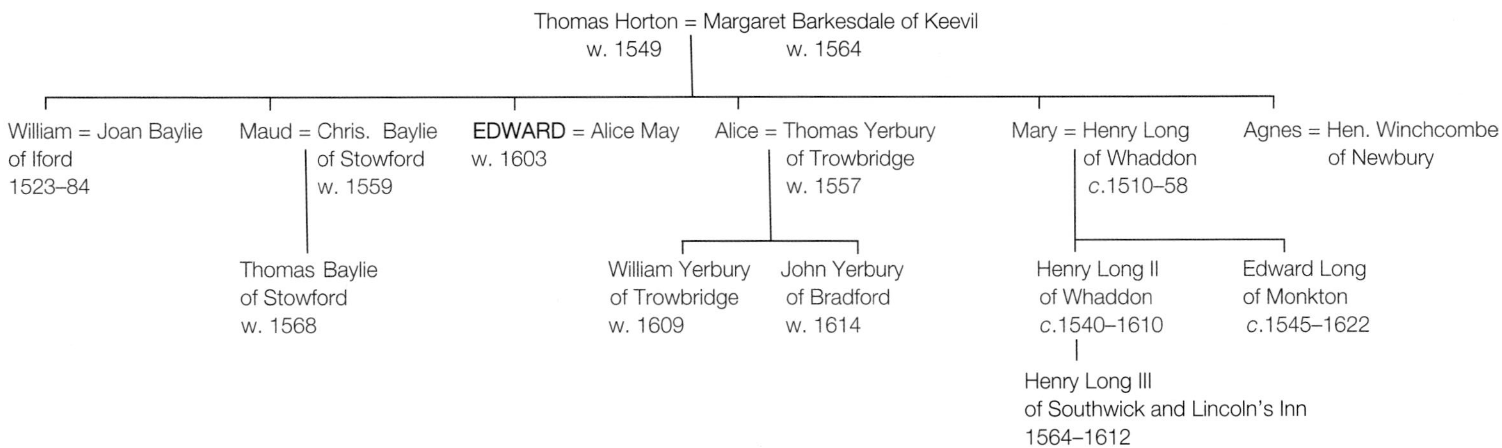

Figure 10.5 Family of Edward Horton of Westwood and Bradford-on-Avon, Wiltshire.

Controlling at least four fulling mills along the Frome and Avon, at Stowford, Iford, Bradford and Whaddon, Horton's network could exert a powerful influence over the marketing of cloths in London.[82] Edward Horton, making frequent visits to the capital, could trade in cloths brought to the mills by lesser clothiers and weavers, who would benefit from faster payment and avoid the cost and risks involved in travelling to and from London. The greater the quantity Horton could offer his merchant customers and the more revenue generated by the cloth trade for the Crown, the more influence he could hope to wield. The marketing advantages the mills brought to the great clothiers vastly outweighed the profits they could make from fulling. In the 1580s a medium-grade cloth could be fulled for 2s 8d, suggesting a maximum annual revenue of less than £70 for a four-stock mill fulling 500 cloths as a service for other clothiers before deducting the cost of repairs, wages and materials.[83] By comparison, the sale of 1,000 cloths per year at about £5 each might yield £750 or more in profit.[84] Horton's sales may have been significantly higher than that.

Horton's importance would have been readily apparent to the leading London merchants. With his family controlling so many manors and mills he could influence production across a valuable territory, well-resourced with sheep pastures, spinners and weavers. This must have been a major factor in maintaining wages in west Wiltshire at a level which seems scarcely to have increased, if at all, throughout the Elizabethan period. The main cost beyond his control was that of wool, where price increases could be mitigated by his own production and any leverage he could exert by buying from others in very large quantities.[85] At the same time Horton and his allies would benefit from any increase in the price of cloth that could be extracted from the London merchants, and this does appear to have risen from less than £4 per cloth in 1547, when the cheapest Wiltshire cloths bought by Thomas Gresham from Thomas Baylie were £36 13s 4d a pack, to the £5 and more paid by Matthias Hoep in 1576 – an increase of nearly 40 per cent.[86] Since skilled labour and wool were the main cost elements, and he had a proprietorial interest in both, it is likely that Horton's profit margins were at least maintained throughout the Elizabethan period, allowing a steady accumulation of cash which may have been well in excess of £1,000 per year.

This trading success drew some of Horton's family into gentry lifestyles. The business strategy of buying estates to secure resources of water power, wool and skilled labour led, in turn, to the need to exploit those estates effectively. In each generation of the Baylie, Horton, Long and Yerbury families only a few sons needed

---

82 The mills were at Stowford, Iford, Bradford and Whaddon.

83 K.H. Rogers, *Warp and weft: the Somerset and Wiltshire woollen industry* (Buckingham, 1986), p. 27.

84 This assumes an average profit of 15 per cent: see Table 10.1 above.

85 The market price for wool fluctuated sharply with demand over the Elizabethan era, but the peak prices of the 1590s were more than double those of trough years in the 1550s and 1560s: P.J Bowden, *The wool trade in tudor and stuart England* (London, 1971), p. 219.

86 This increase comfortably outstripped general price inflation over the same period, which Mayhew's decennial index shows as 27 per cent over the decades from 1550 to 1580, less than 1 per cent per year on average: N.J. Mayhew, 'Prices in England, 1170–1750', *Past & Present*, 219 (2013), pp. 3–39, table 1, citing figures compiled by R.C. Allen.

to be trained up as clothiers; others (including eldest sons) had to manage the lands, which by the end of the century required legal training. A notable example of dynastic commercial strategy can be seen in the upbringing of Horton's nephews Henry Long II of Whaddon and his younger brother Edward Long. From the death of their father in 1558 these boys were in the care of their mother Mary, *née* Horton, and Edward Horton's hand can be clearly seen in their development. Henry Long II would remain a clothier throughout his life, providing advice as such to the Privy Council in 1577 and still being described as 'clothier' in his will of 1611.[87] He married, presumably with Horton's encouragement, Alice May of Broughton Gifford, one of three daughters who were co-heirs of a large estate between Bradford and Whaddon. Of the two other daughters, one married Edward Horton himself and the other married his nephew Jeremy Horton of Iford. These marriages would benefit the clothing business by providing secure and long-term access to sheep pastures in the Avon Vale and to the housing and skilled labour of Broughton Gifford village.[88] Edward Horton and Henry Long must also have concluded that legal expertise would be an advantage, for in 1582 Horton's grand-nephew Henry Long III was enrolled at Lincoln's Inn.[89]

A different path was provided for Thomas Long's chosen heir Edward Long, who was usually described as 'gentleman' and after 1572 made no appearances in the surviving merchants' ledgers or lists from Blackwell Hall.[90] By 1565 Edward married Anne Brounker, sister of the Crown servant William Brounker of Erlestoke, near Edington, who in 1569 married Martha, daughter of Walter Mildmay, Chancellor of the Exchequer.[91] In this way the clothier Hortons and Longs became linked by marriage not only to the Brounkers but to their patrons in the Treasury and the Privy Council. Viewed another way, Walter Mildmay and his brother-in-law Francis Walsingham now had personal ties to two of the major suppliers of English cloth exports. Edward Long had joined the west Wiltshire establishment. He was still operating as a clothier in 1577 and perhaps as late as 1589, but in that year he also received a grant of arms.[92] In 1597 he acquired the manor of Rood Ashton for his own son and heir, Gifford, who would become a JP during the next reign.[93]

From the surviving evidence, it would be unwise to suggest direct political influence accruing to Horton. Nonetheless, there are noteworthy aspects to this new connection to the Treasury and the Privy Council. First, it was achieved while yet another relative of Horton's, the mercer William Burde, held the office – under Mildmay – of Customer Outward at the port of London, where he was responsible for controlling

87 TNA, SP 12/114 f. 4; TNA, PROB 11/117/313.

88 *VCH Wiltshire*, vol. 7 'Broughton Gifford: Manors'.

89 W.P. Baildon (ed.), *Records of the honourable society of Lincoln's Inn: the Black Books*, vol. 1 (London, 1896).

90 Edward Long sold seven azure cloths to Mathias Hoep in 1572: Ehrenberg, *Hamburg und England*, p. 276.

91 W.C. Metcalfe (ed.), *Visitation of Wiltshire, 1565* (London, 1897), p. 8; Ford, 'Sir Walter Mildmay'.

92 Ramsay, *Wiltshire woollen industry*, p. 59; when his younger brother bequeathed him the wool of 'the sheep at Imber': Wiltshire Record Office (WRO) P2/11/43; WRO 947/1866.

93 *VCH Wiltshire*, vol. 8 'Steeple Ashton: Manors'.

the export of cloth from 1560–76.[94] Burde was a close ally and sometimes business partner of Thomas Smythe, Customer Inward and cousin of William Brounker.[95] Second, from 1574 Francis Walsingham was benefiting directly from the export of white broadcloth as grantee of licences to export many thousands of short cloths, and in 1581 he secured a grant of the Hundred of Bradford, Edward Horton's commercial territory. While it might be far-fetched to imagine that Walsingham had the time to deal in detail with such investment, it is reasonable to conclude that others were attending to business for him. In 1582 Thomas St Barbe of Salisbury, a cousin of Walsingham's wife Ursula, made two purchases of land in west Wiltshire from clothiers friendly to Horton; his daughter Mary St Barbe married Edward Langford of Trowbridge, nephew of the clothier Edward Langford, who had been Thomas Webb's master at Freshford.[96] These developments suggest that by the last quarter of the sixteenth century the leading Wiltshire clothiers were as well-connected in the Treasury and the Privy Council as in the City.

Horton's reputation in Wiltshire must have grown with his political connections in London and the West Country and with his family's continuing commercial success. He continued to acquire lands in west Wiltshire at regular intervals, purchasing a Warminster manor from William Burde's son in 1577.[97] Horton was not one of the 11 Wiltshire clothiers who certified to the Council that year that the rising price of wool was the chief cause of the rise in the cloth price, although three of his nephews were signatories: Henry Long and John and Thomas Yerbury.[98] But there is no doubt of Horton's continuing personal activity in the trade on which his fortune had been founded. In 1579 the Privy Council reacted with concern to reports of a robbery planned 'upon the houses of Sir John Horner, knight, and Edward Horton, clothier', confirming his occupation while linking him to one of Somerset's leading gentlemen.[99] In May 1587, when sales at Blackwell Hall were being closely monitored during a short-lived trade crisis in Germany, in one week Horton had the largest quantity of stock in the Wiltshire hall – 77 out of a total of 177 cloths, double that of any other clothier.[100]

By the 1590s Horton had accumulated so much cash that providing credit to the local gentry and trading community became another strand of his business. In this, perhaps, he was following a trend among his customers, the London overseas

---

94 J.J. Howard and G.J. Armytage (eds), *Visitation of London in the year 1568* (London, 1896), p. 68; J. Harley, *The world of William Byrd: musicians, merchants and magnates* (Farnham, 2010), pp. 66–75.

95 B. Dietz, 'Thomas Smythe (1522–91)', *ODNB*; G.W. Marshall (ed.), *Visitation of Wiltshire, 1623* (London, 1882), p. 49.

96 F.W. Weaver (ed.), *Visitations of the county of Somerset, 1551 & 1575* (Exeter, 1885), p. 74; TNA, IND 1/17223 f 6; TNA, IND 1/17224 f 74; J. Evans, 'Clarendon's grandparents', *Notes & Queries*, 22 (1975), p. 28.

97 *VCH Wiltshire*, vol. 8 'Warminster: Manors'.

98 TNA, SP 12/114 f. 48.

99 J.R. Dasent (ed.), *Acts of the privy council of England*, 46 vols (London, 1890–1964), 1579–80, p. 116.

100 TNA, SP 12/20 f. 43. Ramsay, *Wiltshire woollen industry*, p. 67, inferred that Horton was caught by the downturn, but this is a good indication of the scale of his business.

merchants: during the trade crisis of May 1587 Walsingham had observed to Burghley that 'the trade of ten in the hundred, which carries a sure and certain gain, makes the merchants in these doubtful times to employ their stocks for the most part that way'.[101] Horton made loans to landowners and merchants right across west Wiltshire and east Somerset and left the cloth-making business to the next generation. Around 1598 he moved to Bath, where he died in 1603 with his plate in the safe-keeping of the mayor. His inventory recorded more than 180 individual loans totalling nearly £18,000 and debtors including John Thynne II of Longleat (1550?–1604) and five other knights.[102] Since the inventory excluded freehold lands and copyholds, Horton must have been significantly wealthier than any of the Henrician clothiers.[103]

Conclusions: enterprise, resources and the 'achievement norm'

Business enterprise – defined as the aptitude to identify opportunity and to take calculated risks to achieve business growth – was a key factor in the developing economy of Elizabethan west Wiltshire, and perhaps the only one that can explain the region's surge in market share from around 25 per cent of national cloth exports in 1550 to about 40 per cent in 1600. Edward Horton and his nephews and Thomas and Robert Webb present contrasting examples of clothiers making large fortunes in the west Wiltshire countryside in a trade often characterised by historians as stagnant or in difficulty. They were probably the leading broadcloth entrepreneurs of their time, but they were certainly not alone: others can be detected along most of the tributaries of the Bristol Avon, in west Wiltshire, east Somerset and south Gloucestershire. Such men typically built and maintained their businesses within close family groups, but where families were large, or extended by commercially advantageous marriages, they could far transcend the economy of the small master and generate large marketing blocs with significant negotiating power.

In the Elizabethan era the great clothiers who controlled the most productive fulling mills became too powerful to be regulated by the local justices; in effect, they regulated themselves and their cloth was generally of good quality.[104] The 1536 statute requiring all cloths to be sealed had put the mill owners in a controlling position, since it was at the fulling mill that cloths were measured and the seals attached.[105] The great clothiers could thus also regulate the output of their clients. Their importance was clearly demonstrated in the 1570s, when Peter Blackborrow informed not only against Thomas Webb but also against Edward Horton and Henry and Edward Long for cloth-making

101 TNA, SPD Elizabeth vol. 201, ff. 29–30 (May 1587).

102 Society of Antiquaries MS 817/3/f.79.

103 British Library (BL), Add Ms 15559 'The accompt of Henry Long, Gent, one of the executors of Edward Horton'. The value of William Stumpe's estate at his death in 1550 is unknown, but his eldest son and heir had only £1,000 in plate and household goods in 1563, and his lands in Gloucestershire and Wiltshire had been leased for just 700 marks: Baker, 'Sir James Stumpe'.

104 'Leake's treatise on the cloth industry, with proposals for the reform of abuses, 1577' in R.H. Tawney and E. Power (eds), *Tudor economic documents* (London, 1924), vol. 3, pp. 216–17.

105 27 Henry VIII, c. 11: *An act for true making of woollen cloths.*

in the countryside in contravention of the 1558 *Act Touching the Making of Woollen Cloths*, and against the aulnager John Dauntsey for allowing the clothiers to conduct the aulnage as his deputies.[106] Under the statute Blackborrow was entitled to substantial rewards if his information was correct, but even when the Privy Council ordered the Wiltshire justices to investigate and to raise the reward money no action was taken.[107]

In 'Industries in the countryside' Thirsk challenged the then orthodox view that the Wiltshire cloth industry had grown up where it did because of convenient access to water power, fuller's earth and wool supplies. While 'the fulling mill began to drive the industry to the banks of fast-flowing streams and so to the countryside', the decisive factor was not these physical resources but the availability of labour.[108] Industry flourished within a dairy economy that 'required less labour than a corn-growing farm and left men time to engage in a subsidiary occupation'.[109] This narrative has taken firm hold: according to Wrightson, 40 years later, 'the local availability of raw materials, or of swift-running streams to drive the wheels of the fulling mills ... such factors were of small significance ... mill-races could be constructed where they were required'.[110] He follows Thirsk and (through her) Carus-Wilson in dating a shift in location to the late fifteenth century.[111]

But, in the case of the Frome Valley, this view is not ultimately convincing. First, the fulling mills of west Wiltshire were not set up lightly; they were expensive and laborious to construct. Most had been monastic property during the Middle Ages, and early Tudor cloth entrepreneurs bought long leases to secure them before or soon after the Dissolution.[112] Second, as Kerridge showed, much of west Wiltshire did not have a dairy economy; it had a mixed economy, in which grain production was extremely important and sheep were always far more numerous than dairy cattle.[113] It might be objected that the management of sheep was no more taxing than the grazing of dairy cattle, and so Thirk's general argument remains sound. But if, as Coleman observed, 'the clothiers got a cheap workforce' in the late Tudor era this was perhaps because they were 'providers of employment to an expanding population', rather than because the mixed economy was undemanding.[114]

106 Ramsay, *Wiltshire woollen industry*, p. 59; Tawney and Power, *Tudor economic documents*, pp. 190–91.

107 Ramsay, *Wiltshire woollen industry*, pp. 59–60, 139–40.

108 Thirsk, 'Industries in the countryside', *p.* 74.

109 Ibid., p. 87

110 Wrightson, *Earthly necessities*, p. 105.

111 Thirsk, 'Industries in the Countryside', p. 74. For the development of the white broadcloth trade in the Middle Ages see also Postan, *Medieval economy*, pp. 212, 219–20, 234–5, 241.

112 Clifford's Mill at Beckington, Iford Mill and Freshford Mill had all belonged to Hinton Priory: Brett, *Norton St Philip*, pp. 15, 16, 28, 38; *VCH Wiltshire*, vol. 11 'Westwood: Mills'; W. Page et al. (eds), *Victoria History of the County of Somerset* (London, 1906–), vol. 2 'Houses of Carthusian monks: the priory of Hinton'.

113 E.W.J. Kerridge, 'The agrarian development of Wiltshire, 1540–1640' (PhD thesis, University of London, 1951), pp. 53–4; J. Aubrey, *The natural history of Wiltshire*, ed. J. Britton (London, 1848), pt II, c. 9 'Wool'.

114 Coleman, *Economy of England*, p. 78–9.

A more fundamental objection to Thirsk's model is that it undervalues the competitive drive of the Frome Valley clothiers and the commercial advantages of owning fulling mills, especially where capacity was limited, and of grazing large flocks when demand for wool was outstripping supply and forcing up prices. The great clothiers' core business strategy was always to engross: to dominate the output of a specific stretch of water and its hinterland by securing ownership or control of the fulling mills; to buy the entire wool output of a landed estate; to bind their skilled workers into long-term relationships, even when they were not formally employed. The clothiers used their cash resources to counter rising wool prices by buying in large quantities from regular suppliers and by grazing their own large flocks. They co-operated with each other by holding down rates of pay over very long periods. The scale of their output meant they could negotiate with the London merchants from a position of strength. By the last quarter of the sixteenth century the wealthiest clothiers lived in substantial houses and had high-level commercial contacts at court and influence in the Privy Council. Inevitably they also made enemies among the gentry. An unnamed Elizabethan, quoted by Fisher, condemned this new breed of clothier: 'who doth most harm of all other degrees in this land by purchasing land or leases, or by maintaining his son in the Inns of Court like a gentleman or by buying offices for him'.[115] Yet in west Wiltshire their wealth, though dependent ultimately on wool supplies, seems to have been generated (as Tawney himself acknowledged) without significant displacement of the labouring population for enclosure. In that respect Thirsk's model was absolutely correct: the large local resources were readily supplemented from more distant sources.[116]

Ramsay suggested that in the Elizabethan era many Wiltshire clothiers left a depressed trade and invested their wealth in land 'to live at ease upon their rents', fitting Brown's model of the 'achievement norm'.[117] But such a transition does not seem to have been typical. Despite owning a substantial landed estate Thomas Webb (c.1515–85) found a son-in-law willing to trade as a clothier, while Robert Webb's son, Thomas Webb II (1570–1600), married into the family of a wealthy London merchant.[118] He may indeed have been the Thomas Webb, fuller, who in 1594 acquired a 21-year lease of Edward Horton's grist and fulling mills in Frome.[119] Commerce was not lightly abandoned. The fulling mills that could generate wealth for those capable of financing and managing cloth production were far too valuable to be passed outside the family. When no suitable sons were available, sons-in-law or nephews were trained up as clothiers. In the senior branches of the family, Horton's nephews William Horton of Iford and Edward Long of Monkton retained the freeholds of their mills even though they were brought up as gentlemen and would marry into landowning families. It was trading success rather than trading difficulty that sent Horton's grand-nephew Henry Long III to Lincoln's Inn and the bar. Large landed estates provided the essential

115 Fisher,'Commercial trends', p. 110.

116 Thirsk,'Industries in the countryside', p. 71.

117 Ramsay, *Wiltshire woollen industry*, p. 42.

118 *Somerset & Dorset Notes & Queries*, 2 (1891), pp. 17–18; and see Figure 10.4.

119 WRO 212B/7463.

cloth-making resources of water power, skilled labour and at least some of the wool, but landownership demanded new skills to fully exploit those estates. Between 1570 and 1600 the heirs of the most prosperous clothiers entered the Inns of Court alongside their gentry neighbours.[120]

There is no indication that the periodic trading crises emphasised by Ramsay had brought lasting problems for the Elizabethan clothiers; there were few bankruptcies or seizures of property in lieu of debt.[121] Probably the downturns only increased the leverage of those with ready money, particularly those clothiers who had a significant rental income. Few clothier families seem ever to have abandoned the trade; the business of cloth-making simply passed to the most apt in the next generation, if necessary a son-in-law or nephew. Several of the leading clothiers of the last Elizabethan decade can be directly connected to their Henrician forebears, either by descent or as tenants or suppliers.[122] But, during the Elizabethan era, a relatively small number of successful clothing entrepreneurs had established themselves as a new commercial elite with a powerful influence across west Wiltshire. Their wealth was expressed both in architecture and in furnishings. While no Elizabethan clothier would build a house like Longleat, marking the 'High Renaissance of Tudor architecture', by the end of the reign they owned some of the finest smaller houses in west Wiltshire, and spent lavishly on fine furniture, hangings and silver-gilt plate.[123] 'Broadcloth gentlemen' such as Robert Webb and Edward Horton deployed fortunes built through the accumulation of profit over decades and generations, and could align their interests with great merchants such as Hayes, aristocrats such as Cumberland and Crown servants such as Mildmay and Walsingham. There is little reason to doubt that their wealth matched or exceeded that of the Henrician clothiers, and that their enterprise has been significantly underestimated by economic historians.

---

120 Thomas Baylie (June 1578), Christopher Baylie and Henry Long (both Feb 1580/1) were all admitted to Lincoln's Inn: *Records of Lincolns Inn*.

121 A. Conyers, *Wiltshire extents for debts, Edward I–Elizabeth I*, Wiltshire Record Society 28 (Devizes, 1973).

122 Gaisford, 'Capital in the countryside', pp. 232–3 and Appendix 2.

123 J. Summerson, *Architecture in Britain 1530–80* (London, 1953), p. 31. Henry Long II enlarged his manor house at Whaddon around 1575: *VCH Wiltshire*, vol. 8 'Whaddon: Manor'; WRO 947/2190 tab. 2, n. 4. His son Henry Long III acquired by marriage Southwick Court, near Trowbridge, the former home of Lord Willoughby of Broke: E. Kite, 'Southwick Court and its Owners', *WNQ*, 2 (1899), pp. 24–9. The inventory of Edward Horton lists his furnishings at Bath and Bradford in 1603: BL, Add Ms 15559.

Chapter 11

'The fellowship of the town': constituting the commonalty of an English country town, Cirencester c.1200–1800*

David Rollison

> Although the concept of civil society emerged in its thoroughly secularized form only in the seventeenth and eighteenth centuries, its moral and intellectual foundations ... had deep historical roots.[1]

Town and country

Located near the sources of the Thames, 100 miles west of London, at the crossing of three national roads – Akeman and Ermin Streets and the Fosseway – Cirencester was the 'capital' of one of medieval and early modern England's wealthiest 'countries'. Excavation of its Saxon church, demolished to make way for the Augustinian abbey founded by Henry I in 1117–31, 'shows it to have been the longest known in Anglo-Saxon England'. *Domesday* records that Edward the Confessor had five hides and five plough teams, thirty-one villeins, thirteen serfs, ten bordars, three mills, meadows, woods and two free men with two ploughs. 'The wool of the sheep', paid by custom to the queen, was already an important commodity, and a 'new market' was mentioned in 1086.[2] Middlemen based in the town were scouring the Cotswolds for wool before merchants are recorded in twelfth-century sources. A minster supplying priests to the town and several neighbouring villages makes it a strategic place well before the Norman-Angevin hegemony.[3] Henry I's establishment of an abbey (the loyalty of which

---

* I wish to thank Richard Reece for keeping me informed about research conducted since the publication of D. Rollison, *Commune, country and commonwealth: the people of Cirencester 1117–1643* (Woodbridge 2011), and in particular for sending me a draft copy of his *Cotswold Studies 5* (forthcoming), which includes his invaluable analysis of the Register of the Chapel of the Blessed Virgin Mary.

1 K.A. Lynch, *Individuals, families and communities in Europe, 1200–1800: the urban foundations of western society* (Cambridge 2003), p. 21.

2 E.A. Fuller, 'Tenures of land, by the customary tenants of Cirencester', *Transactions of the Bristol and Gloucestershire Archaeological Society* (*TBGAS*), 2 (1877–8), p. 286.

3 A.K.B. Evans, 'Cirencester's early church', *TBGAS*, 107 (1989), p. 113; the Saxon church was '179 feet long with a nave 52 feet wide externally'.

to the Crown could be relied on) built on existing patterns of commercial, religious and political organisation, confirming David Postles' observation that Augustinian houses were founded in 'those types of towns which were archetypal in English commercial organisation'.[4] Cirencester Abbey was founded at the beginning of the twelfth century, when towns 'mushroomed, and the number of their inhabitants and the diversity of their skills and occupations multiplied ... most spectacularly in the Low Countries and the Valley of the Rhine, the Seine and the Thames'.[5]

The abbey's location was determined by commercial considerations. It was an important market, a source of wool, and thus a magnet for enterprising merchants and tradesmen who, for centuries, led and participated in *resistance* to the abbey. Beginning with an account of the rapid development of abbey dominion, this chapter relates the history of commune and commonalty from the early twelfth to the eighteenth century. It shows the commonalty resisting encroaching lordship and creating pre-modern forms of 'civil society'. Communal solidarity centred first on communally funded religious gilds, later on the parish church. Augustinian lordship was imposed at a time when 'formal and legal differences between towns and boroughs had not crystallized'.[6] The secular community, described by its 'elders' in 1209 as 'the fellowship of the town' (*communitate videlicet ville*), petitioned and at times protested violently against encroachments on customs and liberties that they claimed to have enjoyed prior to 1117. The imposition of ever-present and all-embracing lordship not only stimulated repeated episodes of resistance but also, against all odds, recurring customary forms of organisation and repeatedly reinvented *traditions* of solidarity that continued to shape communal politics and government long after the abbots had gone. Although the abbots owned the market, a quotidian sphere of freedom of movement had to be allowed the merchants, craftsmen, traders, woolgrowers and clothworkers to make the market worth having. Commerce underwrote custom. Changing forms of commerce and industry shaped and reshaped conceptions (and selections) of custom throughout the period. The ranks of the commonalty come into sharper focus in the seventeenth and eighteenth centuries. Merchants, wholesalers and capitalist organisers of labour were prominent communal leaders throughout.

From c.1200 to 1400 town and country attracted wool-buyers from the industrial heartlands of high medieval Europe. From c.1400 to 1700 Cirencester was a major conduit to the London markets for mass cloth production in central Gloucestershire and

---

4 A.K.B. Evans, in 'Cirencester Abbey: the first hundred years', *TBGAS*, 109 (1991), p. 99, suggests that the king may himself have initiated building in 1117; D. Postles, 'The Austin canons in English towns c.1100–1350', *Historical Research*, 66 (1993), p. 16.

5 R.I. Moore, *The war on heresy: faith and power in medieval Europe* (London, 2012), pp. 224–5; these urbanising regions 'were building in Europe a common culture under the direction of an increasingly cohesive clerical elite ... [which] flocked to the courts of princes and great lords ... Clerks like these multiplied ... because they could offer better solutions to the problems of their lords.' Richard Fitzmal and Ranulf Glanville, chief counsellors of Henry II, were 'builders of the most developed secular government in northern Europe', pp. 225–7.

6 Postles, 'Austin canons', p. 16.

north Wiltshire. At the height of its economic and political dynamism, roughly c.1380–1660, the 'Seven Hundreds of Cirencester', stretching west across the Cotswolds to the 'Edge' overlooking the Vale of Severn, comprised a hundred parishes, many more manors, dozens of shepherds minding thousands of sheep, a liberal sprinkling of country gentlemen, cloth workers in the Stroudwater Valleys, dozens of mills, scores of yeomen–clothiers, hundreds of husbandmen tilling the 'cotes' or valleys where lay most of the settlements, and strong representations of all the crafts and trades to be found in comparable countries everywhere in England.[7] 'This place is a very great thoroughfare ... particularly from it being the way from London into all the Cloathing Country of [Minchin] Hampton, Stroud, Bisley, Painswick', wrote one of its eighteenth-century ministers. It had been the way into and out of the 'rural' cloth-making districts to its south and west since the late fourteenth century. Fortunes were made by men able in some way to engross local production. 'In consequence [of its location, Cirencester] has the convenience of a Daily Post, Stage Coaches etc.'.[8]

This late source captures the town's strategic location. Cirencester is liminal, one face looking up the Thames Valley, the other across the rich pastures and fast-flowing streams to the west. The highway to Gloucester and Wales drives across the Cotswold plateau to Birdlip, which descends into the Vale of Severn. It was gateway and capital of the Cotswolds, which had rich 'cotes' for husbandry, 'wolds' for pasture, and fast streams for fulling mills. The Thames was navigable from Lechlade, a dozen miles to the west. While in many ways self-sufficient in necessities marketed at Cirencester and at smaller markets at Fairford, Lechlade, Northleach, Cheltenham, Winchcombe, Stow-on-the-Wold, Birdlip, Painswick, Bisley and, later, Stroud, what made local merchants rich was production for 'export' to regional, national and international markets. Wool and cloth brought wealth (and employment) into town and country. Monumental traditions, wealth, a brooding yet fertile landscape and the ancient locations of its hundred or more villages and parish churches made it one of the most prosperous countries in early modern England. Cirencester was its capital.

Manorial dominion

In 1155 'tenants of the king' complained to Henry II that the canons of Cirencester were exceeding 'liberties' granted 38 years earlier. Tenants had fled in the civil wars. When Henry assumed the throne he ordered his officers everywhere 'to restore to his canons at Cirencester their fugitives and natives with their chattels who had fled since the death of Henry I'. He warned the abbot not to 'vex' the 'king's men': there were two freeholders. Henry allocated his manorial rents (as lord) to the canons to complete the abbey's grand chapel, where once the Anglo-Saxon minster had stood.[9]

7 Based on the aggregation and analysis of John Smith, *Men and armour for Gloucestershire in 1608* (Gloucester 1980), pp. 239–317.

8 'Cirencester Parish Book', Gloucestershire Archives (GA), P86/1 IN 6/3, f.80.

9 'Writ of Henry II', doc.75 in C.D. Ross, *The cartulary of Cirencester Abbey* (London, 1964), p. 58; E.A. Fuller,'Cirencester, the manor and the town', *TBGAS*, 9 (1884–5), p. 317.

Richard I sold 'the town and manor of Cirencester in fee-farm in perpetuity, with all its manorial rights, customs, and its weekly market' for £100 down and £30 a year. King John confirmed Richard's charter for £100 and sold the abbot the right to exclude his sheriffs from the manor for another £100 plus 'a palfrey.' The people's rents, market tolls and tallages paid for the building and the series of charters by which their Augustinian lord intensified his dominion. In 1210 the king sold the abbot a license to build a gaol.[10] Twelve years later the abbot completed the purchase of the rectory of the parish church, to add to his collection of 28 benefices as far afield as London, Northamptonshire, Buckinghamshire, Wiltshire and Worcestershire.[11] By the early thirteenth century the parish, the manor, the market and the parish church were firmly in the hands of their ever-present lord.[12]

In 1225 townspeople appealed against the abbot's increasing customary services. The king's agents licensed him to carry on.[13] Under Richard I, John and Henry III abbots added rights to return of the king's writs, custody of prisoners and right to levy tallage whenever the king did so – doubling labour services and financial exactions. Under Richard and John townspeople paid six tallages into the abbot's coffers. Building expenses and royal fees notwithstanding, the scale of the abbey's wealth continued to grow. It contributed nearly a third (£19 6s 9d) of the £66 13s 4d Gloucestershire landowners paid to Richard's carucage of 1198.[14]

Conflict between lord and commune reached a peak in the first half of the fourteenth century. During the crises of the early fourteenth century the abbot, Adam Brokenbury, was a warrior and needed to be. In 1300 'the poor men of Cirencester' complained that he and his men had entered their homes, extorted 'great sums of money', consumed their goods and impounded their beasts. He explained to the court that they refused to have their corn ground at his mills, forcing him to enter their houses to destroy their hand-mills. The king found for the abbot and ordered the townspeople to pay him a fine of 100 marks.[15] In 1308 the abbot abolished the Court of Provostry, believing it to be at the heart of organisation against him. Although their function was to direct weekly labour for the lord, provosts were elected by the men.[16] In 1312 Nicholas of Stratton (aka 'Nicholas the Proctor' and 'Nicholas the Reeve') sued the abbot for an illegal tallage, 'was cudgelled by the abbot's men, and presently died of his injuries'. An inquiry was held, but the abbot 'quietly procured … royal pardons'

10 W. Page (ed.), *The Victoria History of the County of Gloucestershire* (hereafter *VCH Glos*), vol. 2 (London, 1907), p. 80.

11 Welbore St Clair Baddeley, *A history of Cirencester* (Cirencester, 1924), pp. 148, 158–60.

12 The earliest reference naming officials of the parish church in GA, *Hockaday Abstracts Vol. 155, Cirencester 1400–1549*, is a diocesan certificate dated November 1498 naming the prior of the abbey as 'first treasurer' and Dom[inus] John Malvern, a canon, as 'Warden of the Church of St John the Baptist'.

13 Baddeley, *Cirencester*, p. 152.

14 Evans, 'Cirencester Abbey: the first hundred years', p. 109.

15 *VCH Glos*, vol. 2, p. 81; for a comparable episode at St Albans, see Rosamund Faith in R. Samuel (ed.), *People's history and socialist theory* (London, 1981), pp. 50–60.

16 Fuller, 'Tenures of land', pp. 310–11.

for a payment of £200.[17] An *Inspeximus* of 1320 confirmed the abbey's right to charge a 'reasonable tallage' whenever the king did so.[18] A licence (and listing) of 1321 confirms that ruthless acquisition of burgages continued.[19]

In January 1343 townsmen sued 'for recovery of the king's rights usurped and withdrawn by the abbot of Ciceter'. The abbot 'siezed and imprisoned them until they made very grievous fines with the abbot for their ransoms'. They paid up, but he continued 'daily [to] procure them to be indited of felonies and trespasses'. His aim was to so 'vex them who would sue for the king's right [that they] dare not [appeal to the king] for fear of him'.[20] In the same year 'the poor men of Cirencester' produced a charter of Henry I granting Cirencester 'the same privileges as the burgesses of Winchester'. The 'poor townspeople' (they included merchants and landowners) claimed that it was destroyed 'in 1292 (when) the abbot bribed the burgess who had custody of it, got possession of it and burned it'.[21] Twenty 'poor men' were called to Westminster to justify the claim that 'the town and manor had once been independent of one another'. They claimed that 'since the reign of John' the abbots had illegally taken possession of the patronage of the parish church, administered the two hospitals of St John and St Lawrence to their own advantage and habitually disregarded a charter which they claimed had been granted to the town 'allowing it the same privileges as the burgesses of Winchester'. These were 'encroachments on the king's rights and their [i.e. the commonalty's] own'.[22]

The facts were not in dispute. By 1350 the abbot exercised a complete set of powers and liberties in the town and the Seven Hundreds. Edward III's new charter of 1343 confirmed an ascendency that was as complete as it would ever be. The abbot had writings that confirmed all his claims, and writings (genuine or not) went back 'beyond the memory of man'. The abbey held the town's two hospitals, the neighbouring forests, the manor, the parish, the market, the Seven Hundreds of Cirencester with View of Frankpledge and 'tallages whenever the king does'.[23] The lord of the manor had the power to license occupations and trades and hold two markets a week, 52 weeks a year. The 'occupations and trades' never gave up their efforts to limit his powers. It became a custom, something the town was famous for.

---

17 *Calendar of Patent Rolls* (*CPR*) *Ed. II* (26 July 1313): Royal pardon to abbot upon fine made by abbot for acquiring in mortmain in the time of the late king divers small parcels of land, tenements, mills, shops and messuages; Ibid., 127 (24 June 1314): pardon for acquiring in mortmain without licence in Minety; Ibid., 364 (24 October 1315): pardon for acquiring divers lands in Minety; Ibid., 499 (16 May 1316) reports that the abbot and a dozen armed men, including a lay brother of the abbey and one 'William, parson of Cotes', had 'entered the free warren of ... Tettburie and took rabbits, killed four colts of the price of 20 marks, carried away [the keeper's] goods and assaulted his servants'. The abbot was ordered to pay a fine of 100s.

18 *Calendar of Close Rolls Ed. III*, vol. 3, 116 (30 March 1319).

19 *CPR Ed. II*, vol. 4, 29 (19 October 1321).

20 *CPR Ed. III*, vol. 5, p. 593.

21 *VCH Glos*, vol 2, p. 82.

22 Baddeley, *Cirencester*, p. 176.

23 *Calendar of Charter Rolls*, vol. 5 (22 September 1343).

Communal resistance

The founding of Cirencester Abbey and the reorientation of the town that accompanied its construction occurred at a time when the Church and states of Western Europe were girding their loins, loudly and violently attacking heterodoxy, reorganising their instruments and institutions of evangelical repression and authority and avidly repressing alternative sources of legitimacy. Recent studies argue strongly that 'an exuberant variety of religious belief and practice existed more or less everywhere in Europe' at the grass roots.[24] Not least in Norman–Angevin England, in a period of rapid economic and demographic growth, localities were drawn into institutional webs of reforming states which increasingly depended on monks, priests and clerks for counsel and management. We do not know what strains of heterodoxy existed among the commonalty of Cirencester; it is safe to assume that the arrival of recently educated state-sponsored Augustinian canons necessarily disrupted – indeed, replaced – existing relations between the people of town and country and the community of secular canons that had been based at St Mary's Minster, whose task had been to serve the congregations of the district.

By c.1200 religion, secular government and 'the trade of the town, which increased very rapidly in the twelfth and thirteenth centuries, was entirely under the Abbot's control'.[25] For their part, challenges to the abbots' hegemony excited great interest among the people of the district. In 1209 townspeople complained that the abbot was flouting custom by imposing harvest works (or a fee) on every man of working age in the commune.[26] The documents reveal the lucidity of the commune's recitation of custom against the abbey's efforts to escalate labour services and tighten market and trade licences. Two groups, the 'young men' (*juvenes guidem de Cyrencestria domini Regis nativis*) and, testifying to the continuing importance of immigration, 'resident strangers' (*extraneis inhabitantibus sive ad tempus in Cyrencestria*), claimed to be exempt. The sheriff summoned the abbot, canons and servants of the abbey, and the 'young men' and 'strangers', to present their cases to 'the whole halimote court' of the manor. 'Lawful elders' (*legales homines de senioribus*) nominated 19 *electi* to be sworn 'by touching the holy gospel'. Also present were the holders of (or heirs to) two local sub-manors, a merchant (Jordan *le mercat*) and several other worthies.[27]

24 Moore, *Heresy*, p. 296; see also John Arnold, *Belief and unbelief in medieval Europe* (London, 2005).

25 *VCH Glos*, vol. 2, p. 80.

26 The following is based on documents reproduced, in Latin and English, by Fuller, 'Tenures of land', pp. 304–8.

27 'The land of Robert Erkenbald is held on a hunting tenure; the land of Robert Pirie is held by escorting the treasurer of our lord the king': 'Inquisition at the Command of King John', in Fuller, 'Tenures of land', p. 298. The Ercumbald and Pirie lineages held land north and south of what became Chipping (later Dyer) Street; Robert Ercumbald and Robert Pirie witnessed documents relating to the Lady Chapel, established around this time 'for the benefit of the whole parish' (see below); Jordan of Cirencester is probably the man, alternately referred to as 'Jordanus Scotmodi' and 'Jordanus Mercator', who held a messuage in Dyer St and acted three times as a witness to Lady Chapel documents; Ernald Barbast is not traceable, but one Robert Barbast witnessed Lady

Crammed in the church and spilling into the market place, every degree of the lay community was represented, along with 'many others of the district' (*multis aliis de visneto*).

Young men still living at home ('under the rod and power of their fathers') 'were held quit by their parents by reason of the harvest works which they themselves did to the king or his fee-farmer'. Only one member of the household – the head or his nominee – was liable, in their view. Only when the male children of *nativii* 'were become sulfodes … [living by] their own free power, and … by their own labour' (the later 'householders') were they required to serve the harvest works.[28] As for 'strangers inhabiting or sojourning for a while', the elders swore that 'this was the law':

> if a stranger … slept in Cyrencester on midsomer night, and afterwards stayed there till the king or his fee-fermor had his corn reaped … then, whosoever he might be, whether freeman or bondman, male or female (*sive liber, sive servus, sive masculus, sive femina*), he (*sic*) must needs do three bederipes [harvest works] to the king, or to his fee-fermor, for the fellowship that is of the town, which the said man had used and had enjoyed up till that day.

The children of *nativii* and immigrants qualified by custom and communal consensus were entitled to trade as soon as they were no longer 'beneath the rod and authority of their fathers or maintained by their parents'. When they 'attained their own power, and lived of their own labour, and were become reapers … every one of them shall have license to buy and sell freely without toll of any sort', in return for the customary three harvest works and the annual licence-fee. In their eyes, custom worked reciprocally, benefiting the abbots while enabling and encouraging inhabitants' work.

The second half of the twelfth century saw change in the townscape, most obviously in the emergence of what became (and still is) the main street. 'Chipping' (alternatively 'Dyer') Street led from the '*Via Regis*' (Fosse Way) to the existing market place at the junction of the main roads from Cricklade and Gloucester.[29] Recent research suggests Dyer Street was set out over a former open strip field; on the basis of his analysis of donations to the Mary Chapel, Richard Reece 'pushes the existence of the street back towards 1200'.[30] Development of the town's new 'Market Street' bisected two sub-manors held not by the abbot but by two freemen and was almost certainly an initiative of the townspeople. A 'Book of Fees' compiled in 1470 names 24 men who, in c.1250, held small plots and houses on land once held by Richard Pirie in return for guarding the king's treasury, a duty now shared by the 24. They included

---

Chapel documents several times from 1331 to 1353: see Richard Reece,'Lady chapel register', p. 4, and Appendix 4,'Lady chapel index by given names', *Cotswold Studies*, 5 (forthcoming), ff. 17.

28 Sulfodes were people who did not have an inheritance in serfdom and were free to leave their parents' home and live off their labour.

29 The provenance of the alternative names is unclear. Wealthy dyers almost certainly based themselves there, but a rental of 1460 described those who lived there as of 'Chepyngstrete': Richard Reece,'Lady chapel register', Appendix 5.

30 Reece,'Lady chapel register'.

a tailor (*Cissor*), four merchants (*mercator*), one Humphrey of the Barre and another submanor holder, Richard Erkenbald.[31]

By this time a new parish church stood between the dominant abbey chapel (on the site of the Saxon church) and the market place. The church of St John the Baptist was dedicated c.1170 and its nave rebuilt by the parishioners c.1235–50, almost certainly to create a suitable environment for the communal Mary Chapel.[32] The raising of funds to build and maintain the chapel and pay the salary of a chaplain 'appointed by all the parishioners ... to celebrate the Divine Service daily in honour of our Lord Jesus Christ and the most blessed Virgin Mary' was organised by 'good men' 'on behalf of the whole parish'. These were merchants, tradesmen and the holders of local sub-manors, whom later documentation identifies as typical communal leaders.[33] Christopher Dyer writes that later chantry foundations at market towns near Moreton Henmarsh enabled otherwise disenfranchised townspeople:

> to take on some functions of government by developing their fraternities as property-holding organisations ... which had sufficient funds to provide benefits for the inhabitants, such as building schools and employing schoolmasters. They also organised fraternity feasts and other social occasions that brought the townspeople and country traders into contact and provided a service for settling quarrels.[34]

As David Postles writes, 'by 1300, burgesses were thinking ... not only of their ... corporate identity, but also of new types of benefactors for the well-being of their

---

31 Ibid.

32 Evans,'Cirencester Abbey: the first hundred years', p. 113, states that when William of Worcester visited the site in 1488 he commented on the antiquity of the Mary Chapel, suggesting it was older than the then existing nave: i.e. before c.1235; Moore, *The First European Revolution c.970–1215* (Oxford, 2000), pp. 173–5, writes that 'The cornerstone' of Western European monarchical states''attack on the little community' at this time was 'the parochial system, and the authority and influence of the parish priest, under the bishop'. Community-funded chapels thus appear as another form of resistance by 'the little community'.

33 E.A. Fuller, 'The register of the chapel of the Blessed Virgin Mary in the parish church of Cirencester', *TBGAS*, 18 (1893–4), pp. 320–31, citing Bodleian Library, Dugdale Ms. No. 42: 'Register Book of the Wardens', c.1460; Fuller (p. 321) cites a deed saying that the service was 'begun through the zeal and patronage of good men'; the title was in use throughout Europe, of course: for a valuable discussion of the communal/associational contexts of the generic honorific of medieval 'good men' see M.G. Pegg, *A most holy war: the Albigensian crusade and the battle for Christendom* (Oxford, 2008), pp. 26–7; D.A. Postles, *Social proprieties: social relations in early-modern England (1500–1680)* (Washington D.C., 2006), pp. 35, 133, writes that 'The title of goodman ... corresponded with middling status'; 'during the seventeenth century ... Goodmen and Goodwives were symbols of commonwealth, hospitality, and traditional social values, but were being displaced by new commercial culture'.

34 C. Dyer, *A country merchant 1495–1520: trading and farming at the end of the Middle Ages* (Oxford, 2012), p. 211.

souls – chantries and fraternities within the parish churches inside the towns'.[35] This movement certainly took off at Cirencester in the late fourteenth century, but it built on the evident success of the Mary Chapel, founded at least a century earlier.

A later deed says the chapel was 'begun through the zeal and patronage of good men'. 'The prestige and pervasiveness of goodmen,' writes Mark Gregory Pegg of their contemporaries in Languedoc, 'derived from an intense localism focused on a particular village or town ... These villages and towns were like tiny looking-glass cages, with [everyone] constantly watching each other.'[36] Cirencester was a 'face-to-face' community: distinctively urban, yet with no more than about 1,000 inhabitants in the 1380s, rising to 3,000 in the seventeenth and 4,000 in the later eighteenth century. Throughout these centuries, its wealthiest commoners often lived up to the communal *expectation* that their time, wealth and experience of the wider world be placed at the service of the spiritual and material prosperity of the commune.[37]

The people's chapel was a frontier between life and death, and not only in the sense that masses were sung there. In 1348, a year before the Black Death, it was called 'The chapel of the Blessed Mary of the charnel'. The vault was opened in 1867, revealing that 'several feet of the eastern end were completely filled up [with bones]; an outer wall had been made of the bones of arms and legs, and the skulls and other bones [were] stacked behind. The bones of a large number of later bodies were lying loosely in front.'[38] The chapel of the ancestors continuously attracted a flow of small gifts and bequests from rich and not-so-rich townspeople. Its fifteenth-century possessions included an osculatory (a flat wooden representation of Jesus on the cross that was kissed by the chaplain and passed round to be kissed by the congregation), loose beads of jet, breviaries and other books, 'veils, kerchiefs, rings, brooches, girdles, a pearl necklace, several rosaries of amber and a few of jet, and furniture including carpets for the benches, silver chalices, cruets and crucifixes'. In 1458 the wardens received legacies of a bride's cotton veil, two pillows (to rest books on the altar), a ring, 30 small bars of silver valued at 20s and a handkerchief. This treasury disappeared when the chapel was dissolved in 1547, but three years earlier parishioners appointed the wealth of the chapel to 'the keeping of a school'. An eagle lectern worth £5 had already been transferred to the church.[39] Townspeople suspected that their chapels were marked for state plunder and took measures to ensure that the little treasures of nine generations remained in the town, as was customary.

---

35 Postles, 'Austin canons', p. 18.

36 Pegg, *A most holy war*, pp. 26–7.

37 For the significance of this communal ethic in late medieval England, see D. Rollison, *A commonwealth of the people* (Cambridge, 2010).

38 Fuller, 'Register book', p. 324; charnel chapels were used as repositories for bones dispersed or displaced from churchyards during reburials. Mortality (and thus burials) had been exceptionally high in 1316–22 and would be again in 1349; in 1663 a public meeting of Vestry allowed 'Esquire Master' access to the 'charnell house under the Lady Chapel' for a burial place for his family: Cirencester Vestry Book, GA, P86 VE 2.1.

39 Fuller, 'Register book', pp. 326, 329–31.

A collectivity of taxpayers?

Most fourteenth-century English towns had many fewer than the 2,000 souls Katherine Lynch hesitantly uses as a cut-off point.[40] Cirencester probably averaged around 1,000 inhabitants (allowing for sharp fluctuations around epidemic years) from 1300 to 1400. The commune was centred on its merchants, wholesalers, retailers and craftsmen. Immigrants were incorporated into the customs. In the sixteenth century, when its population began to approach Lynch's threshold, its mortality regime was undeniably 'urban'. One clue to the crucial relations between town and country lies in the fact that the surnames of witnesses, chapel trustees and taxpayers of the thirteenth and fourteenth centuries include nearly all the villages of the Seven Hundreds and others, such as 'Scotmody', 'London', 'Northfolke', 'Northerne', 'Waleys', 'Leycester' and 'Lewes', from much further afield.[41] In a recent study of urban protest Samuel Cohn admits that it is usually impossible to know 'whether an insurrection had taken place in the countryside, towns, or both'. Even when we know an episode took place in a town, as in 1209, the sources make it impossible to assess the involvement of participants from surrounding villages. There is a substantive as well as an evidential reason for this. The even spread of many urban places in what we know to have been, by the early fourteenth century, a highly if unevenly commercialised society routinely interconnected by traffic suggests that we need to think in terms of a commonwealth already characterised by something resembling what the sociologist Louis Wirth called an 'urban way of life'. Cohn's observation that 'population is not the crucial variable' in the definition of medieval English towns recalls Wirth's insistence that 'urbanism is not fully or accurately measured by the proportion of the total population living in cities'.[42]

The term 'civil society' refers not only to specific forms of interconnectedness, communications and ideology but also to qualities of sociability and neighbourly good manners that cannot have been easy to maintain in a commune the wealth of which was extremely unevenly distributed.[43] Craftsmen rarely witnessed transactions

---

40 Lynch, *Individuals, families and communities*, p. 27, adds that 'the lower the population size threshold chosen for identifying places as urban, the more continuous the history of European urban life appears to be'.

41 Local surnames include Culkerton, Hampton, Cotes, Woodmancote, Marston, Stratton, Campden, Cheltenham, Colesbourne, Eycote, Oxynton, Baudynton, Lechlade, Mattesden, Gloucester, Rodmarton, Bagendon, Wotton, Yanworth, Ashton, Avebury, Nailsworth, Driffield, Duntesbourne, Ampney, Cerney, Frome, Owlpen and Weston.

42 S.K. Cohn, *Popular protest in late medieval English towns* (New York and Cambridge, 2013), p. 20; C. Dyer, in 'Market towns and the countryside in late medieval England', *Canadian Journal of History*, 31 (1996), writes that small towns could have 300–2,000 inhabitants; my point here is to urge the relevance to late medieval England of the classic interconnected sociological perspective of L.B. Wirth, 'Urbanism as a way of life', *American Journal of Sociology*, 44 (1938), p. 1. '*Trafike*' was an earlier, less abstract word for 'commerce' connoting the movement of people, produce and ideas.

43 Postles, *Social proprieties*, is a path-breaking study of an as yet little studied instrument of social relations at the grass roots, customary titles and modes of address.

concerning the communal Mary chapel. A few rich merchants and dealers dominated. The larger body of craftsmen and shopkeepers constituted a second tier or class of the commonalty: they begin to appear in significant numbers in lists of feoffees of communal fraternities and charities only in the eighteenth century. The wealth of this face-to-face 'fellowship' was very unequally distributed, the self-description of successive petitioners as 'poor townsmen' implying comparison with the relative wealth of the abbot and canons. Assessors of the Lay Subsidy of 1327 divided contributions into three distinct classes.[44] The lowest class comprised 61 tax-payers contributing 6d–18d each. Then there is a distinct gap, with no one paying any sum between 18d and 2s. A 'middle' group comprising 11 individuals paid sums from 2s to 5s 4d. Then there is another clear gap of nearly 10s between the highest payer in the middle group and the lowest payer in the highest group. The moveable wealth of the 61 *minores* (72 per cent) constituted a mere 20 per cent of the total amount; 11 *mediocres* (19 per cent) shared 15 per cent; and a mere eight *majores* (9 per cent) dwarfed the contributions of the other groups with 65 per cent of the total. The *mediocres* and *majores* are also more individualised, all but two occupying a step of their own on the taxation hierarchy: 11 individuals paying between 2s and 5s 4d and the eight of the higher class paying 15s to 21s 1d are spread across 16 'rungs', and each of the top 14 had a specific rung to themselves.

Thirty-eight taxpayers were assigned 'place' and 28 'occupation' surnames. Of 28 craft surnames, 25 paid 18d or less. Only three craft names (Dyer, Walker and Chapman) occur among the middle group. People who made things were not as rich, and usually much poorer, than those who engrossed and traded them. At the top of the list, 10 of the 11 highest payers had place ('Dereham', 'Penyton', 'Crekkelade') or regional ('Scot', 'Northerne', 'Waleys') identifications. The richest men usually brought their wealth and enterprise from elsewhere.

Cirencester paid 547s to the 1381 Poll Tax, when the resident population was probably about 1,000.[45] Comparison with assessments of nearby villages gives an idea of the relativities of town and country.[46] Taxpayers in 1381 included 145 married couples, 65 male singles, 12 female singles, 27 male servants and 31 female servants, and included a much greater range of occupations than did the villages.[47] Most of the

---

44 GA, *Gloucestershire subsidy roll, 1 Edward III, 1327* (privately printed, 1856).

45 Local taxers went from door to door and assessment and collection were conducted on different occasions (xvi); at Cirencester married couples were listed as joint assessments: 1381 Poll Tax, 'Villata de Cirencestra', in C.C. Fenwick (ed.), *The poll taxes of 1377, 1379 and 1381, part one: Bedfordshire to Leicestershire* (Oxford, 1998), pp. 294–7.

46 Cirencester, 547 (100%); Minety, 79 (14 % of Cirencester's total); Sapperton 40 (7.3%); Meyseyhampton 38 (6.9%); Down Ampney 68 (12.4%); South Cerney 63 (11.5%); Harnhill and Driffield 76 (13.9%); Up Amney 126 (23%); Preston 47 (8.6%); Siddington 59 (10.8%); Bagendon 7 (1.3%).

47 R. Goddard, in 'Small boroughs and the manorial economy: enterprise zones or urban failures', *Past & Present*, 210 (2011), p. 7, notes that 'a heavily predominant non-agricultural occupational profile is often held as an "acid test" of an urban space'. Legible occupations in the Poll Tax listing of 1381 included clerk (1), merchants (10), drapers (3), mercer (1), woolmonger (1), goldsmiths

singles, some of the servants, an unknown number of 'passingers' (sojourners passing through[48]) and others too poor to pay, lived in or shared single-room accommodation without cooking facilities: hence the five *hokkestars*, all single women who sold 'small quantities of food in the streets and alleyways or even from door to door'.[49]

The merchants brought their capital and contacts from elsewhere: their names rarely recur after one generation. Yet, up to the dissolution of 1539, such men (including the clothiers and clothmen who begin to appear in significant numbers in the fifteenth century) dominate communal affairs. Being 'foreigners' did not inhibit their involvement in communal as well as personal business, a false distinction in the sense that they were dealing with local producers on a daily basis. The relatively large numbers of tailors, shoemakers and breeches-makers in the incomplete 1381 tax assessment suggest production for 'export' to regional and national markets. When differences came to a head, leading merchants identified with commune rather than lord. Gestures of service to the *commune weal* were a requirement of the culture. Wealthy businessmen of the generations from the Black Death until the dissolution of the chantries in 1547 financed, served as feoffees and wardens, left generous bequests to and wished to be buried in a bevy of new chapels and fraternities of the fifteenth century, as amply confirmed by the sources. New foundations begin with a licence for a Trinity Chapel in 1382 (completed c.1430) and the refinancing of the Mary Chapel in 1392. Two feoffees of the chantry dedicated to the Holy Trinity in 1382 are identifiable in the 1381 Poll Tax list. John Boys *mercat* paid for himself and two servants (3s); Robert Playn *mercator* paid 6s and one of his servants paid 12d. Of the feoffees of 1392, John Cosyn *mercat* paid 6s and his name is followed by three servants paying 12d each; John Baker paid 2s 8d for himself and his wife Isabella and 12d for a servant; and, although most of the entry for William Woodford *Hostelaar* is illegible, he had at least one servant, while another Woodford in the list is designated a draper, usually among the better-off tradesmen.[50]

Cosyn and Poynter figure as witnesses and recipients of Mary Chapel property transactions from the 1370s until their deaths. Cosyn, the highest payer in 1381, was a well-connected commoner, leader of a movement to establish a guild merchant, initiator of a scheme to add a dominant tower to the nave of the parish church (completed by 1420) and very much a captain of the town. In 1400 he led the 'armed crowd of local villeins all armed with bows and sticks' who besieged and captured two earls, three knights and 30 esquires who had barricaded themselves in the Ram Inn following their retreat from London. Cosyn the *mercat* and a young woolmonger, Reginald Spicer, led the prisoners into the market place, where 'thei smote of[f] the

(2), tanners (6), saddler (1), carters (3), bakers (4), butchers (2), breeches makers (7), tailors (10), shoemakers (9), clothworkers (5), cardmaker (1), tilers (2), carpenter (1), fencemaker (1), 'baggers' (makers of sacks for wool?) (2), porters (8), fishmongers (4), cook (1), 'hosteler' (1), spicer (1), shepherd (1), 'workers' (*labor'*) (37) and 'hokkestars' (5).

48 Two centuries later, Shakespeare spells the word for passers-by 'passenger' (on his memorial at Stratford parish church).

49 Lynch, *Individuals, families and communities*, p. 47.

50 Fenwick, *Poll taxes*, pp. 294–7.

Dukes hed of Surrey, and the Erles hed of Salusberye, & mony other moo' to the applause of the crowd.[51]

This was opportunistic communal intervention in national politics calculated to achieve local ends. Following the executions townspeople withdrew customary services to the abbot, and application to a grateful Henry IV for a guild merchant charter was initially successful. The abbot appealed and an increasingly unhappy Henry IV slowly changed his mind. Henry V restored the abbots' liberties and 104 'men of the town of Cirencester' were pardoned in 1414 'for all treasons, insurrections, felonies, trespasses, inobediences, rebellions, negligences, misprisions, maintenances, contempts, councils, abetments, conventicles, confederacies, extortions, oppressions, offences, impeachments and other evil deeds' against the abbey. Fourteen were explicitly assigned occupations, and 15 more had occupational surnames. They included nine weavers, three tailors, three glovers, two dyers, two curriers and single representatives of the trades or offices of carpenter, chapman, spurrier, ironmonger, woodward, baker, draper, smith, stillman and brazier.[52] Once again, the *majores* (merchants and wholesalers), *mediocres* and *minores* (craftsmen and shopkeepers) of the commonalty confirmed their capacity for collective action against their lord. They lost another battle, but developments of the fifteenth century suggest that they were beginning to win the war.

Communal piety, 1400–1600

Withdrawal of the guild merchant charter meant that the commune's efforts to create spaces for its independent life focused elsewhere. The request to license a new chapel in 1382, the refinancing of the Mary Chapel in 1392, the execution of the earls in January 1400 and Henry V's withdrawal of the charter mark the opening of a sustained long-term movement to re-centre the townscape on the parish church. A church with an imposing tower and many altars and chapels financed by different factions of townspeople bodied forth, until the eve of Reformation, an independent, literally congregational (though not in the post-Reformation sense) communal piety, signifying that the town was much more than an imitation or creature of the abbey next door. John Cosyn was 'buried in the new chapel ... before the altar of St Thomas'. He left bequests for a 'chaplain to celebrate ... in the chapel of St Mary', 'Sir John Yonge, chaplain' and 'Walter Kyrkeby, my chaplain'. Smaller bequests went 'to every parish

51 C. Given Wilson (tr.), *Chronicles of the revolution, 1397–1400* (Manchester 1993), pp. 226–34; F.W.D. de Brie, *The Brut or the chronicles of England* (London 1906), p. 361; the identification of Cosyn as a merchant of the town corrects my previous speculation, in *Commune, country and commonwealth*, that Cosyn was a military man or 'Esquire'.

52 *CPR Henry V*, 1.168 (15 February 1414); the men shared a mere 13 forenames but 100 different surnames. They include a 'Malvern', 'Bristow' and 'Nottingham'; beyond these three, place-names had virtually disappeared. Surnames were now routinised: immigrants mostly brought firmly attached surnames with them and it was no longer necessary, except in special cases, to identify them by their place of origin. Only 16 names recur in Richard Reece's cross-referencing of the list with Mary Chapel documents, confirming a high turnover of population.

chaplain' (i.e. not the rector, an abbey appointee), so there must already have been at least half a dozen celebrants, probably more. Twenty shillings went to 'the poor men and women of St John the Baptist' and 40s 'for the construction of a belfry'.[53] The tower, built by communal subscription c.1402–15, overtook the abbey chapel as the dominant landmark. The lord continued to appoint parish priests and wardens until the dissolution of 1539, but by then activity had long shifted to the people's nave.

Rich men are as prominent as in the twelfth century. The walls of Trinity chapel (completed c.1430) were adorned with brass memorials to the most generous merchants and merchant-squires and their wives and children. Less wealthy benefactors, including trade guilds, were named in obits. The Trinity chapel, associated from the outset with the weavers' guild, attracted bequests from clothiers based in Stroudwater and the Vale of Berkeley. The will of one chapel patron, Reginald Dixton, is the earliest Cirencester will written in English. Lollardy was in the wind. Vernacular teaching and ceremonial was proscribed in 1409, yet these words were painted on the north wall of the chapel:

> What man other woman worscip this holi seint Bisscop [Thomas of Canterbury] and mart[y]r every Sunday that bith in the yere wt a pat[ernoste]r and one ave [Maria] Othir ony almus geveth to a pore man or bring ony candill light laff or more he schall have v giftis graunt of god. The firste is he schall have reysonabil gode to his lyves end. The seconde is that his enimyes schall have no pouir to do hym no bodeley harme nor dysese. The iii is what reysonabil thynge that he will aske of god and that holy gent hyt schall be graunt. The iij that he schall be onbourdned of all his tribulacion and dysese. The v is that in his laste inde have schrift [confession] and housil [eucharist] and grete repentaunce and sacramente of an newntinge [extreme unction] and the[y] may come to that blysse that never hath ende.[54]

The tower and nave marked the commonalty's sacred site, in which candles flickered continuously from communally funded altars dedicated to Saints Edward the Confessor, Thomas, John, Mary, Laud, Lawrence, James, Katherine, Eligius, Christopher (always a favourite in countries with streams), Clement, Cuthbert, George, the Holy Cross and Jesus himself.[55] By the end of the fifteenth century the nave housed at least ten chantries and maybe a dozen chaplains and singers, and bequests begin to reveal another massive effort to make the parish church the monumental heart of the town it has been ever since. Merchant Rowland Osmonde, 'buried between the chapels of the blessed virgin Mary and St Katherine' in 1517, left the hefty sum of £20 'for building of the church'.[56] Clothman Robert Rycardes

53 Will of John Cosyn, 1403, GA, *Hockaday Abstracts vol. 155*; see also Will of Thomas Dyare, The National Archives (TNA), Prerogative Court of Canterbury Wills (PCC) Marche 2, May 30 1402.

54 'Copied exactly from the original' by Samuel Rudder, *The history of the town of Cirencester* (Cirencester, 1800), p. 292; for the wider significance of vernacularisation, see Rollison, *Commonwealth of the people*, ch. 3.

55 Will of Richard Nelle, PCC Horne 34, 4 April 1499: GA, *Hockaday Abstracts vol. 155*.

56 Will of Rowland Osmonde, PCC Holder 34, 29 June 1517: GA, *Hockaday Abstracts vol. 155*.

(d.1518), left £20 towards 'the bilding of the midle ile, with such money as I have paide before hands'. 'Between 1515 and 1530 the nave was demolished and entirely rebuilt in the Late Perpendicular style.'[57]

Commercial and religious life went hand-in-hand. The abbey was dissolved in December 1539, and the communal culture built around the church and its fraternities was given a mortal blow by the dissolution of the chantries in 1546–7. A survivalist Catholic cabal led by the abbot's last bailiff ran the manor, for the moment the only effective institution, for absentee lords.[58] He ruled with an iron fist. Alongside him an ex-canon upheld Catholic worship in the parish church until John Hooper became bishop of Gloucester in 1551 and turned the diocese upside down.[59] Hooper's strategy was to encourage Protestant elites in the parishes; at Cirencester this meant a local businessman, the millowner William Partridge, who served as churchwarden many times before his death in 1577, often alongside his son-in-law and successor, John Coxwell.[60] Hooper lodged with Partridge in November 1551, while the bailiff kept his head down and the bishop extracted a written recantation from the surviving Catholic parish priest.[61] If and how Hooper aroused customary sensibilities is not clear. His decidedly Protestant interlude ended with the death of Edward VI, Hooper's imprisonment, and his execution in 1555.

The seeds of evangelical parish and vestry governance were sown by Hooper, but the parish church did not become the unchallenged heart of the town's constitution until after c.1600. First it was necessary to overcome class and sectarian differences that divided town and country in the middle decades of the sixteenth century, which were at their most intense from 1555 to 1585.[62] In 1570 a gathering movement of craftworkers, shopkeepers and petty wholesalers calling themselves 'poor townsmen' cashed in on the papal attack on Queen Elizabeth, petitioning the Privy Council to act against 'the tyranie of infected members called Papists' who 'impoisoned a nomber of good subjects' in the town.[63] The 'chiefest' men behind these 'execrable doings' were the bailiff, the town clerk, the town sergeant and a local Catholic knight: the manorial executive. The legitimacy of the manorial cabal was finally shattered. In the wake of a mortality crisis that killed a third of the population in 1577–9 and a series

---

57 Canon Rowland Hill, *Cirencester parish church* (n.d.), p. 22; for a full account of this movement, see Rollison, *Commune, country and commonwealth*, ch. 6.

58 'Robert Strange, Clothier: see GA, *Hockaday Abstracts vol. 155*,'Oct 5 1553'; GA, D4871 (Strange Family); GA, D2930/3 (61): Strange Family Pedigree.

59 For Strange's muscular style of governance, see depositions in TNA, Stac 2/19/38, 36 Henry VIII.

60 See the emphatically Protestant wills of William Partridge, TNA, prob. 11/61/35, 21 Sept 1578, and John Coxwell, GA, D269B F1.

61 Hooper 'Lodged at Mr Partridge's House', Thursday 12 November 1551: GA, GDR 7.69; 'Appendix: William Phelpes Recantation', in K.J. Beecham, *History of Cirencester and the Roman city of Corinium* (1887, repr. Stroud, 1978).

62 For an account of the dissent and contentions of these decades, see Rollison, *Commune, country and commonwealth*, ch. 9.

63 'Petition of the Inhabitants to the Privy Council', TNA, SPD Dom Eliz Vol LXXI no. 30; transcribed in GA, *Hockaday Abstracts, vol. 156*.

of inflammatory sermons excoriating 'the rich', crowds 'violently resisted the bailiff [Strange], the steward and other officers ... in their duties'.[64] Manorial hegemony *per se*, not abbey dominion, was the enemy. The middling shopkeepers and craftsmen – a clear majority, though by no means the wealthiest of the taxpaying townspeople – revived the guild merchant charter, but were successfully opposed in court by the manorial cabal and, more decisively, by a group at the parish church led by a wealthy puritan businessman John Coxwell.[65] Coxwell was Church Treasurer alongside the lord of the manor, Sir John Danvers, in 1599 and, with other neighbouring gentry, from c.1590 until his death in 1617. If harmonious relations between the classes could be restored and sectarian differences minimised, a borough charter was no longer the best solution.[66]

The reincorporation of the largest class of taxpaying householders as legitimate members of the governing class may have been one of the motives for a series of sermons by 'Philip Jones, preacher of the town' in the mid-1580s. Jones extolled the 'artificer or handicraftes man, labouring diligently in his manuarie trade or science'. Such a 'saint' was defined by the fact that he 'laboured ... to releeve himselfe, and maintaine his familie'. Only such men were certain to be saved; other 'degrees of persons' such as 'Gentilmen', 'princes' and, generally speaking, all 'riche men' were almost certainly doomed to die and never live again. The preacher excoriated 'the riche', quoting Jesus saying that it was 'not only hard but impossible also that a riche man shoulde be saved'. Jones's 'articifer or handicraftesman' lived 'of his own and not in the breath of other men'. He was to be distinguished from two classes of 'spendalls' and 'unthriftes'. Below the saintly artisans were the dependent poor, who 'lived altogether on the town'; 30 years later, vestry would call them the 'wicked poor'. Above tradesmen in 'degree', but not in the eyes of God, were wealthy magnate–rentiers and courtiers.[67] Both classes 'lived altogether on the people'. The preacher identified and strengthened the self-confidence of the largest class of potential tax- and rate-paying householders in very hard times by smoothing their paths into the ranks of the elect. Many of the leaders of the next generation were raised in this movement. New customs and a new culture would emerge.

After a generation of uncertainty in which the legitimacy of centuries-old manorial lordship was undermined by association with Catholicism and efforts to maintain market and trade monopolies, a group of godly merchants, wholesalers, shopkeepers

---

64 Rollison, *Commune, country and commonwealth*, ch. 10 (mortality crises), ch. 11 (sermons).

65 TNA, E178/959: 'Depositions [by Christopher George Esq., Thomas Marshall Esq.,] as to the Office of Bailiff' (c.1580).

66 Specific mentions of Coxwell as Treasurer: GA, P86/1 IN 6/3, 'Cirencester Parish Book', f.142r; John Coxwell Treasurer with Danvers in 41 Elizabeth (1599); with Michael Strange in 1613; with Robert George 1611–17; Mr George Treasurer after Coxwell's death in 1618; last mention of Treasurer was Sir William Master in 1639.

67 *Certaine Sermons preached of late at Ciceter ... upon a portion of the first Chapter of the Epistle of James: wherein the two several states, of the riche and poore man are compared and examined... By Philip Jones, Preacher of the word of God in the same Towne. Allowed by authoritie. Imprinted at London by T.D. for Thomas Butter 1588.*

and tradesmen led by the richest, oldest and most successful of them, John Coxwell, constructed an alliance of classes (rich merchants and gentlemen of neighbouring villages; lesser merchants and wholesalers; shopkeepers and artisans), under the rubric of the godly commonwealth, into an unequal oligarchic democracy of 'the better sort', a term first used in parish writings in 1615. It was vague enough to encompass everyone who voted in parliamentary and vestry elections.[68] Apothecary Albert Eyles, 'an inhabitant for 40 years', summed up the new 'custom' associated with the vestry constitution that took over the town c.1580–1620 in a sworn affidavit in November 1775:

> There is and hath been in the Town and Borough of Cirencester ... from time wherof the mind of man is not to the contrary ... [a customary] right of electing and appointing a person to supply any vacancy ... [that] belongs to and lies and is vested in the Inhabitants at Large of the Town of Cirencester ... who pay or contribute to the Parish Rates.[69]

A custom that had once been innocent and powerless now became the base line of the new order.

The constitutional nexus that dominated from c.1600 to 1753 was an alliance of vestry, ministry and the rate-paying inhabitants.[70] The poor, now legalistically defined as persons too poor to pay rates and, of course, persons actually in receipt of poor relief, were excluded. In practice if not in theology, the ministers who served the parish from the 1580s until 1753 are best described as parochial or congregational independents. Vestry invariably had a lot of say in their appointment and all were happy to work very closely with, and at times defer to, vestry. This was spelled out in 1690, when the diocese threatened to appoint a minister against the wishes of the townspeople. The town candidate, Joseph Harrison, had proved himself as curate to the previous incumbent, Jeremiah Gregory, himself the son of Alexander Gregory, appointed in 1627 by the Feoffees for Impropriations. The Administrator of the diocese wrote that the bishop (currently suspended as a non-juror) had 'recommended another', but, 'Considering how extreamly dependant ye Minister of that Parish is upon ye people, and how many ill consequences may follow upon putting a curate there against their liking', he could not do otherwise than 'chuse to gratify ye people, and therefore I have writ to [the bishop] to know what he would advise me to do. And I

68 'better sorte': GA, P86 VE 2/1, Cirencester Vestry Book, 1589–1886, f. 42, f. 43; the *election* of officers is usually carefully and specifically recorded, e.g. f. 61r, Sunday 2 October 1642.

69 'Parish Book', f. 16.

70 H. French, *The middle sort of people in provincial England, 1600–1750* (Oxford, 2007), p. 27, writes that 'Status as one of the "inhabitants" of a parish signified far more the single geographical fact of residing there ... It meant recognizing that the individual possessed a material stake in the "imagined community" of "the parish".' Being an 'inhabitant' in this sense meant a person was 'entitled to be represented within it, participate in its deliberations, *and pay towards their implementation*.'

hope his answer will be to Mr Harrison's satisfaction'.[71] Harrison was appointed and served until his death in 1753.

The town's parliamentary franchise was also formally democratic. During the sixteenth century there was 'an encrease of near 200 members' in the House of Commons, representing just over half that number of new urban constituencies.[72] One was Cirencester, created in 1571.[73] Following a disputed election in 1624, someone complained that legitimate voters had been denied their right. A House of Commons committee determined that 'The polling, or numbering of the freeholders only was an unlawful and void act, they not being the sole electors.' The custom at Cirencester was 'that more than the freeholders only ought to have voices in the election; namely, all men, inhabitants, householders, resiants within the borough'.[74] This was understood to mean the rate-paying householders.

Class to party: government by vestry, c.1600–1753

A moderate Leveller (rate-payer) franchise became the source of customary legitimacy for what remained, in practice, oligarchic government. What changed was that that around 1600 the parish church, the affective heart of the commune since c.1450, replaced the manor as the hub of government. My impression is of mainly *bons bourgeois* leadership until the end of the sixteenth century. The vestry regime of the seventeenth and eighteenth centuries seems *petty bourgeois*. Patient accumulation and family networking, efforts to accumulate estate and local reputation over several generations, was the new pattern. Certain interlinked families became closely associated with what, when it was challenged in the middle decades of the eighteenth century by a resurgent manor, became known as 'the church party'. They had their counterparts in the large Presbyterian and smaller Baptist congregations, by 1753 in league with new lords, the Bathursts.

From the 1580s until 1639 the chief officers were two Church Treasurers, invariably a financially astute 'town gentleman' (i.e. businessman) like Coxwell, accompanied by someone from a more prestigious (i.e. older) gentry family. It is not clear whether Treasurers were elected, as were churchwardens and lesser vestry officials. The last record of a Treasurer is in 1639: they went out with the civil wars. After that, churchwardens ran the show. Vestry-elected town clerks recorded (or created) the repeated customary practices in a carefully maintained vestry book (later called 'the town book of record'). Failure to record the 'election' of officers by the whole vestry (in theory, every rate-paying householder) is very rare from the 1610s on. The taxpayer franchise even took precedence over religious affiliation. Members of dissenting congregations were elected as Overseers, Supervisors of

71 'The Letter of Bishop Hough (Oxon) Administering the Diocese of Gloucester for Bishop Frampton the Non-Juror': GA, P86/1 IN 4/1.

72 Introduction to John Glanville, *Reports of certain cases determined and adjudged by the commons in parliament the 21st and 22nd of the reign of King James the First* (London, 1775), p. i.

73 Ibid., p. cvii.

74 Ibid., pp. 108–9.

the Highways and, on one occasion, as Constable, on a total of 34 occasions from 1663 to 1689.[75]

From the outset vestry institutionalised a new kind of class-consciousness. On 10 April 1615 it 'met and agreed upon' a set of orders 'to be observed by all such as hereafter shalbe churchwardens of the towne'. Two esquires, three 'gents', two mercers, a chandler, and a wholesale shoemaker were named, along with 'many others of the better sorte of the ... p[ar]ishe'. The named men all lived in the better streets, close to church and market. Only one was under 40 and one treasurer, John Coxwell, was over 100 years of age. It was an oligarchy of comparatively wealthy elders. Four of the named men were designated trained soldiers in the muster of 1608.[76] One vestry 'constitution' they voted in formalised custom regarding vacant church pews. A committee consisting of 'the minister and six other persons of the better sorte of the pishe' was to base its decisions on 'whether the [applicant] be fytt to be rancked with the other tha[t] were in the seate before'.[77] Studiously ranked within, the 'better sort' was defined by its position with regard to other ranks and classes.

A distinction between the class of independent, rate-paying householders and that of the 'dependent' poor was institutionalised in the early seventeenth century and strengthened thereafter. The new order set out to discipline and relieve the poor in the same way as pious independent householders 'relieved' their children, servants, apprentices and journeymen: by employing them. An Order of 1615 lay down that bequests and collections for the poor were to be invested in tools and raw materials so they 'may be sett either to carding, spynning or some other laboure according to their age and habilitye'.[78] In 1619 they appointed a 'beadle of beggars' and carefully codified his functions.[79] Penniless immigrants were not welcome in a time of economic recession: they must 'suffer no strainge beggars in the towne'. The beadle was to 'purge (whip?) wicked poor as are able by their own labour and travayle to earne theire lyvynges'. 'Wicked poor ... may receive noe parte of any chargeable benevolence but be brought to the house of correction', presumably to be 'purged'. 'All alehouse keepers as entertain in their houses such poor as spend the earnynge without all care of wife and children at home' were to be warned, and if they failed to bar wicked carousers the parish officers took away their licence.[80]

Beadles were required to keep 'the office of the towne' (vestry) informed 'of the behaviour of all such poor as are usually relieved by the common almes whether they offend' in any way. 'In travailing up and downe the streets' he was to 'make enquiry what sorte of poore by sickenesse or any other impotencye are fallen into great want'

---

75 B. Hawkins, *Taming the phoenix: Cirencester and the Quakers, 1642–86* (York, 1998), p. 218.

76 Twenty-seven (7.6 per cent) of 353 townsmen listed in the 1608 muster list are designated as 'trained', most of them living in the better streets: 'The burrowe of Cirencester', in J. Smith, *Men and Armour for Gloucestershire in 1608* (1902; facs. edn., Stroud, 1980), pp. 239–43.

77 Vestry Book, f. 43.

78 Ibid., f. 43.

79 Ibid., f. 45r.

80 'The working poor were often the first subjects of scientific social planning': J.C. Scott, *Seeing like a state: how certain schemes to improve the human condition have failed* (Yale, 1998), p. 92.

and to inform 'the [rate] collectors and ... other wele disposed which he thinketh willing and able to relieve them'. Persons vestry licensed to beg were to 'be of good behaviour in their begging of almes eyther of straingers in the streete or at the houses where they begge ... that they give noe offence to such that relieve them'. If they were rude 'they shall receive punishment for it and be put out [of] their part in the ordinary and weekly alms that are geven'. Beadles were to ensure 'no children or yonge people beying above the age of seaven years be suffered to wander about the streets either begging or otherwise but may be sett either to knitting, spinning or some other labour according to their age and habilitie.'[81]

What became a very sharp distinction between 'independent' and 'dependent' households and individuals was central to the propaganda of both sides in the civil wars. Hodgkinson Paine, a clothier, was 'killed with the [town's] colours in his hand' during the royalist siege of February 1643. His memorial described the vocation for which he had died, and which parliamentarians eminently represented. 'The Poore's Supplie his life & calling grac't', it reads, 'Till warre's made rent & PAINE from poore displac't'.[82] What 'gentlemen of town and country' had in common with a common clothier such as Paine, and the master-craftsmen and shopkeepers, was they were all potential employers of labour. The self-conscious vocation that united them, as Paine's eulogist (probably his wife, Elizabeth) recorded, was 'the poore's supplie'.

Royalists reported that 'some of the prisoners confessed ... how that the gentlemen and clothiers threatened them they should have no work'.[83] One thousand one hundred of the defenders were marched to Oxford to meet their fate. The prisoners petitioned to be forgiven and sent home, so that 'many hundreds of people of our towne, who have no other livelihood, may be againe set on work and relieved'. They identified themselves as the employer *class*, the leaders of whom ran vestry government. Forty-six men of the 'better sort' signed. Nearly all were vestry officials in the 1630s and 1640s.[84]

The ascendency of the rate-paying employer class was accompanied by social and economic change. Between 1608 and 1768 the number of different occupations in the town doubled. While most remained entirely compatible with what E.A. Wrigley has called an 'advanced organic economy', one change is noteworthy. Wrigley's hypothesis is that 'in the transition from a traditional society where income levels are low to a modern economy with high average incomes ... the absolute level of

81 Vestry Book, f. 45r.

82 Inscription transcribed from the original; it continues: 'But what made poore unfortunate PAINE blest,/By warre they lost their PAINE, yet found noe rest/ He looseing quiet by Warre yet gained ease,/By it PAINE's life began, and paine did cease;/And from ye troubles here him God did sever,/By death to life, by Warre to peace for ever'; for Paine's death see *A particular relation of the action before Cyrencester ... taken on Candlemas day 1642 by part of His Majesty's army under the conduct of ... prince Rupert* (Oxford 1642/3), pp. 11–12.

83 Ibid., p. 15 (emphasis in original).

84 *The petititon of the inhabitants of Cyrencester whose names are subscribed presented to His Maiestie at Oxford with His Maiestyes answer, printed at Oxford February 28th, 1642*, EEBO. See Vestry Minutes, GA, P86 VE 2.1, and Index, VE 3.1.

demand will rise for the products of all the three main employment categories, but the rate of growth will be least in the primary sector and greatest in the tertiary sector'. 'Tertiary employment,' he explains, 'relates to the production of services rather than material products: the professions, government service; the arts and entertainment; the provision of food, drink and lodging; and transport, for example'.[85] Systematic occupational data from the eighteenth century suggests that tertiary employment grew quite considerably.[86] In 1768 13.2 per cent of householders (73) were employed in tertiary occupations, compared with 7.9 per cent in 1608.

As its tertiary sector increased, the secondary declined. 'Clothing declined because of the lack of rivulets on which to erect fulling mills ... Demands increasing beyond what the clothier could supply, he naturally quit his residence [in the town] and settle[d] where mills might be erected.'[87] The Weavers' Guild continued to meet 'in their hall in St Thomas's Hospital' but 'admit[ted] new members without regard to their line of business ... not any of the company transactions [had] the least relation to weaving'. By then the town's cloth fairs were discontinued.[88] In 1768 one clothier, probably running a fulling mill on the Churn, was providing work for 14 weavers and two dyers.

Abolition of the continental staple for wool and its replacement, in the 1610s, by well-situated English towns such as Cirencester, offered some compensation.[89] The wool market may have flourished to the point where, in the early eighteenth century, Defoe described it as among the busiest in England.[90] In 1753 seven woolstaplers, two woolcombers, two clothiers, a weaver, a mercer and a yarnmaker were among the long list of local employers paid to employ denizens of a 'house of manufacture' established in 1724, replacing ad hoc usage of the house of correction.[91] Cirencester

---

85 E.A. Wrigley, 'Country and town: the primary, secondary and tertiary peopling of England in the early modern period', in P. Slack and R. Ward (eds), *The peopling of Britain: the shaping of a human landscape* (Oxford, 2002), p. 218; E.A. Wrigley, 'The transition to an advanced organic economy: half a millennium of English agriculture', *Economic History Review*, 59 (2006), pp. 435–80.

86 For this calculation I include the following categories as 'tertiary': Transport (7); Alcohol, Food, Entertainment (32); Local Official (5); Services (18); Barbers (7); Apothecaries (3); Bookseller (1); the 1608 figures for transport (13) and A/F/E (14) are comparable and, with a single named local official, produce the considerably lower average of 7.9 per cent overall.

87 The largest occupational grouping in 1608 was labourers; no woolcombers or woolstaplers were listed; in a listing of 717 voters in the parliamentary election of 1768 labourers numbered 77, followed by Woolcombers (53) and Woolstaplers (25): *The poll of the borough of Cirencester, taken March... 1768* (Samuel Rudder, Cirencester, 1768), pp. 8–31.

88 Rudder, *History of Cirencester*, pp. 171–2.

89 G.D. Ramsay, *The Wiltshire woollen industry in the sixteenth and seventeenth centuries* (Oxford, 1943), p. 89.

90 Rudder, *History of Cirencester*, p. 171.

91 GA, P86a OV2.1 Parish Book 1753; these contributed £106 19s 1d (73 per cent); the other employers of workhouse labour were 1 hosier, 1 edgetool maker, 1 hop merchant, 1 gardener, 1 peruke maker, 1 maltster, 1 slatter and 1 carpet weaver; Vestry Book, f. 112r, 15 October 1724, 'Agreement with Gabriel Cooke, Appointment of a House of Maintenance'.

woolcombers and woolstaplers supplied the Stroudwater Valley clothiers with yarn until this final connection was lost in the last third of the eighteenth century. The Cripps brothers, John and Joseph, leaders of the church party, made their fortunes as woolstaplers.[92]

War resumes: church versus manor, 1753–90

> Suppose the Bathursts were extinct and the Manor of Cirencester in the Hands of a Jew: should you like to see a Synagogue in the Park? The Lord of the Manor, you *know* has Power enough. You would soon be stocked with Jews; tho' non-parishioners he could make them Wards-men and Constables and bring a charge *on your parish*. How should you like that?[93]

In 1695 banker's son Allen Bathurst, a wealthy liberal-Tory courtier and placeman, purchased Cirencester manor. For the next 50 years he worked with vestry government, paid his rates, and went along with the customary arrangement for parliamentary elections, in which the lord nominated one candidate, 'the Old Family', the Masters of Abbey House, nominated the other, and the rate-payers elected them both. The 'Old Family' member died in 1753 and the Bathursts, enthusiastically supported by the minister of the Presbyterian congregation, offered two candidates of their own.[94] What henceforth became 'the church party' came together under the leadership of the patriarch of the dominant vestry family, John Cripps (whose wife was daughter of the minister, Joseph Harrison), and an extremely bitter election contest ensued.

The immemorial populist basis of the church party rang out in their propaganda. '[Most of us are] Plain Men … We have been bred up with a view to providing a decent Subsistence for our Families; and in doing that, we enrich our Country by our Industry… I shall therefore, in my homely style, give you my thoughts.' Hard-working 'plain folk' were not about to defer to a haughty intellectual Johnny-come-lately, not the least of whose sins was toleration of jews, immigrants, infidels and 'king-killing' dissenters:

> My Birthright is to do what I please with my Vote; I may vote if I please for two Gentlemen, if I have a mind I may vote but for one, and if none but *Presbyterians* were to stand, I would not vote at all … Fine Gentlemen are mighty apt to think that we Plain Folk have not Common Sense … I was bred up in the Church and I love the Church and will always be for the Church … We are for the Old Family and the Old Principles … We do not like your *Double-Dealings*, nor your *Double-Meanings*, your *Double-Tongues*, nor your *Double-faces*, nor your *Double-Bathursts*. No *turn-coats*; no *Placemen*; no *Slaves!* No *Presbyterians*;

92 John and Joseph Cripps listed as 'woolstapler' in 'Collections' listing, 1753: GA, P86a OV2.1.

93 'Church party' propaganda, GA, R79.111 *The Cirencester contest … letters, papers relative to the election (of 1753)*, pp. 55–6.

94 'The *Presbyterians* think, by going themselves to a certain powerful family, to *lord* it over us. Old England! Old Interest! And the Good *Old Church* for ever and ever!', *The Cirencester contest*, p. 57.

> no *Roundheads*; no *King-Killers! No Jews! NO JEWS!* Christianity for ever! Old England; Old Interest! Huzza![95]

Shortly after the election Joshua Parry, the Presbyterian minister, wrote to a correspondent that 'I, the other day, was complaining to a plain, hard-headed artificer of the ingratitude of the borough of Cirencester, where Lord Bathurst had laid out near 50,000 pounds.'

> 'And pray,' says he, 'has not that borough, for fifty years together, almost uninterruptedly acquiesced in his choice, and was not the predilection for spending his money there originally determined with that particular view? State the account between lord and burgher, the balance is a zero.'

Parry 'urged the appendant rights of an estate, family interest, gratitude etc.', but 'in vain'. The 'hard-headed articifer … laughed at all such considerations and walked away; and yet he had no sort of connection with Cirencester'.[96]

The die was cast. For the rest of the century church and manorial parties were at war.[97] The last vestry-sanctioned Minister, Joseph Harrison, died shortly after the election. Bathurst used his connections to have his own candidate appointed to the parish church, breaking the nexus between rate-paying inhabitants, vestry and minister. The new minister, Samuel Johnson, 'was disliked in the town for taking the part of the Bathursts' and complained that 'Some of his parishioners have by every art and abuse been exciting the others – as many as they could – against him.'[98] The battle shifted immediately to the patronage of church officers. Against the church party's determination to 'render almost every Situation in this Towne elective from the Minister to the Gravediggers', the minister, egged on by Bathurst supporters, insisted

---

95 *The Cirencester contest*, pp. 37–8; the vitriol came from both sides, e.g.:'Some of [the church party] are tolerably well qualified to handle a *Flail*, or to hold a *Plow* … tho' they are only a Degree or two superior to *mere Animals*, there is much Knavery, and some cunning intermingled with their Folly. This appearance in Nature is not in the least uncommon. Tis frequently seen that *Monkies*, nay *Idiots* who are below Monkies, will show themselves cunning in Mischief …'.

96 C.H. Parry, *A memoir of the Reverend Joshua Parry* (London, 1872), pp. 282–3; E.P. Thompson, *Customs in common: studies in traditional and popular culture* (London, 1991), pp. 39–40, wrote that 'the [eighteenth] century saw a growing area of independence within which the small employers and labourers felt their client relationship to the gentry very little or not at all … Working often in their own cottages, owning or hiring their own tools, usually working for small employers, frequently working irregular hours and at more than one job, they had escaped from the social controls of the manorial village and were not yet subject to the discipline of factory labour.'

97 GA, P86/1 IN 6/3,'Cirencester Parish Book' is one of two volumes of notes and transcriptions by Joseph Kilner, c.1790, bound in 1907; two sections are paginated independently; ff. 1–143 are Kilner's account of the constitution of the parish, drawing mainly on what is now GA, P86a VE 2/1, Cirencester Vestry Book, 1580–1887. References that follow are to the second part of IN 6/3, headed'the disputes in the parish', c.1753–1790, which begin again at f. 1.

98 Ibid., f. 39r & passim.

that 'the right of nominating to the Offices belonged to the Minister and Churchwardens & not the Inhabitants assembled in Vestry'.[99] According to supporters of the manor, the church party consisted of 'a very few leading on soliciting and urging on the rest – and in this instance more especially under the beguiling notion of the Town's Right ... prevailing in this and other of their present Contests and Elections'.[100] The Bathursts believed the Cripps 'carried on the war'.[101] By their influence in vestry and as leading employers they were able 'to control a formidable part of the electorate'.[102] In 1775 the elected sexton, town clerk and Registrar of the Parish of Cirencester 'absolutely and expressly surrendered & yielded up into the Hands of the Inhabitants of the said Parish all those said places' according to custom, affirming the church party position that their elective 'mode of appointment is good and wise in itself as well as in the design of it, and has been confirmed by Repetition and a long usage'.[103] In the 1790s Joseph Kilner tried to resolve 'the troubles' by looking for precedents in 'The Annals of this Parish or Register of its Acts in Vestry [which] commences in 1614', concluding that as a result of certain 'alterations' in its constitution there was 'no proof ... to ground a plea of custom on the parishioners' right to elect'.

Kilner blamed 'the troubles in the parish' on 'that baneful and excessive lust of overbearing in Elections and which grow[e]th from and giveth growth to Selfishness and Domineering'. 'The fewer the Elections the more the Quiet and Regard for Duty,' he concluded.[104] A more judicious opinion was offered by a London lawyer, who wrote that 'The greater and more opulent part of the Church people of the town' were, 'to say the least of them, great Anti-Courtiers, and ... in their Borough politics, in great opposition to ... Lordship'.[105] The judgement would have carried the same weight in the reign of Charles I – and, indeed, centuries earlier, in an age dominated by an older species of 'courtiers', the abbots.

Conclusion

Commerce, custom and politics were inseparable aspects of town life. During the first phase of the period covered in this chapter, that of manorial governance (1200–1539), the commonalty used custom to oppose manorial encroachments in 1209, at a time when its leaders were directing their profits into the establishment of a communal guild. These initiatives coincided with the building of a new parish church to house

---

99 Ibid., f. 7, f. 18.

100 Ibid., f. 15.

101 The Cripps brothers 'do all in their power to make the populace believe the contest is between Churchmen and Dissenters, and, of consequence, revive the ridiculous cry of the Church's danger'; Joshua Parry-Henry Bathurst, 10 October 1753, Parry, *Memoir*, p. 35; see also HB-JP, 1760?, *Memoir*, p. 240 and HB-JP, 1 March 1768, *Memoir*, pp. 283–4.

102 'Old Cotswold houses and families VII: the Cripps family of Cirencester', *Wilts and Gloucestershire Standard*, Colesbourne Park Collection (courtesy of Lady Carolyn Elwes).

103 'Parish Book', f. 7, f. 15.

104 Ibid., f. 7r.

105 Ibid., f. 39r: Opinion by J. Mansfield, Temple 7 November 1775.

it, and were followed in the century after the Black Death by the financing of new chantries that signalled an increasingly complex division of labour and the emergence of large-scale cloth-making in the town's hinterlands. Out of the governance of the new chapels and altars emerged the great building project of the fifteenth century, a church tower and eventually a great nave to house the chapels and altars and to body forth the proud aspirations and piety of the commonalty. The institutional basis of this version of communal polity was destroyed in 1539 and 1547.

In my second phase, c.1580–1753, manorial lordship was weak and the politics of the commonalty became the politics of governance. Custom now legitimised a moderate Leveller franchise in vestry (local) and parliamentarian (national) elections. This custom, confirmed by the House of Commons in 1624 and repeated with ever-tighter variations by numerous local commentators thereafter, institutionalised and helped legitimise an ever-sharper division between supposedly independent employer–householders and the burgeoning class of 'dependent' poor, whose continuously declining status was confirmed with the emergence of a workhouse regime during the eighteenth century.

While the economic base of the commonalty changed, a long-standing customary expectation that the wealthier members of the commonalty should assume leadership roles was continuous. A rigid class order was imposed in the early seventeenth century and institutionalised in the division between rate-paying voters and the dependent poor. This order transcended the schism of the commonalty between church (vestry) and manor parties in the mid-eighteenth century. It remained an established part of life in the Cotswolds when manorial order resumed in the nineteenth century.

Afterword

Small places, big questions: reintegrating social and economic history, c.1350–1750

Andy Wood

'Big history' and local history

I want in this afterword to do more than to suggest some possible areas of future work. The fields I address not only require closer empirical investigation but also possess potential for the closer integration of late medieval and early modern economic and social history. In particular, following one of the organising concepts behind this volume, I am interested in themes that move across the boundary between economic and social history – fields that were once united, but in recent years have drifted apart. In some cases, joined-up, integrated thinking about otherwise separated sub-fields might produce some important insights. In others, I have suggested possible areas for further empirical enquiry, especially where there are implications for how we think about social power, the social order and productive relations.

I also engage with a recent polemical work that has attracted a lot of attention among professional historians. This short and constantly provocative work – more of an argumentative essay than a cool and detached survey – represents an attack on what is termed the 'Short Past' in favour of some version of 'Big History'.[1] It is a book that is worth reading, as much for its irritations as its inspirations. In suggesting areas where a closer integration between the economic and the social might be productive, I celebrate the diversity of approaches and subject matter in much recent work. The point at which something becomes a 'definitive' subject is the point at which a field of enquiry dies; we need to be reminded that there is always more to do, and different ways in which to do history.

In contrast to this diversity, and to the emphasis upon the small-scale and the level of lived experience, 'Big History' celebrates the macro-scale of world history; in particular, the authors of *The History Manifesto* have been sharply critical of micro-history. The virtue of the kind of micro-historical approach that has been adopted by many social historians of the period – a micro-history that owes as much to W.G. Hoskins as it does to Carlo Ginzburg – is precisely its attention to the local worlds

1 J. Guldi and D. Armitage, *The history manifesto* (Cambridge, 2014), <http://historymanifesto.cambridge.org> (accessed 15 July 2015).

within which most medieval and early modern people lived their lives.[2] Diversity in historical methodology, subject area, conceptual approach and empirical material has here been the key to historical creativity. The Big History approach currently advocated might well illuminate the growing dominance of a capitalist world order, but it does so by crushing small places and subaltern people under its grinding wheels.

Taking the lead from social anthropology, then, the field of community and regional studies has often helped to answer big questions through the study of small places. So, too, have examinations of individual lives and particular moments.[3] So, more micro-histories of individual episodes that seem to reveal a larger world – what Victor Turner has called 'social drama' – should always be welcome.[4] Robert Darnton's work has been very influential; future digs within legal records, estate papers, diaries and correspondence are likely to produce fresh archival finds in which moments of contestation, embarrassment, anger and inversion reveal something of wider social structures, sensibilities and understandings.[5] Future work in this field is unpredictable – it depends sometimes on chance finds in the archives, or in finding lateral connections that are in many ways intuitive and depend upon serendipity. It entails a kind of archival archaeology, the sifting of the fine grain of manuscripts in search of stories, people or events who don't quite *fit* with the dominant order. This failure to fit is reflective of forms both of dissidence – or just a stolid refusal to budge – and also, by turning the material on its head, of dominant norms.

In contrast to Big History, the protean instability that is embedded within micro-history is difficult to capture in, for example, applications to research councils for project funding, with their demands for clarity, rigour, stated methodology, likely published outputs and so on. But it is in studies of particular moments, or other small communities, that we often find larger worlds revealed to us. We should press on: not

---

2 C. Ginzburg, *The cheese and the worms: the cosmos of a sixteenth-century miller* (1976; Eng. tr. Baltimore, 1980) is a defining text in Italian micro-history; in its own very English way, W.G. Hoskins, *The Midland peasant: the economic and social history of a Leicestershire village* (London, 1957) was equally revolutionary. The best-known example of the Annales School's approach to the field is E. Le Roy Ladurie, *Montaillou: Cathars and Catholics in a French village, 1294–1324* (1975; Eng. tr. London, 1978).

3 Keith Wrightson's recent book, *Ralph Tailor's summer: a scrivener, his city and the plague* (New Haven, 2013) represents a model in micro-historical investigation and is especially important for its self-reflective discussion of historical methodology and the approach to the archive.

4 For social drama see V. Turner, *Dramas, fields, and metaphors: symbolic action in human society* (Ithaca, 1974), pp. 37–42; V. Turner, *The anthropology of performance* (New York, 1987), pp. 34–5; V. Turner, *From ritual to theatre: the human seriousness of play* (New York, 1982), pp. 70–2. For one historian's use of the concept see D. Rollison, *The local origins of modern society: Gloucestershire, 1500–1800* (London, 1992), pp. 136–48. Turner's influence is also to be found in an earlier piece by the same author: D. Rollison, 'Property, ideology and popular culture in a Gloucestershire village, 1660–1740', *Past & Present*, 93 (1981), pp. 70–97.

5 R. Darnton, *The great cat massacre and other episodes in French cultural history* (New York, 1984). See also his discussion of the relationship between cultural history and anthropology in R. Darnton, *The kiss of Lamourette: reflections in cultural history* (New York, 1990).

only does micro-history reveal more of the past to us, but its anarchic unpredictability represents the reverse of the joyless priorities of our governing institutions and their research managers.[6]

As the anthropologists remind us, the local is often the best place to be. This is true for late medieval and early modern social and economic historians in two ways. Firstly, the local focus allows us to approach something close to a 'total' history – or, at least, an *integrated* history – encompassing demographics, landholding, household structure, wealth distribution, gender relations, resistance, literacy, local culture, litigation, belief, authority, social change, landlordship, tenure, custom, governance, ecology, landscape and so on. Secondly, and perhaps more importantly, local histories have done more than just present focused case studies of wider phenomena. Rather, the last two generations of local studies have uncovered the *diversity* of regional and local cultures, social structures and ways of thinking and working. The local, then, is not just a methodological focus: it is also a fluid, shifting historical entity in its own right, and, as such, is as worthy of study as are royal courts or grand diplomacy.

Periodisation and the excluded

This afterword is especially focused upon themes and questions that transcend the late medieval/early modern divide. It is worth noting that what is often called early modern English social history is very often the social history only of the period 1560–1640. This is not just about record survival; in fact, there are very good records for the period 1500–1560. The point is that this chronological focus allows social historians to avoid the contentious areas of the Reformation and the English Revolution. The focus on this 80-year period also allows for synchronic, relatively static analysis of themes such as popular culture, gender, age, class and so on.[7] Equally, much of the social and economic history of the late medieval period tails off around 1450. The result is that there are two significant chunks of the historical past in which there is a substantial lack of a developed social history: c.1450–1560 and 1640–1750. Notably, the economic history of the 1660–1750 period is better served than that of the 1640s and 1650s (the English Revolution awaits its social historian) and of the 1450–1560 period.[8]

---

6 These comments grow out, at least in part, from the current crisis unfolding in Europe, in which neo-liberalism is facing new and unpredictable challenges. Given that a neo-liberal managerial model now predominates within university governance within the United Kingdom, historians may well find themselves living in interesting times. I am partially informed in these comments by Andy Merrified's strange and wild book, *Magical Marxism: subversive politics and the imagination* (London, 2011).

7 For an example of synchronic work that lacks a sense of change over time see A. Wood, '"Poore men woll speke one daye": plebeian languages of deference and defiance in England, c.1520–1640', in T. Harris (ed.), *The politics of the excluded in early modern England* (Basingstoke, 2001), pp. 67–98.

8 Of course, there is some excellent work going on regarding the economic history of the late fifteenth and early sixteenth centuries, most notably that by Jane Whittle. See especially

The political, religious and cultural history of later Stuart and early Georgian England has received a lot of attention: interest has blossomed in confessional and party identities, print culture, the public sphere and gender relations. This has underwritten a fertile interaction between cultural and political history. The main contribution of economic historians to this period has been in the study of consumption; social historians have primarily concentrated on the urban middling sort. In particular, research on patterns of consumption among middling people has eclipsed the relations of production and exploitation that produced the food and goods on which that consumption relied.[9] The consequence of this over-concentration on the polite world of the urban middling sort is a history of Augustan England that is too often blind to social structure, to inequalities of wealth and power and to the lives of ordinary people in rural communities.[10] There is a profound erasure occurring here, in which

---

her monograph *The development of agrarian capitalism: land and labour in Norfolk, 1440–1580* (Oxford, 2000). Yet the social history of that period remains much more patchily covered. This is perhaps especially true of the two generations before the Reformation. The book-length treatments of the following communities and regions commence somewhere in the period 1520–1560: Terling (Essex); Whickham (Co. Durham); Highley (Shropshire); the Peak Country (Derbyshire); Myddle (Shropshire); Chippenham (Cambridgeshire); Hallamshire (Yorkshire); Colyton (Devon); the Forest of Arden (Warwickshire); Earls Colne (Essex). Given the significance of local community studies in early modern social history, this is especially problematic. For an exception see Marjorie McKintosh's dual monograph study of Havering (Essex): M.K. McIntosh, *A community transformed: the manor and liberty of Havering, 1500–1620* (Cambridge, 1991); M.K. McIntosh, *Autonomy and community: the royal manor of Havering, 1200–1500* (Cambridge, 1986). For a local community study (this time of a small town) that covers the *longue durée* necessary to capture, for example, the profound consequences of the Reformation see D. Rollison, *Commune, country and commonwealth: the people of Cirencester, 1117–1643* (Woodbridge, 2011).

9 For further development of this point see Adrian Green's review of A. Vickery, *Behind closed doors: at home in Georgian England*, in *English Historical Review*, 127/526 (2012), pp. 734–6.

10 An exception to this is Steve Hindle's current project reconstructing the social and economic history of the Warwickshire village of Chilvers Coton: see S. Hindle, 'Work, reward and labour discipline in late seventeenth-century England', in S. Hindle, A. Shepard and J. Walter (eds), *Remaking English society: social relations and social change in early modern England* (Woodbridge, 2013), pp. 255–80. An example of the kind of work that could be done is P. King, 'Social inequality, identity and the labouring poor in eighteenth-century England', in H. French and J. Barry (eds), *Identity and agency in England, 1500–1800* (Basingstoke, 2004), pp. 60–86. For 1660–1750 the middling sort of rural England have received greater attention than have those below them in the village pecking order. See, for instance, H. French, *The middle sort of people in provincial England, 1600–1750* (Oxford, 2007); P. King, 'Edward Thompson's contribution to eighteenth century studies: the patrician–plebeian model re-examined', *Social History*, 21/2 (1996), pp. 215–28; for a case study see S. Pearson, 'Threshing out the common in community: the Great Tey riot of 1727', *Rural History*, 9 (1998), pp. 43–56. There is little work on popular protest in the period 1660–1740. Work on rural protest after 1740 has primarily been concerned with food rioting.

historians of bourgeois politeness and middling sort public spheres are active agents. Research on the rural proletariat and poor commoners in late seventeenth- and early eighteenth-century England is badly needed.

Resistance and social relations

One area where there is a need for more micro-studies is that of resistance. We need to know more about village conflicts in the period between the Wars of the Roses and the Reformation: this remains a largely empty area. Meanwhile, the parameters of social conflicts within English villages in the period 1560–1640 have been sketched out.[11] A triangular disposition of lords, established tenants and the migrant or settled poor produced some surprising alliances, such as, for example, where lords established mining operations in regions such as Lancashire, Yorkshire and the North East and hired poor migrants to work in those mines as wage labourers.[12] Attacks by tenants upon these newly settled poor folk, therefore, disguised a lord/tenant conflict. Similarly, for all that tenants presented themselves as the 'poor men', oppressed by 'rich men' and 'gentlemen', this linguistic formulation was often overridden by their economic interests in preventing pauper settlement: men and women who, in one moment, might be describing a bi-polar social conflict between the gentry and the commons might, in the next, be driving poor folk off common land, restricting pauper settlement and whipping their poorer neighbours for stealing firewood from enclosing hedges. Language did not constitute class in this period any more than it did in the nineteenth century. But that does not mean that languages of social classification and social conflict do not matter; more research needs to be done into the ways in which material interest and the linguistics of class interfaced and conflicted, and how this changed over time.

Similar studies are required for the late medieval period. There are some excellent studies of lord/tenant conflict, but it would be good to know more about internal social conflicts and patterns of social polarisation within villages before 1550.[13] Study of

---

11 For a very stimulating materialist overview see S. Hipkin, 'Property, economic interest and the configuration of rural conflict in sixteenth and seventeenth-century England', *Socialist History*, 23 (2003), pp. 67–88. For local studies of these tangled conflicts see S. Hindle, 'Persuasion and protest in the Caddington common enclosure dispute, 1635–1639', *Past & Present*, 158 (1998), pp. 37–78; M. Clark, 'The gentry, the commons and the politics of common right in Enfield, c.1558–c.1603', *Historical Journal*, 54 (2011), pp. 609–29; H. Falvey, 'Crown policy and local economic context in the Berkhemsted Common enclosure dispute', *Rural History*, 12 (2001), pp. 123–58; S. Hipkin, 'Sitting on his penny rent: conflict and right of common in Faversham Blean, 1596–1610', *Rural History*, 11 (2000), pp. 1 35.

12 For now, the best discussion remains J.U. Nef, *The rise of the British coal industry*, 2 vols (London, 1932), I, pp. 305–19.

13 For valuable studies see C. Dyer, 'The English medieval village community and its decline', *Journal of British Studies*, 33 (1994), pp. 407–29; M. Muller, 'A divided class? Peasants and peasant communities in later medieval England', *Past & Present*, supplement 2 (2007), pp. 115–31; L.R. Poos, *A rural society after the Black Death: Essex, 1350–1525* (Cambridge, 1991).

this area in towns and cities is currently being undertaken by Christian Liddy, who has stressed the importance of a vernacular, customary sense of citizenship as a legitimating force in urban popular politics.[14] A lot is now known about customary law in the period 1500–1750, but how did ideas about custom emerge in rural England in what was often the critical period of their genesis, in the years 1350–1500? Work has been done on legal and administrative aspects of late medieval manorial custom, but, in contrast to the literature on the early modern period, the cultural and political dimensions of both manorial and parochial custom in the late medieval period remain an undiscovered country.[15]

The area where further work is really needed across the late medieval and early modern periods is that of the broader field of resistance. Social relations were not only dictated by open conflict; social tensions could be muffled under a blanket of outward deference. Plebeian anger might take the form of threatening letters, animal-maiming or attacks on the landscaped environment of the gentry.[16] The rick-burning campaign in the Captain Swing era had its roots in much earlier forms of resistance: it would be good to know more about these kinds of long-term continuities. Similarly, it is doubtful that the Luddite movement in the Midlands and the North sprang fully formed from the Industrial Revolution. There may well be something particular about the local cultures within which movements such as Luddism emerged; this requires long-term, finely graded local analysis. Social historians long ago moved away from the idea that popular politics was merely reactive and spasmodic, to emphasise instead its active engagement with the world about it.[17] But long-term continuity in popular political language, culture, organisation and mentality remains to be studied.

One such field concerns the relationship between coercion, consent and social cohesion within the village community. The social and cultural meanings of work could be one important subject, so far neglected in the historiography. The exhausting experience of agricultural labour may have been enough to secure the quiescence of early modern labouring people for much of the time.[18] Yet the authority of lords and

---

14 C. Liddy, 'Urban enclosure riots: risings of the commons in English towns, 1480–1525', *Past & Present*, 226 (2015), pp. 41–77.

15 I tried to trace some of these issues in A. Wood, *The memory of the people: custom and popular senses of the past in early modern England* (Cambridge, 2013), ch. 1. But this was really a stab in the dark and much more remains to be said.

16 For a very perceptive essay on attacks on elite landscapes and enclosures see C.J. Griffin, '"Cut down by some cowardly miscreants": plant maiming, or the malicious cutting of flora, as an act of protest in eighteenth- and nineteenth-century rural England', *Rural History*, 19 (2008), pp. 29–54.

17 J.D. Walter, 'The social economy of dearth in early modern England', in J.D. Walter and R. Schofield (eds), *Famine, disease and the social order in early modern society* (Cambridge, 1989), pp. 75–128.

18 M. Hailwood, 'The honest tradesman's honour: occupational and social identity in early modern England', *Transactions of the Royal Historical Society*, 6th Series 24 (2014). For an arresting study see L. Lamphere, 'Work and the production of silence', in G. Sider and G. Smith (eds), *Between history and histories: the making of silences and commemorations* (Toronto, 1997), pp. 263–83.

wealthier villagers depended upon much more than grinding the faces of the poor. Unequal power relations could find softer expression: the gift of cash, food or fuel in a cold winter or a period of dearth, or intercession with other authority figures to secure dismissal of law cases brought against poor neighbours. The grant of long secure leases to copyholders might result not just from the growing assertiveness of the latter but also from a genuine belief on the part of the lord in values of paternalism, decency and charity towards the poor.

All of this was tied up in the concept of what contemporaries called 'gentleness' and 'kindness'. Underpinned by the Scriptures, this sense of social duty was an important source of gentry identity and poorer folk could be assertive in reminding those gentlemen and women who transgressed that perceived duty of their rupture of social standards. This was a form of cultural hegemony – a way of securing the active consent of the governed, binding them into a social contract in return for ceding a certain space and sense of entitlement. But it was also much more than that: the paternalist ideal was underwritten by an emotional economy. The visceral nature of social relations – emotions such as fear, anger, affection, disgust, kindness, responsibility – alongside perceived senses of right and entitlement deserve much closer attention.[19] And, in the end, the unpredictable messiness of everyday life, along with the hornery inability of human beings to observe supposed social boundaries, could create friendships that crossed social boundaries. In his history of his home village of Myddle, for example, Richard Gough tells the story of two big boozers, a commoner called Thomas Jukes and a knight called Sir Humphrey Lea. Of Jukes, Gough remembered that 'he was a bauling, bould, confident person: hee often kept company with his betters, but shewed them noe more respecte than if they had beene his equals or inferiors'.[20] They would play at balls, drink, fall out and then, a few days later, make up and head back to the alehouse. Histories of social relations that focus upon grim class conflict miss these messy nuances and unpredictable complexities. The task for historians is to try to capture these everyday complexities while retaining a sense of the deeper social structures that underwrote everyday life. Yet, for all our grand theorising, social history suggests that there will always be awkward women and men like Thomas Jukes and Sir Humphrey Lea. They have a history too.

Social structure

And so to social structure. Individual community studies – the classic example is Wrightson and Levine's study of the Essex village of Terling – have pointed to growing social polarisation in the sixteenth and seventeenth centuries.[21] This pattern has received very powerful confirmation in Alexandra Shepard's hugely important recent monograph, *Accounting for oneself*. This book – probably the single most significant

19 For a brilliant intervention see H. Taylor, '"Branded on the tongue": rethinking plebeian inarticulacy in early modern England', *Radical History Review*, 121 (2015), pp. 91–105.

20 R. Gough, *The history of Myddle* (London, 1981), p. 97.

21 K. Wrightson and D. Levine, *Poverty and piety in an English village: Terling, 1525–1700* (London, 1979).

piece of work on early modern English social and economic history in a decade – uses court records to get at the ways in which differing social groups understood their level of wealth and hence their place in the pecking order.[22] She finds clear evidence that, in the south-east and East Anglia, middling-sort yeomen came to see themselves as of far greater worth (financially and socially) than their poor neighbours. Related stinting of common rights and restrictions of gleaning likewise deserve intensive study focusing on their shifting periodisation and geography. It would be good to know more about the pattern prior to 1550 – systematic study of early Tudor lay subsidies is one method, especially where combined with local listings. Whatever sources and methods are employed, though, social polarisation in the fifteenth century cries out for a significant study. The geography of social polarisation is also worthy of attention.

Critically, historians need a closer assessment of the development of landlessness and of different forms of proletarianisation. It is starting to become apparent that a larger proportion of the rural population was dependent upon wage labour much earlier than has been assumed: the Lay Subsidy of 1524/5 – used in village studies to chart the distribution of wealth – seems routinely to have under-counted the very poor. Closer studies of village society in the 1520s suggest a significant 'dark figure' of the unregistered poor.[23] More finely tuned studies of late medieval and early Tudor social structure are therefore needed. This is true of both urban and rural communities. Pound's classic study of the social structure of Norwich, for example, is highly revealing – using the 1524/5 lay subsidies, he shows the extent of social polarisation within the city in the early Tudor period, producing a picture of a deeply divided place with a large number of very poor folk (many of them weavers concentrated in slum accommodation in the northern quarter) over whom a small group of very wealthy urban oligarchs attempted to maintain control.[24] How distinct was Norwich in these terms? And how far back in time did that pattern of polarisation go?

Alexandra Sapoznik's chapter in this volume has a special place here. The extensive geographical spread of iron mining and smelting made it a key industry from the earliest date. By the early modern period the kinds of communities supported by such activities – in the Sussex and Kentish Weald, for example, or in the Forest of Dean, covered in this volume by Simon Sandall, had acquired a reputation as 'dark corners of the land', cut off from gentry authority. Of course, we are dealing here with the crude stereotypes of the industrial elite. But how did these communities regulate themselves? Social historians of the law have shown its ubiquity at the local level across England. In the Forest of Dean, institutional arrangements were relatively formal, with the Mine Law Court holding jurisdiction over the industry. But elsewhere both ferrous and non-ferrous mining and smelting arose organically and only gradually (if at all) developed institutional arrangements.

---

22 A. Shepard, *Accounting for oneself: worth, status and the social order in early modern England* (Oxford, 2015).

23 A. Wood, *The politics of social conflict: the Peak country, 1520–1770* (Cambridge, 1999), pp. 45–52.

24 J. Pound, 'The social and trade structure of Norwich, 1525–1575', *Past & Present*, 34 (1966), pp. 49–64.

Riot and rebellion

The records of Star Chamber, which commence (in a fragmentary form) in the reign of Henry VIII and run through to 1641 are – for all their fragmentary survival and opaque description by earlier archivists – a key source for understanding the nature, scale, timing and geography of protest. The records for the Caroline period are virtually non-existent. Very good finding aids exist for the Jacobean Star Chamber (National Archives class STAC8) and so that body of material has attracted a great deal of attention. In contrast, the finding aids for Elizabethan Star Chamber (National Archives class STAC5) are inadequate. This is significant, because it would seem that it was in the latter half of the sixteenth century that – in East Anglia and the south-east – wealthier villagers started to turn their back on the leadership of popular protest. This corresponds with Alex Shepard's startling findings, noted above, concerning changing ideas of self-worth among yeomen in these two regions.

The records of Star Chamber for the period 1509–58 (National Archives classes STAC2, 3 and 4) are better catalogued and so are more open to geographical analysis, or the pursuit of change over time, or thematic studies; yet they remain little explored.[25] The Star Chamber archive is especially important because, among other areas, it held jurisdiction over the prosecution of riotous offences. This has allowed historians to use the Star Chamber records – fragmentary as they are – to draw a rough picture of the geography, extent, leadership and social basis of enclosure rioting across England. One very significant finding from the work of Roger Manning is that enclosure riots in East Anglia fell from 12 per cent of the total in the reigns of Henry VIII and Edward VI to only 3 per cent of the total by the reign of James I. Finer analysis of the precise geography of that rioting within East Anglia shows that the vast majority of the Jacobean disturbances took place in the fenlands, as a result of the attempts to drain the fens.[26] In contrast, enclosure rioting in the period 1509–58 in East Anglia was concentrated deeper in the region, in the arable and sheep-pasture regions of Norfolk, Suffolk and Essex – that is, precisely those counties caught up in the East Anglian insurrections of 1549.

One of the problems of adopting a long-term approach is the complex issue of terminology and how this can influence interpretation. For example, the term 'peasant'

---

25 An exception is the study by Roger Manning, *Village revolts: social protest and popular disturbances in England, 1509–1640* (Oxford, 1988), which often misunderstands individual cases and in its statistical analysis misses out a large body of material. Yet it remains the only attempt to chart large-scale patterns of litigation at Star Chamber over the period 1509–1625, especially as regards rural protest. A more careful and detailed look at the changing geography of agrarian protest would be very welcome.

26 C. Holmes, 'Drainers and fenmen: the problem of popular political consciousness in the seventeenth century', in A. Fletcher and J. Stevenson (eds), *Order and disorder in early modern England* (Cambridge, 1985), pp. 166–97; K. Lindley, *Fenland riots and the English revolution* (London, 1982). The geography of Jacobean Star Chamber cases concerning enclosure riots within the East Anglian region is discussed in A. Wood, *Riot, rebellion and popular politics in early modern England* (Basingstoke, 2002), pp. 82–9.

has proven highly contentious and has developed different meanings across time.[27] In this volume John Broad plays down the historical significance of 'peasant' rebellion; however, the large-scale rebellions of 1381 and 1549 had profound consequences for the long-term development of English society. The events of 1381 helped to break feudalism, at a time when it was already weak. The events of 1549 helped to provide the grounding for the growing domination on a macro-scale of agrarian capitalism and within village micro-politics of middling sorts. Rather than diminishing the role of rebellion and popular politics, the closer study of the large-scale insurrections in 1381, 1450, 1497, 1536–7, 1549 and 1607, along with smaller-scale village and town protests in 1517, 1525, the 1550s, 1586 and the 1590s, reveal a lot about the changing texture of social relations and in many cases had profound implications for economic development. These were emphatically not 'peasant' insurrections. Mostly, they were led by aspirant middling men both from town and country, and their rank-and-file was made up of rural industrial workers, agricultural proletarians and industrial workers. In any case, 'peasant' was a name that the men and women of 1549 would have bridled at – it had already become a derogatory term by that time – witness Hamlet: 'What a rogue and peasant slave am I' (*Hamlet*, 2.II.520). For historians of the post-1450 period, I think that 'peasant' is a term that we can do without.

In a book I published in 2007 I suggested that, in the face of social polarisation and also, possibly, the attraction of Calvinism to propertied groups, the yeoman elite of East Anglia removed themselves from the leadership of popular protest.[28] The basis for this shift was the growing tendency to see poorer neighbours not as 'Christ's poor' – as fellow neighbours within a Christian community – but as a social burden, as immoral, a threat to the village order. This division among the commons removed the basis for joint action and led to the collapse of the tradition of popular rebellion. Empirically, I was skating on thin ice: much of what I had to say represented educated guesses. It would have been important, clearly, to have been able to look at how the pattern of protest changed during the reign of Elizabeth (1558–1603), since this is where the transition was occurring. But the absence of good finding aids meant that I was unable to carry out this task.

There is, therefore, something of a black hole in the history of popular protest in the Elizabethan period. Until such a time as the records of Elizabethan Star Chamber become accessible (and archivists in the National Archives are working on new finding aids that would open up this class of material), perhaps the only way forward is to carry out focused micro-studies of protest and social relations in well-sourced villages or neighbourhoods. In any case, the records of Star Chamber represent a vital – and for the period 1509–1603 – an underexplored body of material. Here, there is potential for a good number of doctoral projects, journal articles and probably also some very revealing monographs.

For all its weaknesses, the records of Star Chamber at least allow us a partial glimpse of the changing nature and geography of rural protest between 1509 and

27 See, for example, J.V. Beckett, 'The peasant in England: a case of terminological confusion?', *Agricultural History Review*, 32 (1984), pp. 113–23.

28 A. Wood, *The 1549 rebellions and the making of early modern England* (Cambridge, 2007), ch. 5.

1625. The nature of rural protest between the 1381 rebellion and the accession of Henry VIII, by contrast, remains only thinly studied. One question concerns late medieval opposition to enclosure.[29] Recent work by Liddy has suggested that, in urban centres, the period 1480–1520 saw intense conflict over use-rights on urban commons.[30] What was the state of such protest in rural communities at this time, and earlier? Liddy was able to use borough records in order to shed real light on his subject; in contrast, manorial records would seem to be generally less revealing. But are they? Jane Whittle has used quarter session records to provide a detailed picture of participation in Kett's rebellion.[31] She was also, through her painstaking work on Norfolk quarter sessions, which start unusually early in the sixteenth century, able to excavate examples of strikes and the undermining of labour regulation.[32] Similar studies have provided evidence of a lordly offensive after the Black Death followed by a rise in peasant resistance which gradually, mostly with little drama, ground down serfdom.[33] But we need a richer sense of the micro-politics of social conflicts in rural England for the period 1381–1509.[34]

One of the most significant achievements over the past generation of early modern social historians has been the reconceptualisation of the nature of the 'political'. From 1989 onwards seminal pieces by Keith Wrightson and Patrick Collinson encouraged a new generation of early modern social historians to break down divisions between politics and society, reconceptualising politics as fundamentally about three things: power, space and resources.[35] This approach was materialist without being Marxist. Importantly, it also broke open boundaries between society and economy, enabling us to write a history of economic life which was, at the same time, a history of neighbourhood, reciprocity, conflict and identity. A number of the chapters in this

29 C.F. Richmond,'The transition from feudalism to capitalism in the archives of Magdalen College, Oxford: a note', *History Workshop Journal*, 37 (1994), pp. 165–9.

30 For early modern conflicts over town commons see H.R. French, 'The common fields of urban England: communal agriculture and the "politics of entitlement"', in R.W. Hoyle (ed.), *Custom, improvement and the landscape in early modern Britain* (Farnham, 2011), pp. 149–74.

31 J.C. Whittle,'Lords and tenants in Kett's rebellion 1549', *Past & Present*, 207 (2010), pp. 3–52.

32 J.C. Whittle, *The development of agrarian capitalism: land and labour in Norfolk, 1450–1580* (Oxford, 2000), p. 286.

33 M. Muller, 'Conflict and revolt: the bishop of Ely and his peasants at the manor of Brandon in Suffolk, c.1300–1381', *Rural History*, 23 (2012), pp. 1–19; idem, 'The aims and organization of a peasant revolt in fourteenth-century Wiltshire', *Rural History*, 14 (2003), pp. 1–20.

34 See, for example, E.B. Fryde and N. Fryde, 'Peasant rebellion and peasant discontents', in E. Miller (ed.), *The agrarian history of England and Wales. Volume III: 1348–1500* (Cambridge, 1991), pp. 744–819.

35 P. Collinson, *De Republica Anglorum, or, history with the politics put back in* (Cambridge, 1989); K. Wrightson, 'The politics of the parish in early modern England', in P. Griffiths, A. Fox and S. Hindle (eds), *The experience of authority in early modern England* (London, 1996). Resources are key to the development theorist Adrian Leftwich's theorisation of politics, work that was influential upon Wrightson's assessment of parish politics. See his *Redefining politics: people, resources and power* (London, 1983).

volume, most notably those of James Bowen on common rights and cottages in early modern Shropshire and William Shannon on woodland resources in Lancashire, builds on and complicates that inheritance in ways that are fresh and illuminating. What is especially satisfying in both pieces is the combination of fresh archival material with a rich sense of local place. A similar sense of place is evident in Simon Sandall's chapter on the Forest of Dean, which offers the sharpest sense in the volume of both the conflictual nature of custom (neither plebeian nor elite, custom represented an available discourse that could be claimed by a variety of contending groups) and the ways in which customary ideals informed social identities.

Coal: the organic energy economy

Coal represented many things in early modern England: it represented heat, smoke, pollution, some flickering light by which to read or to conduct conversation and, of course, harsh, demanding labour. The fuel economy of late medieval and early modern rural communities deserves closer study. I want here briefly to develop one important example, that of the perhaps surprising economic interface between coastal East Anglia and the northern coalfield around Newcastle-upon-Tyne. Alex Brown's chapter in this volume demonstrates the extensive use of coal within the regional market of the north-east from a surprisingly early date, while Postan highlighted the shipment of coal from Newcastle to London from the thirteenth century.[36] By the early sixteenth century coal shipments from Newcastle were arriving in greater numbers not only in the major Norfolk ports of King's Lynn and Great Yarmouth but also in the small fishing community of Blakeney, on the north Norfolk coast. These shipments had profound consequences for the economies of these communities and for those inland areas that traded with them. In the case of Lynn, internal river networks fed coal into Huntingdonshire and Cambridgeshire; Cambridge colleges were heated with coal by the fifteenth century. Yarmouth trade fed the fuel needs of England's second city, Norwich, quite possibly from the early sixteenth century. Coal shipments into small ports without an adjacent river network, such as Blakeney, probably reached a less extensive hinterland, but will have given that village a particularly distinctive appearance and source of domestic heating. The study of the north-east coal trade, therefore, illuminates an important driver in the growing market integration and commercialisation of the English economy.

Of course, the growth of London in the sixteenth and seventeenth centuries would have been impossible without a massive increase in Newcastle coal shipments. Within the rural economy, this had a number of effects. Most obviously, it resulted in the early industrialisation of the northern coalfield of county Durham and Northumberland, breeding proletarianisation, massive landscape change and intense conflict over mineral rights.[37] These village disputes over coal-mining rights remain to be fully

36 M.M. Postan, *The medieval economy and society: an economic history of Britain in the Middle Ages* (London, 1972), p. 222.

37 The key study is D. Levine and K. Wrightson, *The making of an industrial society: Whickham, 1560–1765* (Oxford, 1991).

explored: the records are available to write a very detailed study in both gentry family archives and equity court litigation (for example, the central Exchequer court, Star Chamber and the Palatinate courts of Durham).

The expansion of the northern coalfield created a new kind of rural community: the industrial village. Different in texture to the proto-industrial weaving communities of regions such as the Stour Valley, or the handicraft manufactures of Hallamshire or the Forest of Arden, the proletarian mining villages of the north-east were, at a startlingly early date, already established as fully industrial societies. And the coal that they produced, moved on waggonways to the Tyne, then onto ships from that great port down the east coast, and finally shifted to London or down inland river networks, altered the fuel economies of villages and small towns hundreds of miles from the northern coalfield. Intensive work on inventories, borough records and port books would enable us to chart the development of this energy economy, one that E.A. Wrigley has seen as a fundamental element in England's early industrialisation and sustained demographic take-off.[38] And we should not concentrate on the northern coalfield alone; inland coal industries were also emerging in the late medieval period in areas such as Lancashire, north-east Cheshire and the West Midlands. The inhabitants of Tudor Stockport, for example, were burning coal extracted from nearby Bredbury, on the Cheshire 'panhandle' that reached into the Pennine uplands. Here, too, there is evidence of growing market integration, albeit over much shorter distances.

For those communities that did not lie close to a navigable river or to an emergent coalfield, the primary source of domestic heating remained either peat or wood; for the really desperate, homes were heated by burning animal dung. Access to firewood and peat was dictated by local custom – specifically, the rights of firebote and turbary. Here, too, there is widespread evidence of intense conflict over fuel rights, conflicts that were just as intensely felt and fought as disputes over pasture rights on common land.[39] Following the publication of E.P. Thompson's *Customs in common*, customary rights have recently received much attention, reigniting a subject that had seemed relatively dormant following seminal work by Tawney and the Hammonds. Yet there remain significant lacunae. Work by Shaw-Taylor has, perhaps unsurprisingly, shown that by the time of large-scale parliamentary enclosure in eastern England labourers in smaller communities had largely lost rights to pasture animals.[40] Yet the precise chronology of this shift – micro-political in character – remains to be fully explored. In particular, this will involve attention to enclosure disputes and stinting. Yet pasture rights were not the only

---

38 E.A. Wrigley, *Continuity, chance and change: the character of the industrial revolution in England* (Cambridge, 1988).

39 For a very long-term local struggle see R.W. Bushaway, '"Groveley, Groveley, and all Groveley": custom, crime and conflict in the English woodland', *History Today*, 31 (1981), pp. 37–43.

40 L. Shaw-Taylor, 'Labourers, cows, common rights and parliamentary enclosure: the evidence of contemporary comment, c.1760–1810', *Past & Present*, 171 (2001), pp. 95–126. For an overstated version of the same argument see S. Birtles, 'Common land, poor relief and enclosure: the use of manorial resources in fulfilling parish obligations, 1601–1834', *Past & Present*, 165 (1999), pp. 74–106.

form of customary entitlement; a fuller understanding of, for example, fuel rights will illuminate the interaction of economic and social relations within the village polity, bringing up issues to do with senses of entitlement and social conflict.

Town and country

One of the unfortunate effects of the development of urban history and agricultural history has been a tendency – among both social and economic historians – to identify themselves as either urban or rural historians.[41] This is not helped by the separation of these fields within influential journals that deal mostly with the economic and social history of the medieval and early modern periods – for all their many virtues, titles like *Urban History*, *Agricultural History Review* and *Rural History*, by their very nature, are predicated on the maintenance of an urban/rural distinction.

What I am emphatically *not* suggesting is that historians should not write histories of individual villages or rural neighbourhoods, or of towns and cities. Nor am I suggesting – it would be crazy to do so – that there was no difference between the texture, rhythm or politics of urban and rural life. My point is that historians should write about town and country with a much sharper sense of the dynamic interrelationship between the urban and the rural. We need clearer studies of the market integration of town and countryside. Within highly urbanised regions (such as the South East and East Anglia) and localities adjacent to towns and cities we need studies of migration patterns that are alive to the push/pull effect of the city alongside the demands of lambing and harvest season, as labourers moved into the city in the winter and out again to the countryside in the spring. Urban perceptions of the rural – and rural perceptions of the urban – ought to replace cultural historians' urban bias. But it is sometimes hard to escape established patterns of historical writing, especially where these are implicit or unstated. This has certainly been true of both urban and rural studies. Work on towns and cities tends to refer, in an almost colonial manner, to what they call the rural 'hinterland'. Similarly, most rural studies tend to ignore the importance of towns and cities in driving economic and social changes. The one notable exception to this is Levine and Wrightson's study of Whickham, in the northern coalfield, in which Newcastle looms as a constant presence over the lives of the villagers.

Let us focus, for a moment, on the city of Norwich, for which exceptionally good records survive. Mid-Tudor Norwich people spoke of the 'men of the countrith' as though they were a separate category, yet the borough records are full of examples of rural folk coming and going to the city – trading in the many markets, drinking in the hundreds of alehouses, visiting family, gossiping and spreading seditious words. And the landscape of medieval and early modern cities was more agricultural than we might imagine today. Much of Norwich within its walls was made up of gardens, orchards and playing fields, such as the Gildencroft in the poor weaving parish of

---

41 A very important exception to this is the work of E.A. Wrigley. See, in particular, his essay 'A simple model of London's importance in changing English society and economy, 1650–1750', in E.A. Wrigley, *People, cities and wealth: the transformation of a traditional society* (Oxford, 1987), pp. 133–56.

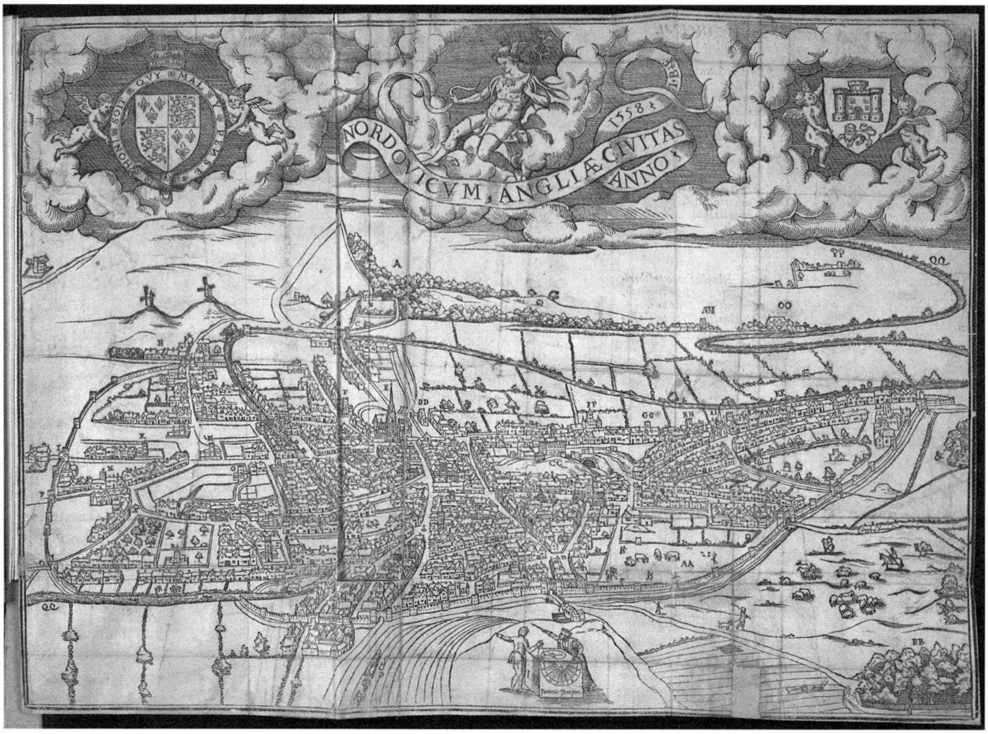

Figure 12.1 Map of Norwich by William Cunningham, 1558. © The British Library Board. The Cosmographical Glasse, conteinyng the pleasant Principles of Cosmographie, Geographie, Hydrographie, or Nauigation. [With woodcuts, including a map of Norwich.] G.6583

St Augustine's, where young men went 'camping' – that is, played football – just as rural lads kicked balls about on 'camping fields' in villages such as Stiffkey.[42] Cunningham's 1558 map of Norwich shows that cultivated fields came right up to the city walls (Figure 12.1). This is confirmed by legal papers concerning the suburbs of the city, such as Lakenham and Eaton. Importantly, those extra-mural fields were actually within the city, in that they fell within the jurisdictional boundaries of Norwich as set by its charters. Medieval and early modern cities were not defined by the people who lived there in terms of relative population density, occupational specialisation or any of the other markers beloved of urban geographers. Cities were defined by their charters, documents that were lovingly preserved within locked and bolted oaken chests in guildhalls. Rural communities, too, took care to preserve the documentary basis of their customary rights. Horses were everywhere. Come market day, the streets would have been crowded with sheep, pigs, cattle and great wains crammed with grain, vegetables, cheeses and fruit. Wherries from Yarmouth were laid up at the

42 D. Dymond, 'A lost social institution: the camping close', *Rural History*, 1 (1990), pp. 165–92.

docks in Conesford and alongside Pigg Lane, dockers unloading coal that had been hacked from the mines of villages such as Whickham in county Durham and shipped down the east coast from Newcastle in big collier ships to Yarmouth. Those same colliers returned to Newcastle loaded with Norfolk and Suffolk grain to feed hungry mouths in the north-east – another example of symbiosis of town and countryside, this time between otherwise distant regions.[43] And engirdling Norwich on its northern and eastern approach was Mousehold Heath, the massive area of common land on which Kett's rebels had gathered in 1549. Although Kett's revolt is sometimes referred to as a 'peasant rebellion', there were many urban men and women among the Norfolk rebels. Significantly, Mousehold was intercommoned by a series of adjacent rural settlements as well as by the inhabitants of the city.

So, in terms of the texture of everyday life, the agricultural experience would have been everywhere within cities – even in London. And rural communities were, likewise, heavily influenced by urban communities. Small towns such as Cirencester – here studied by David Rollison – were especially important, still sitting in the network of minor roads that had been established by the Romans, they represented important trading centres and sources of capital, together with centres of sociability – alehouses; passing players; town and village gossip; political news – for rural people as well as townswomen and men.[44] This swirl of conversation, bargaining and exchanges of ideas, goods and money was known to contemporaries as 'traficke'.[45] And it was what bound what was otherwise a patchwork of local 'countries' and 'neighbourhoods' together, holding it together as a polity, a culture, an economy and – increasingly – as a nation.

---

43 N.J. Williams, *The maritime trade of East Anglian ports, 1550–1650* (Oxford, 1988), pp. 50–68, 138–80. For the broader argument about the growing interdependence of what were emerging as economically distinct regions by 1650 see P. Hudson (ed.), *Regions and industries: a perspective on the Industrial Revolution in Britain* (Cambridge, 1988). That growing interdependence is a key theme in K. Wrightson, *Earthly necessities: economic lives in early modern Britain, 1470–1750* (London, 2002).

44 R. Fleming, *Britain after Rome: the fall and rise, 400 to 1070* (London, 2010), pp. 13–15. Fleming suggests that the collapse of this network of small towns led to the crisis of late antiquity in Roman Britain, as the large country villas that had fed the commerce of the towns turned inward, becoming more like big gentry estates – or even slave plantations, perhaps – than outward-facing suppliers to a market. It is worth remembering that much of the road network within England in the period 1350–1750 was Roman in origin.

45 D. Rollison, 'Exploding England: the dialectics of mobility and settlement in early modern England', *Social History*, 24 (1999), pp. 1–16.

Select Bibliography

Abel, W., *Agricultural fluctuations in Europe. From the thirteenth to the twentieth centuries* (London, 1980).

Adams, M., 'History of the demesne farm at Appledore from contemporary building records', *Archaeologia Cantiana*, 112 (1993), pp. 283–98.

Albion, R.G., *Forests and sea power: the timber problem of the royal navy, 1652–1862* (Cambridge, 1926).

Allen, M., *Mints and money in medieval England* (Cambridge, 2012).

Allen, M., *The Durham Mint* (London, 2003).

Allen, R.C., 'The growth of labor productivity in early modern English agriculture', *Explorations in Economic History*, 25 (1988), pp. 117–46.

Andrews, K.R., *Elizabethan privateering during the Spanish War, 1585–1603* (Cambridge, 1964).

Arnold, J., *Belief and unbelief in medieval Europe* (London, 2005).

Ashby, J. and King, B., 'Statistics of some Midland villages', *The Economic Journal*, 3 (1893), pp. 1–22.

Ashton, T.S., 'Richard Henry Tawney 1880–1962', *Proceedings of the British Academy*, 48 (1962), pp. 461–82.

Aston, T.H. and Philpin, C.H.E. (eds), *The Brenner debate: agrarian class structure and economic development in pre-industrial Europe* (Cambridge, 1985).

Ault, W., *Open-field farming in medieval England: a study of village by-laws* (London, 1972).

Awty, B.G., 'Force Forge in the seventeenth century', *Transactions of the Cumberland and Westmorland Antiquarian and Archaeological Society*, 51 (1979–80), pp. 97–112.

Awty, B.G. and Phillips, C.B., 'The Cumbrian bloomery forge in the seventeenth century and forge equipment in the charcoal iron industry', *Newcomen Society Transactions*, 51 (1979–80), pp. 25–40.

Bailey, M., *The decline of serfdom in late medieval England: from bondage to freedom* (Woodbridge, 2014).

Bailey, M., 'The transformation of customary tenures in southern England, c.1350 to c.1500', *Agricultural History Review*, 62 (2014), pp. 210–30.

Bailey, M., 'Beyond the Midland field system: the determinants of common rights over the arable in medieval England', *Agricultural History Review*, 58 (2010), pp. 153–71.

Bailey, M., 'The form, function and evolution of irregular field systems in Suffolk, c.1300–c.1550', *Agricultural History Review*, 57 (2009), pp. 15–36.

Bailey, M., 'Villeinage in England: a regional case study, c.1250–c.1349', *Economic History Review*, 62 (2009), pp. 430–57.

Bailey, M., *Medieval Suffolk: an economic and social history, 1200–1500* (Woodbridge, 2007).

Bailey, M., *The English manor c.1200–c.1500* (Manchester, 2002).

Bailey, M., 'Coastal fishing off south east Suffolk in the century after the Black Death', *Proceedings of the Suffolk Institute of Archaeology and History*, 37 (1992), pp. 102–14.

Bailey, M., *A marginal economy? East Anglian breckland in the later Middle Ages* (Cambridge, 1989).

Bailey, M. and Rigby, S. (eds), *Town and countryside in the age of the Black Death* (Woodbridge, 2012).

Baker, A.R., 'Some fields and farms in medieval Kent', *Archaeologia Cantiana*, 80 (1965), pp. 152–74.

Barber, L. and Priestly-Bell, G., *Medieval adaptation, settlement and economy of a coastal wetland: the evidence from around Lydd, Romney Marsh, Kent* (Oxford, 2008).

Baxter, D., *Medieval Bourn: a Cambridgeshire village in the later Middle Ages* (Cambridge, 2008).

Baxter, D., 'Roman tumuli or medieval industry? Moulton Hills, Bourn, reconsidered', *Proceedings of the Cambridge Antiquarian Society*, 95 (2006), pp. 49–56.

Beckett, J.V., *The rise and fall of the Grenvilles: the dukes of Buckingham and Chandos, 1710 to 1921* (Manchester, 1994).

Beckett, J.V., *A history of Laxton: England's last open-field village* (Oxford, 1989).

Beckett, J.V., 'The peasant in England: a case of terminological confusion?', *Agricultural History Review*, 32 (1984), pp. 113–23.

Beckett, J.V. and Turner, M.E., 'End of the old order? F.M.L. Thompson, the Land Question, and the burden of ownership in England, c.1880–c.1925', *Agricultural History Review*, 55 (2007), pp. 269–88.

Beecham, K.J., *History of Cirencester and the Roman city of Corinium* (1887, repr. Stroud, 1978).

Beresford, M. and Hurst, J.G. (eds), *Deserted medieval villages* (London, 1971).

Berg, M., *A woman in history. Eileen Power 1889–1940* (Cambridge, 1996).

Beswick, P. and Challis, K., 'Pottery from the medieval iron smelting site at Stanley Grange, Derbyshire', *Derbyshire Archaeological Journal*, 124 (2004), pp. 69–85.

Bevan, B., Doonan, R. and Gale, R., 'Medieval rural lead working: excavations at Linch Clough, Upper Derwent valley, 2000–2001', *Derbyshire Archaeological Society*, 124 (2004), pp. 113–40.

Birrell, J., 'Manorial custumals reconsidered', *Past and Present*, 224 (2014), pp. 3–37.

Birrell, J., 'Peasant craftsmen in the medieval forest', *Agricultural History Review*, 17 (1969), pp. 91–107.

Birtles, S., 'Common land, poor relief and enclosure: the use of manorial resources in fulfilling parish obligations, 1601–1834', *Past and Present*, 165 (1999), pp. 74–106.

Bisson, D.R., *The merchant adventurers of England: the company and the Crown, 1474–1564* (London, 1993).

Blake, J.B., 'The medieval coal trade of north-east England: some fourteenth century evidence', *Northern History*, 2 (1967), pp. 1–26.

Blanchard, I., 'The miner and the agricultural community in late medieval England', *Agricultural History Review*, 20 (1972), pp. 93–106.

Bland, A.E., Brown, P.A. and Tawney, R.H. (eds), *English economic history. Select documents* (London, 1914).

Bolton, J.L., 'What is money? What is a money economy? When did a money economy emerge in medieval England?', in D. Wood (ed.), *Medieval money matters* (Oxford, 2004), pp. 1–15.

Bond, J., 'Medieval charcoal-burning in England', *Ruralia VI* (Turnhout, 2001), pp. 277–94.

Bowden, A.R., *The wool trade in Tudor and Stuart England* (London, 1971).

Bowden, P., 'Agricultural prices, farm profits and rent', in J. Thirsk (ed.), *The agrarian history of England and Wales. Volume IV: 1500–1640* (Cambridge, 1967), pp. 593–695.

Bowen, J.P., '"Before the breaking of the day, in a riotous manner and with great shouts and outcries": disputes over common land in Shropshire in the sixteenth and seventeenth centuries', *Rural History*, 26 (2015), pp. 133–59.

Bowen, J.P., 'Cottage and squatter settlement and encroachment on common waste in the sixteenth and seventeenth centuries: some evidence from Shropshire', *Local Population Studies*, 93 (2014), pp. 11–32.

Bowring, J., 'Between the Corporation and Captain Flood: the Fens and drainage after 1663', in R.W. Hoyle (ed.), *Custom, improvement and the landscape in early modern Britain* (Farnham, 2011), pp. 235–62.

Brandon, P.F., 'South-eastern England', in H.E. Hallam (ed.), *The agrarian history of England and Wales. Volume II: 1042–1350* (Cambridge, 1988), pp. 174–89.

Brassley, P., 'Land reform and reallocation in interwar Europe', in R. Congost and R. Santos (eds), *Contexts of property in Europe: the social embeddedness of property rights in land in historical perspective* (Turnhout, 2010), pp. 145–64.

Brassley, P., *The agricultural economy of Northumberland and Durham in the period 1640–1750* (London, 1985).

Brenner, R., 'Agrarian class structure and economic development in pre-industrial Europe', *Past and Present*, 70 (1976), pp. 34–70.

Bridbury, A.R., *Economic growth: England in the later Middle Ages* (London, 1962).

Briggs, C., 'The availability of credit in the English countryside, 1400–1480', *Agricultural History Review*, 56 (2008), pp. 1–24.

Britnell, R.H., 'The coal industry in the later Middle Ages: the Bishop of Durham's estates', in M. Bailey and S.H. Rigby (eds), *Town and countryside in the age of the Black Death: essays in honour of John Hatcher* (Turnhout, 2012), pp. 439–72.

Britnell, R.H., 'Fields, farms and sun-division in a moorland region, 1100–1400', *Agricultural History Review*, 52 (2004), pp. 20–37.

Britnell, R.H., 'The economic context', in A.J. Pollard (ed.), *The Wars of the Roses* (Basingstoke, 1995), pp. 41–65.

Britnell, R.H., *The commercialisation of English society, 1000–1500* (Cambridge, 1993).

Britnell, R.H., 'The Pastons and their Norfolk', *Agricultural History Review*, 36 (1988), pp. 132–44.

Broad, J., *A common agricultural heritage? Revising French and British rural divergence* (British Agricultural History Society, 2009).

Broad, J., *Transforming English rural society: the Verneys and the Claydons, 1600–1820* (Cambridge, 2004).

Broad, J., 'The fate of the Midland yeoman: tenants, copyholders, and freeholders as farmers in north Buckinghamshire, 1620–1800', *Continuity and Change*, 14 (1999), pp. 325–47.

Broad, J., 'The Verneys as enclosing landlords, 1600–1800', in J. Chartres and D. Hey (eds), *English rural society, 1500–1800: essays in honour of Joan Thirsk* (Cambridge, 1990), pp. 27–53.

Broadberry, S., Campbell, B.M.S., Klein, A., Overton, M. and van Leeuwen, B., *British economic growth 1270–1870* (Cambridge, 2015).

Brooks, C.W., *Law, politics and society in early modern England* (Cambridge, 2010).

Brown, A. and Taylor, C., 'Chellington field survey', *Bedfordshire Archaeology*, 23 (1999), pp. 98–110.

Brown, A.T., *Rural society and economic change in County Durham: recession and recovery, c.1400–1640* (Woodbridge, 2015).

Brown, A.T., 'Estate management and institutional constraints in pre-industrial England: the ecclesiastical estates of Durham, c.1400–1640', *Economic History Review*, 67 (2014), pp. 699–719.

Brown, A.T., 'Surviving the mid-fifteenth-century recession: Durham Cathedral Priory, 1400–1520', *Northern History*, 47 (2010), pp. 209–31.

Brown, R.H., 'The achievement norm and economic growth: the case of Elizabethan England', *Review of Social Economy*, 27 (1969), pp. 181–201.

Bushaway, B., *By rite: custom, ceremony and community in England 1700–1880* (London, 1982).

Bushaway, R.W., '"Groveley, Groveley, and all Groveley": custom, crime and conflict in the English woodland', *History Today*, 31 (1981), pp. 37–43.

Butcher, A.F., 'The hospital of St Stephen and St Thomas, New Romney: the documentary sources', *Archaeologia Cantiana*, 96 (1980), pp. 17–26.

Butcher, A.F., 'The origins of Romney freemen, 1433–1523', *Economic History Review*, 27 (1974), pp. 16–27.

Campbell, B.M.S., 'Agriculture in Kent in the high Middle Ages', in S. Sweetinburgh (ed.), *Later medieval Kent, 1220–1540* (Woodbridge, 2010), pp. 25–54.
Campbell, B.M.S., 'Nature as historical protagonist: environment and society in pre-industrial England', *Economic History Review*, 63 (2010), pp. 281–314.
Campbell, B.M.S, 'Matching supply to demand: crop production and disposal by English demesnes in the century of the Black Death', *Journal of Economic History*, 57 (1997), pp. 827–58.
Campbell, B.M.S., 'Agricultural progress in medieval England: some evidence from eastern Norfolk', *Economic History Review*, 36 (1983), pp. 26–46.
Campbell, B.M.S and Overton, M., 'A new perspective on medieval and early modern agriculture: six centuries of Norfolk farming, c.1250–c.1850', *Past and Present*, 141 (1993), pp. 38–105.
Chambers, J.D. and Mingay, G.E., *The agricultural revolution, 1750–1880* (London, 1966).
Chevet, J.M., 'Reconsidering a rural myth: peasant France and capitalist Britain', in J. Broad (ed.), *A Common agricultural heritage? Revising French and British rural divergence* (British Agricultural History Society, 2009), pp. 37–54.
Clark, G., 'The economics of exhaustion, the Postan thesis, and the agricultural revolution', *Journal of Economic History*, 52 (1992), pp. 61–84.
Clark, M., 'The gentry, the commons and the politics of common right in Enfield, c.1558–c.1603', *Historical Journal*, 54 (2011), pp. 609–29.
Clay, C.G.A., *Economic expansion and social change, England 1500–1700* (Cambridge, 1984).
Clay, C.G.A., 'Lifeleasehold in the western counties of England, 1650–1750', *Agricultural History Review*, 29 (1981), pp. 83–96.
Cleese, H.F. and Crossley, D.W. (eds), *The iron industry of the Weald* (Leicester, 1988).
Cohn, S.K., *Popular protest in late medieval English towns* (New York & Cambridge, 2013).
Coleman, D.C., *Industry in Tudor and Stuart England* (London, 1975).
Coleman, D.C., 'Industrial growth and industrial revolutions', *Economica*, 23 (1956), pp. 1–22.
Collins, E.J.T., 'The coppice and underwood trades', in G.E. Mingay (ed.) *The agrarian history of England and Wales. Volume VI: 1750–1850* (Cambridge, 1989), pp. 484–501.
Collinson, P., *De Republica Anglorum, or, history with the politics put back in* (Cambridge, 1989).
Comet, G., 'Technology and agricultural expansion in the Middle Ages: the example of France north of the Loire', in G. Astill and J. Langdon (eds), *Medieval farming and technology: the impact of agricultural change in northwest Europe* (New York, 1997), pp. 11–40.
Craster, H.H.E., *A history of Northumberland volume VIII: the parish of Tynemouth* (London, 1907).
Crosthwaite, J.F., 'The colony of German miners at Keswick', *Transactions of the Cumberland and Westmorland Antiquarian and Archaeological Society*, 6 (1881–2), pp. 344–54.
Darnton, R., *The kiss of Lamourette: reflections in cultural history* (New York, 1990).
Darnton, R., *The great cat massacre and other episodes in French cultural history* (New York, 1984).
Davis, R., *English overseas trade, 1500–1700* (London, 1973).
de L. Mann, J., *The cloth industry in the west of England from 1640–1880* (Oxford, 1971).
Dickinson, J.C., *Furness Abbey* (London, 1987).
Dimmock, S., *The origin of capitalism in England, 1400–1600* (Leiden, 2013).
Dimmock, S., 'English small towns and the emergence of capitalist relations, c.1450–1550', *Urban History*, 28 (2001), pp. 5–24.
Dirkx, J., 'Wood-pasture in Dutch common woodlands and the deforestation of the Dutch landscape', in K. Kirby and C. Watkins (eds), *The ecological history of European forests* (Wallingford, 1998), pp. 35–42.
Dobb, M., *Studies in the development of capitalism* (London, 1946).
Dobson, R.B., *Durham Priory, 1400–1450* (Cambridge, 1973).

Dodds, B., 'Demesne and tithe: peasant agriculture in the late Middle Ages', *Agricultural History Review*, 56 (2008), pp. 123–41.

Dodds, B., 'Output and productivity: common themes and regional variation', in B. Dodds and R.H. Britnell (eds), *Agriculture and rural society after the Black Death: common themes and regional variations* (Hatfield, 2008), pp. 73–88.

Dodds, B., *Peasants and production in the medieval North-East: the evidence of tithes, 1270–1538* (Woodbridge, 2007).

Dodds, B. and Britnell, R.H. (eds), *Agriculture and rural society after the Black Death: common themes and regional variations* (Hatfield, 2008).

Draper, G., '"Land and marsh": settlement, colonization and consolidation, c.800–1220', in S. Sweetinburgh (ed.), *Early medieval Kent, 800–1220* (forthcoming).

Draper, G., 'Timber and iron: natural resources for the late medieval shipbuilding industry in Kent', in S. Sweetinburgh (ed.), *Later medieval Kent, 1220–1540* (Woodbridge, 2010), pp. 55–78.

Draper, G., 'Small fields and wet land: inheritance practices and the transmission of real property in the Romney Marshes c.1150–1390', *Landscapes*, 6 (2005), pp. 18–45.

Draper, G., 'The farmers of Canterbury Cathedral priory and All Souls College on Romney Marsh c.1443–1545', in J. Eddison, M. Gardiner and A. Long (eds), *Romney Marsh: environmental change and human occupation in a coastal lowland* (Oxford, 1998), pp. 109–28.

Draper, G. and Meddens, F., *The sea and the marsh: the medieval cinque port of New Romney* (London, 2009).

Du Boulay, F.R.H., *The lordship of Canterbury* (London, 1966).

Duby, G., *Rural economy and country life in the medieval West*, trans. C. Postan (Philadelphia, 1968).

Dyer, C., 'The agrarian problem, 1440–1520', in J.C. Whittle (ed.), *Landlords and tenants in Britain, 1440–1660: Tawney's agrarian problem revisited* (Woodbridge, 2013), pp. 19–34.

Dyer, C., *A country merchant 1495–1520: trading and farming at the end of the Middle Ages* (Oxford, 2012).

Dyer, C., 'Poverty and its relief in late medieval England', *Past and Present*, 216 (2012), pp. 41–78.

Dyer, C., 'Villages in crisis: social dislocation, 1370–1520', in C. Dyer and R. Jones (eds), *Deserted villages revisited* (Hatfield, 2010), pp. 28–45.

Dyer, C., 'A Suffolk farmer in the fifteenth century', *Agricultural History Review*, 55 (2007), pp. 1–22.

Dyer, C., 'Conflict in the landscape: the enclosure movement in England, 1220–1349', *Landscape History*, 29 (2007), pp. 21–33.

Dyer, C. (ed.), *The self-contained village?: The social history of rural communities 1250–1900* (Hatfield, 2007).

Dyer, C., *An age of transition? Economy and society in England in the later Middle Ages* (Oxford, 2005).

Dyer, C., *Making a living in the Middle Ages: the people of Britain 850–1520* (London, 2002).

Dyer, C., 'Woodlands and wood-pasture in western England', in J. Thirsk (ed.), *Rural England: an illustrated history of the landscape* (Oxford, 2002), pp. 97–121.

Dyer, C., 'Small towns, 1270–1540', in D.M. Palliser (ed.), *Cambridge urban history of Britain, 600–1540, vol. I* (Cambridge, 2000), pp. 505–37.

Dyer, C., 'The English medieval village community and its decline', *Journal of British Studies*, 33 (1994), pp. 407–29.

Dyer, C., 'Were there any capitalists in fifteenth-century England?', in J. Kermode (ed.), *Enterprise and individuals in fifteenth-century England* (Stroud, 1991), pp. 1–24.

Dyer, C., *Lords and peasants in a changing society: the estates of the bishopric of Worcester, 680–1540* (Cambridge, 1980).

Dyer, C., 'A redistribution of incomes in fifteenth-century England?', *Past and Present*, 39 (1968), pp. 11–33.

Dyer, C. and Jones, R. (eds), *Deserted villages revisited* (Hatfield, 2010).

Dymond, D., 'A lost social institution: the camping close', *Rural History*, 1 (1990), pp. 165–92.

Eales, J. and Hopper, A. (eds), *The county community in seventeenth-century England and Wales* (Hatfield, 2012).

Eddison, J. and Draper, G., 'A landscape of medieval reclamation: Walland Marsh, Kent', *Landscape History*, 19 (1997), pp. 75–88.

Edwards, P.R., 'Competition for land, common rights and drainage in the Weald moors (Shropshire): the Cherrington and Meeson disputes, 1576–1612', in R.W. Hoyle (ed.), *People, landscape and alternative agriculture: essays for Joan Thirsk* (Exeter, 2004), pp. 39–55.

Edwards, P.R., 'The horse trade of the Midlands', *Agricultural History Review*, 27 (1979), pp. 90–100.

Edwards, P.R., 'The development of dairy farming of the north Shropshire plain in the seventeenth century', *Midland History*, 4 (1977), pp. 175–90.

Ekwall, E., *The place-names of Lancashire* (Manchester, 1922).

Epstein, S.R., 'Rodney Hilton, Marxism and the transition from feudalism to capitalism', in C. Dyer, P. Coss and C. Wickham (eds), *Rodney Hilton's Middle Ages: an exploration of historical themes* (Oxford, 2007), pp. 248–69.

Everitt, A.M., 'Common land', in J. Thirsk (ed.), *The English rural landscape* (Oxford, 2000), pp. 210–35.

Everitt, A.M., *Continuity and colonization: the evolution of Kentish settlement* (Leicester, 1986).

Everitt, A.M., 'Reflections on the historical origin of regions and pays', *Journal of Historical Geography*, 3 (1977), pp. 1–19.

Falvey, H., 'The articulation, transmission and preservation of custom in the forest community of Duffield (Derbyshire)', in R.W. Hoyle (ed.), *Custom, improvement and the landscape in early modern Britain* (Farnham, 2011), pp. 65–100.

Falvey, H., 'Crown policy and local economic context in the Berkhemsted Common enclosure dispute', *Rural History*, 12 (2001), pp. 123–58.

Farmer, D.L., 'Prices and wages, 1350–1500', in E. Miller (ed.), *The agrarian history of England and Wales. Volume II* (Cambridge, 1991), pp. 431–525.

Farrer, W. and Brownbill, J. (eds), *Victoria County History of Lancashire, vol. VIII* (London, 1914).

Faull, M.L. and Moorhouse, S.A., *West Yorkshire: an archaeological survey to A.D. 1500, vol. 3* (Wakefield, 1981).

Fell, A., *The early iron industry of Furness and district* (Ulverston, 1908).

Finberg, H.P.R., *Tavistock Abbey: a study in the social and economic history of Devon* (Cambridge, 1951).

Fisher, F.J., 'Commercial trends and policy in sixteenth century England', *Economic History Review*, 10 (1940), pp. 95–117.

Fleming, R., *Britain after Rome: the fall and rise, 400 to 1070* (London, 2010).

Flinn, M.W. and Mathias, P., 'Professor Sir Michael Moissey Postan, 1899–1981', *Economic History Review*, 35 (1982), pp. iv–vi.

Foard, G., 'Medieval woodland, agriculture and industry in Rockingham Forest, Northamptonshire', *Medieval Archaeology*, 45 (2001), pp. 41–95.

Forrest, I., 'The transformation of visitation in thirteenth-century England', *Past and Present*, 221 (2013), pp. 3–38.

Forrest, I., *The detection of heresy in late medieval England* (Oxford, 2005).

Fox, A., *Oral and literate culture in England 1500–1700* (Oxford, 2000).

Fox, A., 'Custom, memory and the authority of writing', in P. Griffiths, A. Fox and S. Hindle (eds), *The experience of authority in early modern England* (London, 1996), pp. 89–116.

Fox, H.S.A, *Dartmoor's alluring uplands: transhumance and pastoral management in the Middle Ages* (Exeter, 2011).

Fox, H.S.A., *The evolution of the fishing village: landscape and society along the south Devon coast, 1086–1550* (Oxford, 2001).

Frankot, E., *Of laws of ships and shipmen: medieval maritime law and its practice in urban northern Europe* (Edinburgh, 2012).

French, H.R., 'The common fields of urban England: communal agriculture and the "politics of entitlement"', in R.W. Hoyle (ed.), *Custom, improvement and the landscape in early modern Britain* (Farnham, 2011), pp. 149–74.

French, H.R., *The middle sort of people in provincial England, 1600–1750* (Oxford, 2007).

French, H.R. and Hoyle, R.W., *The character of English rural society: Earls Colne, 1550–1750* (Manchester, 2007).

French, H.R. and Hoyle, R.W., 'English individualism refuted and reasserted: the land market of Earls Colne (Essex), 1550–1750', *Economic History Review*, 56 (2003), pp. 595–622.

French, H.R. and Hoyle, R.W., 'The land market of a Pennine manor: Slaidburn, 1650–1780', *Continuity and Change*, 14 (1999), pp. 349–83.

Fritzboger, B., *A windfall for the magnates: the development of woodland ownership in Denmark c.1150–1850* (Odense, 2004).

Fryde, E.B. and Fryde, N., 'Peasant rebellion and peasant discontents', in E. Miller (ed.), *The agrarian history of England and Wales. Volume III: 1348–1500* (Cambridge, 1991), pp. 744–819.

Fuller, E.A., 'Tenures of land by the customary tenants of Cirencester', *Transactions of the Bristol and Gloucestershire Archaeological Society*, 2 (1878), pp. 285–319.

Gardiner, M., 'South-east England: forms and diversity in medieval rural settlement', in N. Christie and P. Stamper (eds), *Medieval rural settlement: Britain and Ireland, AD 800–1600* (Oxford, 2012), pp. 100–117.

Gardiner, M., 'Settlement change on Denge and Walland Marshes, 1400–1550', in J. Eddison, M. Gardiner and A. Long (eds), *Romney Marsh: environmental change and human occupation in a coastal lowland* (Oxford, 1998), pp. 129–45.

Gaskill, M., *Crime and mentalities in early modern England* (Cambridge, 2000).

Geddes, J., 'Iron', in J. Blair and N. Ramsey (eds), *English medieval industries* (London, 1991), pp. 167–88.

Giles, K. and Dyer, C. (eds), *Town and country in the Middle Ages: contrasts, contacts and interconnections, 1100–1500* (Leeds, 2005).

Ginzburg, C., *The cheese and the worms: the cosmos of a sixteenth-century miller* (1976; Eng. Trans., Baltimore, 1980).

Goddard, R., 'Small boroughs and the manorial economy: enterprise zones or urban failures', *Past and Present*, 210 (2011), pp. 3–31.

Goldberg, P.J.P., 'Urban identity and the poll taxes of 1377, 1379 and 1381', *Economic History Review*, 43 (1990), pp. 194–216.

Goldman, L., *The life of R. H. Tawney: socialism and history* (London, 2013).

Goodall, I.H., *Ironwork in medieval Britain* (Wakefield, 2011).

Gough, J.W., *The rise of the entrepreneur* (London, 1969).

Gough, J.W., *The mines of Mendip* (New York, 1967).

Grassby, R., *Kinship and capitalism: marriage, family and business in the English-speaking world* (Cambridge, 2001).

Griffin, C.J., *Protest, politics and work in rural England, 1700–1850* (Basingstoke, 2014).

Griffin, C.J., '"Cut down by some cowardly miscreants": plant maiming, or the malicious cutting of flora, as an act of protest in eighteenth- and nineteenth-century rural England', *Rural History*, 19 (2008), pp. 29–54.

Griffiths, E. and Overton, M., *Farming to halves: the hidden history of sharefarming in England from medieval to modern times* (Basingstoke, 2009).

Gross, A. and Butcher, A.F., 'Adaptation and investment in the age of great storms: agricultural policy on the manors of the principal lords of the Romney Marshes and the marshland fringe c.1250–1320', in J. Eddison (ed.) *Romney Marsh: the debatable ground* (Oxford, 1995), pp. 107–17.

Guldi J. and Armitage, D., *The history manifesto* (Cambridge, 2014).

Habakkuk, H.J., *Marriage, debt, and the estates system: English landownership, 1650–1950* (Oxford, 1994).

Haigh, C., *The last days of the Lancashire monasteries and the Pilgrimage of Grace* (Manchester, 1969).

Hailwood, M., 'The honest tradesman's honour: occupational and social identity in early modern England', *Transactions of the Royal Historical Society* (6th Series), 24 (2014), pp. 79–103.

Hajnal, J., 'European marriage patterns in perspective', in D.V. Glass and D.E.C. Eversley (eds), *Population in history: essays in historical demography* (London, 1965), pp. 101–43.

Hallam, H.E (ed.), *The agrarian history of England and Wales. Volume II: 1042–1350* (Cambridge, 1988).

Hammersley, G., 'The Crown woods and their exploitation in the sixteenth and seventeenth centuries', *Bulletin of the Institute of Historical Research*, 30 (1957), pp. 136–61.

Hargreaves, P.V., 'Seigniorial reaction and peasant responses: Worcester priory and its peasants after the Black Death', *Midland History*, 24 (1999), pp. 53–78.

Harley, J., *The world of William Byrd: musicians, merchants and magnates* (Farnham, 2010).

Harrison, C.J., 'Manor courts and the governance of Tudor England', in C.W. Brooks and M. Lobban (eds), *Communities and courts in Britain, 1150–1900* (London, 1997), pp. 43–59.

Harrison, C.J., 'Grain price analysis and harvest qualities, 1465–1634', *Agricultural History Review*, 19 (1971), pp. 135–55.

Hart, C., *The Forest of Dean: new history 1550–1818* (Stroud, 1995).

Hart, C., *The industrial history of Dean; with an introduction to its industrial archaeology* (Newton Abbot, 1971).

Hart, C., *The verderers and forest laws of Dean* (Newton Abbot, 1971).

Harvey, B., *Living and dying in England, 1100–1540: the monastic experience* (Oxford, 1993).

Harvey, B., 'Introduction: the crisis of the early fourteenth century', in B.M.S. Campbell, (ed.) *Before the Black Death: studies in the 'crisis' of the early fourteenth century* (Manchester, 1991), pp. 1–24.

Harvey, P.D.A., *Manorial records* (London, 1999).

Harvey, P.D.A. (ed.), *The peasant land market in England* (Oxford, 1984).

Hatcher, J., 'The great slump of the mid-fifteenth century', in R.H. Britnell and J. Hatcher (eds), *Progress and problems in medieval England: essays in honour of Edward Miller* (Cambridge, 1996), pp. 237–72.

Hatcher, J., *The history of the British coal industry. Vol. 1, before 1700: towards the age of coal* (Oxford, 1993).

Hatcher, J., 'English serfdom and villeinage: towards a reassessment', *Past and Present*, 90 (1981), pp. 3–39.

Hatcher, J., *English tin production and trade before 1550* (Oxford, 1973).

Hatcher, J., *Rural society in the Duchy of Cornwall, 1300–1500* (Cambridge, 1970).

Hatcher, J., Piper, A.J. and Stone, D., 'Monastic mortality: Durham Priory, 1395–1529', *Economic History Review*, 59 (2006), pp. 667–87.

Hatcher, J. and Bailey, M., *Modelling the Middle Ages* (Oxford, 2001).

Hawkins, B., *Taming the phoenix: Cirencester and the Quakers, 1642–86* (York, 1998).

Heath, P., 'North sea fishing in the fifteenth century', *Northern History*, 3 (1968), pp. 53–69.

Herbert, N.M. (ed.), *A history of the county of Gloucester: volume V. Bledisloe hundred, St Briavels hundred, the Forest of Dean* (Oxford, 1996).

Hey, D.G., *An English rural community: Myddle under the Tudors and Stuarts* (Leicester, 1974).

Hill, M.C., 'The demesne and the waste: a study of medieval inclosure on the manor of High Ercall 1086–1399', *Transactions of the Shropshire Archaeological and Historical Society*, 62 (1979–80).

Hilton, R.H., 'Rent and capital formation in feudal society', in R.H. Hilton (ed.), *The English peasantry in the later Middle Ages: the Ford lectures for 1973* (Oxford, 1975), pp. 174–214.

Hilton, R.H., 'The content and sources of English agrarian history before 1500', *Agricultural History Review*, 3 (1955), pp. 3–19.

Hindle, S., 'Work, reward and labour discipline in late seventeenth-century England', in S. Hindle, A. Shepard and J. Walter (eds), *Remaking English society: social relations and social change in early modern England* (Woodbridge, 2013), p. 255–80.

Hindle, S., *On the parish? The micro politics of poor relief in rural England c.1550–1750* (Oxford, 2009).

Hindle, S., 'Persuasion and protest in the Caddington common enclosure dispute, 1635–1639', *Past and Present*, 158 (1998), pp. 37–78.

Hipkin, S., 'Property, economic interest and the configuration of rural conflict in sixteenth and seventeenth-century England', *Socialist History*, 23 (2003), pp. 67–88.

Hipkin, S., 'Sitting on his penny rent: conflict and right of common in Faversham Blean, 1596–1610', *Rural History*, 11 (2000), pp. 1–35.

Hipkin, S., 'The structure of land occupation in the level of Romney Marsh during the late sixteenth and early seventeenth centuries', in J. Eddison, M. Gardiner and A. Long (eds), *Romney Marsh: environmental change in a coastal lowland* (Oxford, 1998), pp. 147–63.

Hobsbawm, E.J., 'A life in history', *Past and Present*, 177 (2002), pp. 3–16.

Hobsbawm, E.J., *Interesting times. A twentieth century life* (London, 2002).

Holmes, C., 'Drainers and fenmen: the problem of popular political consciousness in the seventeenth century', in A. Fletcher and J. Stevenson (eds), *Order and disorder in early modern England* (Cambridge, 1985), pp. 166–97.

Holt, J.S., 'The financial rewards of winning the battle for secure customary tenure', in J.C. Whittle (ed.), *Landlords and tenants in Britain, 1440–1660: Tawney's agrarian problem revisited* (Woodbridge, 2013), pp. 133–49.

Hopkins, E., 'The re-leasing of the Ellesmere estates, 1637–1642', *Agricultural History Review*, 10 (1962), pp. 14–28.

Hoskins, W.G., 'Harvest fluctuations and English economic history, 1480–1619', *Agricultural History Review*, 12 (1964), pp. 28–46.

Hoskins, W.G., *The Midland peasant: the economic and social history of a Leicestershire village* (London, 1957).

Hoskins, W.G., 'Regional farming in England', *Agricultural History Review*, 2 (1954), pp. 3–11.

Houston, R., 'Custom in context: medieval and early modern Scotland and England', *Past and Present*, 211 (2011), pp. 35–76.

Hoyle, R.W., 'Cromwell v Taverner: landlords, copyholders and the struggle to control memory in mid-sixteenth century Norfolk', in R.W. Hoyle (ed.), *Custom, improvement and the landscape in early modern Britain* (Farnham, 2011), pp. 39–64.

Hoyle, R.W. (ed.), *Custom, improvement and the landscape in early modern Britain* (Farnham, 2011).

Hoyle, R.W., 'Introduction: custom, improvement and anti-improvement', in R.W. Hoyle (ed.), *Custom, improvement and the landscape in early modern Britain* (Farnham, 2011), pp. 1–38.

Hoyle, R.W. (ed.), *The estates of the English Crown 1558–1640* (Cambridge, 1992).

Hoyle, R.W., 'Shearing the hog: the reform of the estates c.1598–1640', in R.W. Hoyle (ed.), *The estates of the English Crown 1558–1640* (Cambridge, 1992), pp. 204–62.

Hoyle, R.W., 'Tenure and the land market in early modern England: or a late contribution to the Brenner debate', *Economic History Review*, 43 (1990), pp. 1–20.

Hoyle, R.W., 'An ancient and laudable custom: the definition and development of tenant right in north-western England in the sixteenth century', *Past and Present*, 116 (1987), pp. 24–55.

Hoyle, R.W., 'Lords, tenants and tenant right in the sixteenth century: four studies', *Northern History*, 20 (1984), pp. 38–63.

Hudson, P. (ed.), *Regions and industries: a perspective on the Industrial Revolution in Britain* (Cambridge, 1988).

Humphries, J., 'Enclosures, common rights, and women: the proletarianization of families in the late eighteenth and early nineteenth centuries', *Journal of Economic History*, 50 (1990), pp. 17–42.

Ingold, T., 'The temporality of the landscape', *World Archaeology*, 25 (1993), pp. 152–74.

Jaffe, J.A., *The struggle for market power: industrial relations in the British coal industry, 1800–1840* (Cambridge, 1991).

James, M., *Family, lineage and civil society: a study of society, politics and mentality in the Durham region, 1500–1640* (Oxford, 1974).

Jones, R. and Page, M., *Medieval villages in an English landscape: beginnings and ends* (Bollington, 2006).

Kanzaka, J., 'Villein rents in thirteenth-century England: an analysis of the hundred rolls of 1279–1280', *Economic History Review*, 55 (2002), pp. 593–618.

Keibek, S.A.J. and Shaw-Taylor, L., 'Early modern rural by-employments: a re-examination of the probate inventory evidence', *Agricultural History Review*, 61 (2013), pp. 244–81.

Kerridge, E., *Textile manufactures in early modern England* (Manchester, 1985).

Kerridge, E., *Agrarian problems in the sixteenth century and after* (London, 1969).

Kershaw, I., 'The Great Famine and agrarian crisis in England 1315–1322', *Past and Present*, 59 (1973), pp. 3–50.

King, P., 'The production and consumption of bar iron in early modern England and Wales', *Economic History Review*, 58 (2005), pp. 1–33.

King, P., 'Social inequality, identity and the labouring poor in eighteenth-century England', in H. French and J. Barry (eds), *Identity and agency in England, 1500–1800* (Basingstoke, 2004), pp. 60–86.

King, P., 'Edward Thompson's contribution to eighteenth century studies: the patrician-plebeian model re-examined', *Social History*, 21 (1996), pp. 215–28.

King, P., 'Legal change, customary right, and social conflict in late eighteenth century England: the origins of the great gleaning case of 1788', *Law and History Review*, 10 (1992), pp. 1–31.

King, P., 'Customary rights and women's earnings: the importance of gleaning to the rural labouring poor, 1750–1850', *Economic History Review*, 44 (1991), pp. 461–76.

King, P., 'Gleaners, farmers and the failure of legal sanction in England, 1750–1850', *Past and Present*, 125 (1989), pp. 116–50.

Kitsikopoulos, H., 'Standards of living and capital formation in pre-plague England: a peasant budget model', *Economic History Review*, 53 (2000), pp. 237–61.

Kjaergaard, T., *The Danish revolution 1500–1800: an ecohistorical interpretation* (Cambridge, 1994).

Kowaleski, M., 'The demography of maritime communities in late medieval England', in M. Bailey and S.H. Rigby (eds), *Town and countryside in the age of the Black Death: essays in honour of John Hatcher* (Turnhout, 2012), pp. 87–120.

Kowaleski, M., *Local markets and regional trade in medieval Exeter* (Cambridge, 1995).

Lamphere, L., 'Work and the production of silence', in G. Sider, and G. Smith (eds), *Between history and histories: the making of silences and commemorations* (Toronto, 1997), pp. 263–83.

Langdon, J., 'Agricultural equipment', in G. Astill and A. Grant (eds), *The countryside of medieval England* (Oxford, 1988), pp. 86–107.

Langton, J., *Geographical change and industrial revolution: coalmining in south west Lancashire, 1590–1799* (Cambridge, 1979).

Large, P., 'From swanimote to disafforestation: Feckenham Forest in the early seventeenth century', in R.W. Hoyle (ed.), *The estates of the English Crown, 1558–1640* (Cambridge, 1992), pp. 389–417.

Le Roy Ladurie, E., *Montaillou: Cathars and Catholics in a French village, 1294–1324* (1975; Eng. Trans. London, 1978).

Lee, J.S., *Cambridge and its economic region, 1450–1560* (Hatfield, 2005).

Leftwich, A., *Redefining politics: people, resources and power* (London, 1983).

Levine, D. and Wrightson, K., *The making of an industrial society, Whickham 1560–1765* (Oxford, 1991).

Liddy, C.D., 'Urban enclosure riots: risings of the commons in English towns, 1480–1525', *Past and Present*, 226 (2015), pp. 41–77.

Lindley, K., *Fenland riots and the English revolution* (London, 1982).

Lister J. (ed.), *Court rolls of the manor of Wakefield, vol. 3* (Leeds, 1917).

Lomas, R.A., 'A priory and its tenants', in R.H. Britnell (ed.), *Daily life in the Middle Ages* (Stroud, 1998), pp. 103–24.

Lomas, R.A., 'The priory of Durham and its demesnes in the fourteenth and fifteenth centuries', *Economic History Review*, 31 (1978), pp. 339–53.

Lynch, K.A., *Individuals, families and communities in Europe, 1200–1800: the urban foundations of western society* (Cambridge, 2003).

Macfarlane, A., *The origins of English individualism: the family, property and social transition* (Oxford, 1978).

Madge, S.J., *The Domesday of Crown lands: a study of the legislation, surveys and sales of royal estates under the commonwealth* (London, 1938).

Manning, R.B., *Village revolts: social protest and popular disturbances in England, 1509–1640* (Oxford, 1988).

Marshall, G., *In search of the spirit of capitalism. Max Weber and the Protestant ethic thesis* (London, 1982).

Martins, S.W., *English model farm: building the agricultural ideal, 1700–1914* (English Heritage, 2002).

Mate, M., 'The economy of Kent, 1200–1500: an age of expansion, 1200–1348', in S. Sweetinburgh (ed.), *Later medieval Kent, 1220–1540* (Woodbridge, 2010), pp. 1–24.

Mate, M., *Trade and economic developments, 1450–1550: the experience of Kent, Surrey and Sussex* (Woodbridge, 2006).

Mate, M., 'Tenant farming and farmers: Kent and Sussex', in E. Miller (ed.), *The agrarian history of England and Wales. Volume III: 1348–1500* (Cambridge, 1991), pp. 680–703.

Mate, M., 'Labour and labour services on the estates of Canterbury Cathedral priory in the fourteenth century', *Southern History*, 7 (1985), pp. 55–68.

Mate, M., 'The farming out of manors: a new look at the evidence from Canterbury Cathedral priory', *Journal of Medieval History*, 9 (1983), pp. 331–43.

Mayhew, N.J., 'Coinage and money in England, 1086–c.1500', in D. Wood (ed.), *Medieval money matters* (Oxford, 2004), pp. 72–86.

McDonagh, B., 'Negotiating enclosure in sixteenth-century Yorkshire: the South Cave dispute, 1530–1536', in J.C. Whittle (ed.), *Landlords and tenants in Britain 1440–1660: Tawney's agrarian problem revisited* (Woodbridge, 2013), pp. 52–66.

McDonagh, B., 'Subverting the ground: private property and public protest in the sixteenth-century Yorkshire Wolds', *Agricultural History Review*, 57 (2009), pp. 191–206.

McDonnell, J.G., 'An account of the iron industry in upper Ryedale and Bilsdale, c.1150–1650', *Ryedale Historian*, 6 (1972), pp. 23–48.

McGibbon Smith, E., 'Court rolls as evidence for village society: Sutton-in-the-Isle in the fourteenth century', in M. Bailey and S.H. Rigby (eds), *Town and countryside in the age of the Black Death* (Turnhout, 2012), pp. 245–76.

McIntosh, M.K., *Poor relief and community in Hadleigh, Suffolk, 1547–1600* (Hatfield, 2013).

McIntosh, M.K., *Poor relief in England, 1350–1600* (Cambridge, 2012).

McIntosh, M.K., *Controlling misbehaviour in England, 1370–1600* (Cambridge, 1998).

McIntosh, M.K., *Autonomy and community: the royal manor of Havering, 1200–1500* (Cambridge, 1986).

Meddens, F. and Draper, G., 'Out on a limb: insights into Grange, a small member of the cinque ports confederation', *Archaeologia Cantiana*, 135 (2014), pp. 19–32.

Melikan, R., 'Shippers, salvors, and sovereigns: competing interests in the medieval law of shipwreck', *The Journal of Legal History*, 11 (1990), pp. 163–82.

Merrified, A., *Magical Marxism: subversive politics and the imagination* (London, 2011).

Middleton-Stewart, J., '"Down to the sea in ships": decline and fall on the Suffolk coast', in C. Rawcliffe, R. Virgoe and R. Wilson (eds), *Counties and communities: essays on East Anglian history presented to Hassell Smith* (Norwich, 1996), pp. 69–83.

Miller, E. (ed.), *The agrarian history of England and Wales. Volume III: 1348–1500* (Cambridge, 1991).

Miller, E., 'Michael Moissey Postan 1899–1981', *Proceedings of the British Academy*, 69 (1983), pp. 543–57.

Miller, E. and Hatcher, J., *Medieval England: towns, commerce and crafts, 1086–1348* (London, 1995).

Moore, R.I., *The war on heresy: faith and power in medieval Europe* (London, 2012).

Moore, R.I., *The first European revolution, c.970–1215* (Oxford, 2000).

Moorhouse, G., *The last office: 1539 and the dissolution of a monastery* (London, 2008).

Moorhouse, S., 'The medieval parks of Yorkshire: Function, contents and chronology', in R. Liddiard (ed.), *The medieval park: new perspectives* (Macclesfield, 2007), pp. 99–127.

Morrin, J., 'The transfer to leasehold on Durham Cathedral estate, 1541–1626', in J.C. Whittle (ed.), *Landlords and tenants in Britain 1440–1660: Tawney's agrarian problem revisited* (Woodbridge, 2013), pp. 117–32.

Muller, M., 'Conflict and revolt: the Bishop of Ely and his peasants at the manor of Brandon in Suffolk, c.1300–1381', *Rural History*, 23 (2012), pp. 1–19.

Muller, M., 'A divided class? Peasants and peasant communities in later medieval England', *Past and Present*, supplement 2 (2007), pp. 115–31.

Muller, M., 'The aims and organization of a peasant revolt in fourteenth-century Wiltshire', *Rural History*, 14 (2003), pp. 1–20.

Myrdal, J. and Sapoznik, A., 'Spade cultivation and intensification of land use 1000–1300: written sources, archaeology and images', *Ruralia X* (forthcoming).

Nair, G., *Highley: the development of a community 1550–1880* (Oxford, 1988).

Neeson, J.M., *Commoners: common right, enclosure and social change in England, 1700–1820* (Cambridge, 1996).

Nef, J.U., *The rise of the British coal industry, 2 vols* (London, 1932).

Newman, C.M., 'Economy and society in north-eastern market towns: Darlington and Northallerton in the later Middle Ages', in C.D. Liddy and R.H. Britnell (eds), *North-East England in the later Middle Ages* (Woodbridge, 2005), pp. 127–40.

Nightingale, P., 'Gold, credit, and mortality: distinguishing deflationary pressures on the late medieval English economy', *Economic History Review*, 63 (2010), pp. 1081–104.

O'Donnell, R., 'The creation of ring-fenced farms: some observations from eighteenth- and nineteenth-century Northumberland', *Agricultural History Review*, 63 (2015) pp. 39–59.

Ormrod, D., 'Agrarian capitalism and merchant capitalism: Tawney, Dobb, Brenner and beyond', in J.C. Whittle (ed.), *Landlords and tenants in Britain, 1440–1660: Tawney's agrarian problem revisited* (Woodbridge, 2013), pp. 200–15.

Ostrom, E., *Governing the commons: the evolution of institutions for collective action* (Cambridge, 1990).

Owen, C.C., *The Leicestershire and south Derbyshire coalfield 1200–1900* (Ashbourne, 1984).

Page, W., *The Victoria History of the County of Durham, vol. III* (London, 1905).

Pearson, S., 'Threshing out the common in community: the Great Tey riot of 1727', *Rural History*, 9 (1998), pp. 43–56.

Pegg, M.G., *A most holy war: the Albigensian crusade and the battle for Christendom* (Oxford, 2008).

Pettit, P.A.J., *The royal forests of Northamptonshire; a study in their economy, 1558–1714* (Gateshead, 1968).

Pollard, A.J., 'The north-eastern economy and the agrarian crisis of 1438–40', *Northern History*, 25 (1989), pp. 88–105.

Poos, L.R., *A rural society after the Black Death: Essex, 1350–1525* (Cambridge, 1991).

Postan, M.M., *Medieval agriculture and general problems of the medieval economy* (Cambridge, 1973).

Postan, M.M., *Medieval trade and finance* (Cambridge, 1973).

Postan, M.M., *The medieval economy and society: economic history of Britain, 1100–1500* (London, 1972).

Postan, M.M., 'Hugh Gaitskell: political and intellectual progress', in M.M. Postan, *Fact and relevance: essays in historical method* (Cambridge, 1971), pp. 169–82.

Postan, M.M., 'A plague of economists', in M.M. Postan, *Fact and relevance: essays in historical method* (Cambridge, 1971), pp. 80–91.

Postan, M.M., 'Investment in medieval agriculture', *Journal of Economic History*, 27 (1967), pp. 576–87.

Postan, M.M., *An economic history of western Europe, 1945–64* (London, 1967).

Postan, M.M., 'Medieval agrarian society in its prime: England', in M.M. Postan (ed.), *The Cambridge economic history of Europe, vol. I: the agrarian life of the Middle Ages* (Cambridge, 1966), pp. 548–632.

Postan, M.M., 'Money, population and economic change in late medieval Europe', *Economic History Review*, 12 (1959), pp. 77–82.

Postan, M.M., *British war production* (London, 1952).

Postan, M.M., 'The trade of medieval Europe: the north', in M.M. Postan and E. Miller (eds), *The Cambridge economic history of Europe, vol. II: trade and industry in the Middle Ages* (Cambridge, 1952), pp.168–305.

Postan, M.M., 'Some economic evidence of declining population in the later Middle Ages', *Economic History Review*, 2 (1950), pp. 221–46.

Postan, M.M., 'The rise of a money economy', *Economic History Review*, 14 (1944), pp. 123–34.

Postan, M.M., 'The fifteenth century', *Economic History Review*, 9 (1939), pp. 160–7.

Postan, M.M., 'Recent trends in the accumulation of capital', *Economic History Review*, 6 (1935), pp. 1–12.

Postan, M.M., 'Credit in medieval trade', *Economic History Review*, 1 (1928), pp. 234–61.

Postan, M.M. and Miller, E. (eds), *The Cambridge Economic history of Europe, vol. II: trade and industry in the Middle Ages* (Cambridge, 1952).

Postan, M.M. and Titow, J., 'Heriots and prices on Winchester manors', *Economic History Review*, 11 (1959), pp. 392–411.

Postles, D., *Social proprieties: social relations in early-modern England (1500–1680)* (Washington, D.C., 2006).

Postles, D., 'The Austin canons in English towns c.1100–1350', *Historical Research*, 66 (1993), pp. 1–20.

Pound, J., 'The social and trade structure of Norwich, 1525–1575', *Past and Present*, 34 (1966), pp. 49–64.

Power, E., *Medieval people* (London, 10th edn., 1963).

Power, E. and Postan, M.M. (eds), *Studies in English trade in the fifteenth century* (London, 1933).

Rackham, O., *Trees and woodland in the British landscape* (London, 1990).

Rackham, O., *The history of the countryside: the classic history of Britain's landscape, flora and fauna* (London, 1986).

Ramsay, G.D., *The Wiltshire woollen industry in the sixteenth and seventeenth centuries* (Oxford, 1943).

Razi, Z., 'The myth of the immutable English family', *Past and Present*, 140 (1991), pp. 3–44.

Reeves, A., 'Romney Marsh: the fieldwalking evidence', in J. Eddison (ed.), *Romney Marsh: the debatable ground* (Oxford, 1995), pp. 78–91.

Richmond, C.F., 'The transition from feudalism to capitalism in the archives of Magdalen College, Oxford: a note', *History Workshop Journal*, 37 (1994), pp. 165–9.

Richmond, C., *John Hopton: a fifteenth century Suffolk gentleman* (Cambridge, 1981).

Rogers, K.H., *Warp and weft: the Somerset and Wiltshire woollen industry* (Buckingham, 1986).

Rogers, K.H., *The book of Trowbridge* (Buckingham, 1984).

Rogers, K.H., *Wiltshire and Somerset woollen mills* (Edington, 1976).

Rollison, D., *Commune, country and commonwealth: the people of Cirencester 1117–1643* (Woodbridge, 2011).

Rollison, D., *A commonwealth of the people* (Cambridge, 2010).

Rollison, D., 'Exploding England: the dialectics of mobility and settlement in early modern England', *Social History*, 24 (1999), pp. 1–16.

Rollison, D., *The local origins of modern society: Gloucestershire 1500–1800* (London, 1992).

Rollison, D., 'Property, ideology and popular culture in a Gloucestershire village, 1660–1740', *Past and Present*, 93 (1981), pp. 70–97.

Rowley, T., *The making of the English landscape: the Shropshire landscape* (London, 1972).

Rudder, S., *The history of the town of Cirencester* (Cirencester, 1800).

Sandall, S., *Custom and popular memory in the Forest of Dean, c.1550–1832* (Saarbrücken, 2013).

Sapoznik, A., 'The productivity of peasant agriculture: Oakington, Cambridgeshire, 1360–99', *Economic History Review*, 66 (2013), pp. 518–44.

Schofield, B., 'Wreck rolls of Leiston Abbey', in J.C. Davies (ed.), *Studies presented to Sir Hilary Jenkinson* (London, 1957), pp. 361–71.

Schofield, P.R., *Peasant and community in medieval England 1200–1500* (Basingstoke, 2003).

Schofield, P.R., 'Access to credit in the early fourteenth-century English countryside', in P.R. Schofield and N.J. Mayhew (eds), *Credit and debt in medieval England c.1180–c.1350* (Oxford, 2002), pp. 106–26.

Scott, J.C., *Weapons of the weak: everyday forms of peasant resistance* (New Haven, 2008).

Scott, J.C., *Seeing like a state: how certain schemes to improve the human condition have failed* (Yale, 1998).

Searle, C.E., 'Customary tenants and the enclosure of Cumbrian commons', *Northern History*, 29 (1993), pp. 126–53.

Searle, C.E., 'Custom, class conflict and agrarian capitalism: the Cumbrian customary economy in the eighteenth century', *Past and Present*, 110 (1986), pp. 106–33.

Shannon, W.D., 'Risks and rewards in wasteland enclosure: lowland Lancashire c.1500–1650', in J.C. Whittle (ed.), *Landlords and tenants in Britain, 1440–1660: Tawney's agrarian problem revisited* (Woodbridge, 2013), pp. 150–65.

Shannon, W.D., 'Approvement and improvement in the lowland wastes of early modern Lancashire', in R.W. Hoyle (ed.), *Custom, improvement and the landscape in early modern Britain* (Farnham, 2011), pp. 175–202.

Sharp, B., *In contempt of all authority: rural artisans and riot in the west of England, 1586–1660* (California, 1980).

Shaw, R.C., *The royal forest of Lancaster* (Preston, 1956).

Shaw-Taylor, L., 'The rise of agrarian capitalism and the decline of family farming in England', *Economic History Review*, 65 (2012), pp. 26–60.

Shaw-Taylor, L., 'Family farms and capitalist farms in mid nineteenth-century England', *Agricultural History Review*, 53 (2005), pp. 158–91.

Shaw-Taylor, L., 'Labourers, cows, common rights and parliamentary enclosure: the evidence of contemporary comment c. 1760–1810', *Past and Present*, 171 (2001), pp. 95–126.

Shaw-Taylor, L., De Moor, M. and Warde, P. (eds), *The management of common land in north west Europe* (Turnhout, 2002).

Shepard, A., *Accounting for oneself: worth, status and the social order in early modern England* (Oxford, 2015).

Sieglerschmidt, J., 'Social and economic landscapes', in S. Ogilvie (ed.), *Germany: a new social and economic history: vol. 2, 1630–1800* (London, 1996), pp. 1–38.

Simpson, P., 'The continuum of resistance to tithe, c.1400–1600', in R. Lutton and E. Salter (eds), *Pieties in transition: religious practices and experiences, c.1400–1640* (Aldershot, 2007), pp. 93–108.

Skeel, C., 'The cattle trade between Wales and England from the fifteenth to the nineteenth centuries', *Transactions of the Royal Historical Society*, Fourth Series, 9 (1926), pp. 135–58.

Skipp, V., *Crisis and development: an ecological case study of the Forest of Arden, 1570–1674* (Cambridge, 1978).

Slack, J., *The lordship of Oswestry, 1393–1607* (Shrewsbury, 1951).

Slavin, P., *Bread and ale for the brethren: the provisioning of Norwich Cathedral Priory, 1260–1536* (Hatfield, 2012).

Smith, J., *Men and armour for Gloucestershire in 1608* (Gloucester, 1980).

Smith, R.M. (ed.), *Land, kinship and life-cycle* (Cambridge, 1984).

Smith, R.M., 'Plagues and people. The long demographic cycle, 1250–1670', in P. Slack and R. Ward (eds), *The peopling of Britain: the shaping of a human landscape* (Oxford, 2002), pp. 177–210.

Snell, K.D.M., 'The culture of local xenophobia', *Social History*, 28 (2003), pp. 1–30.

Somerville, R., *History of the Duchy of Lancaster, vol. 1 (1265–1603)* (London, 1953).

Spenceley, G.F.R., 'The origins of the English pillow-lace industry', *Agricultural History Review*, 21 (1973), pp. 81–93.

Stead, D.R., 'The mobility of English tenant farmers, c. 1700–1850', *Agricultural History Review*, 51 (2003), pp. 173–89.

Steele, R., *Mediaeval lore from Bartholomaeus Anglicus* (London, 1907).

Stone, D., 'The consumption of field crops in late medieval England', in C.M. Woolgar, D. Serjeantson and T. Waldron (eds), *Food in medieval England: diet and nutrition* (Oxford, 2006), pp. 11–26.

Stone, D., *Decision-making in medieval agriculture* (Oxford, 2005).
Stone, L., *The crisis of the aristocracy: 1558–1641* (Oxford, 1965).
Stone, L., 'Elizabethan overseas trade', *Economic History Review*, 2 (1949), pp. 30–58.
Stretton, T., 'Women, custom and equity in the court of requests', in J. Kermode and G. Walker (eds), *Women, crime and the courts in early modern England* (London, 1994), pp. 170–90.
Summerson, J., *Architecture in Britain 1530–80* (London, 1953).
Supple, B.E., *Commercial crisis and change in England 1600–1642* (Cambridge, 1959).
Sweetinburgh, S., 'Hythe's butcher-graziers: their role in town and country in late medieval Kent', in C. Dyer, A. Hopper, E. Lord and N. Tringham (eds), *New directions in local history since Hoskins* (Hatfield, 2011), pp. 98–113.
Sweetinburgh, S., 'Overcoming disaster? Farming practices on Christ Church Priory's marshland manors in the early 14th century', in M. Waller, E. Edwards and L. Barber (eds), *Romney Marsh: persistence and change in a coastal lowland* (Sevenoaks, 2010), pp. 97–115.
Sweetinburgh, S., 'Strategies of inheritance among Kentish fishing communities in the later Middle Ages', *The History of the Family*, 11 (2006), pp. 93–105.
Tawney, A.J. and Tawney, R.H., 'An occupational census of the seventeenth century', *Economic History Review*, 5 (1934), pp. 25–64.
Tawney, R.H., 'The assessment of wages in England by the justices of the peace', in W.E. Minchinton (ed.), *Wage regulation in pre-industrial England* (Newton Abbot, 1972), pp. 37–91.
Tawney, R.H., *The radical tradition* (London, 1964).
Tawney, R.H., *Business and politics under James I. Lionel Cranfield as merchant and minister* (Cambridge, 1958).
Tawney, R.H., *The attack and other papers* (London, 1953).
Tawney, R.H., 'The rise of the gentry, 1558–1640', *Economic History Review*, 11 (1941), pp. 1–38.
Tawney, R.H., *Land and labour in China* (London, 1932).
Tawney, R.H., *Equality* (London, 1931).
Tawney, R.H., *Religion and the rise of capitalism* (London 1926).
Tawney, R.H. (ed.), *Thomas Wilson, a discourse upon usury* (London, 1925).
Tawney, R.H., *Education: the socialist policy* (London, 1924).
Tawney, R.H., *Secondary education for all* (London, 1922).
Tawney, R.H., *The acquisitive society* (London, 1921).
Tawney, R.H., *The agrarian problem in the sixteenth century* (London, 1912).
Tawney, R.H. and Power, E. (eds), *Tudor economic documents 3 vols* (London, 1924).
Taylor, H., '"Branded on the tongue": rethinking plebeian inarticulacy in early modern England', *Radical History Review*, 121 (2015), pp. 91–105.
Tebbutt, C.F., 'An abandoned medieval industrial site at Parrock, Hartfield', *Sussex Archaeological Collection*, 113 (1975), pp. 146–50.
Thirsk, J., *England's agricultural regions and agrarian history, 1500–1750* (London, 1987).
Thirsk, J., *Economic policy and projects: the development of a consumer society in early modern England* (Oxford, 1978).
Thirsk, J., 'Seventeenth-century agriculture and social change', *Agricultural History Review*, 18 (1970), pp. 148–77.
Thirsk, J. (ed.), *The agrarian history of England and Wales. Volume IV: 1500–1640* (Cambridge, 1967).
Thirsk, J., 'Enclosing and engrossing', in J. Thirsk (ed.), *The agrarian history of England and Wales. Volume IV: 1500–1640* (Cambridge, 1967), pp. 200–55.
Thirsk, J., 'The farming regions of England', in J. Thirsk (ed.), *The agrarian history of England and Wales. Volume IV: 1500–1640* (Cambridge, 1967), pp. 1–112.

Thirsk, J., 'Industries in the countryside', in F.J. Fisher (ed.), *Essays in the economic and social history of Tudor and Stuart England* (Cambridge, 1961), pp. 70–88.

Thompson, E.P., *Customs in common: studies in traditional popular culture* (London, 1991).

Thompson, E.P., 'The moral economy of the English crowd in the eighteenth century', *Past and Present*, 50 (1971), pp. 76–136.

Thompson, F.M.L., 'The land market, 1880–1925: a reappraisal reappraised', *Agricultural History Review*, 55 (2007), pp. 289–300.

Thompson, F.M.L., 'The social distribution of landed property in England since the 16th century', *Economic History Review*, 19 (1966), pp. 505–17.

Threlfall-Holmes, M., *Monks and markets: Durham Cathedral Priory, 1460–1520* (Oxford, 2005).

Threlfall-Holmes, M., 'Late medieval iron production and trade in the north-east', *Archaeologia Aeliana*, 5th ser., 27 (1999), pp. 109–23.

Titow, J.Z., *Winchester yields: a study in medieval agricultural productivity* (Cambridge, 1972).

Titow, J.Z., 'Some evidence of the thirteenth-century population increase', *Economic History Review*, 14 (1961), pp. 218–24.

Turner, M.E., 'Parliamentary enclosure and landownership change in Buckinghamshire', *Economic History Review*, 28 (1975), pp. 565–81.

Turner, V., *The anthropology of performance* (New York, 1987).

Turner, V., *From ritual to theatre: the human seriousness of play* (New York, 1982).

Turner, V., *Dramas, fields, and metaphors: symbolic action in human society* (Ithaca, NY, 1974).

Tylecote, R.F., *The prehistory of metallurgy in the British Isles* (London, 1986).

van Bavel, B.J.P., Hoyle, R.W. and Brakensiek, S. (eds), *Social relations: property and power* (Turnhout, 2010).

van Bavel, B.J.P. and Schofield, P.R. (eds), *The development of leasehold in northwestern Europe, c.1200–1600* (Turnhout, 2008).

van Bavel, B.J.P. and Hoppenbrouwers, P.C.M. (eds), *Landholding and land transfer in the North Sea area (late Middle Ages–19th Century)* (Turnhout, 2004).

van Zanden, J.L., 'Early modern economic growth: a survey of the European economy, 1500–1800', in M. Prak (ed.), *Early modern capitalism* (London, 2000), pp. 69–87.

Vervaet, L., 'Lease holding in late medieval Flanders: towards concentration and engrossment? The estates of the St John's hospital of Bruges', in Frederic Aparisi and Vicent Royo (eds), *Beyond lords and peasants: rural elites and economic differentiation in pre-modern Europe* (Valencia, 2014), pp. 111–38.

Vivier, N. and Corbin, A., *Propriété collective et identité communale: les biens communaux en France 1750–1914* (Paris, 1998).

Vollans, E., 'Medieval salt-making and the inning of tidal marshes at Belgar, Lydd', in J. Eddison and C. Green (eds), *Romney Marsh: the debatable ground* (Oxford, 1995), pp. 118–26.

Waddell, B., 'Governing England through the manor courts, 1550–1850', *Historical Journal*, 55 (2012), pp. 279–315.

Waites, B., 'Medieval iron workings in northeast Yorkshire', *Geography*, 49 (1964), pp. 33–43.

Walter, J.D., 'The social economy of dearth in early modern England', in J.D. Walter and R. Schofield (eds), *Famine, disease and the social order in early modern society* (Cambridge, 1989), pp. 75–128.

Ward, R., *The world of the medieval shipmaster: law, business and the sea, c.1350–c.1450* (Woodbridge, 2009).

Warde, P., 'Fear of wood shortage and the reality of the woodland in Europe c.1450–1850', *History Workshop Journal*, 62 (2006), pp. 28–57.

Warde, P. and Williamson, T., 'Fuel supply and agriculture in post-medieval England', *Agricultural History Review*, 62 (2014), pp. 61–82.

Watts, S., 'From moss and moorish ground to fertile farmland: the early seventeenth century reclamation of Tetchill moor', *Transactions of the Shropshire Archaeological and Historical Society*, 80 (2005), pp. 125–31.

Wheeler, J., 'The environmental impact of iron-working on the woodlands of Rievaulx and Bilsdale, North York Moors, UK, c.1132–1647', in M. Atherden and T. Milsom (eds), *Yorkshire Landscapes Past and Present* (York, 2008), pp. 61–7.

Whittle, J.C., 'Introduction: Tawney's agrarian problem revisited', in J.C. Whittle (ed.), *Landlords and tenants in Britain, 1440–1660: Tawney's agrarian problem revisited* (Woodbridge, 2013), pp. 1–18.

Whittle, J.C. (ed.), *Landlords and tenants in Britain, 1440–1660: Tawney's agrarian problem revisited* (Woodbridge, 2013).

Whittle, J.C., 'Lords and tenants in Kett's rebellion 1549', *Past and Present*, 207 (2010), pp. 3–52.

Whittle, J.C., 'Peasant politics and class consciousness: the Norfolk rebellions of 1381 and 1549 compared', in C. Dyer, P. Coss and C. Wickham (eds), *Rodney Hilton's Middle Ages: an explorations of historical themes* (Oxford, 2007), pp. 233–47.

Whittle, J.C., 'Leasehold tenure in England c.1300–c.1600: its form and incidence', in B.J.P. van Bavel and P.R. Schofield (eds), *The development of leasehold in northwestern Europe, c.1200–1600* (Abingdon, 2007), pp. 139–54.

Whittle, J.C., *The development of agrarian capitalism: land and labour in Norfolk, 1440–1580* (Oxford, 2000).

Whittle, J.C., 'Individualism and the family–land bond: a reassessment of land transfer patterns among the English peasantry, c.1270–1580', *Past and Present*, 160 (1998), pp. 25–63.

Whittle, J.C. and Yates, M., '"Pays réel or pays légal?" Contrasting patterns of land tenure and social structure in eastern Norfolk and western Berkshire, 1450–1600', *Agricultural History Review*, 48 (2000), pp. 1–26.

Whyte, N., *Inhabiting the landscape: place, custom and memory, 1500–1800* (Oxford, 2009).

Whyte, N., 'Landscape, memory and custom: parish identities c.1550–1700', *Social History*, 32 (2007), pp. 166–86.

Williams, N.J., *The maritime trade of East Anglian ports, 1550–1650* (Oxford, 1988).

Winchester, A.J.L., 'Property rights, "good neighbourhood" and sustainability: the management of common land in England and Wales, 1235–1965', in B.J.P. van Bavel and E. Thoen (eds), *Rural societies and environments at risk: ecology, property rights and social organisation in fragile areas* (Turnhout, 2013), pp. 301–29.

Winchester, A.J.L., *The harvest of the hills: rural life in northern England and the Scottish Borders, 1400–1700* (Edinburgh, 2000).

Winchester, A.J.L and Straughton, E.A., 'Stints and suitability: managing stock levels on common land in England, c.1600–2006', *Agricultural History Review*, 58 (2010), pp. 30–48.

Winter, J.M., 'Introduction: Tawney the historian', in J.M. Winter (ed.), *History and society. Essays by R.H. Tawney* (London, 1978), pp. 1–40.

Wirth, L.B., 'Urbanism as a way of life', *American Journal of Sociology*, 44 (1938), pp. 1–24.

Wood, A., *The memory of the people: custom and popular senses of the past in early modern England* (Cambridge, 2013).

Wood, A., *The 1549 rebellions and the making of early modern England* (Cambridge, 2007).

Wood, A., *Riot, rebellion and popular politics in early modern England* (Basingstoke, 2002).

Wood, A., '"Poore men woll speke one daye": plebeian languages of deference and defiance in England, c.1520–1640', in T. Harris (ed.), *The politics of the excluded in early modern England* (Basingstoke, 2001), pp. 67–98.

Wood, A., 'Custom and the social organisation of writing in early modern England', *Transactions of the Royal Historical Society*, 6th Series, 9 (1999), pp. 257–69.

Wood, A., *The politics of social conflict: the Peak country, 1520–1770* (Cambridge, 1999).

Wood, A., 'The place of custom in plebeian political culture: England, 1550–1800', *Social History*, 22 (1997), pp. 46–60.

Wood, D., *Medieval economic thought* (Cambridge, 2002).

Woodward, D., 'Straw, bracken and the Wicklow whale: the exploitation of natural resources in England since 1500', *Past and Present*, 159 (1998), pp. 43–76.

Wordie, J.R., 'The chronology of English enclosure', *Economic History Review*, 36 (1983), pp. 483–505.

Wrightson, K., *Ralph Tailor's summer: a scrivener, his city and the plague* (New Haven: CT, 2013).

Wrightson, K., *Earthly necessities: economic lives in early modern Britain, 1470–1750* (London, 2002).

Wrightson, K., 'The politics of the parish in early modern England', in P. Griffiths, A. Fox and S. Hindle (eds), *The experience of authority in early modern England* (London, 1996), pp. 10–46.

Wrightson, K. and Levine, D., *Poverty and piety in an English village: Terling, 1525–1700* (London, 1979).

Wrigley, E.A., 'Urban growth in early modern England: food, fuel and transport', *Past and Present*, 225 (2014), pp. 79–112.

Wrigley, E.A., 'The transition to an advanced organic economy: half a millennium of English agriculture', *Economic History Review*, 59 (2006), pp. 435–80.

Wrigley, E.A., 'Country and town: the primary, secondary and tertiary peopling of England in the early modern period', in P. Slack and R. Ward (eds), *The peopling of Britain: the shaping of a human landscape* (Oxford, 2002), pp. 217–42.

Wrigley, E.A., *Continuity, chance and change: the character of the industrial revolution in England* (Cambridge, 1988).

Wrigley, E.A., 'A simple model of London's importance in changing English society and economy, 1650–1750', in E.A. Wrigley (ed.), *People, cities and wealth: the transformation of a traditional society* (Oxford, 1987), pp. 133–56.

Wrigley, E.A. and Schofield, R.S., *The population history of England and Wales: a reconstruction* (Cambridge, 2002).

Wrigley, E.A., Davies, R.S., Oeppen, J.E. and Schofield, R.S. (eds), *English population history from family reconstitution* (Cambridge, 1997).

Yates, M., 'Change and continuities in rural society from the later Middle Ages to the sixteenth century: the contribution of west Berkshire', *Economic History Review*, 52 (1999), pp. 617–37.

Young, B., 'Iron ore in Cumbria', in G. Brooks and C. Irwin (eds), *Master of them all: iron making in Cumbria* (Cumbrian Industrial Society, 2007), pp. 5–25.

Zell, M., *Industry in the countryside: Wealden society in the sixteenth century* (Cambridge, 1994).

Index